Pioneers, Settlers, Aliens, Exiles

J. L. Fisher

Pioneers, Settlers, Aliens, Exiles

The decolonisation of white identity in Zimbabwe

J. L. Fisher

Published by ANU E Press
The Australian National University
Canberra ACT 0200, Australia
Email: anuepress@anu.edu.au
This title is also available online at: http://epress.anu.edu.au/pioneers_citation.html

---

National Library of Australia
Cataloguing-in-Publication entry

Author:	Fisher, J. L. (Josephine Lucy)
Title:	Pioneers, settlers, aliens, exiles : the decolonisation of white identity in Zimbabwe / J. L. Fisher.
ISBN:	9781921666148 (pbk.) 9781921666155 (pdf)
Notes:	Bibliography.
Subjects:	Decolonization--Zimbabwe. Whites--Zimbabwe. Zimbabwe--Politics and government--1980- Zimbabwe--Race relations.
Dewey Number:	320.96891

All rights reserved. No part of this publication may be reproduced, stored in a retrieval system or transmitted in any form or by any means, electronic, mechanical, photocopying or otherwise, without the prior permission of the publisher.

Cover design and layout by ANU E Press

This edition © 2010 ANU E Press

Contents

Abbreviations ix

Preface xi

1. Introduction 1
2. Zimbabwe's discourse of national reconciliation 27
3. Re-inscribing the national landscape. 55
4. Zimbabwe's narrative of national rebirth. 79
5. Decolonising settler citizenship 103
6. The mobilisation of indigeneity 131
7. The loss of certainty 173
8. Zimbabwe's governance and land reform crises—a postscript 201
9. Conclusion 221

Appendix 231

Bibliography 239

Map of Zimbabwe

Showing provincial borders and principal towns

Abbreviations

AAG	Affirmative Action Group
BSAC	British South Africa Company
CCJP	Catholic Commission for Justice and Peace
CFU	Commercial Farmers Union
CZI	Confederation of Zimbabwe Industries
ESAP	Economic Structural Adjustment Programme
FAO	Food and Agriculture Organisation (United Nations)
GOZ	Government of Zimbabwe
IBDC	Indigenous Business Development Council
IBWO	Indigenous Business Women's Organisation
LSCF	Large-scale commercial farm
MDC	Movement for Democratic Change
NCA	National Constitutional Assembly
NGO	Non-governmental organisation
OAU	Organisation of African Unity
RF	Rhodesian Front
SADC	Southern African Development Community
SAPs	Structural Adjustment Programmes
TRC	Truth and Reconciliation Commission
UDI	Unilateral declaration of independence
UNDP	United Nations Development Programme
WFP	World Food Programme
ZANLA	Zimbabwe African National Liberation Army
ZANU	Zimbabwe African National Union

ZANU PF	Zimbabwe African National Union Patriotic Front
ZAPU	Zimbabwe African People's Union
ZBC	Zimbabwe Broadcasting Commission
ZCTU	Zimbabwe Confederation of Trade Unions
ZIPRA	Zimbabwe People's Revolutionary Army

Preface

In the academic literature, 'white'—objectified at the apex of the racial hierarchy—is commonly applied to those who enjoy centring and a sense of agency. Nowhere was this more evident than in Britain's colonies, where the administration imposed categorical identities, locating and positioning people in the social order according to race. Rhodesia provides a case in point. Drawing on difference in this way, Europeans—being the politically and economically dominant party—were invariably experienced by the colonised, the acted on, as racist and oppressive. Bonnett (1997), however, suggests the scholarly reification of 'whiteness' runs the risk of homogenising difference, leaving little room for the recognition of multiple positionings or diversity within. Moreover, categorical representations are not immutable—something recognised by the government of Robert Mugabe when calling for the decolonisation of racial identities at Zimbabwe's independence.

The passing of Rhodesia's settler government in 1980 did not by itself signify the end of the colonial experience. Colonial modes of thought still structured the country's landscape, legislation, language and so forth. The order of the settlers' world was soon challenged when Zimbabwe's newly installed political elite began a programme of decolonisation to assert ownership of and control over the country and its institutions in the name of the black majority. Reworking racial identities would prove to be an intrinsic part of these initiatives, each de-naturalising and raising questions regarding the continuing European presence. How had Zimbabwe's white community understood or engaged with this programme? What were they to 'unlearn' and 'learn again' (Landry and MacLean 1996:4–5) in order to leave whiteness behind? A chance encounter sparked my interest in these issues: a brief conversation late in 1994, not more than the exchange of a few remarks between several whites at a sports club on a hot Sunday afternoon in Zimbabwe's capital, Harare. We were hardly acquainted and I felt in no position to intrude, ask questions or clarify as they muttered and grumbled among themselves about proposed changes to the country's citizenship laws. The local newspaper had carried sketchy details, little was clear and perhaps nothing would come of it. These individuals were, however, clearly worried, mulling over what proposed amendments might mean for their children. Two years earlier in 1992, Zimbabwe's white community had accounted for 0.8 per cent, or about 82 000, of a total population of 10.5 million. Of these, 62 000, or 0.6 per cent, claimed to belong in Zimbabwe as citizens. Nevertheless, they complained of being 'locked out' and 'not wanted', of being outcasts in the country of their birth. At the time, I reflected upon the confidence I held in my identity as an Australian citizen, something I took almost for granted, my forebears having arrived as pioneer settlers in the colony of South Australia during the mid 1800s. At first glance, 'white liberation' from colonialism appeared to be achieved differently in the Antipodes. This study examines the processes whereby Zimbabwe's racial hierarchy has been dismantled and white hegemony overturned, how in effect the Rhodesian homeland has been remade with an African identity, illustrating Bonnett's (1997:177) point that as a historical and geographical construction, 'white' might also be a site of contest and change.

Our conversation took place more than a decade and a half ago now. I have intermittently followed its trail ever since, probing the bonds that bind whites to Zimbabwe and how these attachments might also be broken. One question led to another, my research broadening to encompass issues to do with place making and indigeneity—all part of the production of white autochthony. The result is an examination of various discourses of national belonging, their borders or boundaries, how these are displayed and enclosed, and the supervision they facilitate, as white identity has been reconfigured in power relations since Zimbabwe's independence. As I proceeded, however, it was Spivak's (1990:121–2) concern with unlearning privilege to gain knowledge of the other that held my attention. Hence, at a more abstract level, the following chapters reflect the interplay of colonial memory in making these people what they once were, and what they have now become, the journey from dominance to an understanding of theirs as a failing community. As something is told of what it means to be white in the post colony, the point is made that Europeans are not beyond finding themselves decentred, dispossessed and marginalised in the name of decolonisation and correcting the colonial record. Ten years have passed since I left the country and Zimbabwe is much changed. In view of which, this study offers a retrospective to what is now known as the 'Zimbabwe crisis' and how issues implicated in it emerged and developed before 2000.

With regard to racial nomenclature, I have applied the terms 'European/white' and 'African/black' somewhat interchangeably, while remaining cognisant of the historical period under discussion. As modes of objectification, these labels, while out of favour in Western antiracist literature, are an integral part of everyday language in Zimbabwe, used to describe oneself and others despite regional and class distinctions or differing views on race and the position of whites in the territory. 'Tribe', also out of favour in Western academia, is still occasionally heard in Zimbabwe, for words have their own veracity. The communal areas might, for instance, be referred to using the Rhodesian name: the Tribal Trust Lands or the TTLs. Politicians, government officials, scholars and others also applied the term to political patronage, voting patterns, provincial names, styles of dancing and so forth. Another semantic divide existed with regard to the armed conflict that ended in 1980 and brought Zimbabwe into being. Black Zimbabweans most commonly referred to this war as the liberation struggle.

For whites, it was the civil war, but again these terms were not rigidly applied. I heard this conflict spoken about as 'the time of the killing' by a former black soldier and, comparing it with Australia's engagement in Vietnam, 'our five-minute skirmish' by a white conscript. Places are given the names appropriate to the era, far-reaching changes coming in the wake of political independence.

For obvious reasons, individuals—unless they courted public attention—have not been identified by name. Nevertheless, I would at this point like to sincerely thank the many Zimbabweans who, privately or as members of various institutions, made this study possible. In particular, I would like to acknowledge the support from colleagues at the University of Zimbabwe, where I worked for much of my time in the country. They were rewarding years, first with Professor Victor Muzvidziwa in the Departmental Chair and later with Professor Michael Bourdillon. I also appreciate assistance provided by staff employed at the National Archives and the Central Statistics Office and owe a great debt to those who contributed their time, answering questions and involving me in their daily activities. Thanks go to Professor Nicolas Peterson and Professor Francesca Merlan of The Australian National University for reading and commenting on my doctoral thesis and for helpful suggestions at that time. Special thanks go to Professor Richard Werbner, Director of the International Centre for Contemporary Cultural Research at the University of Manchester, who later in the piece prodded me to revise the manuscript in view of publication. Finally, I would also like to acknowledge the encouragement and support of my husband, Roger, during the many years this work has taken to complete.

1. Introduction

This chapter provides a brief history of Rhodesia as a white settler state. It introduces the Rhodesians, details early bonds developing between them and the territory and their nascent interest in pioneer history before saying something about what sorts of people they thought they were and the society they hoped to create. An account of the key legislative pillars that institutionalised racism and mapped the identities of white and black, settler and native, into the landscape follows. Then the process of data collection is discussed, as well as white engagement with Zimbabwe's public culture, for they have heard a lot about themselves in policy statements and political speeches significant in forming images of their place in the nation. Next, white inner space—the cultural dimensions of their domesticity that are productive of identity—is described before the gist of the main argument presented in the following chapters is outlined.

Establishing Rhodesia as a white homeland

The colonial era began in 1889 when Britain granted a Royal Charter to the British South Africa Company (BSAC) to administer and exploit country north of the Limpopo River. The territory, inhabited by the Ndebele and Mashona peoples, was given the name Rhodesia after the BSAC's founder, Cecil Rhodes. This early act of white dominance suggested an idea about the future envisaged for the place. A year later, after the company's Pioneer Column had arrived in Mashonaland, a vast tract of land was pegged as gold claims and farms by individual pioneers on the strength of promises made to them by Rhodes. The BSAC also took land for mining and agriculture on the basis of dubious concessions—made in exchange for guns, cash, liquor and so on—negotiated by its representatives with African leaders. A significant turning point in European settlement came after the 1903–04 goldmining slump convinced the company that financial success would depend on land and not, as previously thought, on mineral wealth. Consequently, a viable commercial farming sector became an imperative for any future stable settler society. The early 1900s saw the start of an 'agricultural revolution' as the variety of stock, seeds and farming methods expanded and improved and tobacco—soon to become the country's major export crop—was introduced. Once this more stable agricultural economy was established, Rhodesia had made the transition from a frontier to a settler society.

Bad feeling soon developed between the settlers and the BSAC such that in 1922 they voted not to become the fifth province of South Africa and to stay out of the Union. Rhodesia thus changed from company to direct settler rule and administratively became, in 1923, the responsibility of the Dominions Office in Britain (later the Commonwealth Relations Office) rather than the Colonial Office. As a self-governing colony, Southern Rhodesia had its own parliament, civil service and security forces, all answerable to its settler society rather than to Whitehall. While Britain retained the right to intervene in legislative decisions made in Salisbury, particularly with regard to native affairs, it did not do so even when blatantly racist legislation was coming into force. The settlers hoped in the not too distant future to become an independent state within the British Commonwealth, to achieve a status similar to that enjoyed by Australia, New Zealand and Canada. Attracting large numbers of immigrants to fill the country's vast empty spaces was critical to the fruition of their designs. Kennedy (1987) describes in some detail efforts to find suitable settlers—especially those with commercial farming skills—in Britain and South Africa. These initiatives met with only limited success, however, and the majority of early settlers, whether from Britain or South Africa, were usually poor labouring migrants. By World War I, white immigration had all but dried up, and with the Depression, company and government immigration campaigns fell into disuse.

Notwithstanding such setbacks, some whites, even as early as 1903, began to claim that they belonged to the land on the grounds of having lived through the 1890s native uprising—or first *Chimurenga*—when about 10 per cent of the white population were killed.[1] Territorial battles and environmental hardships, as well as the beauty and challenge of a 'new land' and its peoples, all engendered strong emotional bonds, the 'unfolding' of feelings of 'love and loyalty' and 'identity', between the settlers and the country (Howman 1990:100). Within another generation, the Rhodesians began to exhibit interest and pride in their ancestry. They credited themselves with being a practical people, possessing a spirit of initiative and adventure. Historical societies celebrating the pioneer legacy sprang up,[2] memorialising the past and thereby contributing to a white telling of history that supported the settlers' politics of location. The National Archives, also promoting a genre of pioneering stories, opened its doors in 1935 (Gann 1965:315). The inherited prestige of a pioneer background passed to descendants, enabling them to locate themselves within the larger narrative of Rhodesia and its history. In these ways, the land, infused with meaning, began to represent home to the Europeans. This paramount concern shaped their relations with Britain and with the local African population, just as it had in other white settler societies (Weitzer 1990:26).

---

1 Letters written by Edward George Howman between 1896 and 1903 relate the immediacy of this experience (Howman 1990). As a member of the Watt's Column, Howman was sent to relieve Mashonaland and keep the route to Umtali (Mutare) open during the first *Chimurenga*.
2 For example, in 1953, the Rhodesiana Society succeeded the Stanley Society of 1939 and, after independence, changed its name to the History Society of Zimbabwe. The society continues its tradition of publishing articles covering the early years of Rhodesia and the settler legacy in the journal *Heritage of Zimbabwe*.

Establishing the settler colony required the African population be harnessed to the project. The *Land Apportionment Act* of 1930,[3] while giving legal recognition to the freehold/native division already pertaining to the country, classified the colony into 'European', 'Native', 'Undetermined', 'Forest' and 'Unassigned' areas. The act conferred on Africans the right to buy land without competition in only 7 per cent of the country, designated African Land Purchase areas, while also preventing them from acquiring land in much of the rest deemed to be European—always the areas of greatest natural wealth and economic potential. By this means, the principles of racial separation and hierarchy—or Rhodesia's 'ethnic spatial fix' (Moore 2005:14)—were inscribed on the territory's geography. Tax burdens compelled African participation in the labour market at the same time as property and educational qualifications excluded them from the vote.

Mapping the urban landscape followed the geographical division of rural space. The Rhodesians generally thought of urban areas as European. By and large, Africans residing therein were perceived as migrant workers who would, at some time in the future, return to their native homes or reserves. Movement from their 'home districts' to the urban areas was regulated, invariably in a prohibitive manner, by the *Native Registration Act* (1936). Opportunities for black social advancement were further restricted by the creation of two occupational pyramids. Most notably, the *Industrial Conciliation Act* (1934) excluded Africans from the status of employees in wage and industrial negotiations. As white unions also controlled apprenticeships, Africans were confined to menial and unskilled jobs. In short, Africans were incorporated into Rhodesia only in ways that served white economic needs. Taken together, Rhodesian cartography and legal regulations contributed to the colonists' production of power/knowledge that upheld Rhodesia as a white homeland and facilitated the emergence of a white labour aristocracy that, according to Astrow (1983:9), stood 'shoulder to shoulder' with Rhodesia's bourgeoisie on every important occasion.

Immediately after World War II, Southern Rhodesia again began to attract immigrants—predominantly from the United Kingdom and to a lesser extent from Mediterranean countries—most of whom were destined for Rhodesia's urban areas. The European population grew from 80 500 in 1945 to 219 000 in 1960 (Palmer 1977:242). The creation of the Central African Federation (1953–63) during this period, led and dominated by Southern Rhodesia, was a regional

---

3   The *Land Apportionment Act* (1930), renamed the *Land Tenure Act* in 1969, was amended many times. In 1969, all previously unallocated land was removed and the country divided in half along racial lines, the white areas amounting to 44.95 million acres (18.19 million ha.) and the black to 44.94 million acres (18 million ha). African interests were deemed to be 'paramount' in African designated areas, as were white interests in the European areas (Murphree and Baker 1976:391). However, the best agricultural land always remained in white hands. The legislation's basic principles remained unchanged until 1977 when amendments introduced by the Rhodesian Front overturned the paramount interest of each racial group within their designated areas with regard to rural land, other than in the Tribal Trust Territories (*Parliamentary Debates*, 19 December 1978, col. 1799). The de-racialisation of urban areas followed soon after (Caute 1983:225).

attempt to keep political power in settler hands. For its duration the quest for Dominion status was shelved in order that the economic basis for a wider bid for independence was strengthened. Soon after the Federation's break-up, Britain conferred independence upon black-majority governments in less-developed Northern Rhodesia and Nyasaland. The settlers of Southern Rhodesia believed independence to be their entitlement also.

In December 1962, the Rhodesian Front came to power in Southern Rhodesia and state politics shifted to the right. With a grant under settler rule not forthcoming, the Rhodesian Front in November 1965 made a unilateral declaration of independence (UDI) so as to wrest de facto autonomy from Britain and secure the country's future as a white homeland. Reckless though UDI might have appeared, Chennells (1989:124, 132) averred that it was not so much an arbitrary act as a logical step in view of the Rhodesians' perception of themselves as a distinct people that had been maturing for three-quarters of a century. The settler government, in what would soon become a Republic (1970) and be known simply as Rhodesia, then proceeded to assert its sense of colonial nationalism and to institutionalise white rule (Eddy and Schreuder 1988:7). The legislation described above had already established separate administrative structures and apportioned land according to race, thereby mapping the subject position of settler and native on to the landscape. Building on this, the Rhodesian Front set about extending European privilege, entrenching whites as the political, economic and social elite, creating an all pervasive 'apartheid by bye-law [sic] and convention' rather than by grand design, as in South Africa (Murphree and Baker 1976:378).

Prior to UDI, Rhodesia had remained strongly British in composition and outlook, and was envisioned by its settlers as a loyal white colony and an integral part of the British Empire. In the aftermath of the declaration, however, Rhodesia became internationally identified as a rogue state. The subsequent imposition of United Nations sanctions reconfigured the settlers as 'pariahs'. Britain, they now felt, had turned against them, rejecting and turning them into enemies. With the settlers' right to control the character and future of the country in dispute (Jess and Massey 1995:134), their vision of Rhodesia as a larger geographical space where whites belonged appeared less convincing. Perceptions of Rhodesia as a modern El Dorado, full of promise and opportunity, began to give way to a sense of theirs as a beleaguered country, for UDI put an end to any hope of a massive influx of immigrants from Europe. Rhodesian authorities turned their attention to finding settlers in other parts of Africa. Most came from South Africa and newly independent Zambia, with a few from Kenya. The European population peaked in the early 1970s at just under 250 000, or 5 per cent of the total population. The greatest number of post-UDI immigrants arrived somewhat later from the former Portuguese colonies of Angola and more particularly Mozambique—both territories attaining independence in 1975.

UDI also coincided with the first episodes of counterinsurgency in the country. Attacks started in the early 1960s, with incidents in isolated white farming areas, and escalated into a sustained guerrilla offensive late in 1972.[4] Rhodesia's security forces confronted two nationalist armies—namely, the Zimbabwe African National Liberation Army (ZANLA) and the Zimbabwe People's Revolutionary Army (ZIPRA), the troops of Robert Mugabe and Joshua Nkomo respectively. In March 1978, in a vain attempt to return to international legality, stay in control and direct unfolding events, the Rhodesian Front came to an internal settlement of the crisis with conservative black leaders. Elections brought Bishop Abel Muzorewa to head an interim government in April 1979, but did little to foster international recognition. With Mugabe and Nkomo excluded from contesting the election, the ground war in fact escalated, making 1978 and 1979 record years for European emigration (Wilkinson 1980:117) and severely testing the cohesiveness of Rhodesian society. Departure of the young and economically active damaged the country, in view of which alarmists questioned whether the economy of the future Zimbabwe could survive the loss of its professional and skilled white manpower. Critics derided the 'fainthearted'—namely, those leaving for fear of their person and property or fed up with the country's far-reaching conscription commitments and foreign currency restrictions. They were part of Rhodesia's 'hidden exodus', departing ostensibly 'on holiday', never to return.

In sum, establishing Rhodesia was a display of white dominance whereby the settlers located themselves at the heart of the nation—namely, the freehold areas of the countryside and towns, spaces in which the black majority enjoyed only tenuous rights. In this context, to be 'at home' was to be included on the grounds of kinship and race, to be the subject of the national discourse and to enjoy a sense of control and connectedness (Jackson 1995:154). Race was thus a spatial, legal and social marker of difference (Moore 2005:143). Nevertheless, calling Rhodesia home was not an unmediated experience, something reflected in one of the country's more striking features—namely, its throughput of people (Roberts 1978:61). While depicting Rhodesia as a frontier and themselves as pioneers and later settlers, many whites had not in fact stayed to build the white homeland. UDI remade their home as a place of stigma. Impending independence and the devolution of power to a black majority government provoked anxiety in white ranks over the future. With the cessation of hostilities, the question whether

---

4 Zimbabwe's 1992 *War Veterans Compensation Act (Chapter 11, article 15)* came into effect in March 1995 and set the official war dates as 1 January 1962 to 29 February 1980 (*Parliamentary Debates*, 2 October 1997, col. 2157).

they could legitimately belong in light of Rhodesia's history of violence and unjust racial privilege was voiced. Would there be a place for them, or indeed for other minority groups—namely, Asians and coloureds—in the new country?

Data collection

The following chapters address the decolonisation of settler identity, their search for a legitimate national identity within Zimbabwe's discourses of citizenship and indigeneity and their subtexts of belonging and homecoming. To capture the various sides to this issue, I adopted research practices 'attentive' to the range of available forms of knowledge (Gupta and Ferguson 1997b:37). Indeed, data collection proved full of chance encounters and unexpected opportunities. So, while some material came directly from ethnographic observation, much else pertaining to where Zimbabwe's borders of national personhood lay and how these were established and defended, came from other varied sources (Falk Moore 1993:4–5).

I found the State's nationalist discourse embodied in official texts—political speeches, parliamentary debates, policy documents and annual reports—inscribed in monuments and enacted during the gambit of national celebrations. As part of the public transcript (Scott 1990:2), these afforded material about the ruling elite's construction of the Zimbabwean nation and their understanding of vernacular membership therein. In addition, I scoured citizenship statutes and immigration regulations to unearth the thinking behind the recent introduction of amendments, and watched the development of these ideas as bills were debated and passed through the House. Indigenisation guidelines became available during fieldwork. A draft was circulated for discussion among policymakers in the public sector and guidelines were in the process of being agreed upon some seven years into the debate. The state-sponsored national land conference, convened in early 1998, provided another site where multiple representations of indigeneity were canvassed.

Archival sources provided some historical background to the nationalist position. I was able to access findings from various commissions of inquiry, annual reports from departments within Rhodesia's Ministry of Immigration and Tourism, as well as promotional pamphlets campaigning for settlers from the mid 1960s. Educational material and political commentary also shed light on earlier settler constructions of citizenship and indigeneity. Biographies written by settlers Phillippa Berlyn (1967) and Robert Tredgold (1968:13), who 'grew up with the country', and Doris Lessing (1994:160), who was aware that she had been 'part of an extraordinary time, the end of the British Empire in Africa', supplemented material from official Rhodesian records. Recently, a younger generation of whites—such as Angus Shaw (1993) and Bruce Moore-King (1989)—has written specifically about the war years and the futility when they, as Rhodesian conscripts, were sent by their elders to 'resolve what my people had begun' with the Africans (Shaw 1993:vii). Their contributions are also included, for young and old did not always see the war and its aftermath in the same way.

The research also draws on my experiences (between 1992 and 1997) as a locally recruited member of staff at the University of Zimbabwe. These earlier years in the country confuse somewhat the tropes of entry and exit that construct distance and difference between the field and home and thereby 'authenticate' anthropological material (Gupta and Ferguson 1997b:12–13; Des Chene 1997:69–70). I had not, however, previously interacted closely with white Zimbabwean society and so set about gaining ethnographic knowledge of their world by involving myself in recreational and community activities. I attended prayer meetings and reconciliation services, art exhibitions and performances of plays written by fringe members of this community. I was invited to family celebrations, joined social and sporting events and took fishing holidays with people who became friends. I travelled the length and breadth of the country, staying at both productive and derelict farms, visited colonial monuments and graveyards, found myself caught up in demonstrations cutting the country's main rural thoroughfares and joined the 'stay-aways' and protests in town. I shopped, lined up in post offices and banks, frequented the local library and engaged in casual conversations while I undertook the usual activities that occupied middle-aged and middle-class white, as well as black, women. In this way, a picture emerged of the everyday and mundane ways whites attempted self-definition.

I also ensured I was part of the audience at migration seminars—each presentation filled to capacity with young, middle-class Zimbabweans from all races well before the advertised starting time. Some were held at venues in Harare's international hotels, others in the surrounding farming districts.[5] Here, consultants—almost all having some prior connection with the region—set themselves as insiders, their jokes playing on fears as well as suggesting familiarity with commonly held stereotypes. Would-be émigrés were advised, for example, not to mentally convert their savings into foreign currency because 'you have no money, you must start again'. And, once relocated, they were urged 'not to say they originated from Southern Africa for we're the bad boys of

---

5   Some presentations were aimed specifically at attracting people to Australia, others to a range of English-speaking, Western countries. The audience was predominantly white at the former, with a lesser number of Asians and coloureds, while the latter were filled with Zimbabweans of all races.

apartheid; say you're Greek or Irish or whatever'. Perhaps with greater insight, audiences were also told 'you are immigrants, you will have to change to become one of the people of the country of your choice'.

Later in the day, two short-term non-governmental organisation (NGO) assignments offered the chance to pursue my interest in health and welfare matters and at the same time interact with Zimbabweans whose work and political viewpoints put them outside the white mainstream. In this capacity, I evaluated a restorative justice programme for the victims of torture and state-organised violence operating in Mashonaland Central Province. As a colleague and I drove the 'dust' roads, visiting rural clinics and isolated hospitals, 'overnighting' in the townships, I was able to get some sense of the Rhodesian war's meaning for people who lived in what were then called the Tribal Trust Lands. A second engagement brought the opportunity to assess the case management of sexually abused children presenting at one of Harare's general hospitals and, by incorporating indigenous knowledge, to broaden the otherwise Western-oriented medical and psychological intervention strategies. Here again I met Zimbabweans from all races joined by the will to reduce human suffering. While peripheral, both projects nonetheless furthered my knowledge of issues central to my research.

By entering social networks at these various points, I sought to capture a range of subject positions and contending voices from within the white community. At the same time, I hoped to identify families in which members had emigrated, for I was still under the sway of the conversation described in the Preface. I quickly discovered that emigration tales were commonplace and that few families had been left untouched by this issue. I was already aware that white Zimbabweans were generally sensitive to scrutiny and that outsiders' judgements made them feel secondary and defensive. I had met their brusque manners and blunt replies on the streets and in shops. Thus initially, I approached my project with some apprehension, adopting, I hoped, an open, non-judgemental attitude. While not everyone—most notably, younger men—was prepared to be associated with the research, about 30 white Zimbabwean households willingly participated in more focused interviews. Participant observation helped clarify and substantiate data gained through interview, allowing me, for instance, to experience the competitive exchanges between whites as they justified to each other decisions to emigrate or stay in the country. I was also party to tensions between family members, now middle-aged and back on holiday, regarding who had 'done best', as well as the resentment of younger siblings who, left behind, felt abandoned. Something I had not anticipated was that in about one-third of families interviewed, members had left only to return and re-establish a home in Zimbabwe some time later.

We usually met over several sessions at informants' homes and, in one or two instances, at their office or place of business—all significant sites for self-definition and the construction of a collective white identity. Here, I let the conversation flow freely, taking a self-styled shorthand developed as a student and during an earlier career as a mental health practitioner. I recorded historicised accounts of individual and family journeys, white thoughts about citizenship and conceptions of home, as well as their reading of official statements regarding reconciliation, indigenisation and the Zimbabwean diaspora. Although not entirely comfortable with my being employed at the University of Zimbabwe— dubbed 'the Kremlin on the hill'—most welcomed the chance to talk or, in some instances, to 'get the message out' and be heard by a wider Western audience. Some 'enjoyed' the interviews or found the material covered 'interesting'. For others, it proved a cathartic experience, 'a relief' as they engaged with the process. Once, in a slightly hostile fashion, I was quizzed about life in Australia, my thoughts on South-East Asian immigration, multiculturalism and the welfare state—questions that I endeavoured to answer in detail. A few respondents proved offhand or short in reply to my questions—something reflected in an unevenness to quotations in the body of the text. Engagement in community affairs also led me to several members of the white community with privileged knowledge of reconciliation and immigration matters, individuals whom I also approached for more structured interviews.

Many whites I noted held attitudes towards the United Kingdom that were, at best, ambivalent. Elders among them, having escaped dreary postwar Britain for the adventure and vigour of Rhodesia, claimed to 'despise' successive socialist UK governments and described Britain as 'a crowded country of little people and little buildings' and 'a nation which is done for'. Others, born either in Rhodesia or various other British colonies in Africa, also spoke of holding 'no feelings' or 'no nice feelings' towards Britain, the country that 'let us down'. This was not a land to which they wanted to return or a place they would willingly call home. Australia on the other hand was perceived as a place of future possibility, 'the country most like Zimbabwe in climate, language, sport and food', and more often than not, the destination of first choice. Perth, in particular, was seen as 'psychologically and economically closer to Zimbabwe than anywhere else in the world', one person proffering: 'the nationals are settlers like we are, we understand each other.' Yet while Australia was described as 'a golden opportunity' and 'a heavenly chance', the country was simultaneously feared as a decadent, unchristian place where children 'go off the rails', its citizens made 'lazy' and 'soft' by the State's social welfare system.

In keeping with their Australian counterparts, most white Zimbabweans were town dwellers, living predominately in the two main cities of Harare and Bulawayo.⁶ A small but economically and politically significant number associated with the commercial farming sector resided in the countryside and are represented in the following chapters by several farmers and farm managers. Typically, white urbanites were business, professional and trades people, while a few were influential in manufacturing and mining.⁷ Some had significant interests in the private sector. One research participant was the owner-manager of a medium-size import/export business, another a director of several companies, a third the retail manager of a family owned furniture store, and a few more were self-employed in a professional capacity. Generally, however, most were small players in the urban economy and many were employees. The latter included bookkeepers, secretaries, computer programmers, a headmaster and various other kinds of teachers, a pilot for a cargo company and a lowly executive with an indigenous merchant bank. One man was searching for work, another trying to set up a bakery with his wife, whose trade as an informal importer of cheese from South Africa was becoming less and less financially viable with the fall in the Zimbabwean dollar. Also in keeping with this ageing population—of which about half were economically inactive—a significant number of informants were retired or mothers who did not wish to work.⁸ Zimbabweans of European descent were not therefore a monolithic group but were divided along class and, as later chapters indicate, also ethnic lines. That whites were conspicuous in the retail and trade sectors gave Harare a very different feel to other African capitals, such as the cities of Kenya and Malawi (previously Nyasaland) where I had resided and worked during the 1980s. The number of European settlers in these countries declined sharply after independence. The few who remain are now vastly outnumbered by a more recent group of foreigners—namely, expatriates.

Knowledge

Early on, the issue of evidence, or how white Zimbabweans 'knew' what they claimed to know, caught my attention. Questions arose out of an apparent ideological closure surrounding some areas of my research. Informants spoke as if with one voice, in spite of the distinction they made between themselves as liberals or conservatives. Liberals were, for example, particularly keen to draw my attention to their more progressive attitudes, although I found their views not greatly different from others'. Both groups were politically to the right of centre and a far cry from the radical missionary voice of individuals

---

6   Tables 1.12 and 1.13 of the 1992 Census indicate that 64 889 whites were urban dwellers while 17 908 lived in the rural areas, giving a total of 82 797. Note that these figures reflect the total white population and thus include non-citizens who are permanent or short-term residents.
7   See Appendix Table 3.
8   See Appendix Table 3 and Figure 1.

such as Brian MacGarry (1994a, 1994b). In view of this, I was interested in the information sources whites drew on when forming or justifying their opinions, for, by and large, most had little direct experience of state events, described in later chapters, where the ruling party endeavoured to constitute its form of national identity. Nor did they commonly access policy documents or legislation relevant to themselves as a minority and in which the government set out the formal terms of their incorporation.

Instead, informants gleaned some sense of their perception in the wider Zimbabwean society by way of daily, informal interactions with members of the black majority, as well as through contact with lower-level state officials. Bureaucratic practices surrounding passports, identity cards, residence permits, business licences and so forth, in addition to classifications imposed by public enumerators, assigned identities and substantiated for informants the State's limits of national belonging (Wilson and Donnan 1998:24). Here Foucault's (1982:212) work on power and modes of objectification proved useful to understanding how whites were 'attached' to their colonial identity, how in effect they were shaped by imposed 'truths' that others must recognise of them, as well as be recognised by the subjects themselves. In instances described in later chapters, white appellants, resisting subjectification, have resorted to Zimbabwe's courts to challenge the principles state regulatory instruments have been built on—principles that through their administration are further developed and elaborated.

More importantly though, whites formed images of their place in the nation through their engagement with public culture. The role of the media in apprehending one's self in the world, and the ideas about simultaneity that these sources contribute to 'thinking the nation', is well documented.[9] In Zimbabwe, media representations of white subjectivity were instrumental in advising minorities of their status in society, their shortcomings and governmental expectations of them. As one informant put it, 'the President speaks to us through the press', for the country's leaders were otherwise inaccessible and remote public figures. Consequently, the populace generally knew Mugabe and his Ministers—many former comrades in arms who have held one government post after another since independence—by their political pronouncements. These received extensive coverage to all corners of the country in the government's mouthpieces, *The Herald*, *The Sunday Mail* and ZBC TV1, where editorial comment invariably defended the ruling party's line. Whites and disaffected middle-class blacks avidly read another paper, the *Zimbabwe Independent*. This weekly, first appearing in 1996, assigned itself the task of vigilantly exposing corruption and

---

9   See, for example, Anderson 1990; Kemper 1993; Spitulnik 1993; Gupta 1995.

misrule on behalf of the public.[10] It also reported sympathetically on business and farming interests, couched argument in terms of economic rationality and practicality and provided a focus galvanising white opinion in Zimbabwe and abroad, with a Rhodesian web site carrying a link to each edition. Informants drew my attention to particular articles, discussed coverage among themselves and welcomed 'the new openness because we've been whispering for years'.

While media coverage of Zimbabwe's political discourse 'brings knowledge of others to mind', creating images of who is like us, who belongs and who does not (Bowman 1994:140–1), reading or listening to political discourse does not mechanically interpellate the reader/listener within the subject positions produced. Audiences might not recognise themselves or dispute the regimes of truth that, in Zimbabwe, 'compel' whites 'in certain ways' and not others (Sylvester 2000:252). Furthermore, within public culture, other sites drew otherwise invisible whites and blacks into the national arena (Hall et al. 1978:121). Here, in letters to the editor, memoriam columns, feature articles, talkback radio and current affairs programmes, opportunities existed for them to air their views, defend their interests and anxiously discuss and refute their mode of representation. These struggles about 'who we are' proved an integral part of Zimbabwe's decolonisation process. Extracts from contributors are to be found in the following chapters, although in private opinions might be less compromising. Importantly, for present purposes, the extent to which white Zimbabweans recognised a number of common concerns set them apart and defined them as a community, distinct from black Zimbabweans and the expatriate community.

An acrimonious relationship developed between Zimbabwe's two media camps. While Raftopoulos (1992:60) nominated the press as one of Zimbabwe's sites of democratic debate and public participation, the government doubted the 'independence' of the independent press, stigmatising it as 'Rhodesian', 'unpatriotic' and as such destructive to national unity. Media claims and counterclaims were fuelled and supported by the use of questionable statistics. Figures cited could be wildly divergent.[11] If the experience of government statisticians, town councils and social scientists was anything to go by,

---

10 Another paper, *The Financial Gazette,* provided some political comment, although primarily it was a rather dry business newspaper without widespread popular appeal. After I had left Zimbabwe, the *Daily News* appeared on the streets.

11 There were, for instance, no agreed figures for the contribution of various sectors to gross domestic product (GDP) or other important social indices such as the budget deficit as a proportion of GDP, unemployment and inflation levels. Nor was there consensus about how statistics should be constructed. Arguments arose over which goods should be included in the outdated consumer price index (CPI) basket and the appropriate formula for calculating the fall in the Zimbabwean dollar. The Central Statistics Office in particular complained that the information it needed was simply not forthcoming, prompting the suggestion that a media campaign be undertaken to educate the public about the importance of providing data to officials (*Parliamentary Debates*, 9 October 1996, col. 2374).

Zimbabweans were generally not prepared to supply information needed for the constitution of accurate quantitative indicators. To extract data on the age composition, education and economic activities of the white population from the 1992 Census proved a task unto itself, despite generous cooperation from the Central Statistics Office. Thus, overall quantitative evidence tends to be fragmentary, should be treated critically and placed within material drawn from other sources.

The dialogue of mutual mistrust and insecurity, often strident in tone, is reproduced here as it was spoken in Zimbabwe, where it was the nature of political discourse that the ruling ZANU PF party's dominating presence and uncompromising language (De Waal 1990:43) overpowered a more accommodating black *sotto voce*. Perforce, Sylvester (1995:406) describes ZANU PF as 'a monolith', 'an icon' set on narrating 'the best tale about the past' as it sets out 'the proper relationship' between the people and the party.[12] Responding to this, white informants commonly drew a clear distinction between the State's leaders, who purportedly represented the nation, and the people who made up the nation (Gandhi 1998:119). In effect, they separated the State's antagonistic discourse from their relations with the ubiquitous man on the street.

While Falk Moore (1993:2) points out there are 'seldom simple answers to questions about the meaning and consequences of political statements', they do give some indication as to the individuals or parties who expect to set the terms of the debate (Peck 1992:78). The title 'Father of the Nation' credits Mugabe—with his portrait hanging in almost every public place—with personifying the nation. As repositories of wisdom, he and other senior government officials expected respect rather than to be critically questioned. The importance of political oratory is enhanced when, as in Zimbabwe, few clear policy documents exist on many key issues. In point of fact, 'policy' was not infrequently a collection of ad hoc and, at times, contradictory statements made by leaders to sit well with a particular audience.[13] The policy of reconciliation was, for instance, spelt out over the course of a number of Mugabe's speeches detailed in the next chapter. While research was in progress, whites were preoccupied

---

12   Various scholars have analysed the contribution of oratory to political leadership, pointing to its coercive codes. According to Bloch (1975:9), political speech is a means by which control is exerted, where speakers and listeners are tied in a highly structured, hierarchical situation that permits only a one-way relationship. Cohen (1994:50), however, argues that 'the rules of rhetoric as cultural products are nothing without their actualisation in the mouths of creative individuals'. Certainly in Zimbabwe, party figures harangue audiences in a manner not dissimilar to that adopted by Samburu elders, described by Spencer (1965:140–2), who relentlessly berate the young and female members of society, accusing them of gross irresponsibility and lack of respect and collectively shaming them for individual breaches of conduct.
13   President Mugabe shares with the former Congolese leader Patrice Lumumba the tendency to 'blow hot and cold' depending on his listeners, and particularly with respect to the colonial legacy (Sartre 2001:158–9). While accused of inconsistency, both men were the products of the colonial system and its mission education. Opposing conceptions therefore 'coexist' within these leaders and 'translate the profound contradictions of what can only be called (their) class' (Sartre 2001).

with how to make sense of political statements linked to the introduction of a policy of indigenisation outlined in Chapter 6. Where some believed these utterances could be dismissed as little more than 'hot air', others argued that while 'actions were critical, words could be ignored'. The suggestion was also made that politicians were trying to 'outdo each other in their radicalism, just for public consumption'. In private, it was said that political brokers could be counted on to be 'sensible, hard-headed businesspeople'. Still, the inability to 'reliably penetrate' the party's official transcript (Scott 1990:67) engendered confusion, uncertainty and rumour mongering.

Indeed, these were restive years. Where, initially, many whites dismissed the import of the indigenisation discourse, its reality was becoming apparent in events from 1997—evident in, among other things, increasing numbers of farm, business and courtroom invasions. Matchaba-Hove of Zimrights observes that 'mobocracy', where unruly mobs are sanctioned to harass and disrupt, is a legacy of ZANU PF rule.[14] Whites, with some bravado, referred to this practice as 'rent-a-riot', for it was recognised that these were not spontaneous demonstrations but orchestrated and paid for from above. The urgency of what was euphemistically dubbed 'the wealth grab'—holding out the promise of black prosperity and economic opportunities perhaps never to come again—heightened Harare's atmosphere of ferment. Political crises (strikes, stay-aways, price or food riots, coup rumours and Congo war cover-ups) and corruption allegations fell one upon the next. I lived within a few streets of the university, and not uncommonly the sour odour of tear gas hung in the evening air. Thus the research took place against a background of increasing strain, insecurity and repression for all Zimbabweans; a colleague graphically described the ever more visible and brazen presence of the State's security police as 'those men in suits and dark glasses, laughing like hyenas on street corners'.

To know what was happening within the country, many whites—aware that governments before and since independence have practised media censorship and disinformation—said 'one must also look outside'. Mass communications have encouraged them—now spread across the world—to keep in touch in ways that were inconceivable until recently. During crises, I observed a spate of overseas phone calls as friends and relatives shared information gathered from the BBC and CNN and rang to inquire about what was happening on the ground. Rhodesian web sites also kept readers informed of the whereabouts of friends and reunions, and generally encouraged former Rhodesians to see themselves as exiles and 'people the world would like to forget'. Every so often, the government let its anger with the activities of these 'long distance nationalists'

---

14 Matchaba-Hove, *Zimbabwe Independent*, 14 November 1997, p. 1.

(Anderson 1992:12), over whom it had little control, be known. 'Their meddling in politics from afar,' reflected one person, 'does nothing to make life here easier for us local whites.'

Expatriates, in the country on short-term contracts with embassies, aid organisations or multinationals, represented another important cleavage in Zimbabwean society. When I arrived in Zimbabwe at the end of 1990, this was the category to which I as an 'expat wife' belonged. In a few instances, our presence was welcomed, with one local white extolling 'the benefits of cross-fertilisation, for we were like clones, you could tell us a mile off. We wore the same clothes, held the same ideas and fought the same war.' To this particular person, expatriates represented 'the influx of new people coming to us, bringing new ideas and standards, opening new horizons'. To many others, however, expatriates were seen to be no more than 'two or three-year wonders', and accused of being ineffectual, ignorant of local conditions and 'not caring' for Africa. On the domestic front, expatriates were criticised for upsetting the established order, 'ruining it for us' by paying too high rents, wages and so forth. This antagonism stemmed from a variety of factors, not least expatriate access to hard currency, their influx after 1980 in response to majority rule, diplomatic social exclusiveness and to the fact that as temporary residents they would all ultimately depart. That my positioning shifted somewhat in the eyes of black and white Zimbabweans was reflected in questions directed my way. Where local whites initially asked, 'How long are you here for?', this later became 'Are you staying?' or 'Have you bought a house yet?' Middle-class blacks, confusing the transition from temporary to permit resident, inquired 'Are you applying for citizenship?' While such loaded questions, reflecting my unusually long stay in the country, were difficult to answer, they suggested some movement in the eyes of the questioner beyond the status of short-term expatriate contract worker.

But what of my research topic itself? I had toyed with ideas more to do with the courses I was teaching at the time. One in particular looked promising. Sitting in the city's magistrates' court, my interest was piqued by arguments linking customary bride-wealth and modern-day maintenance payments. I was, however, also aware that some members of Zimbabwe's educated elite were uneasy about Westerners 'stealing our heritage' or 'profiting from our cultural knowledge'. Their disapproval reflects the fact that to be the subject of metropolitan ethnography is to reproduce colonial relations.[15] 'Natives', brought into being by anthropologists as well as settler administrations, are today not necessarily enthusiastic about finding themselves the object of Western, anthropological research. Moreover, given the country's development agenda, the subjects of research—often poor or marginalised sections of Zimbabwe's society—expect the end result to be to their benefit. They therefore

---

15   See, for example, During 1987:44; Asad 1991:314–15; Kuper 1994:544–7; Tuhiwai Smith 1999:39, 42.

question when the promised 'help' for their 'problems' due on account of their participation in purportedly useful projects will be forthcoming. In view of these issues, a foreign anthropologist's choice of topic is a political decision set against the inescapability of Western privilege.

Given anthropology's colonial antecedents, East and Central African universities usually subsume and teach anthropology in conjunction with other social sciences or, in some instances, do not offer undergraduate courses at all. The former situation pertained in Zimbabwe, where disciplinary boundaries were not jealously guarded to the extent that they were in Western academies. In addition, local scholars were somewhat sceptical of inexperienced Western students coming briefly to study 'the exotic', depending on local assistants for language translation and in some instances to get the line of their research right. Their cynicism extended to First World academics, who, passing through and perhaps hoping to please their hosts, spoke in radical idioms. These are not new issues for anthropology.[16] Sally Falk Moore (1994:75–86) expresses eloquently the demands of African intellectuals to speak for themselves and claim a share of the scholarly action. Generally, however, the academic literature fails to spell out steps anthropologists might adopt—having recognised that a problem exists—beyond gestures aimed at establishing some token of reciprocity or alternatively registering their dislike of the nationalist or racist overtones of nativist protest (Kuper 1994:547). More productively, Gupta and Ferguson (1997b:23–4) point out that African academics are 'looking for new and less colonial modes of engagement'—a desire that must be set against decades of independence that have failed to bring political, economic or intellectual self-determination.[17] They suggest that to practise decolonisation means 'doing away with the distancing and exoticism of the conventional anthropological "field"' (Gupta and Ferguson 1997b:38) in favour of foregrounding ways in which researchers are socially and historically linked with their area of research.

Cognisant of these sensibilities, I found colonial settlers accepted as a fruitful topic for investigation by my Zimbabwean colleagues, who anticipated difficulty accessing white society themselves. Much had already been written about Rhodesian short-sightedness, their folly and authorship of their own misfortunes.[18] Historians Bhebe and Ranger (1995:2), however, note with some concern that, while material is available on military matters, very little is known about white Rhodesian society, its ideology or the effects of the war on white civilians. Nor, might I venture, has urban white society received sustained

---

16 See, for example, Asad 1973:15–19; Ahmed 1973; Mandaza 1988; Said 1989; Stocking 1991:3–6; Sanjek 1993.
17 See, for example, Loomba 1994:305; Tuhiwai Smith 1999:20.
18 See, for example, Hills 1981; Hudson 1981.

scholarly attention in the post-colonial period. As more than a decade had elapsed since the black majority took over the reigns of power, it seemed opportune to examine what political independence meant to the former colonisers.

After my years away at the University of Zimbabwe and elsewhere, it came as something of a shock to return to an orthodox anthropology department, with its talk of 'going to the field' to study people in small-scale communities, who were very different to the usually Western anthropologist. In light of this, I felt Australian colleagues considered Zimbabwe's white community not worthy of academic attention. On the one hand, my work among informants from the same racial and language group appeared as something akin to doing anthropology 'at home'. On the other hand, colleagues—perhaps taking a moral high ground—appeared unable to concede familiarity, to countenance a common heritage as European invaders, colonists, settlers and migrants. That Rhodesia was tainted by association with South Africa didn't help. Mamdani (1997a:7, 27) warns, however, of the analytical dangers inherent in South African 'exceptionalism', of taking its apartheid regime as intrinsically different to British 'indirect rule' and French colonial 'association', which he perceives as having taken on the character of prejudice. In much the same way, Hansen (1992:12) finds recent feminist writing on colonialism unsatisfactory to the extent that scholarship dwells too long on infamous and eccentric colonial actors in idealised settings. Recognising this academic prejudice did not in itself make writing any easier. Many were the times I packed my material up in cardboard boxes ready for storage only to unpack it weeks, sometimes months, later. The problem was more than the sinking feeling of pleasing no-one and betraying friendships that others had documented. Tracking back and forward between diverse but compelling arguments held strongly by people from various positions proved wearisome. Simply put, good and bad, moral and immoral did not in every instance line up seamlessly with race and history. Reading late in the day Dembour's (2000) recollections of Belgium's colonialism in Congo—an era that officially ended half a century ago—made me more keenly aware of the widely held stereotypes and the poverty of memory in imperial homelands, as well as the distaste felt towards this part of their histories. Collegian uneasiness with my area of research perhaps suggested a deeper-felt Western ambivalence than could be explained as left-liberal anger at colonialism that was supported by their own governments (Thomas 1994:1–2). Possibly it also masks more troubling issues to do with legitimacy in New World settler societies.

Inner space

The following chapters describe a very public and at times heated debate between Zimbabwe's political and intellectual elite and the country's white community. At this point it might therefore be worth saying something about whites' inner space, the cultural dimensions of their domesticity and how their lives were lived in the privacy of their homes during the 1990s.

Harare, where the bulk of research took place, is a city terminologically divided into what are called high and low-density suburbs. During the Rhodesian era, these were racially delineated, with whites domiciled to the north of the central business district. Harare still bears this colonial imprint, although in the low-density suburbs the population mix has changed. The majority of whites resided here, in streets lined with flowering trees: jacaranda, bauhinia, flamboyant and cassia. Their neighbours or landlords were as often as not middle-class blacks. Relations between the two were typically quiet, amicable but distant. Houses were in the main older Rhodesian brick bungalows, serviced with electricity and water, many with security bars across windows and doors in order to discourage petty theft. A shortfall of cement and other materials meant little building took place during the 1980s, contributing to a housing shortage. Homes constructed more recently by members of the black ruling elite were larger, more imposing and multi-garaged. Senior diplomats also tenanted other grand mansions with guards posted at the gates. One could also come across an original low-slung colonial home in the earliest settled suburbs, often dilapidated with timber badly in need of paint, or an African style of house, several mud-brick *rondavels* (circular huts) joined together under a thatched roof. This light and cool alternative was, however, more commonly associated with accommodation provided at tourist resorts. There were also pockets of white poverty, particularly in older, inner-city tenement areas where rented flats or rooms were spartanly furnished. Some of the white poor were former Rhodesian civil servants, whose pensions, not index linked, were worthless. Other old or infirm people depended on church feeding programmes and practical help from service organisations to survive.

White class stratification became all the more apparent as Zimbabwe's economy opened up in response to the government's 1991 Economic Structural Adjustment Programme (ESAP). Trade liberalisation ended 25 years of restricted choice, limited quality and shortages of goods occasioned by UDI sanctions, the liberation war and the post-independence government's earlier socialist intentions. On the streets, Renault R5 and Datsun 120Y cars, several decades old and belching smoke, were regularly seen in 1990. As the decade progressed, however, new Mercedes, BMWs and four-wheel-drive vehicles appeared, as well as a plethora of smaller 'as-new' Japanese models, with the practical, all-purpose *backie* (utility) ever popular among younger whites. A mass of new or previously unavailable goods also arrived in the market. At home, those who could afford it renovated. Formica benchtops, linoleum tiles, dated raffia and crocheted lampshades were all discarded in favour of more modern equivalents.

Imported ceramic tiles and timber replaced older stone or polished concrete floors. Parquet, lifting in places, was overlaid with ever-popular carpet. Local cottons, sewn into curtains, pelmets, bedspreads and cushions, added a splash of colour to walls, which were painted in pastel shades and hung with European prints. A few African artefacts were about—a basket or some item of woodwork—but little more. Thus, where some homes appeared functional, almost barren, others I visited were furnished comfortably in a sophisticated Western style.

White Zimbabweans were hospitable to each other, regularly extending invitations for a drink or meal, entertaining for the most part informally—men in open-necked shirts, shorts or long pants, women in cotton frocks or tie-dyed and wrap-around skirts. Typically, social events began with the man of the house serving drinks from the 'home bar'—beer or spirits, the latter locally produced by African Distillers, or perhaps a glass of wine once trade opened up with South Africa after majority rule in 1994. Where possible, the bar, complete with necessary accoutrements, cane chairs or bar stools, was located in a separate room, otherwise it squeezed into the front hall, verandah or thereabouts. Sporting memorabilia, a team photograph or a trophy or two, maybe a fish caught and mounted some time in the past decorated this centre of convivial activity. Later guests were served European foods, roasts, casseroles or perhaps local freshwater or saltwater fish from South Africa or Namibia. Alternatively, a *braai* (barbecue) was prepared outside around the recently relined glitter-stone pool. In this setting, the host and hostess relaxed with others of their own kind, for these were generally all-white gatherings at which people held similar values and beliefs.

Guests took the opportunity to catch up on what others had been up to, shared news of friends in common, the whereabouts and progress of children and so forth. Most hoped their offspring would attend, at least for secondary education, a private school, some established during the Rhodesian era along ethnic lines, now taking pupils from across the board. At the same time, there were good 'A-grade' government schools patronised by whites. Students intent on pursuing tertiary studies would, in all likelihood, need to apply for the release of foreign currency to meet tuition costs outside the country, usually in South Africa. Places at local institutions were limited and competition was steep. Parents recognised and worried that this option could well close in the future, as South Africa addressed its own need for widespread black education. Otherwise a white-collar job or a supervisory position could usually be found by word of mouth, by networking within this 'bonded' community. 'Know-how' was ranked highly and was considered by some to be just if not more important than 'paper' qualifications, as well as the ability to take on responsibility at a young age.

Commodity prices were another point of general discussion—in particular the interest shown by overseas buyers at Zimbabwe's tobacco auctions—as were the rains, for these things affected the lives of everyone, city and country folk alike. Talk also turned to rising prices and shortages of basic commodities—maize meal, bread, milk, cooking oil—as the 1990s progressed, and to the heady heights of inflation and the falling value of the local currency. Other topics were routinely avoided. International affairs and local politics were not often discussed in any depth except in the small number of better-educated, liberal households. Elsewhere only frustrated comments concerning government ineptitude were aired. The country's civil war was almost never brought up beyond a chance remark describing teenage years spent manning canteens, making cups of tea for the boys just back from a sortie during the 'bush war', or a passing question clarifying regiments served. Only later, in 1998, watching security helicopter gun-ships patrolling Harare's streets from the air, did I hear about the fear felt in Rhodesian playgrounds when helicopters carrying body bags flew over Salisbury, and of mothers too afraid to voice their anxiety because that was called 'rocking the boat'. Female memories such as these were described as 'just like yesterday' and 'still too raw' to express or confide more freely.

Domestic help played an important role in making this pleasant, sociable lifestyle possible. Usually, there was one worker in and one outside, but the number depended on family size and the presence of young children. Outside staff deferred to those inside. Female domestic workers, known as maids, wore crisp cotton uniforms with *doek* (headscarf), a new style released each year, anxiously awaited and available in town at the Farmers Co-op, later known as Town and Country. Male staffers were also uniformed, usually in white or beige, while gardeners were outfitted in brightly coloured blue, green or orange overalls and gumboots. Domestic workers were expected to carry out their tasks according to European standards of punctuality, hygiene and order—skills that in my experience they acquired at mission schools, from previous urban employers or as workers on white commercial farms. Most lived on the property and within the compound's walls that enclosed the main residence and staff quarters, the latter structure distinct from the main house. Employers were generally hesitant to intrude upon an employee's private space. Conversely, house workers knew intimately the ins and outs, likes and dislikes of their employers' domestic domain. While their movement and that of goods—phones, irons, umbrellas and buckets—back and forth across the racial divide blurred somewhat the spatial division of living areas, these domestic arrangements rehearsed white authority and dominance. They were in effect productive of white identity. The presence of domestic help freed fathers, as heads of households and primary breadwinners, to enjoy leisure activities on weekends. Mothers had time to ferry children between school and other activities, pursue business or sporting interests and shop. Most preferred to purchase goods locally or at large suburban shopping complexes such as Avondale, Borrowdale Village or Westgate, making only a minimum number of trips to the city centre, deterred by parking problems and car thefts. Alternatively, housewives would drive to the outer city limits, where Jaggers—the city's first bulk warehouse, which sold everything imaginable—opened its doors to the public in the mid 1990s.

The sun shone most days in Harare in a brilliantly blue sky. The rainy season's tropical downpours passed quickly. This climate lent itself to a casual outdoors life. Sport was a major leisure activity and it was generally considered important to acquit oneself well on a sports field. Results were analysed in detail; the angle of a tennis, cricket or squash shot, the vagaries of a particular golf hole and the bait used on a fishing trip were all part of reproducing whites as an aesthetic community (Werbner 1997:240). After Saturday's sporting fixtures, many whites went out on Sunday for a meal, perhaps at a friend's home or to enjoy *piri piri* (hot and spicy) chicken at a restaurant run by Portuguese émigrés from Mozambique. Alternatively, the venue was a sports club where children could play safely. During the rainy season, families drove out to the Mazowe Dam to check the water level and see it spill. A few made the trip north in 1998 to watch the Kariba Dam's floodgates open for the first time in many years. A day at the races appealed to some older members of the white community but was invariably disappointing, there being so few familiar faces left in the crowd.

Arts and live theatre were on hand at the Repertory; however, this theatre was probably better known for its bar, which was a favourite local 'watering hole'. Video stores did a roaring trade. Satellite dishes also appeared during the 1990s and opened television choices to more than just the government-controlled Zimbabwe Broadcasting Commission (ZBC). Overseas coverage of sporting events was enthusiastically received, turning locals for a while into international participants, although many soon found the quarterly US$45 subscription fee 'way too steep' and opted out of the schemes. Australian programmes avidly watched and taken to reflect life in the West included *Neighbours*, *Home and Away* and *Rex Hunt's Fishing World*. Many white homes also tuned in to the English-language radio station with its mixture of 1970–1980s hit tunes, informative discussions on gardening, home decorating and agriculture and Sunday church services. Few books were available for purchase, bookshops often being little more than stationers; yet Zimbabwe had an established printing industry and Harare hosted an annual book fair that attracted a regional clientele. Some families made use of the suburban libraries where elderly white volunteers helped out and English-language books and an occasional British magazine and newspaper such as *The Telegraph* and *Spectator* were on hand. Titles were, however, outdated and budget constraints meant very few recent publications were added to the collections.

Holidays were usually taken in the company of groups of relatives or friends, commonly to destinations in South Africa, perhaps to stay with people who had already emigrated or to go to the beach. People interested in wildlife would drive to Zimbabwe's game parks or further afield to Botswana or Namibia. An invitation to stay for a few days on a houseboat on Lake Kariba owned by a syndicate of friends was especially popular with men, or fishing and golfing at Nyanga in the Eastern Highlands and the Vumba Plateau outside of Mutare. For the less well off, National Parks' Department huts and campsites, built during Rhodesian times and now showing their age, offered an alternative. These located in pioneer or prime wilderness sites, such as the Matopos Hills and the Zambezi Valley, sustained white identity. I also met individuals who had never travelled as far as the Eastern Highlands, several hours away from Harare by car. Others, growing up in Matabeleland, had their movements confined well into adulthood because of the continuing insecurity in this part of the country—a situation that prevailed into the late 1980s.[19] Only with peace was it possible to safely venture farther afield. While some young whites headed off overseas as backpackers on working holidays, it was only a small minority of the very wealthy who contemplated a holiday in Europe. As part of foreign exchange control, the government set holiday allowances, just as during the Rhodesian era. Others nostalgically remembered times before the war when these trips were possible, the British and Rhodesian currencies being of equivalent value, and they were global travellers.

All in all, these factors added up to a limited exposure to new ideas or contact with the world outside Southern Africa, insularity heightened by foreign currency regulations. Thus white Zimbabweans enjoyed a comfortable, if provincial, lifestyle in which old friends and outdoor activities were crucial. A few used the term 'colonial' to describe it; 'the New Year's Eve dance at hotels in the mountains, watching cricket from beneath the trees, nothing much has changed', they said, 'it's all still very colonial'. And, thanking me, they applied this term to themselves as having somehow fallen behind the times, musing 'it's good to have you come and sit with old colonials like us'. Notwithstanding its limitations, this white lifestyle also provided the model of materiality and domestic assistance that middle-class blacks sought to emulate.

The argument

The new regime of Robert Mugabe, coming to power in 1980, was well aware that decolonisation would require a project of mental or imaginative disengagement

---

19   Kriger (2007:66) notes that more white farmers and their families were murdered in Matabeleland during the 1982–87 conflict than during the liberation war.

(Ngugi wa Thiong'o 1988:90; Nederveen Pieterse and Parekh 1995:4) for whites as well as blacks and their participation in what would prove to be a programme of profound change. Separation from the majority, however, raised questions with regard to white receptivity, their readiness to confront the crisis of identity awaiting them or to 'come home' by embracing an alien mode of life thereafter (Dallmayr 1993:155). Where some among Rhodesia's white educated elite (Broby 1978) had favoured the continuation of European privilege on account of their skills, the incoming government encouraged them to stay, not by offering compensations or incentives, but by announcing a policy of national reconciliation.

The terms offered to whites to stay after independence are outlined in the following chapter. The argument is advanced that reconciliation introduced a debate about racial identity and clarified official expectations of whites who opted to remain in the country. More particularly, by de-absoluting and problematising the present, reconciliation opened up the possibility that things could be different (Falzon 1998:69) and that a new conversation or relationship between the former colonisers and colonised could evolve. Outward signs taken during the 1980s to reflect whites' willingness to reconcile included emigration figures, voting patterns and their preparedness to advance the government's national development goals.

Moves towards black self-determination and sovereignty began with the symbolic and spatial re-inscription of the country. Chapter 3 describes the decolonisation of Rhodesia's national iconography and geographical landscape that mirrored Zimbabwe's shifting social relations. Colonial landmarks and symbols linking Rhodesia's history to the territory were revised during the 1980s and early 1990s, eradicating from the landscape social knowledge that privileged white identity, decentring the settlers and denaturalising their presence. Whites, contesting this, produced an alternative metaphysics of European settlement—also identified in this chapter—which served to root them firmly and legitimately in Zimbabwean soil.

With the removal of white knowledge, the question of what was now to be remembered about the colonial era proved critical to the decolonisation process. Chapter 4 discusses the official critique of Rhodesia's past objectified at Heroes' Acre, a monument that provides a concrete and visual display of the settlers' interpellation in the discursive constitution of national rebirth. The chapter asks to what extent whites recognised themselves and were able to invest in the subject positions on display and suggests that settlers and their descendants were offered only a few limited ways of being in history. Importantly, as a body of knowledge, this icon embedded colonialism as a cognitive frame, thereby putting in place the ideological foundation necessary for the State's future nationalisation projects.

Remaking the country to reflect a black identity also required that moral codes be reworked. Revisions to the scope and meaning of Zimbabwean citizenship provide examples. Chapter 5 describes the 1984 exercise of renunciation of foreign citizenship that was to put an end to the separation of the former colonists and colonised. Here, the State looked for evidence of a sense of commitment from settlers, of loyalty objectified in, among other things, passports, tools in the politics of their identification. Court decisions and legislative revisions, also detailed in this chapter, suggested greater weight being placed on *jus sanguinis*, of belonging in terms of descent, as the basis for citizenship of the country. Consequently, whites had little confidence that their claim to citizenship on the basis of birthright would be accepted.

Ideas about who belonged and how they belonged in racial and cultural terms also surfaced in debate surrounding economic decolonisation. Chapter 6 addresses the prominence given indigene representations from the early 1990s—hitherto a term unheard in Zimbabwe's identity politics—in an anticipatory discourse of black economic empowerment. The grounds on which whites believed that they too could legitimately position themselves as indigenes and call Zimbabwe home are examined. Their perceptions did not, however, enjoy widespread acceptance among the majority. Instead, the black discourse produced whites as aliens, between cultures and countries, and the 'poetics' of their displacement (Kaplan 1990:26) was captured in the designation of white farmland described towards the end of the chapter.

Chapter 7 shifts the focus from pragmatic to affective dimensions of community identification. It suggests how subjectivity and the remaking of identity, emerging out of Zimbabwe's changed power relations, have been felt and interiorised by members of the white community, generating within them a sense of being disconnected from their history and homeland. The question is posed rhetorically whether whites could think, or imagine, a way through estrangement and find a passage out of their current deracination. The search by a few to find common ground and engage with blacks in pushing for government accountability and constitutional reform is then described.

Thus, in large measure, this is a study of Zimbabwe's borders and boundaries from 1980 to 1999, all in one way or another informed by memories of Rhodesia's colonial period. Where some had a taxonomic clarity, others were more a matter of personal definition. Nonetheless, each record structured consciousness, separating people from one another, and reflected the whites' corresponding journey from pioneers to exiles. Reading now scholarly works of Zimbabwe from 2000, I am struck by how much has changed, yet at the same time many underlying ideas appear ever familiar. Chapter 8 provides a postscript that illustrates the continuing purchase of memory in multi-party electoral challenges and land reform that have fed the 'Zimbabwean crisis' at the start of the twenty-first century. In conclusion, the suggestion is made that there is a strong theoretical distinction between the post-colonialism of New World settler societies and the Old World states of Africa and Asia. An undifferentiated use of the term elides radically different ways in which decolonisation has taken place, the possibilities for settlers putting paid to the past and the trajectory out of colonialism for those who elect to make their home in the post colony.

2. Zimbabwe's discourse of national reconciliation

Rhodesia's war concluded with the Lancaster House Constitutional Conference held in London between August and December 1979. Elections[1] the following February brought Robert Mugabe into office as Prime Minister and leader of the Zimbabwe African National Union Patriotic Front (ZANU PF). A policy of national reconciliation was part of the political settlement and, in light of this, plans for the future direction of the nation were established. Elsewhere new governments intent on employing a policy of national reconciliation 'as the official normalisation of a previously abnormal condition' have confronted the dilemma of 'how to remember the unjust or criminal social order that was contested and superseded, while also working for the peaceful co-existence of hitherto antagonistic communities' (Parry 1995:86). This tension is discussed with reference to Zimbabwe, where a policy of national reconciliation set out to address how the former colonisers and the once colonised might live together in the future—a problem predated by identities created by the racial classifications instituted during Rhodesia's colonial era.

This chapter comprises several sections. First, the terms negotiated by the government of national unity in order to achieve peace and national reconstruction are outlined and a space of new possibilities is identified that opened to the former colonists within the politics of belonging. White responses are described, together with outward indicators taken by the government to reflect their acceptance of the new social order. '[A] culture of reconciliation' is not, however, based solely on the promises and expectations of political leaders (McCandless and Abitbol 1997:2). In Zimbabwe, reconciliation has proved to be a multifaceted project, grounded in local initiatives and institutions, which theorise reconciliation somewhat differently to the State. To this end, the discourse of other parties to the process—in particular Christian and civil rights groups—is detailed. Then the government's amnesty—the strategy embedded in its policy of reconciliation for dealing with atrocities committed during the civil war—is examined. Particular attention is paid to the amnesty's capacity to engender insight into the historical legacy, which is necessary to reach some agreement about and to forge a new and just society.

---

1 Mugabe and Nkomo fought the election separately. Mugabe's ZANU party won 57 seats and Nkomo's ZAPU party 20, the polls reflecting their regional support.

The official national reconciliation discourse

On 4 March 1980, in an address to the nation, the Prime Minister Elect, Robert Mugabe, introduced the idea of national reconciliation. He promised to abide by the conditions of the Lancaster House Agreement and acknowledged that peace and stability could be attained only if people felt a definite sense of individual security. Mugabe continued:

> I urge you, whether you are black or white, to join me in a pledge to forget our grim past, forgive others and forget, join hands in a new amity, and together as Zimbabweans, trample upon racialism, tribalism and regionalism, and work hard to reconstruct and rehabilitate our society... Let us deepen our sense of belonging and engender a common interest that knows no race, colour or creed. Let us truly become Zimbabweans with a single loyalty.[2]

The new government hoped to promote a stronger national consciousness and unity across racial and regional lines by encouraging all the people who lived in the country to think of themselves first and foremost as Zimbabweans. Reconciliation was to make 'everyone believe that this country belonged to them', to inculcate 'the spirit of belonging' in the minds of everybody, black and white.[3] There was good reason for this. During the war, Mugabe, Nkomo and their respective troops had been rivals and distrustful of each other (Moore 1995). While both leaders wanted to see the end of white rule, they adopted different strategies for liberating the country. Where ZANLA, the numerically larger, pursued a Maoist-inspired guerrilla war that involved politicising the black population, ZIPRA, with Soviet support, conducted a more conventional campaign (Alexander 1998:152). Recruitment along regional lines reflected the importance of patron–client relations and left each of the liberation armies dominated by a different language group (Alexander 1998; Bhebe and Ranger 1995:16).[4] Moreover, other blacks, about whom little has yet been documented, had joined the lower ranks of the Rhodesian military and police[5] forces.

---

2 Mugabe, Prime Minister Elect, Address to the Nation, Zimbabwe Department of Information, 4 March 1980.
3 *Parliamentary Debates,* 3 March 1998, col. 3648.
4 At the same time each liberating force faced the challenge of generating popular backing. Where Ranger (1985:284) writes of 'a consistent peasant political ideology and programme', Kriger (1988:320) is more circumspect regarding sustained popular support or cooperation with the comrades. She argues that, although they had grievances, the black populace had to be cajoled with future promises and acts of violence to participate in the struggle. The nationalist cause therefore meant different things to the black elite and the bulk of the black population, who were divided also by lineage, gender and class interests (Hodder Williams 1980:104). Kriger (1988:320) further suggests the war was a time for settling old scores within rural communities, 'an opportunity for various oppressed groups to challenge their oppressors', of which whites and the Rhodesian State were but one, and not always the 'most vulnerable or accessible'. 'To accuse people of not supporting the war,' she writes 'became a nationalist disguise for a host of social and political struggles, and many simply petty rivalries'—a point Ranger (1985:285–7) also concedes.
5 See Chaza 1998.

Mugabe's words were directed as much towards black/black relations as they were to the black/white divide, for infighting between the now victorious nationalist forces had been endemic during the struggle (Kriger 1988; Sithole 1987:90). Reconciliation sought to contain these tensions. With independence, three mutually suspicious armies of ZANLA, ZIPRA and the Rhodesian forces, plus the private militias of internal settlement leaders Muzorewa and Sithole, required integration into a single Zimbabwean Army and Police Force. Here the policy was, at best, only partially successful (Alexander and McGregor 2004:81). Competing black leaders now felt it 'necessary for the principal actors to scale each other's strength and will to rule' (Sithole 1991:554). Although Nkomo and a few of his cohorts were included in Mugabe's government, the early years of independence were, at times, unstable, as factional fighting broke out between Mugabe's ZANLA and Nkomo's ZIPRA forces in the major cities (Alexander 1998:154; Astrow 1983:166–71). Disturbances in the south of the country led to Nkomo's sacking in 1982 and presented a more serious challenge to national reconciliation (see below).

The new leadership offered reconciliation to whites—who had fought but lost a war to protect their privileged position—as a demonstration of respect for past enemies, for minorities and, importantly, as magnanimous behaviour befitting victors. Mugabe said 'nothing is so mean as for the powerful to turn vindictive against the vanquished or the victor to press his advantage too far' (Shamuyarira et al. 1995:36). There were to be 'no Nuremburg-style trials' and Zimbabwe's form of reconciliation was a policy of 'no victor, no vanquished' (Shamuyarira et al. 1995 41–2). Certainly, some blacks did not want to reconcile and expected vengeance to be theirs (Kraybill 1994:211), to settle old scores with their erstwhile colonial enemies.[6] So there were instances where reconciliation ran counter to popular feeling and leadership had to take a persuasive role to 'impress the moral correctness' of its policy (Shamuyarira et al. 1995:48). Where this was the case, it was sometimes difficult for blacks to know how to behave towards their former masters since retribution was denied them in Mugabe's speech.[7]

Revenge was foregone in the interest of national development and reconstruction. In light of this, 'past differences had to be forgotten and past crimes forgiven' so that people could get on with tackling the country's social and economic problems (Shamuyarira et al. 1995:39). The government committed itself to building a just society based on the introduction of its version of African socialism. Ferguson (1993:83) describes African socialism elsewhere on the continent as a moralising ideology that extends African family metaphors of sharing, solidarity and mutuality to the nation, and contrasts these qualities

---

6   *The Senate,* 20 January 1982, col. 1187.
7   Ibid.

with European capitalism—a selfish and individualistically acquisitive economic system.[8] Rhodesian settler capitalism, which had seen the exploitation of the majority by a few, would be replaced with 'socialism with a human face' and Zimbabwe's new social order would reflect the communal nature of traditional African society.[9] This objective was set out in the government's *Growth with Equity* document (Government of Zimbabwe 1981:1) and was built into its first *National Development Plan* (Government of Zimbabwe 1982), which targeted, in particular, social welfare spending on health, education and transport, particularly in the hitherto neglected rural sector.

Reconciliation therefore contained the seeds of the State's vision of a just post-colonial society. A more equitable social order was to be achieved through government expenditure and improving the pay and conditions of service, rather than by the redistribution of property. Notwithstanding this, state direction of private enterprise (in the form of marketing arrangements, price and rent controls, allocation of foreign exchange and so forth) was deemed necessary to ensure the economy operated with 'a social conscience' and saw a more equitable distribution of goods and services. The private sector was expected to play its part in meeting goals set by the government through employment creation and foreign exchange earnings. At the same time, as the above speeches suggested, Mugabe was at pains to allay white fears and assure them there was room for all, that they also had a stake in the new country. Civil servants' pensions were assured and individual property rights would not be interfered with unconstitutionally. In effect, reconciliation signalled that socioeconomic transformation would be carried out in an orderly manner (Shamuyarira et al. 1995:32; Astrow 1983:163, 171) and the new society forged within the parameters of the law.

The idea of personal transformation was pivotal to Zimbabwe's reconciliation policy. Official spokesmen were keenly aware that, at independence, whites remained burdened with identities from Rhodesia's past. Zimbabwe's President at the time, Canaan Banana, noted 'white people needed to be liberated from their false sense of self importance—while blacks needed to be liberated from a sense of self rejection' (quoted in Lapsley 1986:6). Colonialism was an affliction they shared in common and decolonisation implied the transformation of both parties to the relationship. At the 1980 independence celebrations, Prime Minister Mugabe had warned that individuals could not afford to be

---

8   See also Grillo 1993.
9   May (1987:35–42) describes in some detail the rights and responsibilities of family membership in Zimbabwe.

backward looking men of yesterday, retrogressive and destructive…
Henceforth you and I must strive to adapt ourselves, intellectually and
spiritually, to the reality of our political change and to relate to each other
as brothers bound to one another by a bond of national comradeship.[10]

Decolonisation would entail active confrontation with colonial modes of thought. Mugabe continued, 'our new nation requires of every one of us to be a new man, with a new mind, a new heart and a new spirit'[11]—that is, metaphorically to be 'born again'. Reiterating this message, other members of the ruling party made it abundantly clear that change, reciprocity and correcting the wrongs of the past were integral to their understanding of reconciliation and provided 'the steps' as it were 'to cross the bridge from Rhodesia to Zimbabwe'.[12] Accordingly, the State's reconciliation discourse opened a dialogue about colonial identity. The policy drew whites into a process of mental disengagement from the past as the means to their liberation and reformation, in order that they be 'freed from the role of an oppressor', a role that had been theirs for decades (Banana quoted in Murphree 1980:4). Their identity would be rebuilt or reconstituted within representations of the new era (Hall 1990:222).

It was not the intention of the new government to drive anyone out of the country. Hodder-Williams (1980:105) made the point that, not only did the transfer of power take place rapidly in Zimbabwe but, having waged a long guerrilla war, incoming nationalist leaders had not been groomed for administration and were therefore ill prepared for government. White skills were needed. It was also doubtful whether the new nation could survive the flight of capital. Political leaders encouraged the minorities to stay. For instance, the Prime Minister requested a meeting with Salisbury Rotarians at which he said:

[T]hose of you with skills will continue to be in great demand…What surprises us in Government is why…some of you should feel either too frightened or too dismayed to remain in the country and play your noble part [in national development]…Of course, if one cannot reconcile oneself to the new political order by adjusting one's mind and heart to the reality of majority rule and the reality of a ZANU Government, then in those circumstances, we certainly would be happier without him and he, I suppose would be happier without us. My concern, however, is not for the negative man…No sane political leaders…can…fail to recognise and appreciate the existence and worth of a community so sizeable and so culturally and economically strong as our white community.[13]

---

10 'The wrongs of the past must stand forgiven and forgotten', *The Herald,* 18 April 1980, p. 4.
11 Ibid.
12 *Parliamentary Debates,* 12 June 1980, cols 772–3, and 30 June 1987, col. 29.
13 'Reconciliation a reciprocal process', Zimbabwe Department of Information, 7 April 1982.

The Minister of Labour and Social Services, Kumbirai Kangai, gave similar encouragement when he addressed white commercial farmers in 1980. He was 'amazed' farmers should be leaving in peacetime after fighting so bravely during the war.

> Through thick and thin you persisted in carrying on and were able to produce substantial outputs. I am extremely concerned to hear that there are quite a number of farmers already giving up, and many more thinking along the same lines…This is your home. We want you to stay.[14]

Farmers who were prepared to remain and give the new government a chance were, he went on, 'true Zimbabweans'. This was also the message taken by government and Commercial Farmers Union (CFU) representatives as they toured the countryside during the early 1980s, talking to various white groups, reassuring them and asking them to stay. White farmers, producing 90 per cent of the country's food requirements, found themselves feted (Palmer 1990:167). The same invitation was extended by the Prime Minister to the Asian community at a dinner they had organised to raise funds for the country's independence celebrations. Here Mugabe pressed Asians to 'feel that they are members of one unified nation', which must make 'maximum use' of their business skills. He made reference to the expulsion of Ugandan Asians in 1972, but reassured local Asians that they were 'citizens of the country' and had a vital role to play in nation building. 'Zimbabwe is your country, take pride in its development,' he said.[15]

On these various occasions, officials signalled white accommodation, the conditional acceptance of minorities and their inclusion on the basis of personal change and contributions to national projects. Letters from members of the black majority indicated that they too were aware of white utility in terms of employment opportunities, wealth creation and until such time as skills could be transferred. Writers suggested that, in recognition of 'the second chance generously afforded them', whites should commit themselves to service to the nation by 'uplifting the black standard of living' so that everyone in Zimbabwe could live in prosperity.[16] Those 'who are not prepared to assist… demolish poverty among Africans…should leave the country'.[17] Evidence of such thinking was to be found during fieldwork. Whites who helped Africans 'to come up' were commended as 'people who know why they are here' (in Africa). Mr and Mrs Connolly from Chidamoyo Mission received this accolade for projects 'geared for the betterment of blacks'.[18]

---

14 'Kangai calls on farmers to stay', *The Herald*, 18 July 1980, p. 1.
15 'PM praises Asian community', Zimbabwe Department of Information, 25 April 1984, p. 2.
16 'Whites should accept change', *MOTO,* 5 July 1980, p. 2.
17 'Fight poverty or leave the country', *The Herald,* 19 September 1980, p. 10.
18 'Black people at heart', *The Herald,* 2 October 1997, p. 12.

Thus, reconciliation, as a liberal-pragmatic regime of truth (Sylvester 2000:145), identified the minorities and co-opted them as potential nation builders despite early indications of their ambivalent identification with the nationalist state. Reconciliation, according to the Minister of Economic Planning, was to harness their energies and abilities in order that the high expectations of the black majority at independence could be met through economic development.[19] As part of 'governmentality' (Foucault 1991:92), the State's discourse 'managed' the former colonists by reproducing them as 'useful and docile bodies' but did not release them from 'the burden of being special' (Ndebele 1998:24). Nominated a special role in nation building served to underline, or highlight, minority difference, just as the role simultaneously incorporated and kept them in structural and racial opposition to the majority.

White reflections

In hindsight, what did white informants hear, or find meaningful, in Mugabe's reconciliation speech? What were their private recollections of that time? First and foremost, white informants heard that there would be no revenge or retribution. This early perception was encapsulated in comments that reconciliation meant 'let[ting] bygones be bygones', 'forgiveness', 'no witch-hunt', 'bringing people together', 'liv[ing] happily together' and 'we'll all be equal'. Several made the point that there were many anxious whites at independence, especially among the ranks of the Rhodesian Front and the security forces. A Rhodesian army officer recalled discussing the impending transition of power 'in a big family meeting'. His, and his wife's, family had lived for generations in Southern Africa:

> We are both able to trace relatives who arrived in Rhodesia in the 1890s. A grandfather, born on the trek north,[20] survived well into his nineties. He therefore lived through the whole colonial era in Rhodesia…This is our home. We decided to stay…even though we thought perhaps we could be strung up from the lampposts in First Street.

Similarly, a conscript, stationed near the South African border during the final months of the war, was aware that retribution was on the minds of captured 'terrorists'. City dwellers also recalled worrying incidents: 'Three months before the end of the war, drunk interim government soldiers trained AKs at us as we walked down the streets of Salisbury.' Mugabe's speech discouraged thoughts

---

19 *Parliamentary Debates*, 5 May 1981, col. 1909.
20 This was an English-speaking trek making its way north from the Cape in South Africa during the 1890s into what had just become Rhodesian territory.

of revenge and called in the guns. Whites such as these heard the reconciliation speeches emanating from representatives of the new government with relief and began to think that perhaps they could remain in the country after all.

Liberals, who had stood in opposition to the Rhodesian Front and argued that majority rule was inevitable, felt they had less to fear. Some initially responded enthusiastically to the idea of reconciliation.

> We were stunned by the sincerity of Mugabe's reconciliation speech… we were all victims of Rhodesian Front propaganda and expected a monster…at the time we felt genuinely glad that we could all be Zimbabweans, we were delighted, but now that this has not been so, there are a lot of disillusioned whites and disappointed blacks.

A conscientious objector, who described the war as 'the lost years, just a big gap of waiting until I could come back home', was in the United Kingdom at the time. He recalled listening to Mugabe's speech on the BBC and thinking 'it was a good start, a typically generous response of the blacks…even after a civil war we can still be friends'. He also wondered, however, whether it was a doctrine that would change ingrained attitudes. In retrospect, he thought not. Someone else who 'hadn't had a war' was also struck by the amicable, friendly black response to him as a white, while walking around a regional centre soon after the end of hostilities. There was 'no spitting-on-you attitude because we'd lost the war, rather smiles and greetings. All the races had a let's-work-together, let's-build-together attitude at that time, but now blacks are far more hard-nosed about politics and business.' A younger man, in his final year at a private school near Salisbury in 1980, had felt that

> the principle of reconciliation was right. At school it was not discussed, but we senior boys knew the whites were no longer in charge after 1980. The only way to sort out our lives together was to do things with the Africans. Reconciliation took time. At first it was strange because, during the war, the white sense of community was strong, we were like one big family. But, we had to forget the past and adjust. We did it naturally; we did not need to be told what to do by our teachers or by the government.

White liberals such as these accepted reconciliation as simply one of the terms of the peace settlement and credited the ruling elite with giving the white community 'a morale boost' in 1980 by including whites in the new government.[21]

---

21 Dennis Norman, David Smith and, a little later, Chris Andersen were included in the government of national unity. After the abolition, in 1987, of the 20 seats reserved for whites under the Lancaster House *Constitution*, ZANU PF has continued to 'absorb opposition' and demonstrate its commitment to reconciliation

Mugabe's notion of personal transformation, of repudiating the colonial ethos, appeared harder to grasp. The idea proved difficult to speak about, was glossed over and described as 'a vague philosophy that did not spell out specifically what was expected between races and ethnic groups in day-to-day living'. The young man in his final year of school cited immediately above nominated the importance of 'doing things together'—notably, in his case, when playing sports. His reflections intimate some recognition of the need to build dialogic relationships of equally placed participants or coevals (Parry 1995:94). An elderly woman understood personal transformation more in terms of confronting cultural difference. Wondering if liberals like herself should have been more sceptical, that perhaps Mugabe's speech offering reconciliation 'had been too good to be true', she asked rhetorically:

> What was it that the government hoped for, or envisaged, from us in 1980? Did they want a homogeneous society? Did they expect us all to become black? What has in fact happened is that urban blacks are becoming whiter materially, educationally, in interests and leisure activities.

Her remarks are touched with some anxiety about the subordination of her own identity in light of the social and cultural restructuring that has accompanied political change. They also suggest she had grappled with the idea of the reconciliation of diverse cultures, set against a backdrop of increasingly rapid class differentiation among the black majority, for as Raftopoulos (2004a:169) notes, there has been limited recognition of countervailing European influences in the making of Zimbabwean identities.

Other, more intransigent, whites dismissed the policy's relevance for themselves, arguing that it had more to do with 'the older' or 'the younger' white generation. Credit for its introduction as a cornerstone of the new government was denied in other ways. Some pointed out that while 'Mugabe was seen as a saint overseas', the British had, in fact, imposed reconciliation on the new government at the Lancaster House Conference. Similarly, remarks such as 'you probably heard more about reconciliation outside the country than in it', as the policy was well received internationally, demeaned its local import. Others saw little chance of reconciliation working between blacks. They made reference to the latent hostility they noticed between blacks, originating from different regions of the country, employed in the army and Forestry Commission soon after independence and they doubted the effectiveness of the doctrine to contain these tensions.[22] A few informants preferred not to comment.

---

by appointing white MPs (Zimbabwe Department of Information, 10 December 1987, p. 2). While research was under way, two whites held ministerial posts: Dr Timothy Stamps, Minister of Health, and, until 1997, Denis Norman, Minister of Agriculture.

22 See also Zaffiro 1984:103; Alexander 1998.

The significance of the policy cannot, however, be underestimated. Vekris (1991:13) describes Mugabe's declaration as a 'unique opportunity, not only to start building a civilised, prosperous and peaceful nation, but also one that brought together peoples from many and diverse ethnic backgrounds into a united community in a way never achieved anywhere else before'. Importantly for present purposes, reconciliation provided whites with the right to remain in the country with the proviso that they engage in personal transformation and decolonise their identity. In effect, the policy invited critical reflection from them, encouraging and fostering forms of cultural self-recreation (Falzon 1998:70); thereby, the 'grim polarities' of Rhodesia's colonial encounter could perhaps be bridged.

Migration as a barometer of reconciliation

Rhodesian leaders had portrayed immigration figures as 'a barometer of the views and the confidence that people outside the country have of us' (Harris 1972:70). Conversely, emigration evoked strong negative emotions as well as secretiveness among them; they were never sure of each other's readiness to stay and defend Rhodesia's 'western standards' and its 'Christian way of life' (Schultz 1975). In mid 1979, the white population totalled 232 000, the figure dropping to 148 000 just over two years later (CSO 1987:15, 17). Many seemingly loyal compatriots had packed up and left with majority rule. About 100 000, known as 'when wes' because of their predilection for referring back to their lives in Rhodesia, settled permanently in South Africa (Uusihakala 2008:1).

The themes of migration and reconciliation were also linked during the early 1980s. The new government employed migration figures, this time as a metaphor for or 'barometer of reconciliation'. The media repeatedly quoted numbers to demonstrate that fewer whites were leaving, more were returning and hence concluding 'reconciliation works'.[23] Certainly, in official thinking, and as articulated by Mugabe to the Rotarians mentioned earlier, emigration was taken to signal that a person could not 'fully accept the reality of the new social and economic order'[24] and refused to live under a black government. A black political activist and thorn in the side of the former Rhodesian government provided some background to this way of thinking:

> There wasn't hatred between the races during the war, but suspicion. Each side was suspicious of what the other would get up to next. Those whites who left did nothing to allay black suspicions, and in the event, let remaining whites down…Suspicion continues today. The

---

23 'Reconciliation works', *The Herald*, 26 June 1985, p. 4. See also Shamuyarira et al. 1995:40.
24 *Parliamentary Debates*, 15 August 1980, col. 1655.

government is suspicious of Rhodies regrouping overseas, and worried about disenchanted blacks, left out of the current wealth grab, following a white leader.

In view of this, it is not surprising to find some whites arguing 'I'm still here, aren't I', as if little more is expected from them. 'Those of us who have stuck it out and are still here have proved we have reconciled...anyone who could not reconcile has left.' It had been a case of 'last in, first out', with subject positioning as a new or old immigrant important to understanding relationships with the country, and 'sojourners' were now long gone. The next informant also alludes to the political nature of emigration:

> When my parents left, they left for good. They bought one-way tickets, sold everything and advised the necessary government departments. My father did not leave a side door open [by buying return tickets and exiting as holiday makers], so he could not come back economically and now he could not come back politically.

The way this couple exited the country sent an unequivocal message. A conciliatory official from the Ministry of Home Affairs in the early years of independence said, however: 'It's the white African who goes from here who is most likely to feel lost. And he is the most likely to come back.'[25] Another, whose letters I will quote from at some length, did just that. The extracts describe the woman's personal transformation in terms of the experience of deracination, emigration and the decision to return to Zimbabwe.

> We began our preparations to leave our home, our country, our friends. All the bric-a-brac collected over years was sorted out, all the things that had been saved 'just in case' ruthlessly dealt with. Possessions were shed, leaving only a minimum, the most loved pieces and the most practical. Somehow, throughout the period of cleaning away, giving away and packing away, I felt I had been anaesthetised, going through all the motions until finally we were people without a past, without a history...We moved in with friends for the last two weeks of our time in Zimbabwe while all the threads of our old existence were neatly tied... Emigration is the transplant of a psyche, the transplant of a body as well as a soul...I felt I was wearing a hair shirt...Nor was I prepared for the ego bashing. At home one has a place in the community...emigration leaves me a tadpole gasping for survival in the muddy periphery of a foreign pond.

---

25 'Zimbabwe's emigrants head back', *The Sunday Mail*, 7 November 1982, p. 1.

The family's subsequent return to the country late in 1984 appeared to the author as the ultimate rite of passage, reflecting her reconciliation with, and recommitment to, the new Zimbabwe.

> Pride is a convoluted human emotion, but we had to be true to ourselves and admit that the move for us, at our age, was the wrong thing. It takes a certain courage to leave one's home and, I think, it took even more to analyse our situation and decide to return…The days in Zimbabwe still dawn sunny and crystal clear, I still look out from our bedroom window…this time rejoicing in the fact that we have been given a second chance…I have achieved a certain serenity from the knowledge that although we have problems here, there are as many on the other side, just different ones…Its [the African continent's] problems are ours, the destinies of its various peoples intertwined, best solved by those who belong here [not expatriates]. Why not seize the challenge of solving the problems, in this place, at this time, rather than looking for another place in the sun where, as an immigrant, one doesn't get the chance to be effective. In fact, make adjustments in one's own country… Our strength is that we belong.

In this passage, the Rhodesian legacy is put to one side, transcended rather than worked through or processed (Parry 1995:89), the writer reconciling with Zimbabwe and its problems by moving beyond the past.

Nation building as reconciliation

Reconciliation was not, however, simply an invitation to stay or even to return to reside again in the country but, more importantly, encapsulated the expectation that the white community should join in nation building. Cognisant of this, the CFU advised its members shortly after the transfer of power to 'keep your head down, don't be provoked, get on with what you do well'—namely, large-scale farming. There would be knock-on effects from this. Farmers were 'desperately unsettled at independence' and 'if they could be persuaded to stay, this gave confidence to urban whites, for agriculture is the backbone of the country's economy'. A former CFU representative retold a joke he had shared with a nervous Afrikaner when party officials addressed a meeting, reassuring farmers and asking them to remain in the country, soon after independence at Bindura, a rural centre 100 kilometres or so north-east of Harare. The farmer approached the CFU official and said, 'I'm emigrating.' 'Where to?' asked the official. 'I'm leaving Rhodesia for Zimbabwe,' replied the farmer. I was to hear this hoary tale in various guises a number of times during fieldwork, always with the notion of the pluri-locality of home (Bammer 1992:vii) and its metaphor of an imagined, transformative migration.

The CFU believed that by doing their job well, and contributing to national goals through food production and foreign exchange earnings, farmers demonstrated their acceptance of reconciliation. A one-time president of the organisation said his body had been prepared 'to work with government' from the outset. He recalled that in the early years he could simply get on the phone and speak to President Mugabe. Another respondent confirmed that the 'CFU leadership wanted to get close to government in order to determine what was expected of whites; they wanted to do the right thing but it took them a few years to work out what that was'. By 1990, however, Mugabe, surrounded by party functionaries, had distanced himself. CFU leaders felt 'shut out' as government officials became more remote from the population at large. National reconciliation had by this time become something of a doubled-edged sword. Farmers, while praised for their agricultural outreach programmes that 'introduce harmony through the races working together, and generate a feeling that all belong to the same country',[26] were soundly rebuked for abusing the policy on other occasions. Speaking to this, a retired tobacco farmer believed that by the late 1980s reconciliation was being employed instrumentally and not as an effort to reach across racial and regional divides.[27] Where reconciliation had at its introduction stood for 'togetherness', the building of trust and a sense of commonality, the meaning, now changed, simply spelt 'one must agree with ZANU PF'.

Dhalla (1993:19, 20) makes the point that reconciliation is difficult to achieve where there is little consensus about the ideologies and values necessary to constitute a new and just society. Tensions between the State and white business leaders, appearing soon after independence, underscore this observation. The predominately white private sector was avowedly for a free-market economy and had worked closely with the Rhodesian Government (Weiss 1994:129). Like the commercial farmers, they too were alarmed at independence. Speaking

---

26 The Minister of Agriculture, explaining the importance to national reconciliation of transferring skills and agricultural inputs between the large and small-scale commercial farmers (*Spotlight*, ZBC Radio 1, 9 September 1997).
27 When, in 1997, officials of the Zimbabwe Tobacco Association argued against the administration of a levy raised by growers for research and development projects being taken over by government, they were 'heavily criticised' by the state-controlled press for abusing its policy of reconciliation (see 'War path? What war?', *The Sunday Mail*, 22 June 1997, p. 8; also *Parliamentary Debates*, 10 February 1999, col. 3682). The dispute also served to highlight class tensions within the white community. For instance, while not disagreeing with the farmers' analysis, an urban white remarked that a wealthy section of white society, 'tobacco farmers should come down and live like the rest of us' instead of provoking the government's ire and drawing unwanted attention to the white community as a whole. Notwithstanding this, whites generally believed reconciliation had, by this time, come to mean largely adopting an uncritical acceptance of the new political order and government actions.

on behalf of the business community in 1984, Mr Thrush MP reported that innumerable entrepreneurs and senior executives in industry had approached and asked him whether 'the government wants us to stay', to which he replied: 'I sincerely believe the Prime Minister to be totally honest in his utterances about reconciliation.'[28]

The new regime was, however, unconvinced of the business community's preparedness to meet its national goals. By retaining Rhodesian financial restrictions and supplementing these with others of their own making, the government set in place a command economy. As far as the State was concerned, evidence of the business community's readiness to embrace reconciliation was reflected in their willingness to support investment and job creation. This role provided the private sector with some leverage over the government. Nevertheless, in the new government's thinking, some in business circles remained uncooperative and unreconciled. The Deputy Minister of Trade and Commerce, Comrade Sanyangare, therefore accused white businessmen of procrastinating and allowing business opportunities to pass them by as if they were expecting Zimbabwe to fail. This behaviour, he said, reflected a lack of commitment to national objectives and as such was a rejection of the policy of reconciliation.[29] Other party officials reiterated the message.[30]

In their own defence, white leaders talked of the links, or commonality, between the fortunes of the country and private enterprise, while at the same time questioning the sincerity of the government's position. They viewed ministerial accusations of industrial sabotage as contrary to the spirit of reconciliation and damaging to business morale. Further government measures (sales tax, lack of foreign exchange allocations, price and rent controls, inadequate and erratic electricity supplies among others) and Marxist-Leninist rhetoric all contributed to the lack of domestic and foreign investment.[31] Partly as a result of this ideological difference, Zimbabwe suffered from too little investment throughout the 1980s (Mlambo 1997:50), with concomitant slower growth and reduced economic and employment opportunities—factors the government had counted on to underpin and promote the process of national reconciliation.

Zimbabwe's policy of reconciliation was, in sum, based firmly on political and economic realism. As a discourse conceived to allay minority fears and dissuade whites from a massive exodus at independence and from acts of

---

28 *Parliamentary Debates*, 18 January 1984, col. 73.
29 'Sanyanagare attends ZNCC meeting', Zimbabwe Department of Information, 24 March 1986, p. 2. See also 'Co-operation between government and private sector vital', Zimbabwe Department of Information, 2 December 1985.
30 In another instance, addressing the Institute of Bankers, the President warned that unrepentant and unreconstructed Rhodesian frontiersmen were hindering social and political progress (*The Herald*, 13 July 1985, p. 1).
31 *Parliamentary Debates* throughout 18 January 1984, 26 January 1984, and 3 February 1984.

sabotage thereafter, the policy met with some initial success. The structures of the Rhodesian economy were not dismantled and the land question was sidelined during the 1980s (see Chapter 6). In light of this, the Minister for Education, Fay Chung (1989:9), suggests reconciliation, by leaving the previous regime's economic structures intact, 'benefited white Zimbabweans tremendously', be they in commerce and industry or commercial farming. She could also have added that the policy facilitated the 'embourgeoisement' of the ruling elite (Dashwood 1996:32),[32] for, despite episodic accusations of economic sabotage, Weiss (1994:148, 156) points out that by the end of the first decade of independence, the government and the business community had recognised their interdependence and come to an accommodation with each other. An 'implicit co-operation' developed between the State and white capital, bringing with it opportunities for patronage and enrichment (Raftopoulos and Compagnon 2003:19).

White voices

Had whites, in a private capacity, expected in the early years to reply to the offer of reconciliation other than by economic contributions and staying in the country? Did they, as later suggested by Bishop Desmond Tutu in South Africa, ask 'What is my role in bringing about reconciliation?'[33] Not much was heard of such questions around the time the policy of reconciliation was introduced in 1980. A liberal and active member of the Anglican Church, however, reflected:

> Pre-independence, we were so anti the Rhodesian Front. People like Alan Savory and Judith Todd, the opposition parties, gave us hope that we could build a multi-racial society…We thought reconciliation was great, we went into town and cheered Mugabe when he came through. I thought 'here's someone new'. Reconciliation held out a promise to me, I took a deep breath and thought at last, the people living in tents [displaced persons] can come home and start new lives…A lot of whites did not hear it, they did not change, but kept going in their own sweet way. There was no official white answer. We felt that the whites had been in charge so long, now we were handing over saying you [the new government] get on with it, we know you can do it, we will fit into your scheme. Therefore we did not feel it was necessary to answer officially, we felt we should now take a back seat. We hoped to be included, not excluded, from the new programme, but in a secondary capacity. When we realised [that a reply was necessary] it was too late. Those

---

32 See also Weiss 1994:xv; Jenkins 1997:586.
33 'Racial reconciliation is not easy in South Africa', *The Herald*, 29 July 1998, p. 3.

who could have answered for us, such as Alan Savory, had gone.[34] The others [political leaders] still here were not interested. We began to feel excluded from the political issues that affect us all.

Her words echo the thoughts of the Anglican Reverend John Da Costa towards the end of the war. At the time of the shooting down of the second Viscount[35] by ZIPRA in February 1979, he said 'others are going to set future standards, and we [the white community] may have to ride out a decade not being asked our opinions. In a word it might be time for us whites to shut up' (quoted in Hills 1981:108).

Both suggest that, as the historically dominant party, whites need to reconcile by de-authoring themselves and 'desist from rising to the top'. Their willingness to silence could be perceived as an act of deconstruction and preparedness to be de-centred. They, like Pakeha New Zealanders described by Mulgan (1989:74), might also signal acquiescence and acceptance of a new social order without the need for further discussion through their silence. Silence can, however, mean, and be read, in other ways. Whites who perceived reconciliation as 'a ploy to win international financial support' and 'a political gambit as the government was looking for 10 years of stability in which to establish itself', felt there was no moral requirement to reply.

Thus, for different reasons, whites individually did not publicly acknowledge the State's offer. Notwithstanding this, the liberal informant above indicated that some looked to white political leaders to speak for them. But who were they? Many such as Alan Savory, known to reformers as a 'voice of sanity', in part because he challenged the Rhodesian Front's interpretation of the war (Godwin and Hancock 1993:100), had emigrated. The whites remaining in Parliament were former members of the Rhodesian Front, the party having won all 20 white seats in the 1980 election.[36] Their contributions to proceedings in the House were frequently not in the spirit of reconciliation. In debate surrounding the export of emigrants' effects, for example, they ridiculed and poured scorn on the notion.[37] Invariably, the priority of white parliamentarians was to protect minority rights by wresting assurances from the new government in the name of reconciliation. Theirs was a vision of a multiracial and multicultural Zimbabwean society where

---

34 According to Auret (1992:101), Savory was 'induced' to leave Rhodesia in 1979 when it became apparent that he was to be framed on a treason charge.
35 The Reverend had achieved notoriety six months earlier when he gave his 'Deafening silence' memorial sermon after the first Viscount had been downed (see Lapsley 1986:App. 8). This sermon, misread Da Costa claims by some Rhodesians, evoked patriotic but anti-Christian emotions among parishioners (Lapsley 1986:61).
36 Soon after independence, the Rhodesian Front party changed its name to the Republican Front, with Ian Smith as its leader. Four years later, it was renamed the Conservative Alliance, although party policies remained the same throughout. A breakaway faction of white parliamentarians, unhappy with Smith's leadership, formed themselves into the Independent Group.
37 See *Parliamentary Debates*, 1 September 1981, cols 1409–506, and 27 January 1985, cols 1123–34.

minority difference was acknowledged and accommodated. Needless to say, parliamentarians backing minority interests inevitably signalled their distrust of majority rule and provoked critics to ask why minorities were singled out for special treatment. Senator Culverwell, about whom more will be said in Chapter 4, exclaimed: '[O]ne of the most profound statements that was made in this country was done on the night that we were told…that we had a landslide victory when the Prime Minister…came up and spoke about reconciliation.'[38] Culverwell therefore found it extremely difficult to understand the whites' need of reassurance and other confidence-building measures.

Mugabe had made the same point when talking of civil service pensions:

> Concern has sometimes been expressed, for example, as to whether government will honour its commitment in respect of the remittability of pensions. In spite of assurances by myself and my government, and in spite of the absence of any action to the contrary on our part, concern is still expressed in regard to our attitude on this matter…these assurances and reassurances cannot become a ritual for us which it is thought we have some sort of obligation to engage in on a regular basis. Let me be quite frank. Those who constantly talk about the remittability of pensions strike us as inordinately selfish and lacking in any degree of commitment to this country. Anyone who regards this country as his home, or who intends to make it so, cannot simultaneously seek repeated assurances…This bird of passage mentality is unhealthy and is certainly unacceptable to us.[39]

The government's vision of a morally just society was a non-racial society, devoid of any racial (or regional) distinctions. In the spirit of reconciliation, special measures based on race and ethnic categorisations were to have no part in public life.

White votes: the 1985 election

The government's frustration with the lack of a positive response from conservative white leaders to its generous offer of reconciliation spilled over after the 1985 election. Before this, concessions to white interests appeared to have been paying off, isolating reactionary white politicians from much of their electorate (Stoneman and Cliffe 1989:46). Prior to the 1985 election, the Conservative Alliance of Zimbabwe, formerly the Rhodesian Front, was left with less than half of the 20 seats it had won in 1980. The white community as a

---

38   *The Senate,* 20 October 1982, cols 1184, 1187.
39   'PM speaks on pensions', Zimbabwe Department of Information, 11 June 1981, p. 1.

whole, however, was taken to have rejected reconciliation when 15 members of the Conservative Alliance were returned to Parliament in 1985, including the former Rhodesian Front Prime Minister Ian Smith. The election campaign had been fought around the issues of national unity and peace. Of 33 485 white votes cast, the Conservative Alliance polled just more than half (18 731) and independent candidates the remainder. Almost one-third of the whites, Asians and coloureds eligible to vote did not bother to go to the polls. Nonetheless, the government viewed the number of Conservative Alliance MPs returned as an act of defiance and a betrayal of reconciliation, in essence a vote for the past[40] and a demonstration of the minorities' failure to transform their attitudes and loyalties.

Cognisant of this, a group of white liberals tried to salvage the situation by forming the Sector Representation Group, which petitioned whites to support the 'Time to Sign' campaign.[41] The campaign posed two questions to the white electorate—namely, 'Do you affirm your loyalty to Zimbabwe?' and 'Do you support the policy of reconciliation?' The response was both encouraging and disappointing, for although whites were prepared to sign, business was not forthcoming with financial assistance. In the event, the group's efforts were overtaken when the abolition of the white electoral roll, already on the government's agenda, came about in 1987.[42] The majority of whites had by this time come to recognise that a separate roll left them highly visible and vulnerable to criticism, so they did not oppose its passing. Thereafter, the vocal and, at times, disruptive (although impotent to influence legislative change) white opposition ceased to sit in Parliament and Zimbabwe became for the next 15 years a de facto one-party state. White interests continued to be represented by industry associations such as the CFU and the Confederation of Zimbabwe Industries (CZI), but not directly at the political level.

In short, the President was by the 1985 election voicing his disappointment with and doubts about the white response to reconciliation. He has become increasingly outspoken on this issue, accusing whites of spurning the policy of reconciliation, of holding back and not accepting the black hand of friendship.[43] As one of the State's systems of knowledge, the policy contains authoritarian overtones identified early on by Hodder-Williams (1980:105) as a legacy of the liberation war's command structure. Accusations of the failure to reconcile have

---

40 'Days numbered for white racists: PM', *The Herald*, 1 July 1985, pp. 1, 5.
41 'White groups dismayed at CAZ victory', *The Herald*, 2 July 1985, p. 5; 'Drive to abolish white roll gathers momentum', *The Herald*, 16 July 1985, p. 5.
42 Constitutional reforms abolished the white electoral roll, introduced an executive presidency and a unicameral parliament. The position of Prime Minister ceased to exist and Mugabe, as the leader of ZANU PF, replaced Banana as head of state.
43 'Saboteurs must leave—President', *The Herald*, 12 August 1988, p. 1; 'Mugabe castigates whites for spurning reconciliation', *The Herald*, 7 June 1996, p. 1.

become a means by which the State stifles debate and prevents discussion of mutually relevant topics. In view of this, the State's discourse of amity and peaceful co-existence had an increasingly hollow ring.

The nation in crisis: Christian approaches to reconciliation

National reconciliation was not, however, a new or novel idea in Zimbabwe. Church leaders of all denominations had repeatedly called for reconciliation of the races since UDI in 1965, and more particularly since the 1969 amendments to the *Land Act* (Lapsley 1986:74). The Anglican Bishop Burrough had spoken of 'the Church's great duty of reconciliation' (Lapsley 1986:27) at his inauguration in 1968. Moral Rearmament emissaries, also active on this score from the mid 1970s, advocated daily 'quiet times' of prayer, moments to 'listen to God' and act accordingly. Like the Anglicans, they perceived rethinking individual values as the key to social change. In addition, church leaders of various denominations could legitimately claim a place for themselves in history for their efforts in bringing various protagonists together to discuss peace initiatives (Kraybill 1994). Some attended the 1976 Geneva and 1979 Lancaster Conferences on their own volition in order to promote the idea of a politically negotiated end to the war in the spirit of Christian reconciliation (Auret 1992:95; Strong 1985:15).

As both Lapsley (1986:74) and De Waal (1990:65) pointed out, however, while there were notable exceptions, such as the Roman Catholic Bishop Lamont and the Anglican Bishop Skelton, too many white clergy expected black Christians to reconcile with their white counterparts, while ignoring the racial disparities of wealth and power that were central to the armed struggle. The Anglican hierarchy—not unusually recruited from Britain and representing one-third (and the largest group) of white church members—often saw itself in partnership with the settlers. Theirs was an attitudinal understanding of reconciliation and, all too often, the Anglican Church's reconciliation discourse appeared to be little more than avoidance of 'a hard moral choice' (De Waal 1990:57).

On the other hand, the Catholic Church and its human rights watchdog, the Catholic Commission for Justice and Peace (CCJP), established in 1972, understood the Rhodesian conflict somewhat differently. They interpreted the war in structural terms and therefore saw the removal of social injustice as an imperative of reconciliation (Auret 1992). To this end, the Catholic Church set about 'listening' to the victims of human rights abuses, 'truth telling' and writing pastoral letters, as well as collecting and publishing data that illustrated the country's socioeconomic disparities—functions it continues today. Not all white parishioners, however, wished to hear what the Catholic Bishops were telling them (Auret 1992:34, 43–6). Aware of this, Vambe (1972:234) makes the point that the Christian Church in Rhodesia 'failed as a symbol of peace, understanding and brotherhood…because it has not been able to influence the hearts and mind of the European'.

After 1980, national reconciliation, although presented by the State as a moral discourse, was not infused with religious values or portrayed as a Christian approach to healing the nation. That church leaders did not play a role in framing the policy was a cause for regret to some. One, banned from talking on radio during the 1970s and present at the Geneva talks, said evangelical Christians, in particular, were concerned that Mugabe's stand regarding reconciliation was essentially political and economic—'a tactic to turn enemies into allies'. He added:

> There were no Desmond Tutus or Alex Boraines in the Zimbabwean context. The Churches in Zimbabwe let an important chance go by. The new government did not involve them, and the churches did not claim a role. The black churches were at the time prepared to let Mugabe deal with the concept politically, whereas white church leaders were too busy dealing with their own racism.

So, in the event, national reconciliation was not defined or discussed with church leaders as it was in South Africa, where religious values and a human rights discourse converged (Wilson 2000). Yet Christians in Zimbabwe felt they could contribute. They believe the State needs the collaboration of the Church, for the Church provides a model of unity for the nation to follow (Zvarevashe 1994:5). Further, political legitimacy derives from a 'moral partnership' (Werbner 1995:99) with God. National leaders therefore have a responsibility to be mindful of and nurture this relationship for the wellbeing of the land and its people. But Church leaders have been disappointed to find that, while the country's political leaders claim national paternity, they do not present themselves as spiritual leaders. As some black religious figures see things, no separation should be made between spiritual and material wellbeing. Rather, these are considered to be mutually reinforcing and the politicians' compartmentalisation of life is, therefore, denounced as 'foreign'.

Although the Mugabe Government did not call on religious leaders to participate, the evangelical churches have, nonetheless, taken it upon themselves to promote reconciliation in their own way, particularly at moments of national crisis. For instance, during the unstable years just before independence, a 'prayer thrust' known as 'A Nation at Prayer' came into being. 'Desperate people needed help as to how to hold the nation before God in a time of fear, transition and transformation' (Strong 1985:23). Thus the movement grew in response to suffering and uncertainty and the desire to see national reconciliation taking place under God (Strong 1985:13). A diary was prepared, setting prayers for each day of the year. This, published for many years as a newsletter in English, Shona and Sindabele and then later in the local paper, provided a practical guide to petitions for the nation, its political leaders and the wellbeing of the country. An estimated 27 000 Christians from almost all denominations prayed in this way every day during the critical years of transition from Rhodesia to Zimbabwe.

While public participation in the national prayer movement had slackened by the mid 1980s, interest revived a decade later, again in response to a sense of national crisis. Advertising the reinvigorated 'Nation at Prayer' in 1997, the National Chairman, Reverend Wutawunashe, noted the many problems and 'the spirit of hopelessness that oppresses the nation'. These were exemplified in, among other things, the serious fall in the value of the Zimbabwean dollar following the war veterans' payout, the volatile political situation precipitated by land designation and the confrontation between the government and the Zimbabwe Congress of Trade Unions[44]—all issues taken up in the following chapters. The solution proposed was 'not to apportion blame' but to 'pray fervently'; '[d]on't complain about it, pray about it'. In your prayers, 'name the major players…in the crisis…and ask God to intervene in their lives'. Another homily in the form of 'Stand in the gap; don't take the gap' was set before those—black and white—who might now be thinking of leaving the country.[45]

The movement's *Prayer Informer* illustrates the breadth of the evangelical vision of reconciliation. This included repentance for national acts of arrogance against neighbouring countries during the war of liberation, atrocities committed much earlier against the Bushmen who once inhabited Zimbabwe and more recent attacks by the Fifth Brigade in Matabeleland (see below). Parishioners at a multiracial, but female-dominated, lower middle-class service held in suburban Harare focused, however, on more immediate issues. Intercessors prayed about the proposed abortion bill, the state of the government's health services, the imminent collapse of the Public Service Medical Fund, the corruption and greed of national leaders, AIDS and Zimbabwe's involvement in the Congo war. Contributions also reflected their authors' inward political desires. One hoped a new Christian political party would grow out of the prayer movement; another felt the offerings were 'too negative' and parishioners should spend more energy 'giving praise'. Thus, it was Zimbabwe's more immediate national problems, rather than the colonial legacy,[46] that were foregrounded in parishioner petitions.

---

44 'Urgent call to nation-wide prayer', *The Herald,* 24 December 1997, p. 6.
45 *The Prayer Informer,* 16 March 1999.
46 The evangelical churches did, however, support a young woman from the United Kingdom who set out on Heroes Day 1998 to walk from Harare to Bulawayo. She carried a large wooden cross—her symbol of reconciliation—to apologise for the actions of her pioneer forefathers. She hoped others would join her

The previous year, in 1996, Harare's various evangelical parishes had joined together to hold a 'Heal the Wounds' service in ZANU PF's Congress Building in central Harare. Several thousand people attended. On this occasion, church members were asked to confess and repent their harboured resentment and unforgiving attitudes. Facing up to these self-truths was referred to as 'the way of coming back', the groundwork required for rebuilding trust and repairing fractured relationships. 'Ask forgiveness for our racial, tribal, cultural and ethnic prejudices. Commit ourselves not to speak negatively of our brothers and sisters, that we might set an example of a Christian family living together for the world to see.' In this, each person was perceived to be answerable ultimately to God and not to the State or any other secular authority. Evangelical Christians did not think Zimbabwe's political leaders set a good example here and accused them of making comments and speeches that stirred up 'racism, disunity, strife and discontent'. In view of this, intercessors prayed 'that the comments and speeches from our leaders would be towards reconciliation, respect and acceptance of all the peoples of Zimbabwe'.[47]

The evangelical churches therefore offered a competing reconciliation discourse that employed psychological and religious metaphors of healing and confession, enjoining a personal relationship with God and respect for the uniqueness and sanctity of others from different racial or regional backgrounds, for they were also God's children. National reconciliation, as propounded by the government, was seen to be bereft of this spiritual dimension that blacks and whites, adopting a Christian approach to reconciliation, considered paramount.

Dealing with the past: Zimbabwe's amnesty

Rosenberg (1999:327), writing the afterword to Meredith's *Coming To Terms*, suggests incoming leaders face a number of choices regarding strategies appropriate to dealing with a country's past. Zimbabwe's policy of national reconciliation contained mixed guidelines on this score. While promising that independence would bestow 'a new history' (the subject of the following chapters), Mugabe also directed at his inauguration that 'the wrongs of the past must stand forgotten and forgiven'.[48] He made clear his concern 'that my public statements should be believed when I say that I have drawn a line through the past' (quoted in Flower 1987:3). In this way, reconciliation provided an amnesty such that the misdeeds of all protagonists—be they former members

---

along the way and that her efforts would engender more harmonious race relations in Zimbabwe. Instead, the woman's appearance was met with incredulous laughter from bystanders and the local press, and after her departure, the gesture received little further comment or media attention.
47 *The Prayer Informer*, 13–14 September 1998.
48 'Address to the nation', *The Herald*, 18 April 1980, p. 4.

of the Rhodesian forces, ZANLA, ZIPRA or the militias—were treated as 'equal wrongs' (Nuttall and Coetzee 1998:2). No investigations were made, no stories told. Nor was the policy embedded in an institutional structure such as South Africa's Truth and Reconciliation Commission (TRC), set up in 1995. Zimbabwe has not publicly examined its past in the same way as South Africa has done. Consequently, the guilt of particular individuals has not been established nor the actions of white or black political figures systematically scrutinised.

Mugabe's blanket pardon, while met with relief by many whites, has proved contentious with members of the black majority. Mention was made earlier in this chapter that not all blacks wanted to reconcile. As the 1980s progressed, there was a growing tendency in some black quarters to view reconciliation as the price to offset massive white emigration and, as such, a sign of government weakness and pandering to white interests. While others argued that reconciliation should not necessarily be taken as a sign of government weakness, it was they, nonetheless, who shouldered the burden of reconciliation. Early on, a reader of the 'In Memoriam' columns had asked: '[I]s it only the African side of the tug of war which is expected to reconcile and forget the past?'[49] Critical comment became increasingly persistent:

> It appears that reconciliation is extended by blacks and blacks only as if we are apologising…They [whites] are supposed to apologise to the blacks for what happened during the colonial era. They are the ones who should have responded positively when the policy of reconciliation was extended.[50]

To date, despite belated calls from members of the black majority to do so,[51] white leaders have failed to acknowledge the crimes of the Rhodesian era. An apology, as an expression of genuine regret, would perhaps have contributed to conditions necessary for meaningful reconciliation. The appearance of amity and consent between the formerly colonised and the colonisers, so desired by Mugabe at independence, could also have gone some way in establishing grounds for white inclusion in the moral community (Tavuchis 1991:7, 22). For these things to be possible, however, former colonisers must be willing to examine and accept unfavourable facts about their history. The South African experience suggests that public hearings and confessions made to the TRC have been significant in opening the eyes of many, and a prerequisite for developing a collective history (Hamber 1997:6; Ndebele 1998:20).

---

49 'Reconciliation: is this the way?', *The Herald*, 16 September 1980, p. 4.
50 *Parliamentary Debates*, 18 February 1997, col. 3415.
51 'Saved by the government', *Sunday Mail*, 27 September 1998, p. 10; 'Queen, Smith must apologise', *The Herald*, 19 February 1999, p. 10.

Back in Zimbabwe, only a small number of whites were prepared to take stock of the past, and this was not encouraged in the early days by Mugabe as the architect of Zimbabwean reconciliation, beyond calls for their personal transformation in the interest of developing a new national identity. One who recognised that some re-evaluation, or processing, of the colonial record was missing, noted, however, that at independence he had hoped, as a 'good white', conscientious objector and Rhodesian Front critic, to be accepted as a member of the new nation. But this did not prove as easy as imagined. Reflecting upon this and Zimbabwe's amnesty in light of the role subsequently adopted by South Africa's TRC, the man believed that the hearings had the capacity to 'give freedom'. Truth telling, confession, repentance and ultimately forgiveness are cathartic experiences for the perpetrators of violence. Willingness to participate and account for one's actions indicates some commitment to recognise and right the wrongs of the past. These steps were not taken in Zimbabwe and, in light of this, another white activist wrote that 'white guilt is collective'. While whites 'are tolerated, we are not free because reconciliation without confession cannot give freedom'. This means that even those who stood opposed to the previous regime, such as this man, are 'implicated in a history we could not stop'.[52] To politically minded blacks, however, these arguments were fundamentally flawed. Proponents overlooked their own privileged position and failed to recognise that, in spite of good intentions and deeds, the beneficiaries and victims of Rhodesia's colonial era were the non-African and African populations collectively. As Karen Alexander (2004:203) points out, whites do not countenance how separate their experience has been from the black experience of Rhodesia.

While Zimbabwe's blanket pardon might have been necessary in order to make a start with problems of national development, by 'forgetting' and 'drawing a line through the past', silence was imposed on former protagonists in the name of reconciling the nation. Mutual distrust and suspicions harboured during the war went unfettered. A representative of Zimrights, a civil rights group launched in 1992, said that 'dialogue has been missing since 1980. When Mugabe reconciled, the whites did not publicly say anything. To date blacks do not know whether they accepted reconciliation.'[53] While seeking government reassurances for themselves, whites had generally not appreciated that the black majority also required some demonstration, or assurance, that signalled whites' preparedness to reconcile (Maveneka 1981:2). Instead, through complaint and refusal to face up to historical issues, they adopted a defensive and ultimately disempowering stance. De Waal rightly questions whether, in fact, the policy of national reconciliation asked too little of whites. 'They tend to think that nothing is required of them, that they do not have to make much effort to alter their attitudes' (De Waal 1990:122). As the former colonialists, however, whites

---

52 'I want my Nuremberg', *The Financial Gazette,* 20 October 1994, p. 4.
53 'Racism continues to haunt Zimbabwe', *The Chronicle,* 28 May 1996, p. 4.

are set apart from all other minorities in Zimbabwe. Not only did they remain economically influential, but independence had to be wrested from white hands. As such they have a special obligation to learn to be Zimbabwean (Vekris 1991:13). It is in their interest, as it is for the white Namibians, 'to walk an extra mile to reconcile with the wronged' (Melber 1993:25). In this regard, De Waal and Vekris argue that the white community, having failed to play an active role in creating 'the new man' or developing a shared future for all Zimbabweans, has allowed a significant opportunity to slip past them.

Reconciliation and human rights

The country's first major challenge to the policy of national reconciliation came not from the racial minorities but in the aftermath of dissident activity in Matabeleland between 1982 and 1987. The State's deployment of the exclusively Shona Fifth Brigade to the region in 1983 led to gross violations of the civil and political rights of the Ndebele people (Alexander 1998; Auret 1992:147–66). Former ZIPRA soldiers, always wary of integration and with a sense of exclusion and repression within the ranks, now defected from the National Army (Bhebe and Ranger 1995:19; Alexander 1998:150, 156). The *Gukurahundi* (the spring rains or 'the rain that washes clean') massacres ceased with the signing of the Unity Accord in 1987 and the appointment of Joshua Nkomo[54] as the second Vice-President. Alexander et al. (2000:Ch. 11) describe in some detail local attempts made since 1988 to deal with this violence, to commemorate its victims and heroes and to heal and cleanse the land and the populace from its effects. Suffice here to point out that while reconciliation as political accommodation might have occurred at the level of party leadership, it failed to embrace the common person, for ZANU PF has neither acknowledged responsibility nor paid compensation for these human rights violations. During fieldwork, simmering anger and the desire for revenge were evident at the grassroots level in Matabeleland and Midland Provinces (Amani Trust 1998:6).

With hindsight, civil rights leaders believe that by leaving in place a culture of impunity the 1980 amnesty compromised reconciliation. Through its failure to acknowledge past atrocities, the amnesty discouraged the development of a human rights culture such that violations like *Gukurahundi* could not be concealed or condoned in the future (Parry 1995:86). The Catholic Commission for Justice and Peace (CCJP and Legal Resources Foundation 1997), developing

---

54 In addition to bringing Nkomo back, Mugabe took several other members from Nkomo's ZAPU party into his government of national unity. However, with Nkomo's increasing frailty and subsequent death in 2000, the Accord appeared under threat, with calls for it to be renegotiated. While Nkomo had been portrayed as the Ndebele leader, he was in fact from a Shona subgroup, the Kalanga. The Kalanga are closely culturally affiliated with the Ndebele and together they make up 20 per cent of Zimbabwe's population.

its 'watchdog' role of the 1970s, played a central role in collecting testimony and publishing reports of the Matabeleland atrocities. The commission and other civil rights groups have called for government accountability and an apology as steps towards healing and reconciling the bitterness that remains. These organisations conceived reparations, in the form of justice, compensation and rehabilitation for the victims of organised violence, to be fundamental to reconciliation. In the light of ZANU PF's continuing refusal to acknowledge the atrocities its forces committed in Matabeleland, a broad spectrum of Zimbabweans believed the ruling party lost the moral authority it had enjoyed at independence to reconcile the nation. Notwithstanding the State's own problems with historical remembrance and accountability, the President continued throughout the 1990s to espouse the idea of reconciliation. It was a principle deployed to support ZANU PF's political platform, and racial and regional minorities were cajoled and threatened to respond. For many, however, including positively minded whites, the discourse had soured within just a few years of its introduction.

Conclusion

In this chapter, the argument was put that, at independence, the State's discourse of national reconciliation represented an attitude of ethical openness, aimed at engendering feelings of belonging in all Zimbabweans in the interest of their peaceful coexistence and national reconstruction. The official discourse opened a dialogic space to settlers, offering a way out of the colonial racial binaries by theorising identity as a production, always in process, and as much a part of the future as the past (Hall 1990:222, 225). Incorporating ideas about transformation towards a new national identity and commonality of interests, national reconciliation provided a potential site of innovation and creativity in race relations at the end of the colonial era.

Dialogue conducive to the emergence of new forms of thought and action failed, however, to emerge. There were a number of reasons for this. Zimbabwe's amnesty discouraged critical reflection of Rhodesian-era hostilities and proved insufficient to the task of building some consensus about the nature of a new and morally just society. Competing ideologies regarding the place of minority rights and the nature of the economy also proved disruptive in the decade after independence. Further, through its refusal to accept culpability or address the role of the armed forces in Matabeleland, the State obstructed the development of a human rights culture, thereby exacerbating enduring regional antagonism. These factors worked against the building of trust and repairing of relationships, which would perhaps have allowed former enemies to move forward and work together for a better future. In time, reconciliation as the State's discourse of enablement and minority accommodation gave way to constraint and discipline. It was perhaps too early in 1980 for the President to call for amity and togetherness across racial and regional lines when Zimbabwe's continuing asymmetries of socioeconomic power—the structural inequalities behind the liberation war—persisted unaddressed for another decade.

In the meantime, the recovery of a previously suppressed history received the State's attention. Although Rhodesia's hierarchically connected territorial spaces had been de-racialised in 1979 and political sovereignty was achieved a year later, the Rhodesian imprint still lay like a mantle across the country. The next two chapters examine the decolonisation of the national landscape and the memorialisation of 'the people's history' as the new government made good Mugabe's promise that 'independence will bestow on us' not just a 'new sovereignty, a new future', but 'a new history and a new past'.[55]

---

55 'Address to the nation', *The Herald*, 18 April 1980, p. 4.

3. Re-inscribing the national landscape

With majority rule, the question arose of what about Rhodesia's colonial era was to be remembered. This issue brings with it a struggle over historicity that has in part been waged over the decolonisation of Zimbabwe's national landscape. Radcliffe and Westwood (1996:28) make the point that there is a diversity of sites where correlative imaginaries between a people and a place can be produced. In this regard, states actively 'distribute space' (Driver 1992:150), setting material and representational boundaries that are formative of identities. These 'imaginative geographies' (Said 1993:6, 271) are contained, for instance, in 'the concrete and precise character' (Driver 1992) of territorial maps and texts, and are experienced subjectively by populations in their daily lives. In Zimbabwe, the re-inscription and repossession of an African identity began with the historical and geographical recovery of the territory. Several aspects of this process are addressed here and the argument is put that decolonisation of the national landscape was envisioned as an upheaval and a challenging step towards the reconstitution of white identity. First, the disassembling of Rhodesian icons, monuments and cartography in order that the landscape could be reclaimed and remade to reflect the majority is described. The white community's response, or rejoinder, to the State's erasure of the Rhodesian memory is then considered, together with the question of why remembrance of Rhodesia and the Rhodesians is an issue of future concern to them.

Dismantling Rhodesian national identity during the internal settlement

The years of contest started in earnest after the signing of the Rhodesia Constitutional Agreement in March 1978 and the accession of Bishop Abel Muzorewa to Prime Minister from April 1979. Thus, as an integral part of memory work, the restructuring of settler identity began during the transition—known as the 'internal settlement'—from white rule and before formal independence. While coming to a political settlement with moderate black leaders, white politicians were mindful of important implications inherent in the decolonisation process. They sought to salvage symbols and landmarks that provided recognition of what they saw as their community's considerable investment in the country. White leaders therefore pressed for some credit to be given to the Rhodesian memory in the externalities of Zimbabwean identity formation and in its revised symbols of personhood that encoded national belonging. The following sections illustrate their concerns with particular reference to decolonisation of the country's name and flag.

The interim government introduced the joint names of Zimbabwe Rhodesia early in 1979. While white liberals expected and were prepared to accept the single name Zimbabwe, more conservative Rhodesian Front MPs argued for the retention of the name Rhodesia. Senator Ritchie's comments indicate the reasons for this. He said Rhodesia, considered to be

> a jewel in Africa [had] developed magnificently since 1924...Let us not in any way suggest that the sacrifices by all our people to carve out this terrific country from virgin bush should be forgotten by removing the name Rhodesia. Our creditworthiness, our products, our minerals, the courage of our young people, our honesty and integrity have won recognition throughout the world for these attributes...in the name of Rhodesia.[1]

In this way, conservative white MPs put the case for having the memory of Rhodesia maintained in the name of the country.

Black MPs, however, stood to condemn the double-barrelled name. A genuine transfer of power would see the name Rhodesia 'come off'. They voiced disappointment and disapproval of the Europeans' desire to hold on to Rhodesia at the end of the colonial era and saw white yearnings as 'petty' and contrary to the spirit of majority rule. According to Mr Bwanya:

> I, as a black man, would like myself to be identified as a Zimbabwean and there is no doubt that the whites would prefer to be identified as Rhodesians. For two people from one country to be identified under two different names I think is very ridiculous.[2]

Instead, black MPs argued for 'a vernacular name', 'a native name' with which the black population could identify. At independence, just over a year later, the country's name was shortened simply to Zimbabwe, meaning 'house of stone', effectively linking the new country to the Great Zimbabwe of an ancient past. These buildings, located some 300 kilometres south of Harare, were once the capital of the Munhumutapa Kingdom that flourished between the thirteenth and fifteenth centuries. As the largest complex south of the Sahara and the work of an African people, the structures have long been a source of black pride (Shamuyarira et al. 1995:16) and references to them have been inserted into the names of black-nationalist political parties since the 1960s (Sinamayi 1998:95).

---

1 *The Senate*, 29 August 1979, cols 280–1.
2 *House of Assembly*, 13 February 1979, cols 2581–8.

3. Re-inscribing the national landscape

The desire of conservative white MPs to hold on to symbols of Rhodesian identity was also evident in the debate surrounding the remaking of the country's flag. As an icon of personhood, flags carry the State's ideology and reflect its aspirations, manner and future direction (Handleman and Shamgar-Handleman 1993:441), so suggesting to the international community and citizens alike how to conceive or think about the nation. There have been a number of Rhodesian flags since 1889 but for present purposes only the three most recent are of consequence. The symbolism of each will be examined briefly, for these shifting articulations of social relations communicate the identity of those holding power, as well as the position of those without (Berry n.d.).

After the breakdown of the Central African Federation in 1963, each of the three territories adopted flags of their choice. In 1964, Rhodesia reverted to flying the Union Jack and its own light-blue ensign with the Rhodesian shield in the corner—similar in all but minor aspects to Southern Rhodesia's pre-federation flag. In 1968, however, on the third anniversary of their unilateral declaration of independence (UDI), the Rhodesians lowered the Union Jack and the Rhodesian flag, replacing them with what became known as the Rhodesian Front flag, which consisted of three alternating green and white panels. Green, the predominant colour, signified the importance of the agricultural base of the country. Superimposed on a central, unremarked-on white panel was the Rhodesian coat of arms,[3] granted to the colony by the Royal Warrant of George V in 1924 (Berry n.d.:10). This flag was hoisted in front of the statue of Cecil Rhodes in the centre of Salisbury (now Harare).

In August 1979, the Muzorewa Government adopted another flag, its design mirroring political changes occurring in the country. A vertical black stripe symbolised the importance of majority rule. Placed prominently on a chevron at the top of this stripe was the Zimbabwe bird, deemed particularly significant by black MPs because the artefact represented an older, pre-colonial source of power and identity.[4] The bird, unique to the area, embodied the essence of Great Zimbabwe after the structure was abandoned. Black MPs therefore perceived the creature as the quintessential symbol of nationhood, a respected icon with the capacity to unite the various African groups making up the nation. The flag also had three horizontal stripes. Red represented the blood spilled in the struggle for majority rule, white the integral part of the European community and other minorities in all aspects of the country's life, while the green stripe reflected the importance of agriculture to the country's wellbeing.[5]

---

3   The Rhodesian coat of arms depicted a gold pick on a green field with a crest made up of the Zimbabwe bird and two sable antelopes, the latter reflecting the country's natural heritage. Lions and thistles copied from the coat of arms of Cecil Rhodes were also incorporated. The coat of arms bore the inscription (in Latin) 'May [Rhodesia] be worthy of the name' (Berry n.d.).
4   *House of Assembly*, 15 August 1979, col. 1148.
5   Ibid., col. 1144.

This Zimbabwe Rhodesia flag, although radically different to its predecessor, had the support of Rhodesian Front MPs because it reaffirmed the importance of the white community.[6] The flag credited their contribution to the country's progress and development and expressed the hope that this legacy would continue in the future. Moreover, while this flag indicated some movement towards white acceptance of the idea of black majority rule, it did not deny the country's origins and thereby jeopardise its future. Speaking to this theme, a white MP said:

> Anyone or any people who deny their origins...deny their own existence. Rhodesia is part of our origins and is the history of our country and our people. If the Zimbabwe bird is considered an important part of our flag, then it is historical and so is the name Rhodesia.[7]

Something more, however, was at stake in this debate. Memories of a prior era embedded in, for instance, national symbols, invoke past identities as they legitimate identities of the future (Lambek 1996:239). To remember is, in effect, 'to place a part of the past in the service of conceptions and needs of the present' (Schwartz 1982:374). In light of this, white MPs perceived the flag to be a 'masterly compromise' that they felt should be acceptable to most people.[8] But to blacks MPs this, for all its alternation, was the flag of Zimbabwe Rhodesia and as such it did not represent much different to the Rhodesian flag. Little popular support was expected for 'the flag with two names'; it was as if nothing had changed. Senator Chief Charumbira put the idea this way: 'I am Zefeniah Charumbira meaning that I am the son of Charumbira. Now it [the country] is called Zimbabwe Rhodesia, this is the son of Rhodesia.'[9] Was Zimbabwe to be forever linked to Rhodesia as its progeny? The co-presence made the reconstituted nation unbelievable and its flag unacceptable. It was not a flag, the chief said, that 'can take us along the path' to majority rule for it did not signify that a distinct break had been made with the colonial past, and it was therefore incapable of projecting the image of an independent African state.

At independence in 1980, several further modifications were made. The horizontal white stripe representing Zimbabwe's minority groups was removed, while a yellow stripe representing the mineral wealth of the country and a white triangle symbolising the nation's desire for peace, development and progress, were added. The triangle also contained a five-pointed red star, indicative of the State's socialist aspirations and place in the international community of nations.

---

6   *House of Assembly,* 15 August 1979, col. 1144; *The Senate,* 29 August 1979, col. 274.
7   *The Senate,* 29 August 1979, cols 280–1.
8   Ibid., col. 278.
9   Ibid., col. 291.

With the introduction of this flag, change had triumphed over any sense of continuity with the recent past. The whites' hope that their memory would receive recognition and be projected into the future through incorporation in the new national flag was not to be realised. They had been downgraded in the imagined community, no longer recognised as 'one of the two dominant peoples'[10] making up the nation. Instead 'one-ness' was to become the new catchall, with Mugabe saying 'we have one national army, one police force, one public service and I should say one national flag that symbolises our oneness, our nationhood' (Shamuyarira et al. 1995:40).

In short, at independence, white MPs were cognisant that remembrance was a moral and an identity-building act (Lambek 1996:249). European identity would be constituted out of what was remembered, and forgotten, about them as a people and their place, Rhodesia. Revised symbols and national names reflected the different ways of their 'being in history' in the future (Bloch 1996:229). Ultimately, however, various white efforts to memorialise the Rhodesian era during the term of the interim government—to be acknowledged in the icons with which the country presented itself to the world—were short lived. The Muzorewa administration was out of office by March 1980 and, with majority rule, the power to 'place make' passed to Mugabe's nationalist government. The process of white de-territorialisation picked up speed during the first decade of independence as the Rhodesian memory was removed from the country's national holidays, maps and monuments through erasing, overwriting and restitution. The State set about constructing another version of nationhood with its own local supporting icons of emplacement, and mapping in this way an African identity onto the landscape.

Remaking national holidays

The post-independence government recognised that public holidays required renaming if the population as a whole was to be afforded the opportunity to mark its most important sacred and historic events and to honour people held in high regard. The Minister for Home Affairs argued that it was 'necessary to move away from the old historical holidays and create new ones for the new nation' in order that the masses could leave the past behind and identify themselves with the new era.[11] In line with this, the State created Independence Day and Africa Day, the latter to celebrate the inauguration of the Organisation of African Unity in 1963, effectively locating the new country within the main body of Africa and no longer as an appendage of 'the white South' (South Africa). May Day was

---

10   *House of Assembly*, 29 August 1979, col. 276.
11   *House of Assembly*, 25 June 1980, col. 1021.

introduced to remind the government that it was the workers who had brought them to power, while Ancestors Day, introduced by the interim government, was replaced with Heroes—now the Heroes and Defence Forces weekend—in August.[12] Heroes Day is the time to remember and 'reflect on the sweat and blood that were spent by our compatriots so that our nation could be born'.[13] The public is exhorted to view this holiday—set aside for commemorating Zimbabwe's revolutionary birth—as a particularly solemn occasion and give it the respect it deserves. They should thus desist from having *braais* (barbecues), getting married and other leisure activities on that day. I will return in the next chapter to the Heroes holiday as a display designed to affirm and naturalise the power and authority of the ruling elite, as it sustains white provisionality.

The white community was asked to accept these changes and adopt the new national days in good faith. A black MP from the backbench said:

---

12 The interim government dropped the Rhodes, Founders, Pioneers and Republic holidays from the national calendar, replacing them with President's and Unity Days and the more contentious Ancestors Day. The last name was selected as a compromise to Heroes Day, also nominated at the time, because of disagreement regarding who could be considered a hero. Some hoped that the more neutral title would 'cut across the colour line', enabling people to remember forebears in their customary or traditional manner (*House of Assembly*, 4 October 1979, col. 154).

13 'Heroes an example to us', *The Herald*, 10 August 1982, p. 3. The national anthem makes the same points—namely that Zimbabwe was 'born of the fire of revolution and the precious blood of our heroes'. It contains a plea for leaders to be exemplary and for labour to receive its just rewards. At independence, Mary Bloom's 1975 national anthem, which depicted Rhodesia as a God-fearing country praying for Christian strength 'to face all danger' and blessed with a magnificent landscape, was replaced (*Rhodesian Commentary*, November 1975; see also Department of Prime Minister and Cabinet 1975). This had been sung to the tune of Beethoven's *Ode to Joy*, which was also the European Community's choice of anthem and, as such, was played annually at Harare's Europe Day celebrations, to the chagrin of senior government officials, who were unaware of its origins. The music's association with Rhodesia also caused a storm of protest when the piece was included in a Christmas organ recital organised to raise funds at a Harare church in 1994. After independence, the popular *Ishe Komborera Afrika (God Bless Africa)* served as Zimbabwe's national anthem. *Ishe Komborera Afrika* was composed in 1897 by South African Enoch Mankayi Sonotoga and was later developed by another South African, Mqayi. It was adopted by the African National Congress (ANC) in 1925 and subsequently became the anthem of Tanzania, Zambia, the South-West Africa People's Organisation (SWAPO) of Namibia and the regional Organisation of African Unity (OAU). Words for a specifically Zimbabwean anthem were chosen in 1990 from a national competition, won by Dr Mutswairo, lecturer in African languages and literature. It took another four years to find suitable music. According to Anderson (1990:132), singing the nation's anthem should be an experience in 'simultaneity…an echoed physical realisation of the imagined community'. Certainly, a local newspaper hoped Zimbabwe's new anthem would engender these sentiments. The editorial explained that 'a national anthem is not a dance song. It is more like a national flag in song and music, something to be proud of, to love, to rally around. So we had better learn it, and sing it with gusto' (*The Herald*, 16 April 1994, p. 2). The public was given the choice of two tunes, but neither satisfied. Many Zimbabweans found them 'tunes of the ear' but 'not of the heart' as *Ishe Komborera Afrika* had been. Others felt the composers 'must be of western-type music, which has no place in independent Africa' (*The Herald*, 7 February 1992, p. 6). So, while the judges settled on one composition, the new anthem had little popular appeal and was largely unknown in the country during the late 1990s.

What the Minister has done is to give the holidays that are necessary and they mark the importance of African aspirations. All we ask of you is that you become Zimbabweans and do not remain Rhodesians. Once we are all Zimbabweans, we will have no conflict of interest.[14]

Taking on board the new order was thus envisioned as an upheaval and reconstitution of white identity. The MP's words suggest that the whites' association with the country could be strengthened if they were prepared to deconstruct their Rhodesian sense of self, embrace the new national holidays and so demonstrate their re-engagement as Zimbabweans. Change thus represented a step towards white liberation, releasing settlers from their colonial history and mentality, and part of making good their personal transformation called for in the State's discourse of national reconciliation. The government kept the holidays of the Christian calendar, offering these as its gesture towards reconciliation,[15] for the decolonisation of the nation's iconic geography ran concurrently with the introduction and development of this policy.

A few years later, the President's birthday was also made a national day with the inauguration of the February 21st Movement in 1986. The movement, built around Mugabe as its role model, invites children between the ages four and fourteen—'the born frees'—regardless of race, creed or parental political affiliation, to a birthday party with the expressed aim of imparting political knowledge to them. Said an official: '[T]his is a national event and we expect all children from various cultural groups to take part.'[16] Black/black divisions had also not been forgotten. In 1997, a decade after the Unity Accord mentioned in the previous chapter was signed, the ruling party proclaimed National Unity Day in recognition of the peace ushered in by the agreement. In this instance, however, the idea of one nation did not hold, for the people of Matabeleland spurned the holiday. Refusing to mark the day with festivities, they effectively threw doubt on the Accord's record in lessening what on this occasion was labelled 'ethnic tension'.

Revising place names

Settler cartography, as elsewhere in the British Empire, was integral to the colonial project (Huggan 1989). Rhodesian maps signified the extent of the colonists' spatial power while colonial inscriptions privileged settler identity (Ashcroft 1997:13). Their place names effaced pre-existing African social and geo-cultural formations, detailed the expansionist aims of the settlers, legitimated these

---

14 *House of Assembly,* 26 June 1980, col. 1080.
15 *House of Assembly,* 25 May 1980, col. 1021.
16 'Children urged to attend celebrations', *The Financial Gazette,* 20 February 1997, p. 36.

against the conquest of an underpopulated land and, in the process, 'called up' the Africans as the subordinate other. Thus a critical task also awaiting black-nationalist attention was to pick apart the settlers' historiography. Returning African place names was part and parcel of taking back control over the location in order to bring the new place Zimbabwe into being. In this the government had the support of the black majority. The following quotations reflect the importance accorded reclaiming local names so that an earlier African history and identity could be recovered. The first comes from an African pastor, the second from a public discussion about African traditions.

> In African tradition no name is innocent; all names make statements. The ancestors, the Christian God and the Devil are all interested in names. Hence names are important, they prophesise, give authority and have power. Name change is empowering; notice in the Bible we read of Jesus changing people's names. Names of nations, towns and provinces influence the nature of the place. Names snare the person who repeatedly uses the name; people can be caught up by the words in their mouth, hence it is important that colonial names are altered in order that past servitude is not perpetuated.[17]

The idea that names carried by people and places are a store of history is also evident in the next contribution.

> History provides identity. Any people to be a people have to know their historical background. We are products of our people of yesterday, it is they who have given us our personhood, our language, family, culture and religion, that is our history as a people. If you use white language, names or gods you have a white man's history. History links up everything, if you want to change you must know your people's history. History is a rallying point.[18]

Names thus link identity to places and, in so doing, introduce the meaning of history into contemporary life. Consequently for black Zimbabweans, name change was empowering to the extent that it fractured colonial hegemony, de-linking a place from its colonial antecedents and returning control over its meaning to earlier inhabitants. Perforce, the 1982 Cabinet Committee on Place Names set about ridding the country of offensive, controversial and misspelt place names, many of these being reminders of the colonial past.[19] A lively debate covering the choice, derivation, appropriateness and spelling of names ensued between blacks in letters to the press. Countrywide, thousands of towns, villages, streets, public buildings, schools, hospitals, nursing homes, rivers, hills,

---

17 ZBC Radio 1, 11 December 1997.
18 ZBC TV, 31 January 1999.
19 *House of Assembly*, 21 August 1981, col. 1218.

forests, communal lands and dams changed names during the 1980s. Where possible, names in use before settler occupation were restored. This proved an energetic top-down programme that employed Emergency Powers Regulations to limit debate in the House and alter 'every colonialist or neo-colonialist or settlerist name...We want to wipe the slate clean and present our image of independent Zimbabwe without these vestiges of colonialism,' explained the President.[20] After a decade of work, the pace of re-inscription slowed. The Place Names Committee transferred the initiative to the people when a directive—to the effect that residents who found local names offensive should notify the Ministry via their local council—was issued in 1993.[21] By this means the decolonising project was transformed into a 'bottom-up' process—something that was not widely known or advertised.[22]

Yet, despite these intentions, there was a proprietary palimpsest to the Harare landscape during the 1990s where African names still stood side by side with settler inscriptions. For example, the copper dial giving directions and distances to various Rhodesian landmarks, thereby inscribing colonial adventure tales and significant events that secured settler territorial possession, continued to grace *Kopje*,[23] Harare's highest point and a popular tourist destination. Municipal notices described this as a 'religious place', the public was requested to 'behave decorously and quietly' and to not vandalise the site. Instances of colonial cartography were also evident in the central business district, where the names Selous, Baines, Fife and Allan Wilson Streets remained uncontested. Overwriting had also not erased other settler identities. For example, midway along its length, Josiah Chinamano Avenue lapsed back into Montague Avenue, then recovered the national hero's name just before the road finished. Other signboards memorialising national heroes Leopold Takawira and George Silundika were contra-indicated on the pavement where Europeans Moffat and Gordon were remembered.[24] Moreover, in Harare's suburbs, much did not change. In the older

---

20 *Parliamentary Debates*, 22 February 1984, col. 701.
21 *Parliamentary Debates*, 13 October 1993, col. 2909.
22 Late in 1998, however, the ruling party proposed to remove provincial names untouched since the colonial era. Preliminary measures created a storm of protest, particularly in Matabeleland, because ZANU PF was seen to have introduced the plan without consultation. The Governor of Matabeleland North, Welshman Mabhena, rejected the notion out of hand. A change of name did not mean a change of heart, he said (*The Herald*, 17 November 1997, p. 11, and 28 November 1997, p. 8). Ordinary people also proclaimed attachment to their provincial names, accusing the ruling party of a programme to destroy Matabele identity, when 'it should be reconstructing our history and identity after the colonial era' (*The Herald*, 20 November 1997, p. 10). Provincial re-inscription appeared to them as a naive solution to the problem of national integration. 'Tribalism and regionalism, blamed on the wrong causes, were being prescribed the wrong medicine' (*The Financial Gazette*, 20 November 1997, p. 9). At the time of writing, the government had made no concrete progress on the matter.
23 *Afrikaans*, meaning small hill.
24 At Rhodes' request, Selous, a renowned hunter, guided the Pioneer Column around Matabeleland and onto the high veld of Manica and Mashonaland (Ford 1991; Gann 1965:93). Baines was a South African who, finding himself unable to develop his land concession, sold it to Rhodes in 1871. Fife was a director of the British South Africa Company; Wilson was a pioneer who took part in the Matabele wars and was killed at the

residential areas, it was not unusual to see inscriptions bearing the names of more senior members of Britain's royal family—the Rhodesians remaining loyal to the monarchy even after declaring UDI—in addition to references to several British generals. Here names also recalled British landscapes and prominent families as well as the first settler farms established in the locality. While bureaucratic oversight could account for the retention of some of these colonial names, the State, mindful of the tourist dollar, had directed that Victoria Falls retain its colonial name. Geographical evidence therefore pointed to a layered, though largely male, history and the interpenetration of imperial, colonial and African locations. The white community would have liked this tangled heritage, reflecting the plurality of the country's origins, to have been given greater recognition in Zimbabwe's new historical truths.

Removing monuments

Public monuments also play a significant role in imposing a permanent memory on the landscape.[25] Rhodesian monuments had established the territory as a white homeland just as effectively as their geographical maps. They made credible particular collective identities and denied or eroded others (Savage 1994:143). For this reason, monuments the world over are an issue of public concern, built and removed by those with the power and public consent to erect and dismantle them. Zimbabwe's new government set about tackling black alienation by disassembling monuments and statues that depicted the colonial era, replacing these with others 'consistent with the new political and social order'.[26] Tasked with chairing the Monuments Committee, Minister Shamuyarira said 'the occasion...is not one of recrimination, but one of reconciliation—reconciling us to the reality of our independence, the death of colonialism and the natural aspirations of the people'.[27] Consequently, the colonial plaque commemorating 'the final halting place of the Pioneer Column' outside Salisbury's Railway Station was taken down, as were other offensive statutes such as *Physical Energy*. The British South Africa Company had presented this grand, bronze sculpture of a prancing horse with rider to Northern Rhodesia in 1960 in Rhodes' memory. Rhodesia had requested and 'inherited' the statue, dismantled just six years

---

defence of Shangani River (Gann 1965:315; Grant 1994). Chinamano, Silundika and Takawira are the names of black political activists, now national heroes. While Takawira died in prison before independence, Chinamano and Silundika distinguished themselves as government ministers after independence. Montagu was a member of the Rhodesian Legislative Council and Minister of Mines (Gann 1965:264). Father and son Robert and John Moffat were missionary advisors to Matabele Kings Mzilikazi and Lobengula, particularly in regard to their dealings with Europeans.

25 See Schwartz 1982; Connerton 1989; Bodnar 1994; Savage 1994.
26 'Rhodes statue moved', *The Herald*, 1 August 1980, p. 1.
27 Ibid., p. 2.

later, from independent Zambia (McCarthy 1994).[28] Another statue to go was that of Cecil Rhodes, which had graced Jameson Avenue in central Salisbury.[29] These were not wantonly destroyed. Zimbabwean monuments are protected under the *Museums and Monuments Act* and artefacts no longer enjoying collective recognition and legitimacy are collected and stored by the National Archives for the education of future generations. Accordingly, Cecil Rhodes was to be found at the back of the archives building in Harare, while Alfred Beit[30] sat at a side entrance. New monuments replaced the outmoded—for example, statues of the Shona spirit mediums Sekuru Kaguvi and Mbuya Nehanda, who inspired the first *Chimurenga*, stand at one entrance to the Parliament building.

By and large, the exercise was to prove an orderly dismantling of the colonial relics. The Rhodesian Front, however, saw it differently. Representatives accused the government of deliberately antagonising the white community and argued that men such as Rhodes and Beit had 'done a tremendous amount of good for the country'. A spokesman continued:

> [W]hile fully supporting the principle of reconciliation in the development of the country, this [RF] congress does not accept that it implies that the white Zimbabweans must meekly accept the denigration of his achievements and past. On the contrary, reconciliation implies acceptance of the white man and his past.[31]

Other statues of explorers and missionaries such as David Livingstone[32] not considered politically provocative were spared during the 1980s. In the mid

---

28   McCarthy (1994) relates the monument's chequered history. Controversy surrounded its choice from the start. The BSAC selected a monument depicting the dynamism and energy of an Englishman, in order to inspire all the peoples making up the Central African Federation and to whom, the company believed, they all owed a debt, at a time when imperial memorabilia was being vandalised and removed in other parts of the empire. The Company rejected criticism that this statue was politically insensitive, as well as the suggestion of Federal Prime Minister, Lord Malvern, that a more appropriate choice could be the representation of David Livingstone's body being carried to the African coast on its way back to Britain. *Physical Energy* achieved further notoriety when Southern Rhodesia's Prime Minister, Godfrey Huggins, likened the Federation's policy of partnership to the horse and rider—a remark taken as a racial insult in Northern Rhodesia and Nyasaland.
29   Jameson Avenue became Samora Machel Avenue and Salisbury was renamed Harare.
30   Alfred Beit (1853–1906) was born in Germany, the son of a Jewish businessman. Later in life, he became a close financial ally of Rhodes and was known for his philanthropic work. The Beit Memorial Committee presented to the town of Salisbury a statue of Beit in 1911. The figure moved locations within Salisbury at least five times between 1920 and 1965. After Beit's death, his wealth was consolidated in the Beit Trust to assist in development and has since contributed to infrastructure and educational projects (Gann 1965:155–6). Blake (1978:412–13) records the extent of his generosity.
31   'RF slams removal of old monuments', *The Herald*, 29 September 1980, p. 2.
32   Missionary and explorer David Livingstone first saw Victoria Falls in 1855, and it was here that a memorial to him was unveiled in 1934 (Gray 1990; Piearce 1992). The bronze statue, likened more to a naturalist than an imperial conqueror, carries the inscription 'the Liberator' in reference to Livingstone's antislavery work. Late in 1996, this epitaph was deemed to be offensive in some quarters and pressure was brought to bear on the Minister of Home Affairs to have the words removed.

1990s, however, a movement for 'The Restoration of Revered African Sites'[33] began to lobby for their removal, and the removal of Rhodes', Jameson's and other settlers' graves from the Matopos Hills, outside Bulawayo.[34] The graves, particularly that of Rhodes as 'the founding father', had by the 1930s become a national sanctuary and place of memory and pilgrimage for Rhodesians.[35] Receiving short shrift from the Department of National Museums and Monuments,[36] the activists issued in 1998 statements linking the presence of the colonists' graves to the unrest sweeping the country. 'The economic and social upheavals dodging [sic] Zimbabwe are the result of dissatisfaction by spirits of the land over the lack of initiative by the living and ruling to redress some of the sacrileges committed against the indigenous people of this land.'[37] An irate British reader of a Rhodesian web site expressed her 'horror' at this campaign and asked, '[W]hat a travesty…are we going to allow this to happen?' Whites were not the only ones to censure the plans. Black critics voiced their suspicions regarding the movement's political aspirations, while villagers in Matabeleland, whose homes were in close proximity to the graves and who derived income from tourists visiting the Matopos Hills, also denounced the activists' statements. The locals believed that the lobbyists, as a pressure group from another part of the country, had no right to speak on this issue,[38] thereby pointing to regional lines along which the Zimbabwean nation threatened to pull apart.

White resistance: refusing historical re-visioning

As the 1980s progressed, Rhodesia began to look like a location that had been fixed more readily mentally than geographically (Massey 1992:11). The response of white politicians to the decolonisation of their landscape has been mentioned above. While not denying the new regime's authority to reconfigure the nation's iconic and physical geography, political spokesmen pushed for some recognition of the Rhodesian era to be incorporated in the collective memory. Their statements are part of the public record, but what can be said about the wider white community's decolonisation critique, their private transcript, spoken and acted on away from official scrutiny? Were they prepared to move from the known to an unfamiliar landscape?

---

33 The Restoration of Revered African Sites is a project of Sangano Munhumutapa, supported by the Affirmative Action Group (see Chapter 6).
34 Ranger (1999:30–2) describes the graves in more detail.
35 See Tredgold (1968:98–101).
36 The Department described itself as an apolitical para-statal service and would not therefore institute change unless directed to do so by the appropriate minister.
37 'Remove Rhodes' remains from Matopos', *The Herald,* 19 February 1998, p. 7.
38 'Rhodes' remains must be removed', *The Herald,* 19 August 1998, p. 7; 'Let Cecil Rhodes rest in peace', *Zimbabwe Independent*, 21 August 1998, p. 4.

In the first decade of independence, most, finding themselves unable to publicly disavow the State's re-visioning project, adopted a somewhat sullen, silent stance. During the second decade, however, with changes to the political climate and dissent emanating from many sections of Zimbabwean society, whites felt more able to speak out. Yet only the most brazen sought to draw the State's attention to themselves or make headlines. The majority stopped short of outright defiance or masked disaffection in anonymity and cryptic humour, for although they did not support the landscape's decolonisation they believed it was foolhardy to confront the State head-on over the issue. To do so was 'to put us all at risk'.

Nonetheless, in various ways, they refused black claims and protested the rewriting of Rhodesian historiography. Their attitude was summed up in the retort 'you can't reinvent history'; it is 'a fact of life that there were 90 years of colonial rule'. Elderly respondents in particular echoed this sentiment. They claimed, for instance, to be 'offended' and 'insulted' by the removal of monuments that documented the Europeans' relationship with the place called Rhodesia. 'You don't tear down history, regardless of whether you like it or not; tearing down the past leaves a gap that can't be filled.' And despite being requested by authorities to rethink and avoid equating Independence Day with the colonial Rhodes and Founders holidays, some whites still referred to public holidays by their former names, thereby announcing themselves as 'men of yesterday'. Significant numbers also spoke of Harare's main thoroughfares and avenues—renamed in 1990 to honour black statesmen, presidents from neighbouring countries and heroes of the first and second *Chimurenga*—using their Rhodesian names. Preferring North Avenue to Josiah Tongogara, a woman remarked, 'What's so offensive about North Avenue? Just because it was so called by the whites is not a good enough reason to get rid of it.' The Rhodesians had established themselves by mapping their identity onto the landscape with these urban locators, drawing equivalencies that confirmed bonds between the Europeans and the territory. Yet, while whites believed they were being stripped of their heritage 'to serve ZANU PF's electoral needs', the meta-communication of the government's actions was not lost on them. They recognised that the geographical dismantling of the white homeland signified that 'the country now belongs to them [the black majority]…there's no Cecil John Rhodes any more; he's out of the history books and they're in'.

In view of this, noticing changes to urban landmarks after his return to Zimbabwe in 1993, a former Rhodesian military officer said:

> When we returned it was all so foreign…change for change sake at great financial cost. It really annoyed me; a pointless exercise because changing names does not change history. Older people still use the old names, while youngsters and expats don't know the difference.

The officer's remarks suggest that, for older residents at least, the old names still embody the real character of the place (Massey 1995b:183). His choice of the word 'foreign' appears as a motif for uprooting and uncertainty. Its application represents a site of difference, a focus for the fears, anxiety and confusion that accompany experiences of transformation (Rutherford 1990:10), as well as white arguments that dismiss and discount revisions introduced as part of the landscape's Africanisation. Another informant, who had watched the coming of independence from the safety of the Cape (South Africa), felt she had 'lost my home the day the country changed its name'. In a more jocular fashion, a third described the dislocation 'of being lost in my own country; I'd hear a name and I'd not a clue where it was'. The ground appeared to be shifting beneath their very feet. Remarks such as these indicate the sense of disruption between the identity of a 'known' place and its colonial past, and the anomalous position in which whites now found themselves as the decentred other in the newly blackened landscape.

One of the knock-on effects of the State's renaming project was that businesses or companies with Rhodesia in their title were obliged to change them.[39] Most complied, but a handful took evasive action. Some inserted the prefix 'rho', or their initials, while others clung to the name 'Rhodesia', saying it was too costly to change—and certainly there was more to changing a company name than just updating the address. The new name had to be registered and advertised, company stationery, licences and vehicles altered and maps revised. The costs were 'a lot to consider for a small business' and 'an expense that needs time and planning'. Three years after independence, more than 40 companies were still registered with Rhodesia, or its abbreviation, in their names. In some cases, the business had ceased trading; but, otherwise, how was this behaviour to be read? Was it simply malaise, 'tardiness' or 'sheer idleness', or perhaps symptomatic of a deeper reluctance to commit to real change? Or was it 'an insult', an act of white defiance, for keeping a name associated with Rhodesia was not in the spirit of reconciliation? A government spokesman deemed it necessary to issue the following warning:

> These companies are showing great disloyalty to the government and the people of Zimbabwe. They must change their colonial names without further delay. Cecil Rhodes died in 1902, and Rhodesia in 1980.[40]

Moreover, under the *Company's Act*, a name should not mislead the public. The Registrar of Companies refused to list any more companies if they had the word Rhodesia in them, saying, '[S]ince there is no such country as Rhodesia I obviously cannot register a company using that name. Such reluctance can only

---

39 'Name of the game is change, reluctantly', *The Sunday Mail*, 13 December 1981, p. 5.
40 'Colonial names muddle in the phone book', *The Herald*, 4 July 1982, p. 1

be regarded with the deepest suspicion.'⁴¹ His words intimate that countries are, as Geertz (1995:21) points out, disjunctive, categorical and exhaustive. Implying that it was impossible to be in two places or countries at one and the same time, the Registrar suggested there was something unnatural or spurious about people who continued to claim to be in Rhodesia. The 'when wes' of South Africa provide a case in point. Uusihakala (2008) describes how they hold the colonial past close by using only the old names, commemorating Remembrance as well as Rhodes and Founders national holidays and surrounding themselves with Rhodesian memorabilia. They have, Uusihakala (2008:6) avers, 'a profoundly felt anxiety' that should they cease to remember and retell, they will no longer exist. They appear unwilling or unable to let go of the past and face the annihilation of Rhodesian identity (Memmi 1965:151), even should this lead to their metamorphosis.

In Zimbabwe, adopting the revised nomenclature was conceived as another form of de-authorisation and consciousness raising by which whites who had stayed on could divest themselves of dominance and privilege and at the same time demonstrate loyalty and national commitment. They, however, proved generally unsympathetic towards the black majority's desire to claim and reshape the country in their own image through cartographic overwriting. The old Rhodesian names anchored white identity, naturalising the relationship between the settlers and the territory, and although many during fieldwork claimed to have 'now adjusted' to the new names, they were resigned rather than enthusiastic. Even spelling changes were deemed to be unwarranted, reflecting European privileging of written over oral history.

Contradictorily, however, many whites spoke of their attachment to 'African history' taught to them at school during the Rhodesian era. A young mother, reflecting upon the responsibility for her children's future in the country, had this to say:

> I'm battling with the new names. I still use the old names in the Avenues. I haven't bothered to learn the new ones, though I don't mind the changes. I try to explain the reasons for the changes to the girls. I bought a book, which gives the meaning of the names, and explains the events that happened at the spot. I loved African history at school…the Matabele Wars, Lobengula and his fat tummy, Mzilikazi and his *impis*⁴² with spears…I like to tell the girls what Harare and Bulawayo were like when I was a girl. The kids say not another 'when I' story. Yesterday we were driving through Eastlea [a lower middle-class suburb of Harare]

---

41 'Companies using Rhodesia won't be registered', *The Herald*, 9 May 1983, p. 2; 'No excuse', *The Herald*, 10 May 1983, p. 3.
42 The term refers to the young, male warriors who made up the Matabele regimental system.

and I told the girls this area used to be inhabited by whites. The girls asked where did the blacks who live in Eastlea now live then. I didn't know.

White affection for the heroes of the Pioneer Column (1890), the Matabele Wars (1893) and the native uprising, now known as the first *Chimurenga* (1896–97), memorialises pioneer heroism as well as the struggles of the first settlers who arrived in what they perceived to be a 'dry, wild and fearful land'. Their lives continued to be celebrated in, for example, the activities and field excursions of the History Society of Zimbabwe, formerly known as the Rhodesiana Society. This telling of the past centres the young mother's forebears, yet overlooks the restrictive and segregationist legislation that kept blacks in the former Tribal Trust Territories or urban townships and out of suburban Eastlea. It is a version that generally gives an 'amicable gloss' to the colonial relationship (Parry 1995:93).

The Rhodesian flags described above were another symbol that some whites appeared loath to forgo. An informant spoke with some amusement of a Gwelo (now Gweru) headmaster, 'no starry-eyed liberal' but also no supporter of Ian Smith, who continued to fly Rhodesia's blue and white ensign until authorities stepped in. The green and white Rhodesian Front flag was waved defiantly by white supporters shouting 'Rhodesia' at the last rugby match to be played against South Africa in September 1980 (Caute 1983:437). It is also the emblem of various Rhodesian web sites, hoisted at 'when we' social gatherings held in South Africa (Uusihakala 2008:169) and the flag that former Rhodesian servicemen have marched under on Australia's Anzac Day. Other informants described holding ambivalent feelings towards the country's current national flag. They complained that the 'clashing' colours, copied from Ghana's flag, the first African country to achieve independence, and now identified as the colours of the 1960s Pan-African liberation movement, compromised the flag's dignity. And, given that a national flag 'shows the world what you believe in', Zimbabwe's revolutionary socialist red star is perceived to project 'a negative image' to the world's financial centres, thereby discouraging foreign investment. When viewed draped over a hero's coffin or defiantly hoisted in 1998 by squatters invading commercial farms, the flag evoked only negative white comment, such as 'this is nothing more than the symbol of those who have looted the country'.

For all of this, however, by the late 1990s, the Zimbabwean flag had become one of the more acceptable national symbols, particularly among junior members of the white community. This appears to have come about through the flag's association with various sports—symbols of popular nationalism in their own right for all Zimbabweans. A young man described his experience thus:

> The change from Rhodesia to Zimbabwe took a while but, two years ago at a cricket match between India and Zimbabwe, I found I was waving the Zimbabwe flag and thinking of it as mine. I didn't think 'Geez, what's this I've got in my hand'; I remember it was a wondering thought at the time, simply the naturalness of it.

He was, I suggest, describing how he had allowed the new flag into his life, employing it in this sporting context to represent his sense of national pride. The young man's sentiments were echoed by an elderly woman who said 'it was heartening to see the surge of nationalism at the rugby recently, where our younger supporters had painted the Zimbabwe flag on their faces'. Similar scenes erupted at Harare's airport when the Davis Cup tennis team returned after beating Australia in the world group first round in Mildura, Victoria, in 1998. These sporting events provided sites where whites situated themselves within the nation. Waving the Zimbabwean flag enabled them to place their biographies within the national frame and thereby connect with a spirit of national belonging. Their patriotism was not, however, altogether innocent, for they simultaneously celebrated the sporting prowess of various minority figures. Whites were mostly antipathetic towards soccer, which is the black Zimbabweans' national passion. Again the majority was disappointed by their lack of involvement as players and disinterest as spectators. In their own defence, however, whites pointed out that soccer—dogged by administrative problems, allegations of corruption and poor performances—engendered at times a sense of national shame in Zimbabweans of all races.[43]

So, in short, the white community generally 'jibbed at changes' made during the 1980s and early 1990s. Informants appeared unwilling to forgo settler dominance over the landscape, signifying as it did control over the place. They perceived black re-territorialisation as downgrading to the Rhodesians and their history and symptomatic of their uncoupling from the place now called Zimbabwe. Elsewhere, coming to a shared sense of time and place requires settlers crediting and identifying with aspects of another culture and history as their representations are renegotiated in the interests of national integration (Clark and Reynolds 1994:41; Parry 1995:88). Generally, however, remarks proffered by white Zimbabweans indicated they would prefer the past to be 'irreversible' and 'inscribed in stone' (Wallerstein 1988:78), suggesting a static or non-negotiable conception of history that ignored the choice of memory as a moral practice (Lambek 1996:235). Although with much to lose, most wished to avoid, or appeared ill prepared to confront, the historical challenges that would facilitate their repositioning within the post colony.

---

43 *Parliamentary Debates,* 18 August 1994, col. 836.

Holding onto the homeland: reasserting otherness

Through non-compliance, evasion, refusal and protest, as described above, Zimbabwe's white community resisted and denied the State's historical re-visioning project. Theirs are the consciously intended, though petty, acts of insubordination, examples of 'the fugitive political acts of subordinate groups', and indicative of a realm of dissent (Scott 1990:xii)—something recognised by politically astute officials at the time. Alluding to the reasons for this seemingly passive stance, an elderly woman, keenly interested in opposition politics during the Rhodesian era, explained:

> Resistance need not be defiant behaviour. The majority of whites have been scared for years. Individuals have been picked up over weekends and held on trumped-up charges. The domestic workers' union frightens people. You're afraid to open your mouth or rock the boat. So I'm glad to see whites now beginning to answer back and speak out about things that are not right. We want meritocracy. If something does not measure up, then they [the government] should be told so. Whites are mostly law-abiding and tax-paying citizens.

Collective white actions were not, however, simply reactive, as she implied. They were also creative and had their own politics (Falzon 1998:55; Ortner 1995:177)—in this instance to reassert otherness and keep creditable aspects of the Rhodesian memory alive. Many informants expressed pride in being raised as Rhodesians—'we learned respect, honour, dedication and commitment'—and in Rhodesian ability. In particular, the white community wanted some recognition of Rhodesian accomplishments that shaped the embryonic state. They pointed to the administrative apparatus—the electricity grid and road, rail and postal systems—that added productivity to the land and that were foundational to today's modern nation. The very permanence of engineering structures such as the Kariba Dam, which, in the late 1950s, was the largest hydroelectric dam in the world, spoke directly to the seemingly legitimate place of whites in the country. Its construction simultaneously built the idea that the Rhodesian way of life belonged in the Zambezi Valley (Hughes 2006b:837). More generally, they sought credit for carving out the beginnings of modernity from what they thought of as an untamed environment, for bringing progress and order and for achieving so much in the short time since white settlement.

The white assertion that at independence the State inherited an infrastructure and economy 'second only to South Africa in this part of the world' was acknowledged in 1997 in the government's *Departmental Committee on Technical Ministries Report*. The Committee tabled its findings immediately after a heated debate over corruption in the public sector and referred its report to this problem. With regard to medical and educational facilities countrywide, the report noted that 'we inherited very good structures in terms of hospitals, schools et cetera, but these are breaking down and we do not want them to break during our presence otherwise history will judge us harshly'.[44] Indeed, what needs to be borne in mind is that some Africans, too, have been proud to come from 'the best' country in the region. Reflecting on this, a middle-aged European said, '[I]t would be far easier to identify with the government and the new Zimbabwe if recognition and credit was given to our achievements.' Other whites spoke of the transfer of knowledge, skills and trades, and contrasted their commitment and investment in the country with the cynical, rootless 'new breed of international expatriates' described earlier. They, like Dembour's (2000:78, 133) colonial administrators who gave their life's work to the Congo, believed they deserved a better record in history, only to find their positive contributions misrepresented locally and abroad. Indeed, some white Zimbabweans would like 'a thank you for a lifetime of dedication to this country'.

The ruling elite and radical intellectuals, however, hotly contested this creditable reading of the colonial legacy on the grounds that the colonists' motives were not to 'teach Africans' but to 'build a second Britain' or 'little England in Africa'. The colonists' role, according to an author writing during the Rhodesian years, should have been 'to bring the advantages of civilization to Southern Africa' (Vambe 1972:86). The white 'initiative and foresight' view of nation building was juxtaposed with a 'black sweat' perspective, which asserted that the country had been built out of African mineral, agricultural and labour resources. The latter, incorporated in current educational curricula, tells of black oppression and exploitation and is a far cry from Rhodesia's 'virgin bush' and potential as a 'modern El Dorado' version of the past.

White historiography was certainly forgetful of colonialism's institutional violence. A pastor located settler reluctance to face up to this other side of the historical legacy within the international context, when he said that 'whites the world over must now pay for slavery and colonialism. The blacks are saying they want their country back and the whites are the colonists. It's easy for you in Australia as the majority; whites here are in a very different position.' The potential cost involved in confronting the colonial past was, arguably, far greater for white settlers living in former intrusive colonies of Africa. Nostalgic memories of Rhodesia, the opportunities the country offered and their investment in its development represented ontological resources, important in the battle to become someone of positive regard. They allowed whites to think well of themselves and, as Davis (1979:36–7) pointed out, muted or filtered out unpleasant aspects of the colonial era. Positive constructs also expanded future

---

44 *Parliamentary Debates*, 26 November 1997, col. 2608.

white options. The telling sustained bonds, linking them to the contested land, and shaped an alternative metaphysics of sedentariness that, with some pride, rooted whites firmly and legitimately in the Zimbabwean soil (Malkki 1992:31). While transcending the past in this way secures whites a rightful place in the territory, Falzon, following Foucault, nominates this a traditional or continuous account of history, one that reads the past only in terms of its initial standpoint. Profoundly uncritical, it is unable to question its own beginning and inevitably finds its own starting point confirmed (Falzon 1998:71). It was not a foundational mythology conducive to seeing the land through African eyes.

Commemorating centenaries

These opposing perspectives came to the fore in disputes over how centenaries, falling during the 1990s, could be commemorated. The State did not take an active organising role itself, leaving the task to local councils, institutions and private interests to mark anniversaries in their own way. Consequently, these reflected diverse and local characters, as each grappled with the question of how to record its colonial heritage.

The cities of Harare[45] and Mutare in Mashonaland attained their centenaries in 1997. The mayors of each city, both party functionaries, candidly admitted having difficulty deciding what to do about the anniversary. While 83 years of white rule could not be condoned or celebrated, nor could the municipalities' beginnings be completely ignored, for 'who had not enjoyed the change in the skyline. Who had not delighted', for instance, 'in comparing the view of Harare from *Kopje* over the last one hundred years and more particularly from 1980 to 1997'?[46] Ultimately, each council projected the year as a time for looking critically at their city's colonial history and as a celebration of their rightful appropriation and enjoyment of the fruits of black labour since 1980. In this way, the centenary was divided into two parts: the cities' first 83 years as 'colonial instruments' and the majority's concomitant struggle against oppression, juxtaposed with a later period of liberation and celebration. The Mutare City Council invited 'old-timers', sometimes referred to as 'colonial fossils', to share their recollections and thereby provoked a boycott of its activities by war veterans. The Harare Council 'overlooked' those with early memories until it was 'too late' to extend invitations to them. This tack did not, however, defuse conflict. For where

---

[45] While the arrival of the Pioneer Column at Fort Salisbury (now Harare) was not marked officially in Zimbabwe, some whites travelled to centenary celebrations held close to the border in South Africa. These, described by Uusihakala (2008:189–210), were organised by South African 'when we' associations and re-enacted the flag-raising ceremony of 1880. Other events held in the Cape were markedly different in content and tone.

[46] 'Centenary is part of our history', *The Herald*, 8 November 1997, p. 4; 'No reason to celebrate', *The Sunday Mail*, 16 November 1997, p. 16.

3. Re-inscribing the national landscape

Harare's Mayor, Solomon Tawengwa, argued that the centenary was a time for looking forward and, as the beginning of the next 100 years, was good for investment, the indigenous business community felt it had nothing to celebrate and ignored the event. As present-day dignitaries attended dinner dances, the general public responded apathetically to calls to clean up the parks and to the switching on of lights in First Street, Harare's main shopping mall.

Private companies, located in the capital, marked the occasion by commissioning the writing of the firms' histories, recording in this way white investment in the country. The exclusive Harare Club contemplated its eminent founding fathers, the 'developing dynasties' in its midst and the 'four-generation straight flush' held by some families (Wood 1997). Two prominent government schools in Harare, both with renowned principals, skirted round the difficulty of representing the colonial past by having heads and teachers from the Rhodesian era talk to the themes of a century of educational excellence and achievement. Old scholars, many now prominent blacks in their respective fields, are generally proud to have attended these schools and are grateful for the opportunities the education they received has since provided for them. Embedded in their nuanced recollections was an acknowledgment that something of value came out of the colonial past, the ownership and benefits of which could be shared. By this means, the challenge of national integration was surmounted.

In contrast with the ambivalence shown by the Mashonaland city councils, the General Manager of Zimbabwe National Railways, based in Bulawayo, presented the anniversary as a 'privilege' and an 'opportunity' enjoyed historically by just a lucky few. He went on to pay tribute to all past generations of railway men and women, black and white, and spoke of 'the proud track record which has been selflessly passed on'.[47] Earlier festivities that had marked the arrival of the first locomotives in Bulawayo in 1887, the year following the Matabele Rebellion and just three years after the region was occupied, when the town had been decorated with shields, *assegais* (spears), flags and bunting, were recalled. Then the slogan had been 'No railways, No Rhodesia—It was as simple as that', for rinderpest played havoc with transport reliant on oxen (Batwell 1996:3). By the 1930s, Bulawayo had become Rhodesia's most populous and go-ahead town, centre of the railways and the country's economic capital (Gann 1965:314). In view of this, the theme of progress, charted by the transition from ox cart to steam and, subsequently, electric locomotives, was linked in 1997 to the memories of some 'colourful [white] characters' of the old days, in particular George Pauling, the engineer in charge of construction (Gann 1965:153). The railway's general manager enjoined today's railway employees 'not to be prisoners of history' but 'trendsetters', deriving inspiration from yesterday's railway pioneers.

---

47 'Celebrating a century of service', Supplement to the *Zimbabwe Independent*, 31 October 1997.

Accordingly, Zimbabwe National Railways energetically marked the centenary with a week-long programme of historical exhibitions, train rides and sporting fixtures reminiscent of events held 100 years earlier.

More usually, however, in the eastern and central provinces of the country, centenary celebrations served to counterpoise contradictory senses of place and history—all part of a process of claiming power through the production of different versions of autochthony (Rose 1995:116). Members of the white community and Mashonaland party cadres competed to have the legitimacy of their historical representations of nation building accepted as the dominant version. In this stand-off, neither side willingly conceded the contribution of the other—for example, that the cities of Harare and Mutare were built together, being structures that neither race in the past century could have built alone. While Clark and Reynolds (1994:1) note the importance to reconciliation of settlers developing a common sense of time and space with the majority, Curthoys (1999:18) reminds us that reconciliation can be obstructed when settlers wish to hold on to foundational myths and sentiments that find little recognition elsewhere. This pertained to Zimbabwe, where whites advanced Rhodesian achievements as conferring rights and productive of their sense of belonging, while the new political regime called up memories that predated the state formations of the colonial era. The new regime's telling linked the origins of modern Zimbabwe to the Munhumutapa Empire and re-presented the colonial era as an aberration, a brief disruptive episode in a longer national narrative. Furthermore, the black-sweat view of nation building located whites in a recent and discredited past as colonial oppressors. Historical re-visioning therefore problematised the whites' future by devaluing and denaturalising the link between people and territory, thereby unmapping white identity from the national space.

Conclusion

The salience of place and memory in renegotiating white-settler identity was addressed in this chapter. The argument was made that the nationalist government considered the geographic mediation of national identity a significant decolonising site, and made the recovery of an appropriate identifying relationship between the African majority and the place Zimbabwe an integral part of its nation-building project. The processes and practices of place remaking simultaneously disrupted the Rhodesians' creditable version of history, disallowing identification with colonialism and thereby disrupting white self-privileging. In this way, the State's retelling of history challenged the colonisers' sense of omnipotence and permanence, as well as their sense of the irreversibility and linear progression of historical events (Memmi 1965:61; Nandy 1983:35, 58).

Clearly, revising and re-presenting the nation's past served to highlight the fragility and contingency of links between people and places (Malkki 1997:86). Where white political figures sought to have the memory of the Rhodesians' contribution to state formation acknowledged officially, thereby drawing attention to the plurality of the country's origins and invoking a moral right to belong in the future, this was not an idea that warranted inclusion by the State in its origin narrative. Denial of the significance of the white role in the nation's genesis problematised the whites' future by disrupting the seemingly natural relationship between the territory and the European population. Zimbabwe's white community found itself de-centred as decolonisation of the nation's landscape unpicked the intimate links, or roots, between the Rhodesian people and what they considered their homeland. In various ways, however, the white community resisted territorial re-formation and generated its own metaphysics of sedentariness, which was reliant on its particular reading of the colonial history and confirmed the white conviction of their rightful place in the territory. Colonial memories, varying between different groups, have therefore been mobilised in battles over the future of peoples and places (Rose 1995:97).

Where this chapter has focused on landscape as a symbolic field of memory and belonging, there are other ways to be in history and constitute subjectivity. The next chapter changes direction to look at the invocation of the civil war within the nationalist discourse of personhood in order to clarify how memory of the armed struggle operates in public life, further challenging white claims to be acknowledged as legitimate members of the national collective.

4. Zimbabwe's narrative of national rebirth

This chapter examines how the new regime has drawn on the memory of the liberation war in order to constitute nationhood and create its own authoritative code of membership. That nationhood is realised not uncommonly through war (Hobsbawm and Ranger 1983:279) was something that Anderson (1990:129–31) understood when he attributed our attachment and willingness to die for the idea as an outcome of the nation's depiction in terms associated with kinship and home. Zimbabwe's war memory provides, as it were, a classificatory scheme, the wherewithal to think about who belongs, and how, to the Zimbabwean nation, for war is no less a force in the development of nationhood where, as in Zimbabwe, the conflict to be remembered is internecine (Grant 1998:163). Objectification of the civil war at the Heroes' Acre memorial complex is described below. The first section details how the Rhodesian colonial past is 'registered and felt' (Hirschkop 1996:v) in the official account of the nation's rebirth. Representations of white subjectivity presented at the site and embedded within Zimbabwe's narrative of national rebirth and its ideology of personhood are identified. Particular attention is then directed to the extent Zimbabwe's whites are able to constitute their subjectivity within the subject positions produced at Heroes' Acre, or recognise themselves among the country's national heroes. Finally, the consequences of the State's narrative for the white community's sense of national belonging are examined.

Perceiving the national shrine

The State in Zimbabwe, as in much of the Third World, has played a key role in national construction. Representations, described in the previous chapter, illustrated that Zimbabwe was reconstituted as an African nation, located politically within the Pan-Africanist movement and committed economically—at least at the outset—to socialism. It is also a product of a civil war fought against settler colonialism. Mugabe, perhaps because some hardliner whites insisted otherwise, made this point very clearly when he said, '[I]ndependence was not given to us at the Lancaster House Constitutional Conference in December 1979; it was won on the battlefield in sixteen long and arduous years of a bitter and hard armed struggle' (Shamuyarira et al. 1995:2).

The memory of the anti-colonial war as the revolutionary founding event is conveyed and sustained most powerfully in ceremonies held on Heroes Day, and re-presented at the state funeral of each newly proclaimed hero. The site for these commemorations is Heroes' Acre,[1] thus far the State's most ambitious national representation, which the government began building in 1981. The memorial complex covers 57 acres (23 hectares), originally set aside for a new Rhodesian Parliament House, on the edge of Harare. It comprises two predominant visual foci. The first incorporates the Statue and Tomb of the Unknown Soldier, the national flag and the eternal flame bounded by a black granite wall engraved with murals depicting the history of the anti-colonial struggle from 1960 to 1980. The second takes in the terraces of Heroes' graves, to which I return later in the chapter. This commemorative complex is described in official texts as the product of 'the masses' desire to be the makers of their own history' and 'a place of pilgrimage'[2] designed to 'arouse national consciousness, forge national unity and identity'. To this end, plans were also afoot to erect a museum at the site in order to tell 'the people's history'.

Kriger and Werbner have described the political significance of this monument in some detail. Kriger (1995:135) argues that ZANU PF's ruling elite has attempted to promote its legitimacy and foster national identity by using the civil war as a symbol of black unity. This exercise has, however, misfired, demonstrating instead the party's tendency for 'hierarchy, bureaucratic control, and top-down decision making' (Kriger 1995:145)—characteristics evident in its choice of national heroes, the majority of whom have been ruling-party political or military figures.[3] Indeed, hero biographies, detailed by the Ministry of Information, Posts

---

1 Elsewhere icons such as this are said to 'root the living in a distinctive cultural identity which assures national pride and self-respect' (Rowlands 1996:10; see also Inglis 1998:115). Flames of remembrance, commonly incorporated in their architecture, pledge eternal commitment to the memory of those who died for national purposes (Inglis 1998:204). Thus, not only do war memorials embody the collective recognition and legitimacy of the memory deposited within them (Savage 1994:136), they provide important sites representing the religious force of national identity (Anderson 1990:18). Scholars point to the importance accorded public participation in design, funding and ceremonial occasions that promotes the internalisation of memory, inviting agency and generating a sense of belonging within a community of memory (Bodnar 1994:74; Rowlands 1996:13–17; Inglis 1998:171–93).
2 ZBC Commentary on Heroes Day, 11 August 1997; Ministry of Information, Posts and Telecommunications 1986:2. Public access to the site was, however, restricted. The shrine was opened daily to the public for the first time in January 1999. Before this, an appointment had to be made with the Ministry of Home Affairs; an official guide indicated that there were fears of vandalism and the monument was considered 'too sensitive' to be opened more freely. Before this was possible, he said, 'the people had to be taught to appreciate their history' and 'to value their heritage'.
3 There were various grades of heroes, with the status of national hero being the most prestigious and the most coveted. When someone important died, a request to grant hero status was made to the ZANU PF Politburo for consideration. The request could come from the party, from the War Veterans' Association or, more recently, from the indigenisation lobby (see Chapter 6). While the process of decision making was shrouded in secrecy, Welshman Ncube, Professor of Law, believed that, ultimately, the President decided (*Manica Post*, 7 July 1996, p. 6; see also *Parliamentary Debates*, 5 May 1999, col. 5249). Only national heroes were buried in Heroes' Acre in Harare. The State paid for their funerals and various financial benefits accrued to widows and any dependants, which were paid through the Heroes Dependants Assistance Fund. Debate about the status of would-be heroes indicated widespread discontent concerning the criteria applied when conferring the status (*House of Assembly*, 15 September 1982, cols 509–16; *The Financial Gazette*, 7 July 1994, p. 4; *Zimbabwe Independent*, 16 May 1997, p. 7; *Parliamentary Debates*, 15 August 1996, cols 736–75, and 17 August 1994, cols 778–815).

and Telecommunications (1998), indicate that around two-thirds were former members of ZANU and/or ZANLA. Many other worthy candidates have been ignored.[4] Kriger (1995:150–2) reports the growing dissatisfaction within the Ndebele 'nation', as well as the increasing distance between the country's elite and the masses that, almost from the start, controversy over candidature brought into sharp relief. Richard Werbner (1998) also discusses the politicisation of the memorial complex, in particular the ruling elite's appropriation of the memory and identity of those who died for state ends. He goes on to trace the rise in popular 'counter memorialism' in light of the ruling party's involvement in the post-independence massacres in Matabeleland, described towards the end of Chapter 2.

These scholars address fissures within the black majority. I wish to focus instead upon white subjectivity, and ask in what ways the Rhodesian memory is projected 'into the weft of the collective narrative' (Balibar 1991:93) fabricated at the Heroes' Acre complex. Insofar as war memorials are simultaneously fictions and principles of social organisation (Bowman 1994:147), it is pertinent to ask whether Zimbabwe's political elite envisaged that Heroes' Acre would embody the memory of those who fought on the losing, Rhodesian side. Is it, for instance, a commemorative landmark that provides dignity for all who died and suffered during the war? What categories of nationals and non-nationals are fashioned out of the war's memory? Were whites also to be accorded a place in the national family?

Early on, political activist, detainee and minister in the post-independence government Nathan Shamuyarira described the Tomb of the Unknown Soldier as commemorating

> the lives of all Zimbabweans—black, white and brown—lost in the cause of freedom and national independence. For example the many white and black missionaries who were killed because of their support for freedom and independence will be remembered alongside our heroes.[5]

Also taking a conciliatory position soon after independence, Mrs D. Stebbing of Greendale, Harare, suggested that 'a statue of a white troopie' should stand in Heroes' Acre, 'side by side or shoulder to shoulder' with the three freedom fighters, two men and a woman, who together make up the Statue of the Unknown Soldier. She continued:

> [T]hen, in gratitude, show the many mission priests, doctors, nuns and teachers who lost their lives while trying to minister to all in

---

4 See, for instance, controversy over the status of George Marange and Edmund Garwe (*Parliamentary Debates*, 30 September 1997, cols 1627–50).
5 'Reconciliation and war memorials', *The Herald*, 1 August 1980, p. 1.

need—whether black or white; to the Red Cross and other health administrators who died helping the sick and wounded, and to the would-be peacemakers.[6]

In this way, Mrs Stebbing asked for a 'vernacular representation' (Bodnar 1994:74), which registered the grief, sorrow and contribution of ordinary people in the front line of war. She finished with the following plea: 'Those of us whites who are staying in the country we love would dearly like to be reassured that we, and those who died to keep us safe, are considered as much an integral part of Zimbabwe as the black freedom fighters.'

Shamuyarira's and Mrs Stebbing's remarks suggest that they considered Heroes' Acre had a role to play in healing the social fabric, as an act of closure and a memorial to the suffering and sacrifice of all of the people, in essence an icon to inclusion rather than to victory. Similarly, a white MP spoke at independence of 'the responsibility to heal' and 'rebuild from the agonies and miseries of war'. With this in mind, he suggested dedicating the public holiday to 'those who have fallen'; in which case the eternal flame could memorialise 'all people who died in the civil war'.[7]

The memory embodied at the shrine is, however, depicted in more circumscribed, familial terms. Official documents specify that Heroes' Acre represents those who fell in the struggle, 'the illustrious' and 'patriotic sons and daughters' of the nation who 'distinguished themselves through profound service and suffering' and 'paid the supreme sacrifice for Zimbabwe to be born and for the masses to be liberated'.[8] Along the same lines, the President, reminiscing in 1995, spoke of the Tomb as honouring 'the many thousands of freedom fighters who died in the forests and valleys of Zimbabwe, Mozambique, Zambia and Botswana', many of whom were not properly buried and have no known grave (Shamuyarira et al. 1995:2). They are 'buried here, far from their homes and their families…they now belong to the large family of Zimbabwe, the whole nation' (Shamuyarira et al. 1995:6). The statue of the Unknown Soldier, whose figures today represent them, are 'in place' for they are 'the happy ending' of the anti-colonial struggle (George 1996:14). With feet planted firmly in the soil and true to the ways of their forefathers, this select group is described in tropes of assurance, fitness and moral certainty. Local and centred, they belong 'naturally' as 'sons' of the national 'soil'. Special mention is also made of the President's first wife, Ghanaian-born Sally Hayfron, who at the time of research was the sole heroine, now cast as 'mother' to the freedom fighters, her patriotic sons and daughters, and the nation (Shamuyarira et al. 1995:1, 7). Zimbabwe's familial ideology was

---

6 'Let us remember all war dead on Heroes Day', *The Herald,* 18 August 1981, p. 6.
7 *House of Assembly,* 4 October 1979, col. 152, 26 June 1980, cols 1081–2.
8 Ministry of Information, Posts and Telecommunications 1986:3–4, 1998:1, 2, 5.

4. Zimbabwe's narrative of national rebirth

concretised through financial backing in November 1997. Earlier that year, war veterans had taken to the streets, shut down ZANU PF headquarters and refused to commemorate Heroes Day. At the time, some bystanders saw only an unruly demonstration of mostly down-at-heel rural men. Others perceived something more worrying—namely, a de facto second army, loyal only to its patron, Mugabe, marching in the streets of the capital. Subsequently, ex-combatants deemed to be part of the 'national family' benefited through an unbudgeted compensation payout that has proved highly divisive. Registered comrades received a one-off payment of Z$50 000, a monthly pension for life of Z$2000 (increased in 1999), plus health and education benefits and a promise of land.[9]

This now pre-eminent version of belonging depicts the Zimbabwean nation in terms of kinship and conduct and the unity of those joined by blood and sacrificial love for the liberation cause. Consequently, for some black nationalists, it had been

> ludicrous to contemplate those who died for Ian Smith and all he stood for—white supremacy, inequality and domination—as heroes of Zimbabwe...There can be no two ways about this. Those who died defending colonial oppression died for a lost cause. Reconciliation dictates that we do not open old wounds. But we cannot sit back quietly while those representing the old guard mock our heroes who made the supreme sacrifice.[10]

As the most important monument of Zimbabwean nationhood and anchor of the civil war's memory, Heroes' Acre could not with credibility include a white Rhodesian soldier, just as the bodies described by Savage (1994:131) as subsumed within American Civil War monuments have been conceived within certain boundaries and allegiances, and typically depict erect, unwounded Anglo-Saxon soldiers. Instead, dogmatic formalism (Bodnar 1994:74) calls for

---

9 This package represented considerable economic wealth and provoked anger among some members of the black educated elite, many of whom had been studying out of the country during the war and who now found themselves shouldering higher taxes to fund the payments. The payout also delivered a severe blow to national unity because vetting of would-be war veterans was carried out by party officials at party district offices (*The Financial Gazette*, 27 November 1997, p. 7). Political detainees, former *mujibas* and *chimbwidos* (the young boys and girls who had supported the liberation forces by providing food, provisions, information on the Rhodesian forces in the area and so forth, described more fully by Astrow 1983:151), as well as other former freedom fighters and those considered 'sell-outs' did not qualify. Sell-outs fought for the Rhodesians and some considered they were entitled to gratuities and benefits under the terms of the Lancaster Agreement. Chidyausiku (1998:7–8) gives the counterargument. This controversy came on the heels of revelations from the Chidyausiku Commission of Inquiry, which showed that the War Victims Compensation Fund had been defrauded of millions of dollars through false, unsubstantiated and multiple claims, prompting its suspension. The 79 major beneficiaries were people prominent in political and military circles (Chidyausiku 1998; Deve 1997; *The Financial Gazette*, 20 August 1998, p. 6). Many other claims were never considered because claimants found it impossible to have their papers lodged by the relevant authorities (Amani Trust 1997:8). Together, these exclusions and controversies raised the fear that the war would be rekindled.

10 'Old wounds', *The Herald*, 12 August 1983, p. 8.

a memorial not to common grief and sorrow, but to triumph, patriotism and national rebirth. Nationalisation of the comrades' lives (and deaths) therefore requires the marginalisation of alternative, non-national war memories and that competing interpretations, such as those proffered by Mrs Stebbing, are downplayed.

Nonetheless, as the monument to the fallen, Heroes' Acre does not exclude memories of the Rhodesians so much as evoke and entrap them as the enemy. The shrine, said Mugabe, memorialises the 'callous nature of those who ruled us yesterday' and serves 'as a reminder of the crimes perpetrated by the Smith regime'.[11] Murals at the commemorative site depict the war in racial terms. They juxtapose the virtues of the liberation forces—men in bulky Eastern Bloc uniforms and women in headscarves and peasant attire—with the rigidly uniformed Rhodesian forces, their lackeys and dogs. The eternal flame represents the people's spirit of independence and infinite desire for freedom. These qualities served to 'defeat the forces of colonialism' and underscore the will to 'defeat external forces of destabilisation and internal forces of reaction' (Ministry of Information, Posts and Telecommunications 1986:6), thereby safeguarding the nation in the future. The contingent symbolic message (Cohen 1994:163) suggested by back-to-back Heroes and Defence Forces national holidays is that the heroes' sacrifice will be protected by the military might on display the next day and that Zimbabwe's independence, won at a price, will be protected whatever the cost. Indeed, the President's 'never again' national vows highlight the regime's resolve to guarantee state security and survival from threats emanating from South Africa as well as 'the fifth column among us'—the enemy within. Passing judgement on the settler regime is therefore a constitutive act of the post-independence government. The war memorial, as a testimonial to and accusation of the colonial era, establishes the dialectic of those who are in place and belong naturally, who are authentic and at home, and the former colonists who, as different and threatening, are out of place and can never belong in the same way.

Zimbabwe's white community, no less than the African-Americans[12] before them (Savage 1994), has found itself unable to perceive the national shrine as

---

11   'Presidential address', ZBC TV, 12 August 1998.
12   Savage (1994:131–5) describes the proliferation of local-level Civil War monuments in the United States that avoid all but the most innocuous representation of the war's origin and significance. In the interest of developing a common white American identity, the conflict was 'recast as a struggle between two ultimately compatible "principles" of union and state sovereignty' (Savage 1994:132), making it possible for former white enemies to appreciate that there were no losers or winners to the dispute. For this narrative to be sustained, however, black American cultural representations were excluded from the memorials and the importance of slavery and the black contribution to the war effort were left unrecorded and so 'forgotten'. Similarly, the Lincoln Memorial, built more than 60 years after Lincoln's assassination, while remembering Lincoln as a nation builder, fails in its inscription to mention slavery as the issue that divided the nation and provoked the American Civil War (Savage 1994:138–41; Rowlands 1996:15).

a memorial to its dead or to realise its identity in the Heroes' complex. Some have chosen to ignore or subvert the memorial's meaning and in everyday, mundane ways reassert self-determination and tell a different version of history. For instance, in the years soon after independence, when the front pages of the daily newspaper were dominated by the ruling party's commemoration of Heroes Day, the small print at the back inscribed another memory. The 'Roll of Honour' and 'In Memoriam' columns carried a dozen or so notices in memory of the Rhodesian security forces—the Selous Scouts, Rhodesian Light Infantry, the Southern Battalion Rhodesian Regiment, the Second Engineers Squadron, the Old Puritans[13] and Police Reservists who gave their lives between 1965 and 1980; 'may all those who fell be remembered for they were men of men'. Another entry was dedicated to all 'those who fought and died for the green and white flag'. A third, more inclusive note referred to 'the proud memory of men and women from all races who died or were maimed for the right they believed in. Let us now not fail in this gift of reconciliation and peace.'[14]

While memorials such as these were no longer published in the press, material collected during fieldwork suggested the sentiments they reflected were still keenly felt. Informants believed that Heroes' Acre represented neither the Europeans killed nor the majority of the Rhodesian security forces, who were black. As the young mother, having trouble with the new street names in the previous chapter, saw things, '[H]eroes' is not ours'. Having said this, she asked, somewhat defensively, 'Where are our soldiers buried? Is it in Warren Park [public] Cemetery? I suppose their families have left…our war vets should receive payouts as well, most of our soldiers came from Matabeleland.' Certainly, it would have been impossible for the white minority to conduct the war if a significant number of blacks had not also contributed to the white cause and continued to serve its public administration (Hudson 1981:205). This point has led some scholars to argue that Zimbabwe's was not so much a mass revolution as a confrontation between two elites: the majority of white Rhodesians on the one hand, and an educated black elite on the other—the fighters of both sustained by forces outside the country.[15]

Other informants described the Heroes Day commemoration as a 'one-sided occasion' and the shrine 'a waste of taxpayers' money'. A former Rhodesian officer said, 'Heroes Day is a needle in our sides, a meaningless alienating symbol; let them [the government] call them [the comrades] what they want, I know what they really were [terrorists].' A conscientious objector, who supported the black cause before independence, felt that 'Heroes' Acre does more harm than good.

---

13 Former students of Plum Tree High School, located in the west of the country close to the Botswanan border.
14 See *The Herald*, 11 August 1981, p. 7, 11 August 1982, p. 7, 18 August 1982, p. 8.
15 See Hodder-Williams 1980:104; Hudson 1981:206–8; Kriger 1988; Alexander 1998.

It commemorates a lot of dead, forgotten people.' He continued in reference to the price riots that rocked the country in January 1998: 'the needs of the people are being ignored. It's ironic that the State gives more attention to the dead than the living.' The riots were in fact a direct result of the war veterans' payout, as the government had raised the sales tax on basic foodstuffs from 2.5 per cent to 17.5 per cent to cover their gratuities. An elderly man, who also saw Heroes' as 'looking backwards', believed 'the government should stop this nonsense of appointing heroes'. Others, bitter, argue that the white community too should be entitled to remember and honour their dead, for the white community generally considers that it is prevented from constructing public monuments[16] to its fallen. Thus, without a sense of authorship and unable to position their identity within the State's narrative, white Zimbabweans have failed to develop a sense of national belonging out of the civil war memory.

Experience elsewhere, however, suggests that it is unrealistic to expect that the defeated, white or black, will find a creditable place in public memory. The Japanese and Germans were either discouraged or forbidden to build military cemeteries at the close of World War II (Gillis 1994:12), while blacks, without 'cultural privilege', had their representations 'overlooked' in the design of this sort of monumental legitimacy after the American Civil War (Savage 1994:136). Yet in Zimbabwe memorials do exist, albeit of a less visible nature. A Rhodesian web site carries the Roll of Honour giving the names and details of whites as well as blacks who died for the previous regime, and without whose support the Rhodesian State would not have remained in charge for as long as it did. Visits to the tiny churches in the Eastern Highlands, where there was fierce fighting, revealed a more private family grief inscribed in a pew or church window.

The Heroes Day epitaph 'We remember. We must never forget' also proved contentious. Several informants took exception to it and queried 'Does that sound like reconciliation to you?' Echoing this idea, others felt 'the party won't let the war be forgotten; it continually rubs salt in the wounds'. Alexander et al. (2000:259) note the widespread use of 'old wounds' as a marker of historical violence and 'opening' them as a metaphor for public probing. In this instance, whites allude to ZANU PF's invocation of war memories as 'salt' that keeps the wounds not just open, but inflamed. Remembering differently has, in effect, made it difficult for past protagonists to recognise each other as part of the same nation. Any 'mutual affirmation of past interactions—our introjection of one another' (Lambek 1996:239)—was hard to perceive or accept with the nation shaped by what it stood against. Zimbabwe's memorial complex as a record of what 'must

---

16 Whites also complained that gathering to mark Armistice Day was treated with official suspicion. Coinciding as it did with the anniversary of UDI, it was, however, perhaps understandable that, to the State, such gatherings represented an act of insubordination, or an instance of what Scott (1990:19) termed low-profile resistance characteristic of non-dominant groups.

never be forgotten', of what must never be lost, has proved deeply divisive and failed to produce the effect of unity by virtue of which all Zimbabweans were made to appear 'as the people' (Balibar 1991:93). Consequently, Heroes' Acre, as a commemorative landmark, was unable to provide symbolic compensation to all who had suffered on account of the war.

Reverends Mashopa[17] and Zvarevashe (1994) shared different concerns. Developing a familial analogy on Heroes Day 1998, Mashopa argued that national days should be days for 'serious national prayer, led by the nation's father'. 'Remembering past injustices and glorifying war memories,' he went on, 'does not contribute to meaningful reconciliation.' To talk of 'heroes as an achievement' is to adopt a secular vision, devoid of the sacred qualities that characterise Biblical heroes such as Noah, Moses and Isaiah. Without personal faith and prophetism, this form of heroism runs the danger of 'degenerating into self-centeredness, pride and greed'. Along the same lines, Zvarevashe (1994) said 'big days' such as Heroes Day should 'not appear as a one-man show'. He believed 'the only way to honour the dead, is to pray for the eternal rest of their souls with the ancestral spirits'. Instead of jet flypasts, deafening gun salutes and political rhetoric, Mugabe should be seen leading the nation in prayer. A number of Christian Church leaders should then be invited to come forward and offer prayers for all those who died. For both men, displays of might had ousted 'the religious element' that they deemed appropriate when commemorating sacrificial death.

Remembering entails engagement with the past, leading Renan (1990:11) to suggest that perhaps forgetting is a crucial factor in the creation of a nation. Indeed, by the time this research was under way, the war, according to some younger more positively minded whites, had 'become a common experience. We now work with the people we fought and we've forgotten we were on different sides', they said. 'It's all in the past, we've moved on to another country.'[18] For them to perceive commonality, past atrocities had to be forgotten or at least memories be fashioned by the requirements of reconciliation. For the ruling party, however, the opposite held true. Party rhetoric justifies the erection of Heroes' Acre on the grounds that 'the people' are forgetful and must be taught to value their heritage. The State asserts that the general populace needs education in 'the people's history' and 'development' as citizens. Its memory of the armed struggle is conceived as a moral imperative that must be transmitted to the next

---

17 Reverend Noel Mashopa, 'Heroes of the Faith', ZBC Radio, 1–9 August 1998.
18 Weiss (1994:161) describes the mutual respect felt by a former ZIPRA fighter and a Rhodesian lieutenant-colonel having found themselves in the same work setting after independence. Godwin (1996:331–4) relates a similar experience in his autobiography, *Mukiwa*. Preparing during the mid 1980s the defence case for Matabele 'dissidents', in particular the former ZIPRA Commander Lookout Masuku and Head of Intelligence, Dumiso Dabengwa, Godwin discovered the commander and his section of the Rhodesian Army had previously fought each other during a civil war engagement.

generation. All of which underlines the importance the political elite accords to 'not forgetting' and suggests some anxiety about the credibility of its idea of nationhood.

Thus, without a doubt, nationalisation of Zimbabwe's war memories had its import for state purposes. Commemorations constructed a great moral distance between the evils of the Smith regime and the virtues of Mugabe's, thereby establishing the new political elite's credentials to rule by refracting its image off the illegality of the colonial regime. In this way, memorialisation of the war as the contingent event of Zimbabwean nationhood introduced a barrier to social memory and provided a means to impose discontinuities on the population and history. To employ Foucaldian terms, 'not forgetting' provided the rationale for the production of knowledge that was self-interested and reflected the State's 'will to power'.

Heroes as exemplary citizens

Heroes' Acre is, however, more than a memorial site that attempts to 'fix the meaning and purpose of the war in an enduring form' (Savage 1994:128). Built in order to inspire all Zimbabweans to emulate the ideals and values of the heroes, it also embodies prescriptions for future behaviour.[19] Accordingly, the Heroes Day holiday is a time for self-reflection and rededication. Each year, the Presidential address links the themes of patriotism and sacrifice to other topical political issues such as reconciliation, the relationship between the party and the courts, black economic empowerment and the land issue. Citizens are then asked to consider how they measure up to the example set by the nation's heroes. Were they walking in their footsteps? Did they, for instance, submerge individualism to the collective will and forsake personal gain for the greater good?[20] With these questions in mind, I will look briefly at the patriotic lessons to be learnt from heroes who originated from the country's racial minorities and ask to what extent they inspired admiration among their compatriots.

The single white national hero[21] is Guy Clutton Brock, a British missionary who arrived in Rhodesia in 1949. He worked for a decade at St Faith's Mission Farm in the Eastern Highlands, where he met and became lifelong friends with future politicians Didumus Mutasa and Maurice Nyagumbo. Clutton Brock

---

19 According to General Dube, the concept of national heroes was borrowed from the socialist countries where many comrades studied and received military training before 1980 (ZBC Radio 1, 11 August 1998).
20 Special Correspondent, 'Who is a hero?', *Parade,* August 1990, p. 28.
21 John Conradie, of Afrikaner and German descent, was awarded the lesser rank of liberation war hero in 1998. Conradie joined the struggle in the mid 1960s and received a 20-year prison sentence in 1967. After serving 11 years, he was released in 1978 on condition that he left the country. He returned after independence and established the Kushanda self-help project.

was instrumental in the formation of the Southern Rhodesian African Congress in 1957. In the late 1960s, he assisted the Tangwena people to resist removal from their home area, which had been classified as European under the 1930 *Land Apportionment Act* (Clutton Brock 1969). He also took an active part in establishing two multiracial farming co-operatives in Rhodesia: first, Nyafaru Farm in the Eastern Highlands and later Cold Comfort Farm on the outskirts of Salisbury (Chater 1985:7–15). Because of the political nature of these activities, he was briefly detained in the late 1950s, and later stripped of his citizenship and deported by the Rhodesian authorities in 1971. President Mugabe, reminiscing with family and friends on Clutton Brock's eightieth birthday, wrote, '[W]hen, in the fullness of time, after our long and bitter struggle, I was called on to form the government of the new Zimbabwe, the example of the Clutton Brocks made it easier to adopt our policy of reconciliation' (Clutton Brock 1987:132). Clutton Brock was declared a national hero after his death in 1995 and his ashes were scattered at the Heroes' Acre shrine. This subdued affair, devoid of the customary pomp and media attention, barely received comment from the white community. Clutton Brock had left the country one-quarter of a century earlier, at which time he had been ostracised by his own race. He was virtually unknown to them at the time of his death. He was not a person most whites chose to emulate or aspired to follow, although his thinking had a profound impact on older African nationalists.

It was, however, not without regret that some whites found 'their kind' unrecognised in the State's pantheon of national heroes. Putting pen to paper a few weeks before Clutton Brock's death, Mr Bennett of Harare described watching

> with sadness and some pride the televised burial of Joe Slovo—pride because the black people of South Africa are willing and able to acknowledge that there are whites in Africa who deserve the accolade of National Hero…South Africa has been able to move further down the road to reconciliation in less than one year, when this country has failed after fifteen years…Are we to believe that not one of the many whites who fought for the rights of blacks in what was Rhodesia, and who have subsequently died, did not deserve to be recognised and honoured as National Heroes.[22]

White liberals, in particular, would like to be credited for their stand against the Rhodesian Front, even if they were unable to espouse a more radical understanding of the black-nationalist political cause. The next contribution, prompted after the President in 1996 publicly castigated whites for their disinterest in Heroes Day, began:

---

22 'White heroes forgotten', *The Financial Gazette*, 19 January 1995, p. 5.

> [A]s in every war there are undoubtedly atrocities on both sides. There were also heroes on both sides…In Spain, a country which went through a very bitter civil war, I believe there is a memorial which simply says 'In memory of all the brave men who gave their lives in the war'. If only we had something like that, which we could all share, in Zimbabwe.[23]

Here again the importance of common memories, of having 'something to share', is raised. Assessments made in the privacy of a white home or an office tended, however, to be more hard nosed. While informants did not consider the official heroes as their heroes, they had other ideas of who they believed qualified. 'There were white heroes—they may have fought on the wrong side, but they are still our heroes.' UDI sanctions busters—'those who sold our tobacco and beef to Europe and flew new jets back from the USA'—were mentioned. A man who had fled the country finding himself 'unable to shoot at the likes of our gardener' nominated conscientious objectors, 'those brave enough to stay in Rhodesia and refuse to fit in'. A more contemporary candidate, admired for standing by her principles, was the outspoken journalist and popular critic Lupi Mushayakarara, respected by many whites for exposing government hypocrisy and disinformation during the 1990s. A sizeable number also nominated the former Rhodesian Front leader Ian Smith for the following reasons:

> Ian Smith has stood by his principles; he continues to live by them till this day. Smith has not left Zimbabwe, not even when his wife died. He has brought his people to this place in history; he will not abandon them, especially the elderly who are here alone.

And again:

> He's here, he didn't desert the old people, he votes, he keeps his mouth shut and that must take some discipline. My brother talked to him the other day. Smith said, 'Don't get fazed by the riots, hold your head high, do not be afraid, show you are not budging and the government will leave you alone.'

Smith's popularity was evident in the lines of whites waiting for his signature when his autobiography was released in Harare at Christmas in 1997. They were captured, hiding their faces and turning to the wall, as television cameras recorded their 'betrayal' for the evening news. However, not all whites felt this way. Some liberals considered Smith, who died in 2007, as well as his Rhodesian Front colleagues, traitors, believing their refusal to repent and acknowledge the errors of their regime had resulted in all whites being tainted with the same crimes (Moore-King 1989).

---

23 'Remember them all', *The Herald*, 17 July 1996, p. 6.

The second minority hero—whom I include for mention because a few research participants were members of the coloured community—was Senator Joseph Culverwell, Deputy Minister of Education and Culture from 1980 to 1988. Culverwell thus achieved a high position in the post-independence government. Tributes paid to him by fellow MPs at the time of his retirement were revealing. Culverwell was praised for, among other things, his 'jovial' and 'encouraging attitude'. 'Light heartedly we referred to him as *muzukuru*. He is our link between blacks and whites…He is more committed to black than white, he lives with us and works with us and indeed he enjoys to be with us.'[24]

'*Muzukuru*' denotes a male relative from one's mother's lineage. Applied as an honorific, it indicates a cordial and intimate bond. A senior *muzukuru* has certain ceremonial functions and, more importantly here, political standing. He is able, for instance, to publicly rebuke a chief for failing to live up to community expectations (Bourdillon 1987:35). The MP quoted above used the analogy to refer to Culverwell's reputation for speaking directly to whites, for 'putting them in their place' during Senate debates soon after independence. Known affectionately as Uncle Joe and *muzukuru*, Culverwell was accorded national membership in terms of fictive kinship, denoted on account of his personal characteristics and political loyalty.

Among his own people, Culverwell was admired for his charitable and community work, 'for pulling us [the coloured community] together' at the national rather than simply the local level. Accordingly, he was a well-known figure, and when he died in 1993, was considered an appropriate choice by his compatriots. Regardless, coloureds did not look on Heroes' Acre any more favourably because they believed the complex gave the impression that 'only ZANU PF can rightly claim to have liberated the nation'. Coloureds joined ZAPU, and to a lesser extent ZANU, the latter being less receptive to non-Africans, during the 1960s (Muzondidya 2005:223–5, 256–60). Coloureds and Asians also fought with the comrades, but were denied registration as war veterans in 1997 and consequently missed out on the monetary payout. At that time, an informant said angrily, 'Our fathers fought with the liberation forces…They are not being written into the history of this country. The promises made to us during the war have not been kept.'

This community leader recognised the importance of having his people's role in the liberation struggle recorded for posterity, particularly when the coloured community was accused of 'fence-sitting'. A second representative also sought to initiate authorship in the narratives of national liberation when he said:

---

24 *Parliamentary Debates*, 30 September 1992, col. 2619.

> The coloureds also sacrificed for independence. We want to document our contribution to the liberation struggle. We need to make our community more aware of its heroes—Foya-Thompson, Berman, Cecil Smith and others—all of whom fought and were detained during the war.

These informants pressed the point that the war was a collective effort. Many contributed in different ways, including members of the coloured and Asian communities, taking risks that have gone unrecognised. For example, Foya-Thompson, Cecil Smith, Frank Berman and others provided urban safe havens as well as moral and material support, raised finances for the families of restricted nationalists and were active in recruitment and underground activities (Muzondidya 2005:224–5).

The liberation struggle had been heavily dependent on civilian help (Alexander and McGregor 2004:83). In addition to the *mujibas* and *chimbwidos* (the youngsters providing food and information in the countryside), there were town dwellers filling orders for the freedom fighters and staff at the mission hospitals who provided medical attention. Others made sacrifices to feed and protect them. Countless more suffered due to the insecurities that war inevitably brought. The signing of the Unity Accord, which saw ZANU PF and ZAPU merge in 1987, offered academics and politicians the chance to reappraise the official version of the liberation war and review ZIPRA's contribution, as well as that of other sections of society, to the armed struggle (Bhebe and Ranger 1995:3). By the mid 1990s, former ZIPRA soldiers 'could present themselves with justification as the unrecognised and persecuted heroes of the liberation war' (Alexander and McGregor 2004:96). Since then, a few former ZIPRA combatants and ZAPU members have been interred at Heroes' Acre—a gesture designed 'to give some semblance of ethnic equation' at the shrine.[25] In 1998, for instance, the remains of Comrades Mangena, a ZIPRA Commander and Makonese, a ZAPU political leader, killed towards the end of the war, were exhumed, brought back from Zambia and interred at Heroes' Acre.[26] Both had been 'overlooked' as candidates for hero status during the 1980s (Kriger 1995:152). Speaking after the Presidential dedication, Mangena's brother described the family's 'obsession' with the 'mysterious circumstances' of his death in a 'landmine accident', intimating that Mangena had been a casualty of the friction between Mugabe's and Nkomo's forces, mentioned earlier. 'Having heard nothing from the current government,' he went on, 'our mother's tears had never dried', suggesting the government's recent attempt at a corrective gesture hadn't washed with the deceased's family.

---

25 Independent committee should adjudicate hero status', *Zimbabwe Independent*, 16 May 1997, p. 7.
26 'Let's rededicate ourselves to freedom fighters' goals', *The Herald*, 10 August 1998, p. 10; 'Remains of Mangena and Makonese reburied', *The Herald*, 12 August 1998, p. 1.

Rather than offering a moment of familial 'recountability' (Werbner, R. 1998:1) where, in the face of official violence a citizen's memory is acknowledged and made known publicly, the ruling elite continued, as before, to stand accused of misrepresentation and the gross distortion of history.[27] The unresolved circumstances surrounding these, and other, deaths threw up contradictions within the liberation war's history. For instance, the families living in Bango chiefdom, south-western Matableleland, and described by Werbner (1995:107), did not remember the liberation war as a unified or heroic struggle, or even a time of triumph. Their narrative suggests it was more an experience of division, suffering and moral ambivalence, where it was survival itself that was heroic (Werbner 1995:108). The state apparatus seems intent on silencing such disparate memories, just as it is prepared to deprive the coloured community of its war memories, for only certain groups and individuals are credited with 'founding' or 'fathering' the nation, and only this section of society unequivocally belongs. Notwithstanding this, state normalising judgements decree that all the minorities are duty bound to give thanks, for they too have enjoyed liberty and peace brought about by the Heroes' sacrifices.

White national commitment: the obligation to participate

Although whites debunk the State's official heroism and refused to pay lip-service to memories that were incompatible with their sense of historical truth, the existence and commemoration of historical injustices nonetheless raise the question of their rectification. In this regard, Connerton (1989:9) asks what obligations do those responsible for past injustice have towards others who suffered because of them. What ought they do, he asks, in order for the historical slate to be cleansed of their illegitimate acts (Connerton 1989)? I suggest the ruling elite expected, among much else, the white community, young and old, to support its national events as a token of their loyalty and the new regime's legitimacy. The following statement issued soon after independence and directed to 'white and brown Zimbabweans' indicates the importance the State attaches to the minorities' investment in its discursive formations:

> National Days should be observed by all Zimbabweans. They are unitive [sic] days, and in a young country still struggling to crystallise and consolidate its nationhood, they should be taken seriously...it is not

---

27 'Opposition urges government to respect unsung heroes', *The Daily Gazette,* 15 August 1994, p. 4.

enough to simply give donations towards national events. Rather there is an obligation [to] experience and concretely share our national oneness [in order] to build a cohesive nation.[28]

A decade and a half later, the same themes continued to be repeated:

Until all the different races in Zimbabwe start paying equal respect to state occasions that are landmarks of our evolution as a nation, the people of this country will never truly believe that they share a common national identity. And without a common identity, the people will never feel they share the same destiny.[29]

Taken together, these statements point to Foucaldian practices of discipline and training that reconstruct and ultimately produce new kinds of people (Rouse 1994:95). Experiencing collective phenomena, which the State articulates in nationalist terms, provides, according to Fanon (1965:155) and Memmi (1965:89), opportunities for colonialists to be liberated from their 'disfigured' and 'oppressive' selves, to develop a 'new consciousness' and thereby form a common bond with their fellow countrymen. Thus, speaking of 'how Zimbabwe was won', Mugabe noted that whites 'had to be fought and won over' through a combination of education and force.[30]

The ruling party also expects children to take part in national events created specifically with them in mind. The President voiced his disapproval of white parents who confined their children to a cultural, political and social laager by not encouraging their attendance, for it was the State's wish that they be socialised in its form of national belonging. Similarly, the Vice-President, Joshua Nkomo, confronted white parents with the prospect of civil strife if their children continued to exclude themselves from 'anything to do with Zimbabwe as a nation'. He asked, '[W]here are your children? Do you want us to fetch them out so that they can participate in national events? They are our children too. There is absolutely nobody who has the right to hide them.'[31] In part, these utterances reflect the notion that children belong not just to their immediate families but to the wider community, and hence all adults have a responsibility to see that children are properly socialised. The President, however, continued, 'they don't want to hear our revolutionary stories, they don't like to be reminded' of the nation's history.[32] They would rather forget than learn from Mugabe as 'the

---

28   'National days', *The Herald*, 19 September 1982, p. 4.
29   'Our history still a tale of two cities', *The Sunday Mail*, 16 August 1998, p. 8.
30   'How Zimbabwe was won', *The Sunday Mail*, 16 February 1997, p. 1.
31   'Opt for racial harmony or risk civil war', *The Sunday Mail*, 15 May 1994, p. 6.
32   'How Zimbabwe was won', *The Sunday Mail*, 16 February 1997, p. 1.

father of the nation'; they were not prepared to absorb the elders' wisdom. Yet the word father (*baba*) is 'a heavy word'; it means respect; 'you cannot refuse your father'.

So, in short, white attendance at Heroes and other national days was conceived to be transformative—of decolonisation through familiarisation with another history—and an act of volition by which to become nationals. The white community, however, refused to accommodate the State on this score. They were familiar with the State's public transcript, well aware that the government was 'pushing the idea of one nation' and expected them 'to join the people' and commemorate or celebrate national events. An informant said, 'Mugabe is angry about our lack of involvement and has begun a dialogue with us through the press about it.' Others, irritated by surveillance, complained that politicians and government officials appeared preoccupied with how poorly whites were represented on national days. Countrywide, however, low turnouts are commonplace, for the majority of the black population does not participate.[33] Provincial Heroes' Acres lie in disrepair, lending some currency to critiques referred to above that assert that the war was neither a mass movement nor a peasant revolution (Hudson 1981:205; Kriger 1988:306). Indeed, relatives were not always happy for their loved ones to be interred at these sites, preferring instead to bury their kinsmen at the family homestead where accessibility was assured and the grave could be tended and visited regularly. Alexander et al. (2000:259–61) describe the impossibility and eventual failure of constructing this sort of monument at Pupu in Lupane, Matabeleand. Despite all of this, it was the invisibility of whites that was repeatedly censured in the government-controlled media. In this way, the white community was made the object of a system of knowledge that defined it and was applied to it through discipline. Before considering the narrative consequence of the State's construction of the nation as a community of obligation, I wish to consider some of the ways in which white resistance to discipline was framed.

---

33 Despite annual exhortations to 'show solidarity with the fallen heroes' and attend commemorative activities out of 'a sense of national duty' (*Sunday Mail*, 10 August 1997, p. 8), attendance nationwide was generally poor. In suburban Harare, a substantial number of smaller shops opened for business, flea markets were in full swing and weddings were under way during commemorations in the early 1990s. This was also the case in 1996, the centenary of the first *Chimurenga*, and was roundly condemned as 'a national shame' (*Sunday Mail*, 10 August 1997, p. 8). Entries in the Heroes' Acre official register also indicated that, apart from relatives, the majority of those who visited the shrine were school groups and tourists. Questioned about this, a guide indicated his disappointment with Zimbabweans who claimed 'we don't need to come, we know our history, we were part of the struggle'. The appearance of social solidarity was also difficult to sustain on some ceremonial occasions. In 1997, war veterans disrupted proceedings at the national shrine in their campaign for a compensation payout, while in 1998 security forces removed the heroes' widows who were trying to demonstrate their poverty and the government's careless attitude towards them. Yet, from the start, there was little attempt to encourage popular participation in the monument's construction. The design did not originate from local artists but came from North Korea. Thus Heroes' is, in many ways, a failed monument when compared, for instance, with the public's response to the Vietnam War monument described by Rowlands (1996:14–16).

A decade after independence, a returnee wrote of her own weakening sense of nationalism and the experience of her son, who lived overseas. She and her husband emigrated to Australia soon after independence. The following passage, written in reflection on Heroes Day 1989 and some three years after their return to Zimbabwe, began:

> My life seems to have been divided into BA and AA—before Australia and after. Before Australia, my pleasure in my home was much more intense. Now it's an effort to remain interested. I do enjoy things aesthetically pleasing, but somehow I feel the circumstances in this country, like impetus, long term involvement, is there any peace for us here? I mean by that the feeling of belonging. We don't really belong any more. Even John, my son, has commented on how strange it is not to feel that one belongs, and that he feels an outsider when observing the pride of other nationalities in their country…Today official statements allude to white and black Zimbabweans. There is no doubt in my mind that the former is not wanted here. Every so often there is a complaint that the white Zimbabweans don't attend the celebrations that include tribal music and dancing. No one ever seems to point out that our cultures differ so widely, and that it's not a slight, it's just too diverse to interest us.

Hers is an instance of identity failure (Gupta and Ferguson 1997a:15). Unable to link up with the anti-colonial rhetoric, she, like many other informants, talked to ethnocentrism. Distancing herself, she pointed out that 'we're not emotionally involved with the liberation movement' and 'it is alien to our culture to attend parades and mass celebrations'. Whites generally claimed that it was inappropriate to attend funerals of people or families they did not know. They invoked cultural incompatibility and a litany of other justifications— the heat, the crowds, the possibility of pickpockets and car thefts—to express their reluctance to participate in any of Zimbabwe's national days. Arguments of this particular cast invoked 'culture' in Said's (1993:xiii, xix) sense of a source of identity 'blind to histories, cultures and aspirations of others'. As a site of political struggle, white invocations had acquired a distinctly pragmatic, defensive purpose, insulating them from the official discourse that took participation to be a measure of their national commitment.

There is, however, another important reason proffered for white reticence. Comment was made in Chapter 2 that authoritarianism was a feature of the Zimbabwean State. Dissent has led to the humiliation and repression of citizens (Jenkins 1997:592). At national events, whites were often targeted for criticism; funerals and public holidays had become a 'time for sniping at whites about the past'. On Heroes Day in 1988, for instance, whites were accused of throwing 'the magnanimous gesture of reconciliation back in the government's face'.[34] The President has also earned a reputation for his outbursts at funerals in language reminiscent of Fanon[35]—for instance, at the incarceration of the forty-third national hero, Comrade Stanford Shamu, who was buried at Heroes' Acre in 1996. On this occasion, the President labelled whites 'enemies [who] deserved to die from a hail of our bullets, your carcasses being thrown to the dogs and vultures'.[36] This was not a narrative of nationhood that the white population was able to invest in. At another funeral a few months' later, whites were again singled out as 'the oppressors of yesterday, they are still oppressors today of our liberated people'.[37] Thus, ceremonial events taking place at Heroes' Acre provided what Falk Moore (1993:2) termed 'summarising occasions' or 'moralising moments'. References to colonial atrocities, adding 'a moral tone to a political position' (Falk Moore 1993), were part and parcel of ZANU PF's discourse regarding how society should be understood and organised.

The President's 'moralising moments' served to construct white identity and strengthened their sense of community. Distinctions made earlier between themselves as liberals or conservatives were put aside or blurred somewhat through the recognition of a common, post-independence oppression. And, while the presence of a Western tourist or hapless backpacker at national functions received extensive media attention, the majority of Zimbabwean whites never, to use their parlance, 'pitched up'. As elsewhere in the world, the message intended by political mobilisers was not always accepted at face value (Falk Moore 1993:1). Mugabe, it was said, was 'playing the white card' for his own purposes. Whites perceived themselves to be demonised in the national narrative, 'rejected' and 'driven into a laager', and remarked that 'the government will have to change its attitude before we are seen at any national events'. Being accused of crimes and publicly stigmatised led them to ask, 'What did we stay in the country for?'

Instead, they left it to their community leaders to sometimes put in an appearance. Senior figures from the CFU, for instance, attended the funeral of popular Zimbabwe Farmers Union President Gary Magadzire at Heroes' Acre in 1996. As the representative of small-scale black farmers and a successful farmer in his own right, Comrade Magadzire spoke not of race but of a community of farmers sharing common interests. 'By working beside each other we can learn,'

---

34   'Saboteurs must leave', *The Herald*, 12 August 1988, p. 1.
35   Zanu PF propaganda was also couched in Fanonist language and supported by photographs of colonial atrocities. See, for example, ZANU PF's advertisements in *The Herald* on 12 August 1994, 11 August 1997 and 18 April 1998.
36   'Mugabe castigates whites for spurning reconciliation', *The Herald*, 7 June 1996, p. 1.
37   'President Mugabe, funerals and white oppressors', *Zimbabwe Independent*, 25 October 1996, p. 10.

he said, 'by staying separate we are perpetuating what we fought against' (quoted in Alden and Makumbe 2001:227). Speaking of the CFU's 'oversight' in the early years, an informant said:

> [O]nce the CFU realised it was hurtful, a slight, not to show that you identified with the nation by attending the celebrations…once the CFU realised this, then the leaders and the local CFU councillors made it a point to attend with their wives…mind you, it took a few years for them to discover this.

As the government-controlled press would have it, however, it was not until 1997 or thereabouts that CFU officials in the Midlands and Manicaland Provinces made an appearance, in this instance at Independence Day festivities. Local dignitaries praised them, saying 'this marked a turning point in the race relations' and 'a milestone in the country's history'.[38] Editorial comment was not so generous. The farmers were rebuked for not coming of their own volition, but only in response to 'special invitations', which were a reflection of fundamental white difference. Again, whites had been marked out in practice by dis-assimilation and special dispensation where various senior party officials believed they should be issued with orders and instructions, and turned into nationals through the process of social and cultural assimilation. *The Herald's* editorial continued:

> The point to deduce from white reticence is that they do not belong. They do not belong and their offspring are made not to belong as well…People should come to the stadium willingly…The independence anniversary is something true Zimbabweans, with a commitment to this country, should feel obliged to participate in. It should be a personal commitment.[39]

Yet the majority of whites had difficulty perceiving the issue in this way. To attend national days would be to assent to, or collude with the State's version of historical truth. The white community was not prepared to concede this. Their counter-discourse rejected their representation as a conquered people and asserted that they did not lose the war on the ground but at the negotiating table. Settlement was 'forced' on them by the international community—in particular Britain, the United States and, ultimately, South Africa. Accordingly, they discounted or made light of national days as 'a black or ZANU PF thing', rituals that the party organised for itself. Nor were white parents prepared to send their children to Mugabe's birthday celebrations, for they considered these to be nothing more than an attempt to promote the party and build a personality cult around the President. Their dismissive remarks did not credit this conflict

---

38 'It's a turning point', and, 'Governor praises white farmers', *The Herald*, 19 April 1997, pp. 6, 8.
39 'Whites don't need special invitations', *The Herald*, 10 April 1997, p. 8.

with the importance it deserved for, I suggest, the whites generally failed to apprehend its narrative consequences. As indicated above, white participation in national days was taken by the ruling party to be a measure of commitment and a corresponding moral right to belong. In this way, nationalism emerged as a trope for belonging, bordering and commitment (Brennan 1990:47). Having failed, however, to be re-socialised in the State's form of national inclusion and unable to recognise the revolutionary new Zimbabwe as their own, the white community was no longer perceived to be legitimately at home in the territory.

National disunity: identification and counter-identification

At independence, the ruling party took responsibility for keeping alive the memory of those who had died during the armed struggle and recast their deaths as a sacrifice given without accounting for national rebirth. Having delegated itself the custodian of their memory, the party constructed a public transcript out of the civil war that served to support its interests and ideological position, as well as define national membership. The party's Marxist-Leninist rhetoric linked the ruling elite to the peasants and workers as freedom fighters and victors in a revolutionary, anti-colonial war. The civil war memory therefore provided a source of state legitimacy; 'nation' building had established the hegemony of ZANU PF and 'sameness' came to signify unity.

For its transcript to be credible, however, the ruling elite required a show of discursive affirmation from below, a settling of historical accounts through repudiation of the old regime and celebration of the new, a performance of deference and consent in reply to its portrayals of mastery and power (Scott 1990:58). As pointed out above, however, the white community refused to provide an audience to ceremonies that marked their own defeat or offer other symbolic gestures of subordination as the erstwhile colonial enemy. To acquiesce would have been to accept the State's representation of white Zimbabweans as the vanquished and defeated beneficiaries of the unjust colonial regime. Their oppositional stance is an example of counter-identification, of white resistance to the subjectivity imposed on them within the ruling party's discourse (Childs and Williams 1997:195). They rejected the basis of the debate about their identity and the terms of their incorporation. Moreover, white counter-narratives introduced inversions that violated the heroic/sacred character of the new regime and unmasked the State's self-interested production of knowledge. These called into question official realities by drawing attention to instances—for example, the abuse of power in Matabeleland—in which state-sponsored violence contravened the official transcript, and in so doing challenged the validity of the nation's revolutionary new beginning. Minority acts of resistance and non-compliance not only indicated the white community's sensitivity to the State's national integration project, which they perceived as oppressive, they signalled that the dominance of the ruling elite was nothing more than a tyrannous exercise of power. In this way, the white counter-narrative sought to wrest from ZANU PF some moral high ground and control over the parameters of the debate regarding the nature of a just society. The incapacity of the State to prevail, despite ordering the white presence at national events, was a measure of its weakness. It was neither successful in annexing white loyalties to its symbolic forms of nationhood nor able to compel the white community's acquiescence.

While the official transcript served to affirm the ruling elite, defining the nation by that which it opposed also meant society remained 'haunted' by its 'definitional other' (Welsh 1997:51). The official narrative of the country's rebirth failed to induce a dialogue out of the violence of the colonial encounter. Instead, as the past was interpreted, a pattern of mutual hostility and misunderstanding, of 'schismogenesis' (Bateson 1958:175, 187), was set in train for the future. Here, in cumulative interactions, the personalities of both communities were distorted as each, perceiving themselves as reacting rather than initiating conflict, blamed the other for their discomfort. Their ever-more alienating utterances and gestures described in this chapter built and amplified difference, introducing into the present and future the politics of confrontation and hostility, out of which the old, adversarial categories of colonist and colonised re-emerged, polarised and hardened (Said 1993:19, 21). This process of increasing differentiation or, in Mbembe's (1992:4) words, their 'mutual zombification', robs all parties of their vitality and, in the longer term, offers only a restrictive and embattled vision of Zimbabwe's future. Ultimately without restraint, schismogenesis could lead to either the assimilation or the elimination of one or other group and the breakdown of the relationship (Bateson 1958:183).

Conclusion

Much of what is officially remembered depends on state decisions about what to record (Hirschkop 1996:v; Lambek 1996:250). In this chapter, attention was directed towards some of the ideas Zimbabwe's ruling elite believed deserved representation at Heroes' Acre, the country's premier monument of nationhood. The cultural work done at the site provided, among other things, the meaning of the war, patriotism and sacrifice and, in the process, nationhood was constituted out of the memory of the liberation struggle. The argument can be made that the war memorial, as a monument to decolonisation, restored black historical identity and asserted nationalist pride in reclaiming the territory—geographically and historically—from the colonists. Perhaps, just as importantly, however, the iconography delineated a core nation, distinct from the population as a whole, with legitimate claims to ownership and control of the State (Brubaker 1996:5). This comprised the freedom fighters and their supporters, who were tied 'naturally' to the national collective, their membership described with familial tropes. Those who fought for Rhodesia will never belong in the same seemingly natural way. This exclusionary national ideology divided the population into the anti-colonial and the colonial, the deserving and the non-deserving, the indispensable and the dispensable. By this means, the colonial intruder and their supporters are cast outside the national family, set apart from the nation by a politics of difference, for the Heroes' complex also objectifies a system of knowledge that reflects the political elite's ambivalence towards the Matabele 'nation' and denies authorship in its narrative of national liberation to the minority coloured and Asian communities. Consequently, reconciliation, conceived as settling accounts from the past, bringing to an end the cycle of accusation and counter-accusation (Asmal 1997:47), has been denied to many.

Thus the State's discourse employs the civil war memory to establish white identity as 'the alien other' in the national consciousness. The struggle over what is to be remembered is intensified, rather than put to rest, when equivalence continues to be drawn between race and history thereby sustaining colonial subject positions and permitting settlers and their descendants only a few limited ways of being in history. Whites have not acquiesced without complaint. In part, this could be attributed to the inflexibility of colonial attitudes and distaste at their interpellation as a conquered people. Equally, however, a case can be made that they are resisting the hegemony of the State's discourse, its homogeneity and containment. Their marginalisation has been compounded by the State's assimilation project whereby whites are required to assume the views of the political elite. Failing in this resulted in their representation as anti-nationalist with no moral right to belong in the country.

With whites unable to share memories and not permitted a new beginning through forgetting, the question that comes to mind is whether it is possible for them to be incorporated in myths of a common destiny. Although they are denied a creditable position in the State's community of memory, are whites able to belong in terms of having a shared programme to put into effect in the future despite differences of history and race (Renan 1990:19)? Oommen (1997a:19) suggests that citizenship, as another subject position and idiom of belonging, has a role in reconciling these tensions. He writes that, as an instrument of equality and inclusion, citizenship has the capacity 'to provide non-national ethnic and minority populations…with a sense of belonging and security' (Oommen 1997a:28). In this way, citizenship provides a 'partial compensation for their remaining within the state in spite of their different identity from the mainstream dominant nation or nations' (Oommen 1997a). I propose to look at these ideas in the next chapter.

5. Decolonising settler citizenship

The academic literature suggests citizenship produces a connection between individuals, the State and the community in which they live, and establishes a relationship containing the element of a common destiny, of stakeholders who have an investment in a shared future (Kaplan 1993:250; Kratochwil 1994:487). Stasiulis and Yuval-Davis (1995:19) believe this to be particularly important in settler and post-colonial societies where myths of common origin are divisive or contentious—a case put for Zimbabwe in the previous chapter. To realise these objectives, a state's citizenship ideals need to be inclusive, capable of drawing people in on the basis of their birth and residence, effectively uncoupling citizenship from nationality, rather than excluding them on account of their historical origins or racial and cultural difference (Castles 1996:170; Kaplan 1993:257). It is therefore pertinent to ask whether, and in what ways, Zimbabwe's 'new past' described in the previous chapters makes an appearance in the country's revised citizenship provisions.

At independence, Zimbabwe's citizenship criteria, like much else, required decolonisation and restructuring in order to assert sovereignty, reflect African ideals and end separation of the former colonisers and colonised. To regulate access to citizenship, it was also necessary for the State to define who constituted the people of the country. This chapter suggests that the State has looked for—indeed taken an active role in directing—the decolonisation of minority citizenship. To this end, the construction of and contestations surrounding the eligibility and meaning of Zimbabwean citizenship are addressed below. First, however, it is important to historicise these issues and, for this reason, the chapter starts by examining the ways citizenship was realised by blacks and whites in Rhodesia. Next, the citizenship provisions worked out at Lancaster House as part of the country's decolonisation process are noted. Then the criteria employed by the post-colonial state as it constructed its form of citizenship are established. Against this backdrop, the extent to which settlers who have chosen to remain in Zimbabwe are able to identify with and to commit themselves as citizens to the country in the ways expected by the new regime, is questioned. Finally, attention is directed towards the State's technologies of power, applied more recently to redefine some whites as aliens rather than citizens, and which serve to disengage those of questionable membership.

Rhodesian paths to black and white citizenship

Archival material spanning the liberal and hopeful years of Federation, its subsequent collapse, followed by the move towards conservatism in Rhodesian politics during the late 1960s reflects the paths to full societal membership for black and white youth during the colonial period. Comment here will be confined to two publications that highlight the critical role attributed to education and the acquisition of skills in transforming Africans from subjects to citizens. A third text suggests a different route to social and political participation for white youth. Each will be discussed in its chronological order.

The first is a report written by British consultants Hunter and Hunter for the Capricorn Africa Society, a non-racial organisation[1] formed in 1949 to promote the material advantages of a united Central and East Africa (Hancock 1984:30). The Capricornians supported the federation of the two Rhodesias and Nyasaland and pushed for the recognition of Africans as wage-earners and consumers (Hancock 1984:31). The society believed that African potential needed to be 'unleashed' through the attainment of citizenship qualifications that would develop an appreciation of Western civilisation (Hancock 1984:40) and, at the same time, reduce the attraction of African nationalism. Accordingly, the society engaged consultants to assess the establishment of colleges, their mandate being the creation of 'a sense of common citizenship between members of the different races by a better understanding of the economic, social, administrative and cultural problems of their country' (Hunter and Hunter 1959:2).

The Hunters' findings suggested that citizenship, as a sense of ownership and sharing in the country, was unlikely to develop among Africans and Asians without some kind of training for employment. At the time, African education remained a territorial responsibility whereas that of Europeans had become a federal matter (Faber 1961:43). The consultants noted that the outstanding weakness in Southern Rhodesia was 'the quite startling shortage of facilities for Africans or Asians to get training for a job in life…whether by apprenticeship, full-time training or evening classes' (Hunter and Hunter 1959:19). The Hunters' surprise was perhaps unwarranted, given the apprehension felt by white artisans, potentially faced with African or Asian competition (Gann 1965:326). That adult education and vocational pursuits were perceived as critical prerequisites for the development of a sense of 'patriotism' and 'nationhood' (Hunter and Hunter 1959:1) suggested an essentially materialist approach to the generation of citizenship. Evidence of this understanding could still be seen in Harare in the 1990s where Ranche House, providing adult training courses of short duration, outdatedly described itself as a 'College of Citizenship', for the constitution of citizenship had moved on and been recast since independence.

---

1 The Capricorn Africa Society, with financial backing from overseas, saw material advantages in federation (Hancock 1984:30–3). The society's citizenship project originated from the conference entitled Education for Citizenship held in 1958. Hancock (1984:47) noted that many future nationalist leaders were Capricornians during the 1950s, when Africans constituted about 65 per cent of the society's members. For instance, Shamuyarira, Takawira, Chitepo and Vambe, mentioned in these pages, were all at one time members of the society.

5. Decolonising settler citizenship

By 1960, the Capricorn Africa Society had largely run its course. Its agenda had not caught the white imagination nor, as indicated below, had their political parties embraced its ideals (Hancock 1984:47). Coincidentally, bans placed on nationalist organisations in the late 1950s led Africans to question whether they could achieve their citizenship rights within the normal political life of the country (Auret 1992:20–2).

A second, somewhat later publication that also traces the path to African citizenship in Rhodesia is Elsener's *My Life Tomorrow—A teachers' guide* (1965), distributed by the Catholic Church for use in its schools. Here, the huge contribution of mission schools and, in particular, the Roman Catholic Church to African education should be kept in mind. The book presents 'Christian teachings integrated with the practical life of Africa's youth' in order to 'form them into upright adults, useful citizens and apostolic Christians of whom the family, the country and the church can be proud' (Elsener 1965:1). To be effective, training needed to be grounded in the customs and institutions of the local society. Visits to a nearby mine or headman's court, studying parliamentary debates in class and school projects focused on developments in the country such as the Kariba Dam were some of the methods used to introduce children and young adults to their place in a community that extended beyond the family and the village, while simultaneously supporting traditional African authority. Elsener's *Guide* unabashedly sought to instil patriotism in pupils by, for instance, making them aware of Rhodesia's unique features and teaching the hymn *Ishe Komberere Afrika*,[2] justifying this on the grounds that 'love for one's country is the Christian way of good nationalism' (Elsener 1965:31). The virtues of responsibility, tolerance and objectivity imbued instructions regarding relations with elders, marriage partners, neighbours and employers. Respect was purported to be the 'key' for 'getting along with people of other races' and building a nation together. The importance of obedience and paying taxes, the need for an efficient and honest civil service, as well as the conviction that it was not the task of government to replace the efforts of the people, were other prominent principles. Forms of government, the benefits of colonial rule and an appreciation of the migratory history of all people then living in Rhodesia were also deemed relevant to preparing African youth for citizenship and colonial capitalism legitimated within a Christian framework.

The tone and endeavour of these publications have much in common, despite citizenship being predicated on an economic foundation in the first, while character formation and values given spiritual underpinning are central to the latter. Both consider education and training to be appropriate tools for building 'good citizenship'. The texts pass on the colonists' own political experience and reflect their certainty in the superiority of Western democracy in which an

---

2   See Chapter 3, note 13.

individual's vote epitomises, above all, full political participation. Content was aimed at enhancing black receptivity to Western political ideas and forms of government, which, the authors assumed, would encourage African decisions in keeping with white interests in the future. Thus, during the colonial era, citizenship was an intrinsic part of the European civilising mission, its objective being the preparation of the African minor for membership in the modern world. Chakrabarty (2000:9) nominates this as an evolutionary or 'stagist' approach to citizenship, the colonists envisioning a preparatory period of education and employment before conferring the right to social and political participation.

About the time these texts were published, however, distinctions between the races were being written ever more deeply into Rhodesia's franchise. Although blacks who attained a certain level of education, means and property[3] were eligible for incorporation by a system of qualified franchise from the time of the first Legislative Assembly in 1898 (Clements 1969:277; Quenet 1976:21), in practice, the shortcomings identified in the Hunters' report cited above limited the numbers of African voters. And, while some liberal thinkers, such as members of the Capricorn Africa Society, supported racial parity founded on a common electoral roll of qualified franchise (Hancock 1984:46), property and educational criteria became more restrictive for African voters as Rhodesian politics turned further to the right (Shamuyarira 1966:148–50). The 1961 and 1965 Rhodesian *Constitutions* enshrined a more gradual time frame, foreshadowing majority rule at some successively more distant date. Further, the 1969 *Constitution* established for the first time separate racial voter rolls—one for Africans and one for all people other than Africans—and, while continuing the earlier educational, means and property qualifications, it made the number of African representatives in the House of Assembly dependent on African income tax contributions. As a result, more than six million blacks were represented by 16 Members of Parliament, only half of whom were elected by popular vote, the remainder being chosen by traditional African leaders (Blake 1978:402), while about 250 000 whites elected 50 representatives to Rhodesia's House of Assembly (Auret 1992:75). The number of black representatives could theoretically increase to that of non-Africans, but thereafter could not exceed that level until the black population contributed about one-quarter of all income tax[4] (Palley 1970:30). Evidence presented to the Commission of

---

3 Historically, Southern Rhodesia followed a system of qualified franchise based on voting arrangements in force in Cape Colony. Africans and non-Africans were required to meet property and educational qualifications (Shamuyarira 1966:148). This colourblind franchise was introduced in part to keep poor whites, notably Afrikaners, off the Rhodesian roll (Gann 1965:144). While property qualifications were not particularly onerous for most other whites, they disenfranchised all but a few blacks. Educational requirements also meant Africans had to achieve a certain level of approved schooling and demonstrate an adequate knowledge of English by completing and signing the necessary registration forms (Clements 1969:279).
4 In 1967, the African population paid 0.42 per cent of income tax receipts received by the State, although they contributed revenue in other ways through indirect taxation (Palley 1970:30). To link African seats in the House to income tax therefore made it impossible for black representatives to outnumber white in the

Inquiry into Racial Discrimination (Quenet 1976:22) indicated that it was the electoral division into races, rather than the voting qualifications per se, that most angered blacks, for citizenship was exclusionist and elitist, the Rhodesian sense of colonial nationalism not including the majority as citizens (Eddy and Schreuder 1988:3).

A third publication, aptly called *The Business of Living: A guide to good citizenship* (Pascoe:1969), suggested that the route to citizenship for young whites was conceived differently. A prominent insurance company printed this pamphlet as a 'service to the young people of Rhodesia', although the topics and illustrations pointed directly to white youth. Advice is provided on money matters—budgeting, hire purchase, writing cheques, the share market and income tax—as well as medical aid, hospital services, unemployment insurance, road safety, driver's licences, the voters' roll, military service, the reading of marriage banns (church notices) and so forth. These rights and duties of citizenship were to be taken up when the age of majority was reached. Much else was taken for granted—for example, race relations were not mentioned, nor were thorny questions regarding the relevance of European immigration. The privileges of citizenship seemingly unproblematically followed the attainment of adulthood.

A scheme of local citizenship and enactment had, in fact, come into effect in 1949. Allowing this, the imperial centre treated Rhodesia administratively not as a colony but as if it were a self-governing dominion, comparable with Australia, Canada or India (Palley 1960:754). The Southern Rhodesian *Citizenship Act* (1949) closely followed legislation in place in the United Kingdom and permitted plural citizenship. Rhodesian authorities presumed that the settlers belonged to the territory in which they were born, whose citizenship they claimed and whose passports they now carried, at one and the same time as they also qualified under the 1948 British *Nationality Act* as British subjects by descent (Nicol 1993:257; Palley 1960:746, 1186). Within a few decades, however, settler presumptions were to be challenged when racial identities were reworked and Rhodesian citizenship became a matter of dispute. The 1978 *Salisbury Agreement*, and amendments to the country's immigration regulations the next year, suggested white politicians had some inkling of this. Hurriedly passed legislation guaranteed entitlement to dual citizenship and gave an automatic right of residence to citizens, people born in Rhodesia whose parents were permanent residents, people born outside the country to permanent residents and who came to reside there before their third birthday, plus the wives and children of these categories. These generous provisions indicate some apprehension that questions regarding the acceptability and legality of the European presence would imminently arise.

---

foreseeable future (Blake 1978:148).

At the 1979 Lancaster House Constitutional Conference, Britain asserted itself as the decolonising power, something its representatives claimed long experience in accomplishing (Stedman 1991:176). Britain's working documents provided the basis for the negotiations and, mindful of Rhodesian anxieties regarding majority rule, contained a number of provisions protecting minority interests. Relevant here are the provisions regarding citizenship. Automatic citizenship was to be granted to all settlers, even the 40 per cent who had arrived after 1965, when Rhodesia was deemed to have become a rogue colony (Wiseman and Taylor 1981:8). In addition, the provisions allowed settlers to hold dual nationality indefinitely (Davidow 1979:57).

The Patriotic Front[5] challenged Britain's underlying assumption of its leadership role at the talks. The Front instead projected itself as representing the people of Zimbabwe and, as such, the effective decolonising factor (Wiseman and Taylor 1981:7). Patriotic Front representatives strongly objected to special provisions for racial minorities, including the proposed citizenship clauses. Mugabe argued that

> [a]ll people who live in Zimbabwe should consider themselves as citizens of that country. Is it possible to call a section of the community European? Surely there can be no such thing as a European in Africa… This is a racial approach and repugnant to our delegation. (Quoted in Stedman 1991:181)

While not disagreeing with this line of reasoning, the British delegation saw the Front's solution as utopian. They believed the political realities of the past could not be ignored, nor could the new state's dependence on white skills (Stedman 1991:179). Consequently, dual citizenship provisions were written into the Lancaster House *Constitution*. Back in Zimbabwe, their inclusion was generally welcomed by settlers who saw in them a form of protection, a safeguard intended to create reassurance and confidence in the minds of many Zimbabweans, being mainly if not entirely white. Subsequently, the provisions were described as measures to win confidence and stem the European exodus.[6]

Settlers as loyal citizens of Zimbabwe

In international thinking, state boundaries define the inside and outside of citizenship (Hintjens 1995:2). Decolonisation can complicate the process but, ultimately, domestic laws determine who is, and who is not, a citizen. Indeed, the sovereign right to determine who belongs, and how they belong, to the State enjoys widespread recognition. In Zimbabwe, the rules, rights and

---

5   Mugabe, Nkomo and their supporters negotiated as a united Patriotic Front at Lancaster House.
6   *The Senate,* 20 October 1982, cols 1184–5.

protections citizenship confers are set out in the country's *Constitution* and its *Declaration of Rights*, in the *Citizenship Act* and immigration regulations. The last two of these are based on the Rhodesian legislation of the same name and provide access to citizenship on the grounds of birth, descent, registration and marriage. The contours of citizenship have therefore been appropriated from the colonial regime and, although amended since independence and influenced by Zimbabwe's international treaty obligations, their origins lie nonetheless in their Western heritage. The legislation is therefore structured according to European ways of thought and practice, with its notion of universal applicability.

The reconstitution of citizenship was neatly caught by the new government's slogan 'One person, one country, one nation, one citizenship', for the incoming ruling elite held that a person could not be loyal to both Zimbabwe and another state.[7] Consequently, the 'theoretical document' produced at Lancaster House required modification so that it fitted and reflected 'the identity of its people'.[8] Midway through the First Parliament, an enabling bill amended the *Constitution* such that it was silent on dual citizenship. Introducing the bill, the Minister for Legal and Parliamentary Affairs, Eddison Zvobgo, said 'this constitutional transformation process will be a major test of loyalty for all non-African citizens in this country. The longer they cling to undeserved prerogatives and privileges—the more they irreparably damage national reconciliation and irretrievably prejudice their own standing in Zimbabwe.'[9] Zvobgo continued: 'we want our citizens to owe allegiance only to Zimbabwe.' He explained that, as far as the government was concerned, dual citizenship had only ever been

> a stop gap in order to give people time to recover from the ravages of the war and decide which country they wanted to call their own. More than two years later, there is no justification whatsoever for anybody to continue to waver between Zimbabwe and any other country.[10]

Nominal citizens, or citizens of questionable belonging, were subject to a programme of national integration. In this the Minister had the support of the majority, if not all, black MPs. A colleague succinctly expressed his sentiments as follows: 'My country right or wrong, my country poor or rich…That is what every Zimbabwean should say.'[11] The MP averred, 'if you can always say that we are here temporarily because I am holding my passport to somewhere else and we can always go…then definitely your loyalty is divided'. With the benefit of hindsight, perhaps more notice should have been taken of the President when he addressed the local white population during the early and generous days

---

7 'Way cleared for citizenship bill', *The Herald*, 25 August 1982, p. 1.
8 *Parliamentary Debates*, 16 July 1982, col. 814.
9 *Parliamentary Debates*, 14 July 1982, col. 692.
10 Ibid., col. 693.
11 *Parliamentary Debates*, 16 July 1982, cols 814–15.

shortly after independence. 'Foreigners,' he said, 'who don't want to take up Zimbabwean citizenship will not be victimised...If you just want to serve the country and return home, you are free to do so. We will not deprive you of the right to make that choice.'[12] While reassuring, his words also reproduced anyone thinking of opting for permanent residence as 'foreigners' or strangers with homes elsewhere to which they would one day return.[13]

Many urban Africans, however, also find themselves 'torn' between homes (Wermter 1987:1). In their case, the term 'home' refers primarily to the rural area where ancestors are buried and which gives a person a totem and clan identity. Urban workers, most of whom wish to retire, die and be buried at the rural home, invest in property and social relationships centred on this location throughout their working lives (Kabweza 1987:1), their ties to the rural home demonstrated by the almost obligatory 'month's end' journey home with provisions and cash. During fieldwork, Irene Zindi, MP, alluded to the significance of her rural home when, putting her case for preferential treatment as a new entrant in the tourism industry, she said, 'I do not have a second home as Zindi. This is my soil and I have nowhere else to go and this is what I enherited [sic] from my ancestors and I will die here and remain here. I will never go anywhere.'[14] In her address, Zindi defines Zimbabwean society organically rather than functionally, on the basis of descent rather than simply by birth or long-term residence (Safran 1991:86). She gives primacy to the principle of *jus sanguinis* rather than *jus soli*. Zindi's appeal also bears out Appadurai's (1988:37) observation that 'natives are not only persons who are from certain places, and belong to those places, but they are also those who are somehow *incarcerated*, or confined, in those places'. Hence the possession of a second passport makes its owner intrinsically different. To the extent that its owner need not be confined, the person may choose not to be present when the country is wrong or poor and is not, therefore, considered to belong authentically as a native. Other black representatives, putting a more positive gloss on immobility, remarked that 'true Zimbabweans' were 'black Zimbabweans because...they will stay in the country'.[15]

Passports have thus become a critical nexus linking 'white' to 'Zimbabwe' in the public domain. Time and again, the debate turned on the ambiguous, unknowable and inherently antisocial character of dual citizens. 'A person who holds dual citizenship is like a person standing between two roads and he does not know

---

12 'No witch-hunt over citizenship, Mugabe pledges', *The Herald*, 19 July 1982, p. 1.
13 Also suggesting a parallel between passports and other homes, Mr Shambambeva-Nyandoro said 'no blacks can have three homes. You cannot have a home in Malawi, a home in Zambia and a home in Zimbabwe. How many can afford to do that? But the majority of whites can do that' (*Parliamentary Debates*, 30 August 1994, col. 1110). Another black MP, also drawing boundaries and perhaps exasperated with those who did not fit his moral map, asserted that 'if people become Zimbabwean citizens we will know who our people are' (*Parliamentary Debates*, 16 July 1982, col. 816).
14 *Parliamentary Debates*, 24 February 1998, col. 3497.
15 *Parliamentary Debates*, 30 June 1982, col. 327.

what to do.' Or, he is 'like a man married to two wives…his attention is divided…
We cannot afford polygamous citizenship.'[16] Cheater and Gaidzanwa (1996:194)
make the point that black male assertions such as these ignore the realities faced
by the exogamously married women of Southern Africa's patrilineal societies
who, throughout their lives, juggle at one and the same time loyalties to natal
kin and affines. Nonetheless, ambiguity as citizens reflected black uncertainty
regarding white loyalty, given 'there are no genuine citizens who hold two
passports'.[17] Law-enforcement agencies warned that the mobility afforded these
footloose people by modern transport systems must be thwarted by the vigilant
application of immigration regulations.[18] These sentiments reflect, to be fair, a
measure of official anxiety regarding the possibility of a white-supported civil
war (Flower 1987:277), as well as anger over the destabilisation of Zimbabwe by
South Africa during the first decade of independence (Dzimba 1998:55; Martin
and Johnson 1986).[19] In light of this, the government looked for some indication
of commitment and loyalty from the white and Asian communities as a whole,
for some indication of their preparedness to remain domiciled in the country in
the longer term and their willingness to accept its legislation, to integrate and
live according to the social values of the black majority.

In reply, white MPs, protesting their personal loyalty while also claiming to
speak for various worried members of their constituencies, could not see why
dual citizenship need weaken their commitment to Zimbabwe, as it had not to
Rhodesia. In an effort to get this point across, a white MP used—not altogether
successfully—a familial analogy:

> Everyone is born into a family. Now, when you grow up you get married,
> you find an attractive girl and you marry her and you live with her. But
> that does not mean to say you sever all connection with your family, and
> that is the connection I see between a person in this country who holds
> a British passport and is a Zimbabwean citizen, or who holds British
> citizenship and not necessarily a British passport. That was his home,
> where he grew up, where he gave service…as I say, you do not have to,
> when you marry, cast off your family, you are still part of that family but
> you have different loyalties to your wife and to your parents…it is better
> to have some sort of loyalty to the country of your birth as well as the
> country of your adoption.[20]

---

16 *Parliamentary Debates*, 16 July 1982, cols 814–16.
17 Ibid., cols 816, 818; *The Senate*, 20 October 1982, col. 1190.
18 Department of Information, 22 October 1984, p. 5; *Principal Immigration Officer versus O'Hara*, (1) ZLR 69 (s), 1993, p. 72.
19 See also *Parliamentary Debates*, 13 September 1994, col. 1621.
20 *Parliamentary Debates*, 25 June 1982, col. 259.

The MP does not conceive of the fundamental mental transformation expected of him as suggested by Memmi (1965:23) and Fanon (1965:35, 52). He hopes, as Memmi (1965:40) predicts, to be part of the new country at the same time as he 'reserves the right' to maintain the citizenship of his country of origin. Other white contributors to the debate added the now commonplace arguments, pointing out the danger of driving white skills and capital out of the country and frightening away foreign investment by tampering with the fundamentals of the Lancaster House *Constitution*.[21] So, while the ruling party linked citizenship with loyalty and commitment, most, but not all, white MPs resisted the linkage. One dissenting voice was that of Rhodesia Front backbencher Mr Micklem, who recognised that the amendment was looking for a more fundamental change of white attitudes, 'a token of allegiance to the country, a token of patriotism, perhaps a token even of reconciliation',[22] and subsequently voted with the government.

During the proceedings, Senator Hungwe also highlighted the importance of consensus, saying, 'in African thinking, opposition is something that must be done away with. The Zimbabweans, black, white, [and] coloured, must unite and dedicate themselves to making this country a good place to live in for all those who wish to make it their home.'[23] Scholars also noted repeated references to consensus, the calls for 'oneness and unity', suggesting that the ruling elite conceived of politics as communal, where 'responsible citizens evolve organically out of communally embedded identity and customary norms of fellowship' (Applegate 1992:70). They are thought of not so much as a free-floating possessor of essential human rights but, rather, as a person of place (Applegate 1992). In this context, fully fledged citizens not only conform to the laws of the land, but, importantly, they demonstrate loyalty by acting in ways that reflect the wishes and interests of the State. The citizenship that counts is grounded in organic solidarity, unquestioning compliance and identification associated more usually with kinship relations.

In sum, minority or white commitment was assumed categorically by the State on the basis of passports, regulatory instruments of residence, travel and belonging, which, by allowing people to span borders, reconfigured them as highly ambiguous beings. Statements to the effect that should the minorities wish to belong in Zimbabwe they must embrace the citizenship of that country and no other[24] make explicit the requirement that settlers sever links with the imperial centre. Two questions followed from this. How were they to go about

---

21 *Parliamentary Debates,* 21 July 1982, 16 July 1982; *The Senate,* 20 October 1982.
22 *Parliamentary Debates,* 21 July 1982, col. 895.
23 *The Senate,* 20 October 1982, col. 1179.
24 *Parliamentary Debates,* 30 August 1994, col. 1127.

breaking ties with their countries of historical origin? And, second, would they confront their ambivalence and, as Zimbabweans, take their place by the side of their black compatriots?

The 1984 renunciation exercise

Shortly after independence, it was clear that non-Africans would be required to decide where they belonged and which citizenship they wished to keep. There was a lag between the passage of the enabling legislation in 1982[25] and the provisions of the Zimbabwean *Citizenship Act*, not made available until 1984, after which time minorities had 12 months to respond. So, initially, people were uncertain about the options they had. Minority MPs felt they were being asked to agree to 'the unexplained and the unknown'.[26] Remarks by the Minister for Home Affairs, Dr Ushewokunze, that the new citizenship bill would 'drum out' the non-belonging and provoke 'fireworks'[27] were remembered as 'not reassuring', prompting speculation about the content of the new provisions. Would longstanding residents who did not opt for Zimbabwean citizenship be prejudiced in any way? Would they, for instance, lose pension rights in the country whose citizenship they forfeited? As aliens, could they hold land, act as company directors or continue in business? Would they need to apply for work permits; what of promotion possibilities within the civil service? And were they entitled to holiday allowances if they elected to keep their foreign citizenship?

The government took it as axiomatic that any citizen-by-registration must hold another citizenship, valid or invalid.[28] Those who wished to retain Zimbabwean citizenship were directed to go to the passport office, register and surrender their foreign travel documents. If they failed to do so their Zimbabwean citizenship automatically lapsed at the end of the grace period. There was some confusion regarding the appropriate action for locally born whites who had an entitlement to foreign citizenship by descent, but did not hold a foreign passport, having used Southern Rhodesian, Federation, Rhodesian or Zimbabwe-Rhodesian passports in the past. 'To be on the safe side', officials advised all those born outside the country, or with a parent(s) born outside, to submit a renunciation form.[29] The renunciation process was in fact simpler for these people. They could send the completed document to the Registrar-General by post. In this way, a register was compiled of all non-Africans who acted in accordance with government directives by one or other means. The Citizenship Office continues

---

25 Table 2.3 in CSO (1987) indicates that in 1982, 114 920 of a total white population of 146 880 claimed Zimbabwean citizenship.
26 *Parliamentary Debates*, 21 July 1982, col. 886.
27 *Parliamentary Debates*, 14 July 1982, col. 697, 3 August 1982, col. 962, 24 February 1998, col. 3497.
28 *Parliamentary Debates*, 26 March 1986, col. 1594.
29 'Citizen steps for "foreigners" outlined', *The Herald*, 25 September 1985, p. 1.

to verify citizenship against this roll when processing passports. When the new citizenship bill (subsequently the *Citizenship of Zimbabwe Act 1984*) was released, it provided that dual citizens who did nothing and those holding only foreign passports but domiciled in the country would become permanent residents. As such, they would be entitled to reside in Zimbabwe, work, vote, own property and 'generally do all things that are done by persons ordinarily resident in this country'.[30] Another decade was to pass before the implications of the amendment were to be fully understood.

In the meantime, the minority's slow and indecisive response to the government's publicity campaign was disappointing, 'hardly demonstrating an eager, whole hearted acceptance of the country in which they live and work'.[31] Various foreign governments, the United Kingdom's and Australia's included, placed advertisements in the local papers advising their citizens of the choices open to them.[32] The British also produced a pamphlet and embassy staff addressed at least one public meeting on the matter.[33] Many informants recalled information provided through these channels, drew my attention to it and came to their decisions bearing it in mind. They credited the British Government with recognising that they were 'acting under duress' and explained that both countries allowed those who wanted to retain Zimbabwean citizenship to hand their Australian or British passport to the Zimbabwean Registrar-General. He could not 'stamp cancel or surrender on it' because the passport was the property of a foreign government. In due course, the Registrar-General, Comrade Tobaiwa Mudede, forwarded the document to the appropriate High Commission from where it could be, but was not always, retrieved at a later date. The British, in particular, made it clear that to renounce British citizenship required that a person approach the High Commission and make the renunciation under the law of that country. Due to differences between the two countries' legal systems, signing the declaration required by the Zimbabwean authorities would not affect their position in British law. Their standing in the United Kingdom was not a matter for the Zimbabwean Government.[34]

---

30 *Parliamentary Debates*, 14 August 1984, col. 802; *Principal Immigration Officer vs O'Hara*, (1) ZLR 69 (s), 1993, p. 73.
31 'Disappointing response', *The Herald*, 5 December 1985, p. 4.
32 See 'Citizenship—to all dual British-Zimbabwean citizens, note from the British High Commission', *The Herald*, 15 July 1985; and 'Note to Australian/Zimbabwean dual citizens', *The Herald*, 16 November 1985.
33 'Citizenship deadline extended till Monday', *The Herald*, 26 November 1985, p. 1; 'Registrar clarifies dual citizenship', *The Herald*, 27 November 1985, p. 1. See also *Parliamentary Debates*, 16 August 1984, col. 930.
34 During the publicity campaign, Zimbabwean officials initially directed dual citizens to renounce foreign citizenship at their respective overseas missions and then proceed with evidence to the Zimbabwean citizenship office. This advice, however, was overturned by the Registrar-General. 'Correcting' the 'wrong information' emanating from his office the previous day, Comrade Mudede said that there was no requirement for dual citizens to inform foreign embassies. Rather, his office would process the renunciation and advise the necessary delegation (see *The Herald*, 10 April 1985, p. 1, 11 April 1985, p. 3). It was therefore on the basis of the Registrar-General's instructions that the renunciation exercise proceeded as it did.

Then came a last-minute rush. Almost 20 000 mostly whites renounced their foreign citizenship in Harare by the deadline.[35] A Rhodesian-born woman recalled the event:

> I remember the long lines of whites at the Drill Hall[36] grounds, reluctantly queuing to establish their Zimbabwean citizenship. We had to appear in person; there were many elderly in the line and [there was] nowhere to sit. We went in the front door to register as Zimbabweans and to pass in foreign passports. I had two to give in. Then around to the side door for thumb prints and photos for our identity cards. It was a bunfight, understaffed, we were bench shuffling, the disorganisation was totally alien to the previous regime.

Another, also locally born, said 'when I saw the chaos at Drill Hall I wondered, what am I doing here, why am I doing this? The whole thing was a nonsense.' A third described the day as 'a dehumanising and humiliating experience', so hinting at the psychological violence inherent in denying one's sense of self.

While whites found it a disquieting indication of the future, of 'other' rather than 'our' way of doing things, the editorial of Harare's daily newspaper described the renunciation exercise as having an Alice-in-Wonderland quality about it.[37] What was to have been a demonstration of loyalty had been diminished to the irritation of form filling and tedious waiting in white lines, through outside intervention by the former colonial power and other settler states. Local white procrastination, in conjunction with the actions of external governments, had made it apparent that, although born in the country, whites could also be considered to belong elsewhere by virtue of descent and associated ethno-cultural factors. This inevitably prejudiced their relationship with the Zimbabwean State, within whose borders they resided and whose citizenship they claimed. As a result, whites, including those who passed in other passports, were dubbed 'dubious' and 'bogus citizens', 'rootless strangers' and foreigners bringing in their wake different behavioural mores.

---

35 'Over 19,000 opt to be citizens in Harare', *The Herald*, 4 December 1985, p. 1. Figures indicating dual citizen numbers were not available in Zimbabwe. For obvious reasons, the national census simply asked people to nominate a single citizenship. Some idea of the magnitude was, however, reflected in the British House of Lords debate on the Zimbabwean land issue. Their report—indicating some 30 000 dual citizens and 15 000 mono-British citizens residing in Zimbabwe—was later tabled in the Zimbabwean Parliament (*Parliamentary Debates*, 10 March 1998, col. 3838). These figures should be treated critically as Zimbabwe's 1992 Census gives a lower figure of 10 654 sole UK citizens (CSO 1994:Table 1.14).
36 Drill Hall was renamed the Makombe Building early in 1985, but informants generally used the old name.
37 'Dubious citizens', *The Herald*, 28 September 1985, p. 4.

Decision making

How had informants come to their respective choices? What factors were important in weighing up the decisions they made? The collage that follows gives some impression of the range of positions whites held on the matter of their future citizenship.

A middle-aged woman described her mother-in-law's thinking in the following terms:

> Her husband had died in 1981. She kept her Zimbabwean citizenship because she wanted the country to work, and to demonstrate her faith in the future. She also owns property in Cameron Street [Harare's central business district].

The daughter-in-law, on the other hand, had 'lost' her 'birthright' (see below), but nevertheless continued to believe she had a right to live in the country, 'to belong because I was born and resided here for many years'. Citizenship can be earned or acquired through birth—earned, she thought, through behaving responsibly, paying taxes, being patriotic and supporting the country. Her husband, still a citizen, also implied that commonality was performative when he added, 'I've been desperately trying to learn Shona, to know what people are saying around me...it's ridiculous that we were taught Afrikaans at school'.

A locally born couple with entitlement to UK citizenship by descent adopted a 'wait and see' attitude. 'We seem to have spent our lives wondering what the outcome will be. UDI, the Republic, the war and so after independence we decided to hedge our bets with the passports.' Others, also locally born, said, 'I took the Zimbabwe route, my wife went British. As a company director and property owner, I decided it was sensible to keep my Zimbabwean passport.' The man's wife concurred: 'We divided the options between us; it might work out for the best.' Before this, the man had, however, applied to immigrate to Australia, but was rejected as being 'too old'. He accepted his failure philosophically, saying:

> We are fortunate that things have panned out better here than expected. We were prepared to stay [after 1980] if education and law and order were maintained. But the future is uncertain. What we did not foresee at the time was the frustration ahead in the business environment.

More positively, a retired couple welcomed the change of regimes. Their commitment to the country, 'to making independence work', cannot be doubted (see Chapter 7, note 14); however, they described themselves as being both anxious and realistic in 1984…We felt suspicious of the government but, at the same time, as a minority ethnic group, we had to be realistic…we knew the rules could change, so we went to [the] Drill Hall and passed in our Rhodesian and foreign passports in favour of the Zimbabwean.

Others held a single, paramount concern. 'As a recently divorced mother of three girls, I felt I had to protect the family home, which I received as part of the divorce settlement', so she passed in her British passport. Conversely, a widow chose to relinquish Zimbabwean citizenship and remain domiciled as an immigrant with permanent residence rights. She had left Britain as a seventeen-year-old bride at the end of World War II. In Rhodesia, her husband established a successful metal-fabricating business. After independence, however, the company was refused foreign exchange, 'squeezed out' and sold at an undervalued price. The family lost money and moved into a tiny flat. The widow was still 'bitter towards the new government about this'. Citizenship decisions came up as the business folded. She said:

> I never thought of changing; I wanted to stay British. My Rhodesian-born son thinks of himself as Zimbabwean and has a Zimbabwean passport for work purposes; he travels to Botswana on his job. But I say to him, you wouldn't be a Chinaman just because you happened to born in China.

Her son, on the other hand, appeared to have taken some tentative steps towards transforming his identity and mentally adopting Zimbabwe as his homeland. His disaffected mother would not consider leaving Zimbabwe without him, her only child left in the country. 'He's my baby, he'd have to go first.'

Reacting to her fears of family disintegration, a woman who had grown up in what she described as a 'possessively close family', recalled telephoning her siblings, urging them to take the necessary steps to secure local citizenship. One of four children born in various countries in Southern Africa to British settlers, she had availed herself of a Rhodesian passport in 1976 in the vain hope of winning a scholarship. In 1985, the woman was particularly concerned that her sister, living temporarily in South Africa on a work permit, would become 'stateless'. In the event, none of her siblings responded to her pleas and all bar herself left the African continent within the next few years. She, however, thought of Zimbabwe as her homeland. As a citizen, she expected to be able to own land, work and vote. She also believed that 'if you don't vote, you have no right to criticise'. Her husband, a third-generation Zimbabwean, spoke Sindebele fluently. The couple joked that he had held passports to five different states—Southern Rhodesia, Federation, Rhodesia, Rhodesia-Zimbabwe and now Zimbabwe—but never moved countries. At the time we met, they had just signed a 25-year mortgage on a house plot in Harare and hoped 'to be still living here when the bond is paid off'. They adopted a Christian approach to reconciliation, supported a local soccer team, possessed only local passports and were philosophical about government shortcomings. On these grounds, they believed themselves to be 'committed to the country'. Nonetheless, the woman also thought that she had the right to 'live my life in peace, doing what I think is right, and make my own decisions about national holidays'.

The grandson of an immigrant from Goa, India, who had initially identified himself as Portuguese, and was then on his way to Australia, countered some of their arguments:

> I chose to keep my Portuguese citizenship in 1984, even though the Portuguese are reluctant to recognise me, or extend my passport, and do not consider me a citizen. I can't speak Portuguese and I've never visited the country, but it's a European passport and gives rights to live and work in Europe. My paternal grandfather came to Southern Rhodesia from Mozambique for opportunity. I thank him for that. I want to open opportunities for my own children. But citizenship is not enough; it is worthless without work…economic opportunity is more important than citizenship.

A little later, the businessman continued:

> African governments are not known for respecting civil rights. Everyone, regardless of race, is afraid here; there's no freedom of expression. Friends have the same view of the political situation as me. Some are diehards and would not think of leaving, but they are blinkered, not listening to what the government is saying about minorities in Zimbabwe. They're out of touch with the government's agenda. The government was forced to accept minorities at independence, but they would like us all to leave.

Interestingly this informant, with ancestors who were Indian labourers brought to Southern African countries by various imperial powers, supported the Hunters' view of 50 years earlier that citizenship as a sense of ownership and common destiny was unlikely to develop without employment. A Zimbabwean-born farm manager, also about to leave for Australia in the wake of land designation (see Chapter 7), had other concerns:

> I thought I'd always be here, so I stayed with the Zimbabwean passport. My father's family has been farming here, first in South Africa, and now Zimbabwe, for generations. But some years after independence I went on two working holidays to the UK and got my British right of domicile, through my mother, stamped in my Zimbabwean passport, because you can put everything you've got into a farm but, at the end of the day, the government could take it anyway.

Uncertainty featured in much of what he had to say. 'We are all waiting for the time we have to leave; extra passports are additional boltholes; the more the better.' His precautions, however, could in fact prejudice his future. The experience of another informant indicated that having entitlement to British domicile inserted into a Zimbabwean passport would compromise his standing as a Zimbabwean citizen when he came to renew his passport in the years to come.

A former Rhodesian officer took an opposing position to almost all others when he supported the government's ban on dual citizenship, arguing 'you can't live with your feet in two countries'. The government was, he felt, quite reasonably looking for 'tangible proof of commitment from whites with expertise'. One of the few to put effort into 'reading all the information' put out by Mugabe's government, he 'decided to give it a go' and joined Zimbabwe's newly integrated armed forces. But, in July 1982, his immediate senior and junior officers 'went to work and never came home'. They were accused of plotting to overthrow the new regime. Martin and Johnson (1986:49) describe the sabotage at Thornhill Air Base that lay behind these accusations as a South African operation, perhaps with help from inside.[38] In its aftermath, the informant felt 'at risk, aware of being under suspicion, and afraid of being set up'. He reflected, 'You can't hold on to the past, you have to make a commitment to the new country. I was totally Rhodesian, then I gave my loyalty to Zimbabwe. Once they betrayed me, I had to give my loyalty to someone else [Australia]...I can't live in two worlds.'

However not everyone had choices to consider:

> I was twenty-two years old in 1985...I had no decision to make. I've only ever had one passport and I only have one now: it's Zimbabwean... my parents have only ever had local passports...their grandparents came from South Africa. In 1980, my parents just went with the flow. Independence meant the war was over, Dad could stay home. No more worrying about his safety when he did call-ups. We were anti-Smith, so Dad was fighting for a cause he did not believe in. We [she and her husband] were war babies. I have no memory of what life was like before the war.

Similarly, a coloured couple found they 'had nothing to decide'. Unsure of their ancestry, and unconcerned about 'who' arrived 'when', they said, 'We grew up in Zimbabwe, we know nothing else but we are aware of being second-class citizens even though we're indigenous.'

Thus, generally speaking, people made pragmatic choices around the legal rights they believed citizenship conferred with regard to property and employment.

---

38 See also Astrow 1983:172; Alexander 1998:156.

Local citizenship 'secured' things and within the country a Zimbabwean passport held considerable value.[39] Importantly, at least as far as minorities are concerned, local passports confer passage into the national territory. Citizens were those who enjoyed freedom of movement and, in particular, had the right to enter the country at will, to remain and work without permits, putting them in effect in a position to establish and maintain a home. It was on these legal grounds that a migration consultant advised clients to hold on to Zimbabwean citizenship as a safeguard against future uncertainties. He pointed out that entitlement to British or South African citizenship through descent could not easily 'be lost', at least for the foreseeable future.

While a few of those cited above did not identify Zimbabwe, the land of their current residence, as their homeland and country of citizenship, others were ambivalent, aware that their claim might not be accepted. Although born and raised in and perhaps wishing to adopt Zimbabwe as their homeland, they, cognisant of the discrepancy between legal terminology and the public discourse, were not sure they would be 'allowed to belong'. A small number expected as citizens to participate actively in civil society by, for instance, voting in general elections—a right that until 2000 Zimbabweans, black and white, treated antipathetically. Yet even they questioned whether their claim to belong would be accepted by the majority. Would they ever be more than 'honorary citizens' still sealed in their whiteness in some African eyes?

Uncertainty, due in part to the wide discretionary powers invested in immigration and other officials in Zimbabwe and abroad, encouraged whites to embrace multiple identities.[40] During the years I spent in the country, academics, farmers, journalists and businesspeople critical of the government were 'called' to present themselves at the relevant state agency to discuss their standing. 'Calls' to attend the Office of the President, immigration or citizenship departments announced that the individual was a questionable member of the moral community. As 'disloyal' or disaffected Zimbabweans, they—just as in Rhodesian days[41]—were threatened with the cancellation of their citizenship or permanent residence status, making local citizenship itself the source of insecurity and anxiety. Indeed, lack of confidence in the future proved critical

---

39 When accepted as a document affirming local identity, passports secured lower charges at hotels, national parks and hospitals, less departure tax, as well as access to educational facilities and employment opportunities. Passports were also necessary for whites to register as voters before the 2000 elections.

40 Zimbabwe's High Court judges called in 1997 for a Board of Appeal to provide a forum for the review of departmental decisions and to protect against the corrupt practices of immigration officials (see the *Report of the Departmental Committee on Security Ministries,* tabled in Parliament on 13 May 1997, cols 4771–7; *Zimbabwe Independent,* 31 July 1998, p. 1).

41 As part of social control, Rhodesia's Minister of Immigration could withdraw the citizenship-by-registration of people who made statements that caused despondency or brought the government into disrepute (*House of Assembly,* 21 November 1972, cols 25–32). Some of the many who over the years fell foul of authorities, and were deprived of their citizenship and immigration rights, included Bishop Lamont and Guy Clutton Brock (mentioned in Chapters 2 and 4 respectively). The Rhodesian *Citizenship Act* also provided

to decisions made by many. Most would concur with the insights of the farm manager cited above when he said, 'Everyone is worried about the day when we have to run, leave in a hurry. A rush of white emigration is going to happen, and I don't want to be in it.'[42] He recalled the distress he felt in 1972 when witnessing the line of cars driving south through Livingstone in Zambia, across the Zambezi River into the tourist town of Victoria Falls, as Asians expelled from Uganda sought refuge from Idi Amin's regime (see Mamdani 1973). Although not welcome in Rhodesia, their plight nonetheless contributed to the shadow of doubt that had fallen over the country's future as a white homeland. White anxiety about what tomorrow might bring reflected an uncertain vision of the country's future, and their place in it. They saw their fears refracted in African countries to the north and raised the spectre of repeating the histories of Uganda, Congo and Mozambique. Nonetheless, efforts to assert some control over the future inside and outside the country—their contingency plans to, in Moore's (quoted in Dhalla 1993:36) terms, 'fix the outcome' with passports and residence stamps—served to make tomorrow's anxieties an important part of today.

Thus, while the majority complied in one way or another with the government's renunciation exercise, lack of trust in their identity as Zimbabwean citizens generated a desire to obtain or retain a second, foreign passport. Said (2000) alludes to the 'talismanic' quality of passports, residence stamps and identity cards reflecting his and other Cairo-based Palestinian families' vulnerability given their privilege in the changing political situation of the Arab world after 1948. Zimbabwe's minority citizens felt much the same way. Passports were hedges against insecurity and inconvenience, for the general public, black and white, held little confidence in the country's civil service. What must be remembered is that it could take up to a year to receive or renew a Zimbabwean passport, and, in order to deter criminal activity,[43] a lost passport would not be replaced for two years because, among other things, it contained the record of holiday allowances. Bureaucratic explanations for these delays covered staff shortages and the manual and lengthy processing systems involved.

---

for the cancellation of citizenship-by-registration of young whites intent on refusing military commitments. Thus, the use of immigration and citizenship provisions to exile and muzzle critics was an established practice in Rhodesia.

42 These comments go some way in explaining the high take-up rates of Australian citizenship by Zimbabweans; 80 per cent of Zimbabweans became citizens once eligible (Australian Bureau of Immigration, Multicultural and Population Research 1995:3, 24).

43 Crime figures indicate that, as Commonwealth passports allow entry into many countries without visas, Zimbabwean passports are much sought after. At least 50 were reported to have been stolen and fraudulently sold each week during 1993 in South Africa, where a ready market existed for them (*The Sunday Mail*, 14 November 1993, p. 1). By 1997, the figure had shot up to 40 a day—some being sold outright by their owners—and the price, the Registrar-General alleged, was 'very attractive' (*The Herald*, 26 March 1997, p. 1, 16 December 1998, p. 1).

As far as a government official was concerned, however, any inconvenience should be accepted patriotically. 'Our citizens have to be proud whether black or white, and say this passport is Zimbabwean. Whatever consequences I may suffer because I hold this is what I have to endure. I am proud of my country. I have to suffer accordingly.'[44] 'Suffering' was an idiom used commonly by black Zimbabweans to describe their lives. Suffering brought entitlement (Moore 2005:2). Suffering, it was also said, promoted resilience and learning and consequently suffering in childhood made for 'strong adults'. 'Suffer—Continue' was a maxim painted on buses. To accept one's suffering stoically was to live as a native. Some whites, however, perceiving the virtues of efficiency as self-evident, wanted other passports in order to avoid the inconveniences that could arise from mono-citizenship. They were not alone in holding instrumental attitudes. African traders, finding themselves short of the fare home after shopping in South Africa, would leave their travel documents with bus companies as security against future payment. Despite the government's promise of full, participatory citizenship for the black majority, in reality this had not been realised by the poor and, particularly, not by African women (Gaidzanwa 1993). Passports thus provided a form of currency to women who were otherwise unable to realise many of the rights of citizenship.

So, while many whites responded to the letter of the renunciation process, the spirit the State hoped to see as evidence of an inner mutation was not forthcoming. A spontaneous, decisive act, taken to indicate genuine identification with the country and its people, was usually lacking. Whites perceived the exercise not so much as an opportunity for them to become aware of, and confront, their ambivalence about where they belonged, but as 'vindictiveness' and 'a show of authority' on the government's behalf and as 'a loss of a freedom' they had hitherto enjoyed. Informants repeated the view that 'you can't legislate for loyalty', nor can loyalty be equated with holding a passport, or passports. While one recalled hearing other people saying 'we're proud to be Zimbabwean, to hell with other passports', she was not thinking that herself. Indeed, I heard few unconditional responses similar to that of Mrs Crafter of Glen Lorne, Harare, who presented her travel document as announcing her home country, saying 'I'm Zimbabwean *and* I travel on a Zimbabwe passport'.[45] Or the patriotic action of a Cheredzi farmer, held up as an example by authorities, who was purported to have renounced his British citizenship under the 1984 Zimbabwean provisions and then gone to the British High Commission to do the same according to British law.[46] Such unequivocal statements of national pride, expressing love of the country, faith in its future and the desire to be fully identified with it

---

44 *Parliamentary Debates*, 16 August 1984, col. 929.
45 'Whites can also be indigenous', *The Herald*, 9 July 1996, p. 2.
46 *Parliamentary Debates*, 30 August 1994, col. 1118.

as a citizen according to the criteria of the new government, were few and far between. 'Perhaps,' reflected another respondent dryly, 'they will regret this patriotic attitude later.'

The decolonisation and renegotiation of citizenship in Zimbabwe therefore revealed distrust on both sides. Whites, refusing to turn themselves into a subject of others, were quick to point out that the renunciation procedures were legally flawed and therefore, in their eyes, invalid, overlooking the new consciousness the exercise was designed to engender. Regardless, the Zimbabwe *Citizenship Act* of 1984 prohibits all citizens from holding dual passports, regardless of race. The statute makes it an offence to obtain and/or use a foreign passport, the penalty for which is the automatic and immediate loss of local citizenship.[47] The statute's provisions effectively criminalise many minority-group citizens, who otherwise pride themselves on being law abiding. Further, what is widely known is that it is not just minorities who possess second passports. The children 'of big gurus'[48] and Deputy Ministers, indigenisation lobbyists[49] (see Chapter 7), as well as others who have had the opportunity to study abroad hold foreign passports for the educational, employment and business benefits they confer in Western countries. The authenticity of their identity as citizens, for these members of the black elite, was not at issue. Partial application of the law, however, allowed minority-group citizens to believe the statute's administration impacted disproportionately, and that the parity promised by citizenship was refused them.

In sum, local passports were an intrinsic part of the State's project of moral regulation, critical to the processes of control and surveillance as the State set in place measures to oversee the movement of minorities, and conferred or denied the right of residence to them. The issue had not been conclusively resolved when I left the country. At that time, research participants were mostly unaware that the government had reopened the question of foreign citizenship in 1994 when it tabled amendments such that, in future, dual passport holders would be required to renounce their foreign citizenship according to the law of the foreign country concerned.[50] Further, the Minister of Home Affairs suggested that all

---

47   During the 1990s, officials usually handled the indiscreet use of a foreign passport administratively. Luggage was searched at the country's entry points and, should a second passport be found, the Zimbabwean document was confiscated and the offender told to regularise his/her situation with the Immigration Department. This meant providing evidence that the person was domiciled in Zimbabwe before the offence. If satisfied, the authorities issued a permanent residence permit in place of the passport. If domicile could not be determined satisfactorily, the person had to apply for temporary residence on the usual grounds, which could well be denied.
48   See *Parliamentary Debates*, 30 August 1994, cols 1104, 1120.
49   See, for instance, the international mobility enjoyed by failed tycoon Roger Boka in the later months of 1998 after the courts had confiscated his Zimbabwean passport. Raftopoulos and Compagnon (2003:27–8) provide details of Boka's controversial business dealings.
50   *Parliamentary Debates*, 30 August 1994, col. 1080.

those who complied in 1984–85 make a fresh renunciation.[51] Raising again the question of minority citizenship was difficult to explain in terms of earlier destabilisation arguments, as South Africa had achieved majority rule in 1994. The world had changed in other significant ways and elsewhere globalisation prompted a rethinking of citizenship (Kaplan 1993:259). In the new world economic order, less attention is paid to birthplace, patriotism or lineage and rather more to opportunities afforded by mobility. Dual passport holding can in fact benefit a country. In Zimbabwe, however, parliamentarians rejected this argument in favour of continued exclusivity, and a second renunciation exercise was scheduled for 2001.

Contesting birthrights and classifying the citizenry

Some in the white community put the case that their right to recognition as citizens was not discretionary, hinging neither on their participation in the 1984–85 renunciation exercise nor on meeting the government's ideals described above. Instead, they speak of being 'Zimbabwean born and raised' or 'Zimbabwean by birth'. They claimed it as a 'birthright', a term in vogue in the Rhodesian era, to reside in and return to the country in which they were born and grew up, a right set out, they argued, in the 1979 *Immigration Act* and recognised in British and Commonwealth precedents. 'My parents, my children, the rest of my family and I were born in this country. Therefore we see ourselves as children from the Zimbabwean soil.' In essence, they conceived membership of the territory according to the pre-eminence of the principle of *jus soli*, or law of the soil—entitlement grounded in a relationship with the land. The historical fact that they were born and have lived in the territory for many years and know no other place of domicile invests them, in their view, with a right to stay and be recognised as citizens. How were they able to sustain this untenable position?

Throughout much of the debate surrounding the Constitutional Amendment Bill (No. 3) and new citizenship regulations, MPs of all persuasions focused attention on the issue of dual passport holding, almost to the exclusion of every other aspect of citizenship. The government created the impression that the substantive rights of permanent residents would not be very different from the benefits of Zimbabwean citizenship.[52] Many whites felt they had been led to

---

51 While winning support on the floor (*Parliamentary Debates*, 13 September 1994, col. 1611), the amendments were later withdrawn for further consideration by the Parliamentary Legal Committee, in order to determine whether the bills or statutory instruments were contrary to the *Constitution* or its *Declaration of Rights*. At the time I left the country, the amendments had not yet been re-tabled, although this was promised after the passage of enabling constitutional amendments, and came about in 2001 (*Parliamentary Debates*, 17 September 1997, col. 1355, 25 March 1998, col. 4397).
52 *Parliamentary Debates*, 9 April 1986, col. 1951.

believe, in fact incorrectly, that the only rights permanent residents would not share with citizens was the right to vote. One person, however, aware that the implications were probably more far-reaching, cautioned:

> [W]hat this bill seeks to do is to remove the birthright of citizenship of the country of one's birth as if by the stroke of a pen this umbilical cord can be severed…Most people would hesitate to throw away any link with the country of their birth.[53]

These words, overlooked in debate at the time, were to prove prophetic. For, although an example was made of several sporting figures[54] who failed to renounce foreign citizenship before the end of the grace period, whites generally were not confronted with the reality of their position until the 1990s. As citizens by birth or registration,[55] or as permanent residents, they had little trouble leaving or re-entering the country. This, however, has now become more difficult, as the 1993 O'Hara case illustrates.

Terence O'Hara was born in Southern Rhodesia in 1958 and raised there, the son of a British migrant who held UK citizenship and was ordinarily resident in Rhodesia. O'Hara thus acquired a domicile of origin in Zimbabwe and was entitled to citizenship by birth. In 1984, O'Hara failed to renounce his British

---

53   *Parliamentary Debates*, 21 July 1982, col. 892.
54   An early casualty was cricketer Kevin Curran, barred from playing for Zimbabwe against New South Wales early in 1986. He held both Irish and Zimbabwean passports and failed to surrender his Irish passport by the 1985 deadline, making him ineligible to represent Zimbabwe.
55   Citizenship was also a status that could be conferred. Naturalisation, with its cultural overtones and invitation to join the national family (Anderson 1990:133), was heard only very occasionally in Zimbabwe (see *Parliamentary Debates*, 26 March 1986, col. 1594). The preferred terminology for this process was citizenship-by-registration. During Ian Smith's time, Rhodesian citizenship-by-registration or naturalisation could be granted in two years to privileged white immigrants. It could also be lost through failure to remain domiciled in the country. In contrast, Zimbabwean authorities claimed to be 'jealous' of the country's citizenship and were reluctant to confer it. Criteria were restrictive and based on stringent and largely unpublished factors, beyond the commonplaces of 'deserving' or 'earned by having contributed towards the development of this country' (*Parliamentary Debates*, 13 September 1994, col. 1616). Amendments in 1984 and 1994 extended the waiting period to five and 10 years respectively before permanent residence would be granted and only thereafter could an application for citizenship be submitted. In the interim, temporary permits of two or three years need repeated renewals. Citizenship-by-registration is thus difficult to obtain and consequently a rare occurrence today. There is nothing unusual in this. Creating connections through naturalisation or registration between an individual and a state is generally made with regard to the benefits the State sees accruing from the process (Kaplan 1993:253). By definition, citizens-by-registration were those who did not qualify as 'natural-born' citizens of Zimbabwe. Their citizenship was discretionary, dependent on meeting character and residence requirements before and after the event. These distinctions have been built into passports. Since the mid 1990s, 'born-ins'' passports are accredited for 10 years, whereas 'not-borns' must be renewed every five years. 'Not-borns' lose their citizenship if they stay out of the country for more than five years; they must come back to 'validate both their passports and their citizenship' (*Parliamentary Debates*, 30 August 1994, col. 1080). 'Born-ins' can stay away as long as they like without jeopardising their citizenship. Citizens-by-registration claimed that this administrative distinction made them feel 'unwelcome' in the land 'we have chosen to call home' and in which they had qualified for citizenship. They preferred instead to portray their decision to 'adopt' the country as something moral and deserving. To the African majority, however, to choose one's nationality appeared 'unnatural', given that the nation was conceived in familial terms.

citizenship, to which he was entitled by descent, and thus ceased to be a citizen of Zimbabwe. In effect, he became a permanent resident with the recognised right to live and work in Zimbabwe. In 1987, he left for four years, training as a helicopter pilot in South Africa (Dumbutshena 1993:7). On his return in 1991, he was prevented from residing and working in Zimbabwe and reclassified by immigration officials as an alien. Under common law, domicile of origin cannot be extinguished by an act of the owner. The O'Hara dispute proved that in Zimbabwe this was not the case. In judgement, the Supreme Court recognised that its ruling departed from common law, but argued that the *Citizenship Act* of 1984 overruled the 1979 immigration regulations when it found that O'Hara's claim to a domicile of origin in Zimbabwe was not held in abeyance but rather lost by his departure and choice of domicile in South Africa (*Principal Immigration Officer vs O'Hara*, [1] ZLR 69 [s], 1993:69–79). In effect, the appellant had a second home, excising his claim to Zimbabwe as his domicile of origin and regardless of his intention to return to his place of birth.

The O'Hara case, and others like it, fuelled anger within the white community, who perceived this to be a human rights issue as well as a legal matter and themselves as discriminated against in the application of the State's citizenship laws and immigration regulations. They, like O'Hara, presented themselves as citizens on the basis of birth in the country. But in the O'Hara case the court's decision suggested otherwise. For whites therefore, title to citizenship on the basis of birth has proved a less than satisfactory method of determining social membership. 'Facts' of birth have been construed as nothing more than 'accidents' of birth where other cultural, linguistic and racial connections to the country are lacking. Judgements handed down in the Zimbabwean courts reflect the importance of belonging not simply in terms of *jus soli* as a place of birth, but in terms of the principle of *jus sanguinis,* or law of blood, where descent is ascribed on the basis of cultural and historical factors indicative of a genealogically common past. Consequently, whites, unable to metaphorically trace a blood connection to the Munhumutapa Empire, are thought not to be part of a nation into which their ancestors were not born. Instead, their citizenship is founded on a colonial history. As racial and cultural aliens, they are termed 'children of Britain' and are advised to 'join their cousins' in the United Kingdom, the country whose language is their natal tongue and whose citizenship they may carry by birth or descent, but nonetheless a land they do not know in terms of domicile or employment.

O'Hara demonstrates the anomalous position in which some whites find themselves, caught between the legal provisions of the former colonial power and the post-colonial state, which highlights their discordant attachments. At one and the same time, they belong and do not belong; as insiders and outsiders, they assert a local and a diasporic identity. Apropos of which, various informants raised concerns about becoming stateless in the future—a possibility when descent determines citizenship within a shallow number of generations after which entitlement was lost. They were aware that British immigration law had become successively more restrictive since the late 1960s (Brah 1993:23; Hintjens 1995:19, 23). The passage of the 1981 *Nationality Act* confined the automatic right of abode in the United Kingdom to citizens and those who had established their patriality prior to the enactment of the law in January 1983 (Nicol 1993:266). While access remained possible according to a range of limited visas, Zimbabweans, black and white alike, reported difficulty entering the United Kingdom or registering themselves or their offspring as citizens.

Back in Zimbabwe, would-be citizens were being shed in other ways. Constitutional Amendment Number 14 (Clause 2) of 1996 removed the right of citizenship for children of parents who normally and lawfully resided therein but were not citizens. Before this, children born in the country of permanent residents had, at the time of their majority, the opportunity to nominate which citizenship they wanted to embrace. This was no longer the case. The amendment posed a problem not only for whites, but more particularly to second and third-generation Zambians, Mozambicans and Malawians whose parents or grandparents came to the country as migrant labour during the Rhodesian era. The constitutional amendment potentially rendered their children, as well as those of whites who stayed on as permanent residents, stateless in the years to come.

Another clause of the same amendment (Clause 8) abolished the automatic right of foreign wives to reside in the country. Previously, foreign husbands had enjoyed no such right, the current and the Rhodesian regime (where the regulations were applied to discourage Indian immigrants) perceiving it as 'unnatural' for a man to move and live with his wife's family. In this matter, the predominantly male legislators of both eras shared a common patriarchal ideology. For some years, human rights and feminist groups had lobbied the government to remove this source of discrimination. They advocated more liberal, gender-blind immigration regulations such that the rights applying to foreign wives be extended to foreign husbands. In support of their petition, feminists claimed that local women, if they wished their marriages to survive, were forced to leave the country, because applications for the renewal of their husband's temporary permits must be lodged from outside the country.[56] Instead, the State decided in favour of conservatism and exclusivity, extending the encumbrances experienced by foreign husbands to foreign wives.

The next informant is a case in point. She described herself as 'Zimbabwean by birth'. She, like many other young Zimbabweans, was out of the country on a

---

56 See also Galvin (1991:65–8).

working holiday in 1985 and took no action.[57] She met her husband overseas and, once married, they decided to settle in Zimbabwe, where her husband held local citizenship. She was

> shocked to find that my birthright was not recognised. I assumed I had a right to residence because I was born here. I am angry about this. Zimbabwe is one of the few countries in the world that does not recognise birthright. I feel unwelcome and rejected. I only have a tenuous right to be here. I am on a temporary permit that expires in April 1999. Then what? Do I have to reapply? I feel uncommitted [to the country] partly because they [the State] won't commit to me.

She suggests recognition as a fellow citizen would help infuse space with meaning, thereby evoking in her a sense of belonging (Shotter 1993:115; Peck 1992:78), aiding and supporting the production of the geographical location as her home (Gupta and Ferguson 1992:73). Now, however, classified as a foreign spouse, she found herself in the invidious position of having no moral claim to residence in her place of birth at a time when she knew no other place as home.

Thus, under the 1996 Constitutional Amendment (No. 14), made purportedly in the interests of gender neutrality, all foreign spouses are now subject to the same screening processes. Residence rights are granted according to skills and merit, not marriage per se, although the marriage may be a 'material factor' that immigration officials wish to consider.[58] Justifying this decision, male MPs argued that girls should be 'seriously encouraged' to marry local husbands. Marriages to foreigners were suspected to be nothing more than a 'matter of convenience'. Consequently, they are subject to oversight by the State. Fearing these marriages introduced Western customs incompatible with local traditions and lifestyles, legislators deemed abolishing restrictions on them would be harmful to the social fabric. Grounds immigration officers saw as sufficient to bring a marriage of convenience to court were, in the Hambly case, age differences, although this was not unusual where polygyny was practised and, more importantly, an intention not to procreate.[59] While the case was ultimately dismissed, the criteria reflected the assumptions of the African majority—that a marriage was not a marriage without children, and that where bride-wealth was paid, childless marriages were usually ended within a few years.

---

57 The government's 1984 publicity campaign regarding the renunciation of foreign citizenship did not extend beyond state borders or overseas. I heard various complaints that approaches to Zimbabwean missions outside the country had been rebuffed in one way or another. Applicants were told the mission could not provide a service on citizenship matters and were advised to go back to Harare to regularise their status. In other instances, after 'asking a lot of questions', authorities took passports but they were never returned. I sought to substantiate these problems with an immigration consultant. He confirmed them and indicated that the bulk of his work entailed submitting applications for the reinstatement of citizenship.
58 *Parliamentary Debates,* 3 September 1996, col. 1052, 30 April 1997, col. 1971.
59 Judgement No. SC 147/98 in the Supreme Court.

In sum, independence set in train the transformation of the white population from privileged citizens into citizens of precarious status and disputed membership. Zimbabwe has moved away from the Rhodesian definition of citizenship as a status determined primarily by birth or residence, to place greater weight on common descent. Where this has been the case elsewhere, it has proved difficult for foreigners to become citizens (Castles 1996; Peck 1992). And while, 20 years on, white Zimbabweans continued to argue their case for citizenship in terms of human rights and Western criteria embedded in legal rules whose veracity could be determined by appeals to the courts, these very same legal rules and administrative regulations provided for their governmentality (Rouse 1994). Through their application, Zimbabwean authorities entered the lives of minorities and remade them as second-class citizens and aliens, their ambiguous status an outcome of state instrumentality.

Conclusion

During the Rhodesian era, citizenship was the prerogative of settlers. Africans, unable to meet European 'standards', were confined to the inferior position of subjecthood. Citizenship was therefore hierarchical and exclusive, conferring little on the majority as racial classifications largely determined rights and access to resources. With independence, civic space was de-racialised and the discourse of citizenship reconfigured. The new regime extended the legal, political and social rights of the settler regime to all Zimbabweans regardless of race. Public statements, made soon after ZANU PF came to power, also contained proposals for redefining citizenship rules and the integration of minorities, proposals that were subsequently incorporated in legislative changes aimed at reshaping minority citizens. Today what matters is their preparedness not only to adopt Zimbabwe as a territory but, more importantly, to adapt to local culture, to live as a native in terms of immobility and inconvenience, to be present when the country faces hardships and to demonstrate the solidarity and loyalty of kinsmen. As an unequivocal expression of identification with the majority and confidence in the country's future, social legitimacy in Zimbabwe has more to do with meeting these ideals and is rather less about defining citizenship in Western terms as a bundle of distinctive rights, with attendant concern for access and equality issues (Kratochwil 1994:485). Thus, assimilation, now expected of non-Africans, has remained central. It is perhaps only under these circumstances that embracing local citizenship may be considered a form of decolonisation and an avenue for transcending the inequality of the colonial relationship (Memmi 1965:40, 149). Another discourse, dovetailing with citizenship and appearing in the 1990s, brought this point to the fore.

Pioneers, Settlers, Aliens, Exiles

6. The mobilisation of indigeneity

Representations of the indigene and, more particularly, the process of indigenisation became prominent during Zimbabwe's second decade of independence. According to Horowitz (1991:4), the introduction of new terms designating categories of people invariably reflects aspirations of an improved collective status or a different conflict alignment. Changes in language therefore indicate the setting or shifting of borders and reveal other, alternative configurations regarding who properly belongs within them and how these people are connected to the land. The ways in which the subject position of the indigene have been constructed, represented and mobilised (Brah 1996:191) and, at the same time, the question of white ethnicity brought into sharp relief, are discussed in this chapter. First, the Rhodesian narrative of the indigene and the lines along which Rhodesian, and later Zimbabwean, society was divided terminologically are addressed. This is followed by an account of various representations of the indigene that have appeared since 1990 and, in particular, how these have played out in the economic sphere. Towards the end of the chapter, the implications of the revised term for white autochthony—their right to be of the land—are examined.

Representations of the indigene during the Rhodesian era

The 1969 Rhodesian *Constitution* and *Land Tenure Act* for the first time explicitly divided the population into European and African, and provided definitions of both. A European was

> any person who is not an African, and an African, any member of the aboriginal tribes or races of Africa, and the islands adjacent thereto… and any person who has the blood of such tribes and races and who lives as a member of an aboriginal native community. (Quenet 1976:21; Murphree and Baker 1976:388)

Rhodesian society was thus divided constitutionally into two main races, a division reflected judicially in land apportionment, the electoral and education systems and employment opportunities (Quenet 1976:4). In practice, the Rhodesians' crude racial border was not something new. In 1898, a Southern Rhodesian Order-in-Council established two administrative hierarchies— structures that reflected the racial division of the land. The Native Affairs Department had from early in the colonial era administered the lives of Africans, the collective other. European 'Native Commissioners' made up the department's senior staff and the government-subsidised native chiefs and headmen manned the lower echelons (Gann 1965:148–9; Bowman 1973:11). The department was in effect 'a state within a state', appointed exclusively to oversee African affairs (Gann 1965:276; Day 1983:169).

Importantly, while producing Rhodesia in this way as a country with 'two races', the colonial discourse stressed that neither was in a position to claim descent from the 'original' inhabitants of the area (Lewis 1973:3). This designation fell to the San—or, to employ Rhodesian terminology, the Bushmen—hunter-gathering Stone Age peoples who lived on and around Zimbabwe's Central Plateau from about 3000BC and who had now all but disappeared (Beach 1980:4). Testimony to their habitation existed in the numerous rock paintings across large stretches of the country. Consequently, Ian Smith described both Bantu[1] and Europeans as 'immigrants to this part of the world, neither are birds of passage—both are here to stay for all time'.[2] Certainly the Rhodesians did not deny that some arrived earlier than others. The early Iron Age predecessors of the Shona came from north of the Zambezi River in three waves during the first millennium AD (Beach 1980:6–9). The Ndebele, a Zulu offshoot from the south, moved into the land during the mid 1800s, not long before the first Europeans appeared towards the later part of the century. In the official Rhodesian discourse, however, 'the Shona, the Ndebele and the Europeans were all migrants, conquerors and settlers and all of them now know no other home. They have established for themselves and their successors the right to remain in this country in perpetuity' (Whaley 1973:31).

Claims to permanent settlement were at the forefront of European representations. Rhodesian Front supporter, and later Senator, Sam Whaley remarked that

> there was never any question of Europeans residing in Rhodesia on a temporary basis in order to develop the land and then hand it back to earlier settlers...Rhodesia is the permanent and rightful home of people of different origins and backgrounds and does not belong to one race alone. (Whaley 1973:31)[3]

For some of Whaley's contemporaries, the legitimacy of the European, as well as the Ndebele, settlement lay in conquest. The Rhodesians had fought for and won the land for themselves and future generations during the Matabele Wars and the first *Chimurenga* of the late 1890s.[4] Immigrant blacks had arrived with and fought alongside the Pioneer Column, making them part of the invading

---

1 The term includes both Shona and Ndebele.
2 *Rhodesian Commentary*, November 1975. See also Whaley 1973:31.
3 His statements were made despite ample evidence to the contrary. For instance, Professor Roberts (1978:61) commented in an article published by the Rhodesian Historical Society that, for every 100 immigrants arriving, between 60 and 80 were leaving, even at the height of the postwar and Federation boom.
4 See Murphree and Baker 1976:38; Palmer 1977:55; Chennells 1989:124

force and giving them a vested interest in settler capitalism (Muzondidya 2002:13). Thus, in a very short time, the Shona found themselves the victims of two aggressive invasions.

Other Rhodesians downplayed conquest in favour of 'winning' legitimacy. Father Lewis, for example, used historicist preoccupations surrounding notions of civilisation and modernity to justify European settlement.

> In a single lifetime an almost empty wilderness has been transformed into a thriving, modern western style state…One can not unscramble the past. We inherit it…The European has won his place in Rhodesia, not by conquest, but by his immense contribution to it. His place is his by right, for himself and his children…Mr MacMillan's[5] [sic] winds of change put him under no obligation to pack his bags and go. (Lewis 1973:4, 6)

Thus, while Rhodesians Ian Smith, Father Lewis and Sam Whaley[6] recognised the notion of aboriginality as historical priority, they did not take this to preclude the presence of others in the territory. Instead, they argued that the land belonged to all the people who inhabited it, and whites, as latter-day immigrants, were also legitimately placed in the country.

Behind these claims, however, and sharing much in common with other settler states, lay the history of European invasion and oppression (Stasiulis and Yuval-Davis 1995). 'Uncontested belonging is a luxury' (Read 1996:xi) not realised in, for example, Australia or New Zealand, where histories of invasion and dispossession also call into question the legitimacy of these settler societies. 'Latecomers' (Read 1998:173) need somehow to remove their alienation vis-a-vis the natives whose roots in the territory are deeper and more profound. Goldie (1989:12–14), writing of Canada, has identified two avenues by which settlers as sign makers generally attempt to erase illegitimacy and separation that arises from their colonial past. They might both valorise and superficially incorporate the other, most commonly by joining indigenes in their association with nature and thereby becoming indigenes themselves. Or, alternatively, they might reject or deny the other. While this second option is 'not an openly popular alternative' today (Goldie 1989:13), it is nonetheless the flip side of the coin and the Rhodesian rejoinder to arguments regarding the illegality of their presence.

The Rhodesians denied the indigene when they represented the country as 'beginning' with the arrival of the whites. This discourse set the industry and

---
5 Father Lewis refers here to British Prime Minister Harold Macmillan's 1960 'Winds of Change' speech that was delivered in South Africa and flagged Britain's intention to divest its African colonies.
6 W. R. (Sam) Whaley was a prominent Rhodesian lawyer; Father Lewis was an Anglican priest. Both were Rhodesian Front supporters and later senators.

civility of the modern settlers against native indolence. The native problem was a labour problem[7] which various colonial administrations tried to ameliorate by attracting 'external' or 'foreign' African labour from Mozambique, Nyasaland (now Malawi), Zambia and various regions of South Africa (MacKenzie 1974:8). These migrant labour schemes had their critics. For example, in 1900, the Resident Commissioner, Sir Marshall Clarke, defended the rights of 'indigenous' labour against infringement by 'external' African labour (quoted in MacKenzie 1974:9). The Resident Commissioner's use of 'indigenous' denotes a locally born, or 'on-site', African inhabitant of Rhodesia. Some years later, D. G. Clarke (1974:22) chose the same term when he compared the unwillingness of indigenous African labour to work on plantations with the migrant 'well-looked-after-farm-boy', or, in the language of the 1930s, 'alien' native (Gann 1965:270). Alien natives' offspring were issued with registration certificates 'that were different from those of the locals and were clearly marked non-indigenous African. That hurt', said the son of an immigrant farm worker after Zimbabwe's independence but before land reform in 1997, 'because, although we knew no other home, we were considered alien in the then Rhodesia' (Masina 1988:11). Thus Rhodesian administrators issued Africans with identity documents that set in place rigid, terminological borders between local and migrant, indigene and non-indigene, based on descent.

Each racial group was encouraged to 'preserve' its identity and coexist, rather than intermix with others (Whaley 1973:31). Hybridity,[8] as the interdependence and mutuality of cultures, met with little acceptance in Rhodesia. As far as white leaders were concerned, 'compulsory integration...was opposed' (Whaley 1973:32). Nonetheless, the settlers concurrently forged, through opposition to both British and Afrikaner, a distinctive culture that was neither metropolitan nor native. The pioneer population had lost its frontier character by the time of self-government in 1923 (Roberts 1978:59; Kirkwood 1984). First Column terminology gave way to 'settlers', or occasionally 'modern settlers', meaning the Europeans, and the Cape Coloureds and Africans who arrived with them, in contradistinction to the earlier influx of Shona and Ndebele. Gann (1961) documents the changing image of the colonial settler during the post-Victorian

---

7   See Gann 1965:172–82; Clarke 1974:18; MacKenzie 1974:1; Kinloch 1975:108–10.
8   The idea of new forms emerging through contact and intermixing, of indigeneity as the product of exchange and adaptation, was to be found in terminology used to describe new animal and plant species. Rhodesians applied the term to cows and pigs, the progeny of animals brought to the Cape 200–400 years ago by European and Chinese trading ships, and now adapted to local conditions though interbreeding. Bulls, imported from South Africa after the rinderpest outbreak at the end of the 1800s, had interbred with African Sanga cattle, commonly found in the Tribal Trust Lands (Stubbs 1994:139). Initially, their progeny, the indigenous animal, was depicted as 'the poor relation' of the exotic European stock. By the 1950s, however, the hybrid, proving more able to withstand African drought and disease, had caught the interest of Rhodesian commercial farmers. The term indigenous continues to be heard in this sense today. For instance, permaculture programmes in Zimbabwe distinguish between exotic trees, which require planting and watering, and indigenous species that 'self-seed' and need little care thereafter.

era and a swing in opinion against empire in the wake of World War I, with the first calls for independence some years later. The once-exalted image of the settler as the idealised representative of empire became deprecatory (Gann 1961:30–1). The term lost acceptability in Rhodesia as well. Whites began to refer to themselves instead as Rhodesians. Africans, the object of the white racial discourse, were not described in this way. Some referred to themselves as 'white Africans', but not generally as 'native'. The term 'native' intimated people whose customs were more distant, or different, to those of the European (Anderson 1990:112; Appadurai 1988:37). 'Going native' in the form of assimilating or adapting to local conditions by adopting African dress, housing and language, or entering an African marriage, although not illegal, was frowned on in white circles (Kennedy 1987:173). The Europeans also separated themselves into the old and the new. Salisbury's fledgling repertory company, established in 1931, was fraught with tension between the two groups (Cary 1975:117). Similarly, Berlyn (1967:87), around the time of UDI, draws a line between herself— Rhodesian born and bred—and more recent European immigrants, 'who come to my country to milk it of its wealth and desert it in its time of need'.

The situation on the ground, however, was more complicated, varied and fluid (Muzondidya 2002, 2004). The ambiguous, intermediate category of 'coloured'[9] blurred Rhodesia's official terminological boundaries. From the 1930s onward, this community, comprising immigrants from South Africa as well as offspring from unions between local European men and African women, became increasing self-aware and pleaded unsuccessfully for official recognition and inclusion (Gann 1965:321; Quenet 1976:88). Instead, the nascent community was 'encouraged to find, or establish, its "own place" in society' (Kinloch 1975:113). Another intermediary, coming in the wake of European settlement, was Indian, known locally as 'Asian', arriving either directly from the Subcontinent, via South Africa or from the Portuguese colony of Mozambique. This term also incorporated a small number of Chinese and Malays. These 'subject races' (Muzondidya 2004:213) occupied an unstable middle ground. Categorised as European with regard, for example, to identity cards and national service and for electoral purposes, they, like Africans, faced discrimination in other areas, such as residence, employment, schooling and the right to own firearms.[10] Asians were also subject to a series of legislative and administrative restrictions, notably with regard to immigration.[11] The Rhodesians, having first distanced themselves from these two minority communities, began in the 1960s to try to draw them into closer political and social participation in order to counter rising nationalism (Kinloch 1975:114).

---

9 Muzondidya (2004:213–14, 2005:31–3) outlines the complexity of the groups subsumed under this label.
10 See Good 1974:13; Murphree and Baker 1976:396–7; Quenet 1976:29, 31–3, 102; Murapa 1984:58.
11 See Gann 1965:178; 319; Stigger 1970:5; Quenet 1976:87; Roberts 1978:58; Kennedy 1987:97.

In sum, Rhodesia was a place where identity was reduced to a racial binary of civilising and modernising European colonisers, pitted against a largely undifferentiated black, colonised people. The racial hierarchy intersected with a discourse about indigeneity that foregrounded themes of migration and conquest, settlement and nation building, and the maintenance of cultural difference. This body of knowledge produced Africans as natives, indigenous or foreign, and Europeans first as pioneers and settlers, and then as Rhodesians of longer or more recent standing in the country. It was a pluralistic discourse, which allowed whites to be positioned as one of several indigenous groups, all legitimately connected to the land, while also maintaining white separation and dominance.

Post-1980 representations

After independence, Africans were officially positioned to write themselves as the subject of the indigene narrative. Control of semiotics was for the first time in their hands. Hence, it is pertinent to ask how questions of race, culture and historical origins have been mobilised within African representations thereafter.

While the new political elite envisioned Zimbabwe as a non-racial society, it was also a black nation, and black advancement was necessary to redress historical imbalances. To this end, the Ministry of Labour, Manpower Planning and Social Welfare collected data on educational enrolments, employment, occupational profiles and much else according to race.[12] At the same time, some official effort was also put into using terms that referred to ethnic rather than racial categories. For example, census questions asked for ethnic rather than racial origins, although contradictorily, respondents were—and are today—given the choice of African, European, Asiatic, Coloured or sometimes 'Mixed'. In everyday parlance, the colonial code of European/African was put aside in favour of a black/white distinction.

The most notable example of measures taken by the new government to correct racial proportions in employment and other facets of life such that they reflected the demographic make-up of the country was the Presidential Directive of May 1980. At the time, this programme of accelerated African placement and promotion was discussed in terms of 'achieving a suitable representation of the various elements of the population'.[13] In effect, the Directive meant the Africanisation[14] or blackening, of the Public Service. Within a few years, its

---

12 See, for example, the 1984 and 1986 *Annual Review of Manpower* (Ministry of Labour, Manpower and Planning and Social Welfare 1984, 1986).
13 See Panter-Brick 1983:224; Murapa 1984:72; Sithole 1987:94.
14 Twenty months after the introduction of the Presidential Directive, Africans accounted for 83 per cent of employees in the Public Service and 47 per cent of senior posts. Two years later, the figures were 92 per

implementation created a civil service with an 'African personality' that, 'in structure and in spirit, would work in consonance with the policies of the new government' and would be 'manned by officers whose destiny lies in the country' (Timbe 1991:5, 72). The Presidential Directive was therefore an act of sovereignty, affirming and asserting an African identity for the Public Service, which was largely absent during the colonial era. The programme contributed significantly to stratification within the black majority, as senior civil servants joined the new political elite and lower-ranking officers became part of the petite bourgeoisie (Weiss 1994:133).

During the first decade of independence, some historical revision also took place, challenging the veracity of the earlier Rhodesian indigeneity discourse. First the San[15] were sidelined as the original inhabitants, although their paintings continued to provide tourist interest and motifs introducing the evening news on ZBC television. Instead, the Bantu from the north were foregrounded as the first people 'to settle' and cultivate the land, rather than simply pass through the area (Ushewokunze 1984:14). By this means, the Shona appropriated the mantle of the first people—descendants of the original settlers who by right enjoyed greater legitimacy and priority in the polity. Second, the colonial era (as argued in previous chapters) was re-presented in ZANU PF's master narrative as an aberration, a time of distortion and dislocation, and whites were configured as colonists, immigrants and settlers. And third, equivalence has been assigned the 'so-called coloureds' and Asians to the 'Rhodesian nationality'. Their position in the country was never fully addressed or defined at independence (Muzondidya 2004:221). Having in the past worked closely or been associated with the settler economy, they were seen as both the instrument and beneficiaries of colonialism. Without representation at Lancaster House and despite protest from some quarters at the time, they were excluded from the common voters' roll. They were placed instead on the white electoral roll and in this way were conspicuously aligned with the criminal past of the white man (Muzondidya 2005:275).

Outlining the reasons for the last of these to an Asian and coloured gathering in 1982, the Honourable Comrade Ushewokunze[16] pointed out that, as largely

---

cent and 72 per cent respectively. These changes were made possible by expanding the service and accepting the resignation of many whites, who either emigrated or joined the private sector. Timbe (1991:268, 273) also notes that 'younger whites were conspicuous by their absence'. Disaggregating 1992 census figures indicated that 25 positions, or about 1 per cent, of senior posts were held by whites, whereas in 1978 they held 90 per cent of these (Weiss 1994:126).

15 A San community remained in the Tsholotsho District of Matabeleland North, close to the Botswanan border. Forced to settle after independence, they have largely been ignored by the government ever since. The community lived in poverty and faced discrimination when it came to receiving food aid. Their language was dying out and some tried to conceal their identity by using Ndebele or Kalanga names (*The Herald*, 16 September 1998, p. 10).

16 Dr Herbert Ushewokunze held various ministerial posts in the ZANU PF government, including Home Affairs during the reworking of citizenship provisions described in the previous chapter and, more recently,

urban communities, both had forged a closer bond through economic ties with the Rhodesians than with the Bantu speakers. Privilege was the colonists' hallmark. Having 'lived and worked in the economy' set up by the Europeans, Asians and coloureds enjoyed some privileges that natives had not and had benefited in other ways from the black/white divide (Ushewokunze 1984:15). Where it had been advantageous to assert a non-African identity (Muzondidya 2002:5) Ushewokunze ignores the fact that while some Asians and coloureds supported the colonial regime, others did not (Stigger 1970:6). Instead, he treats colonialism as an existential condition, which was lived or shared differently (Parry 1995:84), regardless of one's political loyalties. On this basis, Asians and coloureds have been reclassified, despite their protestations that it was not just Africans who suffered under colonialism. In addition, Ushewokunze (1984:16) projected stasis into the future when impressing on his audience that, following independence, the factor common to all groups subsumed under the Rhodesian category was 'their failure to identify with the mainstream politics of our country'.[17] In this way, he reinstated closure through categorisations that compromised individuality and forced people from the racial minorities to belong to Zimbabwean society as members of a collective (Cohen 1994:12).

At the time of this research, the Asian community maintained, as it had done historically, a low public profile. Coloured representatives, on the other hand, wanted objections to their community's classification heard. They claimed that the relationship between the coloured and African community 'is a kindred one', embodied in blood,[18] and they insisted 'we are your cousins'. Some raised by black mothers in the absence of white fathers argued their rightful place was as an integral part of the black community. Another urban group, raised speaking English, 'wanted to be white', but, finding themselves rebuffed, turned to blacks for inclusion at independence. Both groups disavowed the social capital of miscegenation. Instead, coloured representatives argued their community was in some ways historically 'more oppressed than the blacks'. For instance, the *Land Act* confined Salisbury's coloured community to the areas around *Kopje* and Arcadia. 'There were no elite suburbs, such as Marimba Park'[19]—where wealthy black businessmen and professionals lived in a manner

---

the Minister of Health. He was proclaimed a national hero after his death in 1995.
17 Ushewokunze suggested one way to escape such criticism was to join the ruling party. The process involved nomination, vetting of the applicant's political history and a financial payment. While some informants, in particular small-business owners, had considered early on that it was 'sensible' to do this, by the 1990s, party membership had lost its cachet due to widespread disenchantment with the party and accusations that people were 'just buying party cards' without any commitment.
18 For example, in 1998, Rachel Stewart responded to questions regarding whether she was suitably qualified to hold the title Miss Universe Zimbabwe by pointing out that she had 'the blood of all three races in my veins'. She therefore embodied the nation. Earlier the local press had questioned the authenticity of another coloured girl, Dionne Best, when she was crowned Miss Zimbabwe in 1995, asking her whether she considered herself worthy of the title since her skin was not black.
19 This suburb housed a small, modern black elite whose prosperity was built on professional skills or business ownership, in particular general stores and bus companies (see Kileff 1975).

not dissimilar from whites—'for the Coloured. Getting only crumbs from one's father's table is not benefiting, it's degrading', stressed the speaker. 'The fact that we were classified as white for some purposes did not mean we liked it. We were also subject to racial discrimination.'[20]

Nor do coloured informants believe much has been done for their community since 1980. Africans 'were provided with schools and training. Black lawyers, doctors and such like were to be found even during Smith's time, while coloureds were restricted to jobs as teachers and artisans.' Furthermore, they say, the government's 'new policy of indigenisation will be used to discriminate against us; we will not benefit from this doctrine'. Indeed, coloureds found themselves unable to source small-business loans that became available as part of the indigenisation programme in the mid 1990s (see below). Miscegenation does not appear to be of much assistance in achieving insider status, either before or after independence. In the absence of significant social and cultural assimilation, mixed unions are refracted through the lens of race as privilege and, depending on gender, are dubbed either prostitution or 'up-classing'.[21] The coloured community continues, as before, to be caught in the middle.

So, in short, during the first decade of independence, Africanisation, localisation and black advancement were the terms used to refer to the process of correcting racial imbalances, thereby opening historically white space to blacks in the public and private sectors.[22] Little was heard of the term 'indigene'.[23] As part of historical re-visioning, however, state representatives put in place ideas that enabled the realisation of indigeneity during the 1990s. By continuing in its commitment to count and classify the population, the State racialised, elaborated and circulated knowledge about the social body.[24] Critics believed this heightened awareness of race, rather than making race irrelevant in Zimbabwe thereafter.

---

20 *Newsline*, ZBC Radio 1, 26 February 1997.
21 McFadden (1994) documents the controversial nature of black/white relations.
22 See Zimbabwe Department of Information, 18 February 1986, and 29 January 1990.
23 The term had, however, been introduced into parliamentary debate and academic writings, which, more recently, revisited and reworked the Presidential Directive and ancillary events (*Parliamentary Debates*, 22 February 1995, col. 4890; Timbe 1991). Timbe (1991:6, 170), for example, draws a distinction between 'indigenous' and 'non indigenous citizens' when calling for the 'effective control of the national government and other state apparatus by a majority of the people…by virtue of its inherited claim on the country through its ancestors'.
24 See, for instance, questions regarding the racial make-up of individuals granted stand allocations by local councils, the prison population and the Harare agricultural show organisers (*Parliamentary Debates*, 10 June 1998, col. 5189, 17 September 1997, col. 1250, 21 February 1996, col. 4088, 20 August 1997, col. 434). Data were also collected annually on school enrolments.

The rise to prominence of the terms 'indigene' and 'indigenisation'

By 1990, the Zimbabwean Government was voicing its concern over the country's poor economic performance and, in particular, low levels of investment and serious unemployment.[25] The shortcomings of African socialism were acknowledged and an Economic and Structural Adjustment Programme (ESAP), designed to foster new business opportunities, began in 1991 (Government of Zimbabwe 1991:1; UNDP 1998:26). Its introduction gave moral legitimacy to capital accumulation by blacks that had been largely absent during the socialist 1980s (Raftopoulos 1992:68). At the same time, members of the government and the educated elite were aware that economic reform programmes could benefit multinationals, large companies and wealthy members of society rather than small, 'indigenous' enterprises and the poor (Government of Zimbabwe 1991:20; Mlambo 1997:xi, 10). In view of this, African entrepreneurs, backbenchers and pressure groups[26] began to lobby the government, demanding measures be put in place to protect and promote black economic empowerment. The term coined to describe this process was 'indigenisation'.[27]

The case for indigenisation was grounded in the illegality of the 1888 Rudd Concession, the treaty made by the BSAC with Lobengula, King of the Ndebele, on which the colonial state was founded.[28] Proponents, introducing the idea of indigenisation to Parliament, took as their time frame 1890 to the present— namely, the colonial and post-colonial periods. The agreed goal of this 'mother of all motions' was to 'uplift black Zimbabweans', in particular the disadvantaged, in order to 'place the commanding heights of our national patrimony in the hands of Zimbabweans for the well-being of our patriotic broad masses'.[29] Thus, the indigenisation programme, couched in nationalist and patriotic terms, and the materiality of land called up a subaltern history that retold and re-inscribed the narrative of European invasion and colonial exploitation.

Indigenisation, as the 'second phase of our revolution', was also mindful of the 'unfinished business' of independence. Reference has been made to the belief in some black circles that reconciliation has not been taken in the spirit in which it was enunciated. Evidence of the minorities' failure to reciprocate was to be

---

25 See Bloch and Robertson 1996:3; UNDP 1998:19.
26 The three most notable were the Indigenous Business Development Council (IBDC), the Affirmative Action Group (AAG) and the Indigenous Business Women's Organisation (IBWO). Relations between them, however, often lacked unity and were soured by mistrust and infighting over tenders. See, for instance, the Telecel tendering saga (*Business Herald,* 10 September 1998, p. 6).
27 In early presentations, Zimbabwe took Malaysia's Bumiputra (sons of the soil) Movement as its model.
28 *Parliamentary Debates,* 12 March 1992, cols 4338–403.
29 *Parliamentary Debates,* 3 April 1991, col. 3875.

found in the 'ownership structure' of the economy.[30] Consequently, national reconciliation was re-presented as only a 'stopgap'. For example, political analyst and lecturer John Makumbe used a boxing analogy to explain that the policy of reconciliation was simply a cease-fire that brought about 'the end of the fighting'. Reconciliation allowed both sides 'to get back in their corners'—namely, the low and high-density suburbs.[31] Other members of the black urban elite began to pose difficult questions, not just to Zimbabwe's minorities, but to the government. For instance, Sichone (1997:26) asked 'if this [reconciliation] is what you will offer our former enemies, what will you offer us, your own people'. Sichone's and Makumbe's remarks reflect a growing realisation that reconciliation cannot be spoken about outside a dialogue of economic equity. They, like Parry (1995:88), question whether reconciliation and historical remembrance can ever be aligned with radical social, economic, political and cultural restructuring, which renders the colonial past as properly superseded. To their way of thinking, reconciliation demands reciprocity of some kind, restorative justice in the form of compensation or reparations, not just for individual victims of political violence but for communities as a whole, in order that the urge for retribution be extinguished (Parry 1995:88). Indigenisation, by 'dis-investing' whites and Asians in favour of blacks thus flagged, according to Makumbe, the start to 'the end of the war'.[32]

Calls for indigenisation appeared as well as 're-Africanisation'—an attempt to exert some control and 'gain mastery' (Furusa 1998:53) over Zimbabwe's future development. There was a perception among academics, policymakers and in business circles that Zimbabwe was being integrated into the world economy on less than equitable terms. Zimbabwe looked to be one of globalisation's 'notable losers' (Goldin and van der Mensbrugghe 1993:10). The forces of globalisation seemed outside 'our control…All we have is the word indigenous and nothing else'.[33] These comments reflect the lack of agency felt by many Zimbabweans. 'Internationalism' was said to be missing.[34] Again Africa found itself dominated by the West, which remained insensitive to economic disparity and cultural diversity. Indigenisation, here in the guise of re-Africanisation, attempted to get rid of Euro-centric ideas and institutions in favour of centring that which was local. Western cultural practices were seen to be, at best, inappropriate and, at worst, incompatible and polluting and should therefore be kept separate. Proponents of this position searched for 'indigenous solutions' for various social ills and advocated indigenisation of the legal code, the film industry, professional

---

30 *Parliamentary Debates*, 31 May 1995, col. 318.
31 *Insight*, ZBC Radio 1, 20 August 1996.
32 Ibid.; *Parliamentary Debates*, 3 April 1991, col. 3875.
33 *Parliamentary Debates*, 22 February 1995, col. 4990.
34 See papers presented to the seminar Globalisation: Challenges and Opportunities for Zimbabwe, co-hosted by the Zimbabwe National Chamber of Commerce, the Confederation of Zimbabwe Industries and the Friedrich Ebert Stiftung Foundation and held in Harare in November 1998.

practice and so forth. Images and institutions required decolonisation in order that they reflected African culture and 'the people' could see their own lives and experiences portrayed before them. In this context, indigenisation referred to a desire to reconnect with Zimbabwe's cultural heritage and to develop its institutions and values, rather than being a search for atavistic purity or a return to a 'traditional' past. Thus indigenisation represented a step towards constructing a new and modern African society whose identity was not conferred from outside (Zoungrana quoted in Appiah 1991:134).

In sum, when the term indigenisation first appeared in the early 1990s it had a somewhat unfocused social, cultural and economic agenda that included levelling the economic playing field, redressing the inequalities of the past and promoting the inclusion of blacks into the mainstream society and economy. Subsequently, public attention shifted to the means by which indigenisation's economic goals in particular were to be met. Black and white liberals, including some members of the ruling party, spoke of wealth creation via an expanding economy. Steps to broaden black participation included deregulation of the financial sector, making capital available on easier terms, privatising parastatals and warehousing the shares for indigenous investors, removing legislation that inhibited the entry of entrepreneurs into the formal and informal economies, sourcing donor funds for disbursement to indigenous companies and convincing multinationals and large companies to allocate discounted shares to indigenous Zimbabweans. Some liberals also agreed to the idea of individual title being made available in the communal areas and resettlement schemes as a means for blacks to raise capital by using land as collateral. Liberals therefore supported a programme of wealth creation and accepted that economic empowerment of the black majority needed facilitating procedures in order to overcome past discrimination.

Also supporting indigenisation as wealth creation were the more conservative black captains of industry who either had established their own companies or held senior positions in multinationals and other large companies. Already successful in their fields, they tended, however, to perceive much of the accompanying affirmative-action rhetoric as somewhat demeaning. Other conservatives included chiefs who, as traditional leaders, wanted to 'develop' their localities but did not support individual title to land in the communal areas.[35] They believed land distribution, as their power base, had been usurped by state-run rural councils since independence.[36]

The more radical approach to indigenisation adopted by lobby groups, war veterans and some MPs rested on wealth repossession and redistribution. For

---

35 *Parliamentary Debates*, 26 August 1997, col. 653.
36 See Cheater 1990:189.

instance, the Affirmative Action Group (AAG) advocated that 'the thing to do is to take what they [whites] have no right to possess and restore it all to the rightful owners'.[37] Lobby groups projected themselves as the 'liberators in Zimbabwe's economic jihad' and accused the government of dragging its feet over the issue. Indeed, the need for an indigenisation programme was in itself a criticism of ZANU PF's years in office, and the ruling party, law courts and lobbyists not infrequently clashed over who should be directing the process. In part, this conflict reflected generational tensions, as senior political leaders, having established their careers during the liberation war, still held office. Political and economic leadership had not passed to younger men, and clearly certain lobbyists were interested in entering the political sphere, which was known to offer lucrative business opportunities.[38]

Consequently, the indigenisation programme meant somewhat different things to different players, particularly in the absence of a clear government policy.[39] For some, the new term replaced reconciliation as a 'new attempt at real independence'.[40] Stronger than Africanisation, localisation or black advancement, indigenisation transformed 'the whimper for advancement' into the self-assertion of control.[41] The term created commonality among blacks through recognition of the mutuality of suffering and their desire to move beyond colonial disadvantage. While blacks were united by their common history, there was, however, less agreement about the present and future direction the country should take. While plans to rectify colonial inequities through economic empowerment and compulsory land acquisition (see below) marked another start in the process of restructuring Zimbabwean society, different sectors offered alternative proposals for how imbalances engendered by the colonial past were to be addressed.[42] More importantly for present purposes, the multiplicity of interacting indigenisation discourses established the visibility and 'otherisation' of Zimbabwe's minorities, stimulating questions about race and authenticity with concomitant implications for white autochthony. Nowhere was this more apparent than in competing representations of the indigene.

---

37 'Debate goes on', *The Herald*, 15 April 1996, pp. 5, 7; 'Black empowerment has been hijacked', *Zimbabwe Independent*, 10 May 1996, p. 5.
38 The 2000 election saw political office opened to the driving force behind the AAG, Philip Chinyangwa, and the Chairman of the War Veterans' Association, Dr Chenjerai Hunzvi.
39 Cabinet did not approve the Indigenisation Policy Framework document until February 1998 (*Parliamentary Debates*, 20 May 1999, col. 5995).
40 'What does "indigenisation" mean to you?', *The Financial Gazette*, 3 March 1994, p. 12.
41 Editor, *SAPEM*, June 1990, p. 2.
42 *Parliamentary Debates*, 3 April 1991, col. 3889.

Competing black images of indigeneity

The Cabinet Task Force set up in 1992 to look into these questions failed in the body of its report to describe an indigene, although the glossary referred somewhat ambiguously to indigenous Zimbabweans as 'those who inhabited Zimbabwe before colonial rule and thereafter' (Cabinet Task Force on the Indigenisation of the Economy 1994). The policy's objective was spelt out as 'economic justice between the races' and, alternatively, 'democratisation of the economic system by eliminating the racial and ethnic differences such that disparities between the races and provinces are a thing of the past' (Cabinet Task Force on the Indigenisation of the Economy 1994:1, 3). A later document put out by the Department of State Enterprises and Indigenisation, Office of the President and Cabinet, also skirted around exacting definitions. The second report did, however, use the terms 'indigenous' and 'non-indigenous' in conjunction with 'citizenship' and 'enterprises' in order that 'the ownership structure of the economy is reflective of the population composition of the country' (Department of State Enterprises and Indigenisation 1997:1–2). Importantly, both documents made a clear distinction between foreign and domestic ownership of the private sector. Foreign ownership by transnational corporations was estimated to be about 80 per cent. Domestic ownership, while dominated by non-indigenous enterprises, was the small and weak junior partner, a situation that appears unchanged since the *Growth with Equity* document of 1981 (see Chapter 2).

Introducing the motion on the floor of Parliament, Mr Mangwende was less ambiguous regarding which sections of society qualified as indigenes. As the future Chairman of the Indigenisation Task Force referred to above, he spoke in terms of 'foreigners' and 'white settler stock' in contradistinction with the black patriots and the broad masses.[43] 'Indigenous business…equates to ourselves' and is 'not a foreign body or something that is peripheral to the whole social and economic fabric of this country'.[44] An indigenous businessman was, for example, a 'patriotic businessman, sympathetic and supportive to government', someone who did not threaten to dis-invest whenever the government introduced new regulations.[45] Other parliamentarians, debating the various interim reports of the Indigenisation Committee between 1991 and 1997, also applied the term indigenous to 'patriotic' or 'bona fide Zimbabweans'. Minorities were simply 'Zimbabweans' or 'our other' or 'quasi citizens'. And, repeating analogies heard in the earlier citizenship debate, indigenes 'demonstrate a national character of staying' while 'our other citizens lack this national character'. 'Here to stays' were 'people who were born here, who stay here, who die here and who have

---

43 Ibid., col. 3877.
44 Ibid., col. 3886.
45 Ibid., col. 3888.

no second home'[46]—that is, not white. They were 'wholly Zimbabwean' and 'dedicated party cadres'.[47] Thus, representations privileged immutable heritable signifiers and cultural indicators of indigeneity, while also challenging the rootedness and loyalty of those who were foreign or peripheral.

At the same time, more conservative parliamentarians aired cautionary tales of unpatriotic black entrepreneurs. They referred to the 'briefcase businessmen' of the 1980s who sold their foreign exchange allocations at a premium to those starved of hard currency, the 'fronts' who allowed themselves to be used by foreign businesses and 'telephone farmers' holding vast tracts of under-utilised land for status and speculative purposes.[48] Added to these were black professionals leaving the country during the 1990s in search of better remuneration elsewhere.[49] Labelled 'mercenaries' and 'fortune seekers', they, like their white counterparts, could not realistically expect to own a modern house, car or provide education for their children in Zimbabwe's economic climate.[50] They emigrated to earn foreign exchange, in order to be better able to establish themselves financially in Zimbabwe at a later date.

Members of the lobby groups (AAG, the Indigenous Business Development Council and the Indigenous Business Women's Organisation) were the more militant contributors to this debate. They and radical parliamentarians were not timorous with definitions. Indigenous simply meant 'black'.[51] Lobbyists were forthright in calling for 'the wholesale dismembering of white businesses' in favour of blacks. Indigenisation was to 'transfer the unimpeded opportunity of accumulating wealth on the home front to the descendants of the people who were here long before the money economy arrived'.[52] Thus, lobbyists embraced an 'Africanist' view that allowed only two categories: the indigenous to whom the country legitimately belonged and settlers who came from elsewhere.

To achieve these lofty goals, high-profile lobbyists urged African businessmen to decolonise their thinking, to 'think big' and have the courage to pursue 'big ventures'.[53] In addition, they advised Africans intent on entering the economic sphere to actively support, rather than undermine, each other. Entrepreneurs

---

46 *Parliamentary Debates*, 21 May 1992, col. 6371.
47 *Parliamentary Debates*, 3 April 1991, col. 4086.
48 *Parliamentary Debates*, 24 April 1991, col. 4460.
49 *Parliamentary Debates*, 3 April 1991, col. 3893.
50 The government set the hourly rates charged by professionals and interest rates for building societies. Building societies ceased to offer bonds (mortgages) during 1997 (*The Herald*, 24 April 1998, p. 16; *Business Herald*, 3 December 1998, p. 9). They were unable to attract depositors' funds, for they could not compete with interest rates offered by other financial institutions. At the time, banks were charging 40 per cent interest on loans over 20–25 years.
51 *Parliamentary Debates*, 13 February 1997, cols 3381, 4082.
52 'What does "indigenisation" mean to you?', *The Financial Gazette*, 3 March 1994, p. 12.
53 *Parliamentary Debates*, 19 March 1992, col. 4666; 'Think big indigenous business people told', *Business Herald*, 12 September 1996, p. 5.

should be prepared to pool resources and form partnerships rather than rely only on their most trusted family members, take out insurance policies instead of putting their faith in *muti* (African medicine) and the protection of their ancestors,[54] and further, they should keep business records. It was accepted that many businesses failed because of demands from kin and inadequate accounting. Without these innovations, 'we remain colonised, we shall never go anywhere, we shall remain natives'.[55] Here 'natives' were those confined by beliefs and 'modes of thought' (Appadurai 1988:37) that obstructed wealth creation. Lobbyists also supported individual ownership of land, arguing that the 'traditionalist view that the indigenous never owned land...is a serious handicap...that does not measure up to the pressing and necessary needs of present day economic development'.[56] Indigenisation therefore called forth 'a new breed' of businessman, willing to 'extricate himself from traditional beliefs and practices' and prepared to embrace a Western style of business management (Chipeta 1998; Bloch and Robertson 1996:49–51). In effect, indigenisation was about capital accumulation and 'becoming modern' by moving away from, or breaking, restricting practices associated with kinship economies while, at the same time, remaining true to other aspects of African culture. It was a discourse that did not set up an adversarial relationship between modernity and African identity. Rather it created progress by adapting business acumen derived from the West to accord with local conditions and values.

By the late the 1990s, however, the euphoria that accompanied the introduction of indigenisation a few years earlier had waned. Lobby group leaders, some obviously well off, provoked the general public's ire. The empowerment rhetoric appeared to be emanating 'from the wrong mouths', from, for instance, a lobbyist professing to be already 'stinking rich'. Some found the lobby groups' confrontational attitude and 'demands to spill [white] blood' worrisome and wondered whether this 'could delink us from the international sphere'.[57] Also taking stock, local businessman and writer Chido Makunike prudently cautioned that blacks should remain sensitive to the rights of other groups if they were not to damage their moral cause by becoming, or being perceived to be, the 'new oppressors'.[58] Disquiet over just who was really benefiting from the programme prompted some terminological refinement. Critics, such as Chief Makoni, began to refer to 'the authentic indigenous' as poor blacks:

---

54 Without insurance cover, many black retailers were unable to restock or reopen their businesses after the 1998 price riots.
55 *Parliamentary Debates,* 24 March 1992, cols 4447, 4756.
56 *Parliamentary Debates,* 12 March 1992, col. 4344.
57 Mr Chanika, the chief executive of a financial institution, gave this warning at the 1997 Confederation of Zimbabwe Industries Conference (*Zimbabwe Independent,* 7 January 1997, p. 13).
58 'In might, let's be sensitive', *The Financial Gazette,* 16 May 1996, p. 7.

6. The mobilisation of indigeneity

> What you [parliamentarians] call indigenisation, it is only the rich we are talking about who are not even indigenous. Some say we are Zimbabwean and we are indigenous. If you want to see the indigenous proper, go to the rural areas, go and uplift the indigenous rural people… The rich, you have failed this country.[59]

A year earlier, Chief Mangwende said very much the same thing,[60] for it was apparent that those living in the rural areas had not benefited in the same way as urban dwellers.[61] The government's Social Dimensions Fund, which was to have offered some protection from the effects of structural adjustment to the very poor, proved ineffectual (UNDP 1998:28), while the 'embourgeoisement' of officials appeared to have undermined the political will to channel resources to lower-income groups.[62]

Chief Makoni, cited above, draws a parallel between indigeneity and those who continue to suffer the material conditions of subjection, in contradistinction with indigeneity as a status shared by all who were once historically marginalised. Many taking advantage of the indigenisation programme could no longer be described economically or politically in this way. Plagued by corruption, it was obvious that only a handful of wealthy, politically well-connected families had benefited.[63] Zimbabwe's indigenisation drive looked as if it had been 'hijacked' by 'pirate' entrepreneurs, with contracts awarded to firms ill equipped to complete the work[64] and funds spent on consumption rather than invested in the productive sector.[65] Consequently, employment opportunities the poor hoped would flow from wealth creation had not materialised.[66] Against this background, the term indigenous became a word of contempt. Trade unionists, urban workers and farm labourers used it to describe an 'emergent businessman' or an 'emergent commercial farmer' who did not pay workers award rates, or did not pay on time, or was socially irresponsible in other ways.

---

59 *Parliamentary Debates,* 11 March 1998, col. 4035.
60 *Parliamentary Debates,* 11 March 1997, col. 3959, 2 September 1997, cols 892–6.
61 See, for example, the disbursement of the Z$720 million World Bank loan for enterprise development, the bulk of which stayed in Harare and its satellite Chitungwiza (*Parliamentary Debates,* 25 February 1998, col. 3528).
62 *Parliamentary Debates,* 10 March 1998, col. 3733; Dashwood 1996:32; Jenkins 1997:594; UNDP 1998:7.
63 See Jenkins 1997:594; Mandebvu 1997:12; Sylvester 2000:75; *Parliamentary Debates,* 12 February 1997, col. 3325.
64 For instance, the public anger over the failure of a construction company to successfully complete the Mundi-Mataga Dam, which was to have supplied water to thousands of Mberengwa families (*Parliamentary Debates,* 2 September 1997, col. 880).
65 *Parliamentary Debates,* 8 January 1995, cols 4051, 4058, 22 February 1995, cols 5055, 5059, 31 May 1995, col. 255, 12 February 1997, col. 3333. Also 'Truth Commission needed to probe instant millionaires', *The Financial Gazette,* 2 November 1995, p. 4; 'Violence preached as answer to white oppression', *Zimbabwe Independent,* 19 July 1996, p. 4.
66 See also 'Pastoral statement by the Zimbabwe Bishops Conference', *The Sunday Mail,* 11 May 1997, p. 8.

Moreover, disquiet was being voiced over just which regions of the country were benefiting from the government's programme. People from areas that missed out on development funds and opportunities earmarked for indigenisation projects started to apply the term more reservedly. An indigene narrowed to someone 'from within the province'. This usage reflected the anger mounting over the perceived 'Shonaisation' of the country's wealth and culture.[67] The lack of development in some parts of the country appeared as part of a deliberate government strategy and key factor behind 'the revolt' or split between backbenchers and members of cabinet during 1997.[68] The needs of the Tonga, for example, residing in the remote and impoverished Zambezi Valley and accounting for 1 per cent of the population, have been ignored by the State. So too have districts in Matabeleland, where few growth points, sealed roads, water projects or decent schools are to be found.[69] The 1987 Unity Accord had fed hopes of reconstruction and development as a reward for Matabele participation in the agreement (Alexander et al. 2000:232). Instead, continuing neglect appeared as ethnic and regional discrimination. Consequently, competition, tension and antagonism marked relations between various indigenous groups from different parts of the country.

Black feminists added the dimension of gender to indigene representations, a perspective largely absent in the discourse of government and lobby groups (Gaidzanwa 1997:2). They argued that after independence 'black males stole the pie'. Women were largely excluded from the opportunities that opened to blacks at around that time. They vowed not to let this happen again and pushed the idea that the indigenisation process should be about helping the greatest number of the most disadvantaged members of society—namely, women. To this end, black businesswomen, alert to their exclusion and marginalisation, set up their own lobby group, the Indigenous Business Women's Organisation (IBWO). Paradoxically, while 'well-empowered' MPs were frequently seen haranguing rural women and the resource poor to greater effort, directing them to try harder and come up with ideas for their own economic betterment, male students, administrators and academics alike vigorously resisted an affirmative-action programme, introduced in 1995, to encourage female applicants to enter

---

67 Talmu 1994; *Parade*, February 1995, p. 2; *Parliamentary Debates,* 12 February 1997, col. 3322, 14 October 1998, col. 1051.
68 Mandaza 1997:5; *Parliamentary Debates,* 18 February 1997, cols 3444, 3452, and throughout 27 November 1997 and 19 December 1997.
69 For extensive coverage of this issue, see speeches by Mr Matura, MP for Gokwe South, Midlands Province, and Mr Ndlovu and Mr Sibanda from Matabeleland constituencies (*Parliamentary Debates,* 18 March 1997, cols 4142–77). Also note the anger fuelled by poor administration at the National University of Science and Technology, itself an indigenisation initiative designed to develop human resources through education (Cabinet Task Force on the Indigenisation of the Economy 1994:3). Although located in Bulawayo, the institution took only 20 of its 500 first-year intake from Matabeleland. Figures such as these were taken as evidence of regional discrimination that resulted in a lack of skills and future underdevelopment (Amani Trust 1998:5).

university. Women were also generally wary, in the light of experience in other parts of Africa, of individual title to land becoming available. Where the lineage holds corporate rights to land, females in their capacity as kin can, if need be, expect to reside and draw a livelihood from land allocated to males, over their lifetimes. When freehold title was introduced, however, as for instance in Kenya, registration was invariably made in individual male names and women were alienated from access rights to land (Okeyo 1980). Locally, they have found themselves discriminated against in land dispersal at state resettlement schemes, despite the passage of the 1982 *Legal Age of Majority Act* that conferred legal majority on black women. Thus, feminists were sensitive to the fact that indigenisation and black empowerment were profoundly gendered processes, finding all too often the authentic indigenous Zimbabwean appeared as a black male (McFadden 1996:41).

So, in brief, introduction of the terms indigene and indigenisation signalled change in the making and the shifting and reframing of Zimbabwe's borders of national personhood. While indigeneity was understood to be the preserve of those whose origins were pre-colonial, and indigenes the nominated beneficiaries of a programme of economic empowerment, there were competing representations about who among the black majority this might be. Was a distinction to be made on the basis of individual material disadvantage? Or was it a status to which all blacks qualified on historical grounds? Would locally born descendants of migrant labour brought from neighbouring countries during the colonial era also be entitled to use the term? At the same time, indigeneity, like class and ethnicity, is constructed and refracted through gender. In short, the term's use gave rise to dissension out of which emerged a hierarchy of those depicted as authentically indigenous. How did whites speak about and construct their ideas of indigeneity, how did they constitute and convey their connection to the country at a time when they faced economic loss and dispossession?[70]

White representations of indigeneity

White informants put the case that indigenous did not necessarily mean only 'black' or 'original inhabitants'. Instead, they typified indigenes 'as those born in' and occasionally added 'and those who have registered as citizens and travel on a Zimbabwean passport'. Alternatively, 'indigenous means born, educated, employed and still resident in Zimbabwe'. This terminology created

---

70 At the time of fieldwork, invasions of white as well as some black and state-owned farms and multinational plantations by war veterans and villagers had begun. These were to become more systematically organised and widespread in the run-up to the 2000 elections. In the cities, some 'white' and 'Asian' businesses, clubs and schools were also harassed by members of the AAG and Sangano Munhumutapa during the mid and late 1990s.

commonality between fellow nationals regardless of race. Indeed, just after 1980, Mr Pratt, a 'patriot' from Marandellas (Marondera), had written, 'as one who was born here, I consider myself an African in the same way that a Harlem Negro is an American'.[71] Thus, without regard for their historical recentness or colonial antecedents, whites appealed for legitimacy on the grounds of birth and residence. It was on this basis, and their love of the land, that they constructed an image of themselves as indigenes. The term denoted a sense of association and attachment, of properly belonging to a place, and did not refer, as the lobbyists cited earlier, to a human condition of suffering, confinement and incarceration.

The majority of whites, city and country folk alike, spoke in this way of their love of the bush, the smell, the light, the heat, the sunsets and 'the raw beauty of the red soil and the long brown grass', 'the great granite boulders strewn across the land'. An urban worker said, 'I feel Zimbabwean in the bush, my second home, especially fishing in the Zambezi Valley.' This remote wilderness region provided the inspiration and background for numerous wild-game stories. The whites' keen ecological knowledge was evident in conversation and on display at amateur painting and sculpture exhibitions. Extensive 'insider' knowledge of the country's flora and fauna also privileged them and set them apart from the endlessly mobile expatriates and other 'rootless' foreigners. These references and representations of the beauty of the Zimbabwean landscape and expressions of love for the country sustained a sense of belonging and their right to be of the land, and helped 'fix in place a powerful association between a culture and home' (Hall 1995:182). Some felt bonded to the continent as a whole. 'I read somewhere that we whites are like seeds scattered in the wind by our forefathers, scattered across Africa, an exciting, turbulent, colourful continent. So we are. We've put down roots and become native to the continent.' Transformation had begun with their ancestors' migration and adaptation to the new environment. A unique cultural production then emerged out of the formative influences of geography and climate and their bonding to the land.

Other scholars have written of the ties formed by settlers with the land where they were born and laboured.[72] And yet in Rhodesia a paradox existed. Literary critic and lecturer Anthony Chennells (1995:109) wrote that Rhodesian novelists were 'torn between allowing their characters to live in harmony with the wilderness as a means of recovering their essential humanity, and transforming the wilderness into a space where agricultural, mining and industrial capital could flourish'. Certainly that pertained with regard to the Kariba hydroelectric scheme. Hughes (2006b) charts the whites' initially ambivalent response to the damming of the Zambezi River's waters. They were filled with sadness and regret by the environmental destruction (Hughes 2006b:825); however, with

---

71 'White patriots also help this country', *The Herald,* 25 September 1980, p. 12.
72 See Handler 1988:34; Goldie 1989:157; Dominey 1993; Read 1996:70.

time, their 'triumphalist narratives of progress' rewrote the African landscape (Hughes 2006b 829). In effect, they destroyed the wild only to remake it in their own image (Hughes 2006b:838). Chapter 3 indicated the pride many still held in Rhodesia's development, in their transfiguring the landscape into a modern and Western Rhodesian location. Indeed, a few still thought of themselves as Rhodesians. 'I call myself Zimbabwean, but that's only because the word has changed. When I use the term, in my heart I think of Rhodesia, the country still in my heart is Rhodesia, which is where I made a name for myself.' Here memories of youth and sporting prowess, opening windows to another place and time, are nostalgically linked to life during the colonial period, the era when he felt he belonged. A second informant denoted himself in this way because of his alienation from the current political situation: 'I'm a Rhodesian, not a Zimbabwean, because I can't identify with this new government.'

For others, however, 'being called a Rhodesian grates. I'm offended when people refer today to Rhodesia or Rhodesians. I say "that is not the name of my country". It is usually the "when wes" [of South Africa] and people from overseas who use the term'. It was a deprecating term. 'To be a Rhodie is to be a Smith man, a "God's own country" man' and a 'class of person who wears *veldskoens* [a bush shoe or suede ankle boot] and boxer shorts, a lager lout whose mates come before all else'. Progressive whites contrasted themselves with the 'when wes' who, while galvanised by political developments in their former homeland, vowed to remain Rhodesians forever (Uusihakala 2008:25, 199). Living in the past, 'when wes' were a source of irritation, perceived to have ossified rather than changed to meet the new political dispensation. Thus the majority of whites self-referred as Zimbabwean with 'no hyphens' and 'no qualifications'. Very occasionally, a younger white described him or herself as a 'new-breed Zimbabwean', indicating attitudes different to those held by the older generation.

Members of the ruling elite also made a terminological distinction along these lines, between Rhodesians, who had the temerity to take members of the government to court, and white Zimbabweans who 'support the President' and recognised it was not patriotic to do so.[73] Cognisant of this, a young man, looking for an apolitical term, chose the self-referent 'white African'. By this means, he, as Hughes (2005:160) suggests, skipped the nation-state and claimed citizenship of the continent as a whole. The young man confirmed earlier observations that

> whites here are very bush oriented, they're knowledgeable, they know the names and habits of even the most rare animals…I've asked myself why are the whites so ill informed about their history when they know so much about the flora and fauna…I think it's because they followed

---

73 *Parliamentary Debates,* 29 September 1993, col. 3491.

the British school system and the English curricula...the history taught was the history of the British Empire and [was] ethnocentric. This British history was followed by Rhodesian history, followed by ZANU PF's version.

He, like Read's (1996:29) European exiles, preferred to use a generic term to describe himself and his origins. His father also called himself a white African but for different reasons. An elderly man, in poor health, he said towards the end of his life 'all my most meaningful relationships are with Africans'. Another old man shared in greater detail the sense of belonging that friendships engendered:

> I started my life in Ciskei [South Africa], outside Fort Beaufort in Red Xhosa country, before Ciskei became a homeland. I call myself first and foremost an African. I was an only child, I grew up fighting with sticks,[74] up before dawn, riding to mission school with the Africans on tiny ponies...We [he and his mother] left, and I spent the next 50 years in Rhodesia. I love the rural African people and the smell of the African bush. Squatting down with the old men, talking in Ndau [a Shona dialect] about the old days, it gives me such pleasure! I miss hearing Xhosa so much that I speak to myself in their tongue when in Australia...sometimes when I disagree with someone, and don't want to be rude, I tell them so in Xhosa, they never ask what I said...My heart bleeds for Africa.

His narrative expressed the sense of himself at home in Africa when speaking its languages or, as Hollander (1991:47) noted, when 'the way they talk is yours'. An image of himself as a 'white African' points to some recognition of affinity, born out of interaction with others. The term reflected a changed consciousness, of having moved beyond European ethnocentrism evident in white aesthetic representations, which while taken from the African landscape and its wildlife, depicted the national space as largely devoid of an African presence. Notwithstanding this, in 1992, a census enumerator disallowed the old man's self-identification. The notion of a non-black African proved problematic and he was recorded as a European. Bureaucratic practices therefore marked a boundary of personhood and compelled him to render himself in ways that were not of his own choosing (Cohen 1994:12). Yet, mulling over these memories, he said, 'I'm an African, I'll never lose it.' The enumerator's decision was not, however, out of line. To be 'white' and 'African' was perceived as enigmatic. Generally, white claims to being an African or white African called forth both

---

74 Sparring with sticks is a popular pastime among Red (rural traditionalist) Xhosa youth. See Mayer and Mayer 1970:164–72.

laughter (Hills 1981:113) and angry retorts from members of the black majority of the ilk that 'no white man should tell me he is Zimbabwean by virtue of being born here. Whites are alien to this country and Africa as a whole.'[75]

Terminological disputes such as these were one means by which black and white competed for autochthony—'the transcendent moral right to be of the land' (Thornton 1994:12). Similar concerns are evident in the academic literature covering settlerism in Australia and New Zealand, countries where indigenes and non-indigenes also dispute physical possession of, and emotional attachment to, the territory. Antipodean settlers seek to achieve legitimacy in their new lands and to erase their 'separation of belonging' (Goldie 1989:13, 215) by themselves becoming indigenes through claims built around birth and residence. Their representations call up a definition of indigeneity that is not tied to a specific historical moment. In much the same way, white Zimbabweans arrogated indigeneity to themselves by virtue of their birth, adapting and putting down roots in the country. Where initially pioneers and early settlers could not be considered indigenes, their descendants' status has changed. After a century of white presence, they believed the term indigene could no longer be applied exclusively. Recognition by others is, however, critical, leading Goldie (1989:13) to describe indigenisation as 'the impossible necessity' not satisfactorily resolved in the New World, where the settler–native boundary remains an 'anxious and ambivalent one' (Bhabha 1994:116); nor in Zimbabwe where, if not credited with indigene status, the whites' image would be that of foreigners and aliens, or worse—'the fifth column amongst us' and 'the enemy within'. Remarks from white and coloured informants that 'we call ourselves indigenous and the blacks indigenous-indigenous' suggested an appreciation that while some were more entitled to use the term than others, the minorities were nonetheless also legitimately able to consider themselves as indigenes. Thus, they were not so much arguing for authenticity on the same terms as blacks as trying to establish a discourse within which they too could speak of a sense of belonging, connection and placement. Economic factors worked, however, to obstruct the realisation of their desire.

Indigenisation of the economy

Zimbabwe's indigenisation debate brought to the fore complex questions regarding 'ownership' of the economy, the distribution of wealth and the means to correct historical imbalances and get the racial proportions right. For their part, white Zimbabweans deeply resented, as non-indigenes, being added to a category of 'whites and foreigners' who purportedly owned and controlled the

---

75 *Parliamentary Debates,* 18 February 1997, col. 3416.

economy. The future Chairman of the Indigenisation Task Force, Mr Mangwende, stated that 98 per cent of the economy in the private sector was owned by 'foreigners [multinationals], Europeans and Asians' as an off-the-cuff statistic in Parliament in 1991.[76] His figure was repeated by other committee members, adopted by the lobby groups and reproduced uncritically in the Zimbabwean media.[77] Mangwende's figure was, however, not subsequently supported by his committee's report.[78] Whites believed talk of a white 'stranglehold' or 'white-owned' economy was 'mischievous'. Not only was the statistic incorrect, it gave the minorities a prominence they did not deserve and blurred Zimbabwe's equally problematic class, gender and regional wealth disparities. Certainly, statistics such as this legitimated the notion that the economic empowerment campaign was the continuation of the armed struggle.[79] What was also beyond dispute was that minorities were over-represented in terms of the private sector's demographic profile, and that Zimbabwe's wealth was distributed unequally, with 20 per cent of the population receiving 60 per cent of the income (UNDP 1998:12–13; Ministry of Public Service, Labour and Social Welfare 1995:81).[80] Female-headed households and rural rather than urban dwellers carried the burden of poverty.

---

76 *Parliamentary Debates*, 3 April 1991, col. 3877.
77 For example, another committee member, Mr Mudariki, claimed that 99.9 per cent of the economy was in Asian and white hands (*Parliamentary Debates*, 29 September 1993, col. 3482) and lobby groups such as the IBDC based their arguments on these statistics. The IBDC depicted 'market forces'—namely, multinationals, large companies and the stock exchange—as 'white', whereas 'blacks' were just 'consumers' (see IBDC advertisement sponsored by Roger Boka, *The Herald*, 14 March 1996, p. 12). Local economic commentator Eric Bloch (Private correspondence) noted, first, the lack of consensus regarding the basis of measurement, which could variously be the market value of assets, according to income or contribution to GDP. He then estimated that in excess of 70 per cent of the economy lay in non-white hands if calculated according to net asset value or contribution to GDP.
78 The *Policy on Indigenisation of the Economy* (Cabinet Task Force on the Indigenisation of the Economy 1994:1) divided the economy into seven sectors—manufacturing, mining, financial, energy, construction, transport, and wildlife and tourism—and indicated that whites and Asians predominated in manufacturing and tourism and wildlife, the latter being a new sector developed since 1985. Investment in the other sectors was largely in the hands of multinationals, the government and/or local blacks (pp. 10–18). Agriculture was treated separately with its own sectoral policy papers. Tobaiwa (1998), examining racial ownership and control of the economy by shareholding and directorships, found that determining the racial category of shareholders was fraught with difficulties. Identifying data were not available through the Zimbabwe Stock Exchange, which had been active only since 1992 (Tobaiwa 1998:3, 4). Ultimately, Tobaiwa found it more meaningful to analyse shareholding along institutional lines. A major proportion of listed equities were held by Zimbabwean insurance companies and pension funds, in addition to companies such as Astra and Delta Corporations, in which the government was a major shareholder (see also *The Financial Gazette*, 24 February 1994, p. 5, 7 March 1996, p. 6). In terms of chairmanships and directorships held in each sector's four major companies, whites were over-represented, accounting for 17 of 26 chairmanships and 153 of the 221 directorships. Blacks held the remaining nine chairs and 68 directorships (Tobaiwa 1998:23, 24). No breakdown along regional lines was available. Tobaiwa's findings also indicated that the white and Asian-dominated manufacturing sector was the most diverse and competitive, with the four largest players producing only 8.1 per cent of the total sector output. This was followed by the black-dominated services sector, whose four major companies accounted for 9.3 per cent of that sector's total output (Tobaiwa 1998:7–8).
79 'Confusing signals', *The Sunday Mail*, 21 September 1997, p. 10.
80 While the Ministry's findings were not disaggregated by race, empirical observation indicated that the average white per capita income was greater than the black (*The Financial Gazette*, 7 March 1996, p. 6).

Economic Structural Adjustment also impacted unevenly on Zimbabwe's population (Friedrich Ebert Stiftung/Zimbabwe Economics Society 1997). In some ways, urban dwellers benefited from a variety of newly registered, indigenously owned financial institutions. Material goods not seen in stores since the 1960s reappeared and transport queues became a thing of the past. Commercial farmers were among the beneficiaries, adjusting to globalisation by moving into horticulture for the European markets. The declining dollar, however, due in part to globalisation as well as to government ineptitude (Harvey 1998:6), undermined the purchasing power of lower-income earners and rural folk in particular. Many on fixed incomes, including elderly whites, found themselves on the breadline. Nonetheless, indigenisation lobbyists promoted the equivalence of local whites and multinationals, parties that benefited from SAPs, while blacks 'suffered' (Mlambo 1997:10). This struck a responsive chord among Africans, to whom producing wealth looked 'easy' for whites given they faced fewer competing demands diverting capital from economic enterprise. Blacks, however, found the expectations of money and assistance from their extended families irksome, for these made capital accumulation difficult at a time when the cost of borrowing was also prohibitive (Mlambo 1997:10).

Asked where responsibility for economically empowering the majority lay, whites replied that first and foremost the government must create an enabling environment; 'it must get the macroeconomic climate right'. The government recognised this 'primary responsibility' in an early version of its policy document (Cabinet Task Force on the Indigenisation of the Economy 1994:1). As the major spender in the economy, the government was well positioned to direct tenders to indigenous firms and decentralise procurement to the provinces. Yet it had been slow to act on these and actively obstructed black entrepreneurs who were not 'party faithfuls'.[81] Nevertheless, the then Minister of Finance, Ariston Chambati (1994:12), indicated 'a definite role' of 'genuine and selfless commitment' for white entrepreneurs to play in the indigenisation process. Whites certainly perceived themselves as agents for the realisation of national economic goals. That they took some pride in their assignation was borne out by comments such as 'we're an economic plus for the country' and 'the yeast that makes the economic cake rise'. At the same time, organisations such as the Zimbabwe Tobacco Association did not believe its members received the kudos they deserved for their considerable efforts to promote black tobacco farmers. Also aware that whites were blamed for 'not doing enough' to promote blacks in agriculture, business, sport and so forth, a data processor with a local computing

---

81 For instance, the highly publicised case of Strive Masiyiwa, who became a folk hero when his efforts to set up a 'cell' (mobile) phone network were repeatedly frustrated by senior party officials and went unsupported by the affirmative action lobby groups. His treatment provoked the question of when was an indigenous indigenous, and when was an indigenous not indigenous (*Parliamentary Debates*, 13 March 1997, col. 4105), as well as cartoons in the papers.

company asked whether it was realistic to expect measures taken by less than 1 per cent of the population to 'liberate' the black majority. Talking of 'levelling the playing field' by closing the skills gap, she noted that 'since independence skills transfer has worked, blacks are now competent and confident in their work...But the meaning of indigenisation is lost when you talk of empowering and promoting 98 per cent; the focus disappears'. Many whites would probably agree with Mulgan (1989:49) that blacks, as the majority and having achieved full political independence, should be able to turn this to their advantage and, giving up the colonised's dependence (Fanon 1963:74), assume the economic initiative.

While a few informants felt they had missed out on opportunities as a result of black economic empowerment—passed over for promotion, fishing and tourism licences cancelled and reissued in favour of indigenous companies, and so on—most did not overstate their case, one man describing them simply as 'pinpricks'. Adopting a regional perspective, an informant, who at the time was finding it an uphill battle establishing a bakery ('two years and I haven't turned my ovens on yet'), had this to say when comparing the skylines of the main cities of Mashonaland and Matabeleland:

> I'm indigenous. Indigenisation is certainly taking place, but it won't get in my way. White business and professionals need not be threatened by it. Only the poorly qualified should be concerned. And even so whites are such a minority that it won't change much for whites in business. But Harare has lots of new buildings, [it's] a boomtown, go ahead. Bulawayo is a ghost town, stagnant, dying, hardly a new building in 20 years. Perhaps Matabeleland should declare UDI, they're the ones losing out!'

Indeed some whites found that indigenisation worked in their favour, as businesses benefited from the increased spending power of middle-class, urban blacks (expensive flower orders on St Valentine's Day, money spent on outfitting young boys in suits and so forth). A woman who had expected to be appointed to a senior position was, however, less enamoured as she related her experience of indigenisation:

> When the old boss retired, there were two of us in the running for the top job: myself, with better qualifications, and a black Zimbabwean with a year's more seniority who got the job. For 18 months, I was unhappy and when an opportunity came I raised this with the parent company. They admitted not treating me fairly, but asked why I could not be content being 2IC. Afterwards I thought about this remark and came to the conclusion that I could come to terms with this. But I wonder if they [management] would ask a black male if he would be content with a white woman being promoted over him as his boss.

This informant indicates she is aware that race and gender intersect in contradictory ways in affirmative-action programmes, where one person is promoted over another equally or better qualified person because he is black and male. For their part, parent company representatives asked whether she would divest herself of the superior position that she had assigned herself, rethink and accept a non-leadership role, or would she insist on dominance.

There was also widespread concern among whites regarding the longer term. White farmers discussed looking for land in Zambia, Mozambique or Angola, where governments were perceived to hold 'a more positive attitude to investment'. Another family spoke of moving their kapenta[82] fishing operation from Zimbabwe's Lake Kariba to Cabora Bassa in Mozambique. More immediately worrying for most was the anti-white sentiment contained in a series of what became known as the 'Boka advertisements', condoned by the President, which ran in the daily papers during 1996.[83] Racism seemed to be coming 'from the top down'. One person, recently returned to Zimbabwe, said:

> I became aware of this push through the Boka ads. I'm for indigenisation [as economic empowerment], but not racism. I got the feeling they don't want us. I hadn't expected that. Whites can be indigenous, but the criteria seem a race thing. I noticed the old-timers take no notice. Now I rarely buy a newspaper. I'm learning to switch off and to ignore it.

Also concerned was the elderly 'white African' described at some length above, who said 'this is dangerous political talk in that it holds out false hope to the unemployed and uneducated. Yet ordinary black folk are not anti-white.' A retired tobacco farmer quipped, 'Is it just political rhetoric, is it for real, and how do you tell the difference?' Another individual described his sister-in-law's increasingly circumscribed life on a plot outside a town in the south of the country, from where their family had originated.

> She restricts her life, she's withdrawn, she focuses upon her Christian group, Weight Watchers and the small acreage on which she and her husband keep chickens. They are trapped in a fool's paradise. The racism makes whites more insular; they retreat into a laager mentality and evangelical escapism.

---

82 A small, sardine-like fish.
83 These were funded by business tycoon Roger Boka. See, for example, 'The whys and why nots?' and 'Hunter becomes hunted', printed in *The Herald* (22 February 1996 and 14 March 1996), and Sangano Munhumutapa's 'The African tragedy' of the same dates. The advertisements vilified whites and, in Western countries, would have been actionable for inciting racial hatred.

Such is the purchase of racial hostility on inner life. The man suggests his sister-in-law has distanced herself mentally and physically from external political realties, retreating to the private or domestic domain. Ghettoised, she, like many whites, hoped to avoid contestation while also resenting being excluded.

> The white role is upliftment, but not to share in the new initiatives that come from economic liberalisation. We are also excluded from the political debate. If you're white and question government, you're called a racist; if you're black, it's puppet or Uncle Tom. This makes for public apathy and no accountability on the part of government. At the end of the day, whites are not welcome. The inner circle of government does not want us. The general population is apathetic. They don't care if whites are here or not. A huge gulf exists between the politically and ideologically motivated and the population in general.

Taking a similar tack, a woman mused:

> The government does not mean what it is saying. The genuine meaning of indigene is born in. Indigenous is used by the government to mean black, Shona and cronyism. It is excluding and elitist rhetoric which divides us into first and second-class citizens. Whites, as second class, are told that they are not real citizens but settlers, colonialists and thieves. We are citizens but not allowed to participate in the share issue, for example. We would support economic empowerment if it had been called economic promotion. But then whites, like my son, would have applied and competed for a soft loan. Indigenisation excludes us and protects blacks from competition.

She and a sizeable number of others believed whites were scapegoats for government inaction. The race issue effectively shielded the government from criticism over economic mismanagement and earlier sidelining black entrepreneurs. State officials enriched themselves during the 1980s, in spite of the Leadership Code introduced to prevent the amassing of wealth by those in public office, while reconciliation distracted attention away from the black majority's need for 'economic emancipation'.[84]

The discourse of indigeneity, however, did more than this. The terminology made whites aware that others did not share their vision of a future Zimbabwean society. 'The indigenisation rhetoric showed us that some Africans, like the Rhodies, are not interested in building a multiracial society.' Many felt offended by media coverage, which fixed whites in particular racial positions, and the militant lobby groups' exclusive image of the indigene and discourse of dispossession. Privately, whites feared that indigenisation could come to mean

---

84 See also *Parliamentary Debates,* 24 April 1991, col. 4471.

'blacks can take what they want under the guise of empowerment'. For example, the 1992 *Land Act* (see below) allowed for the compulsory acquisition of land for not only agricultural purposes but a number of other, unrelated reasons (von Blanckenburg 1994:35). Thus dispossession in the countryside could well spread to the cities.[85] The discourse refuted white claims to legitimacy and permanence, because 'in the longer term, indigenisation implies that neither I nor my children have a legitimate right to earn a living in Zimbabwe'. Thus, whites perceived indigeneity as the language of their exile and alienation (Brah 1996:203). They and black liberals would have preferred making entrepreneurial promotion and wealth creation national development priorities in terms that were not first and foremost about race and historical origins. Also making this point, local economist Eric Bloch wrote, '[I]t's time to cease thinking in terms of race and ethnic past and instead build a nation of all Zimbabwean peoples, united in pride and love of their country and the common aspiration for an improved life.'[86] Bloch's vision of national development is forward looking, whereas discourses of national attachment that foreground ties of custom and tradition are exclusive and regressive. Compulsory land acquisition in 1997 proved, however, to be the contingent event that crystallised national membership in indigene terms.

The land question

At independence, Zimbabwe inherited a highly inequitable distribution of land ownership along race lines (Government of Zimbabwe 1998a:4; Palmer 1990:165). During the 1980s, the government acquired, as agreed at Lancaster House, land for resettlement on a willing buyer/willing seller basis, with the United Kingdom underwriting half of the cost of land purchases (Palmer 1990:166, 168). In the early years, 55 000 families were resettled—well below the projected target of 162 500, and not always with the infrastructure or capital necessary to work their land productively (UNDP 1998:32). After 1983, the domestic budget could not sustain the programme and the numbers declined substantially for the remainder of the decade.

At the expiration of the entrenched constitutional conditions in 1990, the government set out in the National Land Policy[87] plans to acquire land compulsorily and legislated in 1992 to enable this. Several farms were designated soon after.[88] The government was concerned that land reform redressed the

---

85   See *Horizon*, November 1992, pp. 7, 50; MacGarry 1994b:Preface; *Parliamentary Debates*, 11 March 1998, col. 4002.
86   'Racial bigotry retards economic recovery', *The Financial Gazette*, 24 September 1993, p. 6.
87   *Parliamentary Debates*, 25 July 1990, cols 1216–52.
88   Political factors were prominent in compulsory land acquisition from the start. Two of the earliest farms to be compulsorily acquired in 1993 belonged to government opponent Ndabaningi Sithole and to Henry Elsworth, a recidivist Rhodesian. Sithole's farm, on the outskirts of Harare, was home to 4000 people, who

historical racial imbalance at the same time as productivity was maintained in large-scale farming areas, and commercialisation of agriculture was to be promoted in communal areas.[89] To this end, late in 1997, the government gazetted 1471 commercial farms for compulsory acquisition[90]—about 30 per cent of all large-scale farms and 40 per cent of that sector's land area. Criteria set down to guide land identification included derelict or under-utilised land, multiple and absentee farm ownership and proximity to urban and communal areas.[91] Thus, the criteria did not aim to sustain or recreate historical or customary ties to particular areas, although on the ground this proved to be a priority of some traditional leaders.

While all stakeholders agreed on the imperative of reform, the land question re-emerged as a political issue in changed local conditions (Palmer 1990:174). For a start, the black population had almost doubled since independence[92] and, by 1994, between 400 and 500 of the country's black elite had become large-scale landowners (von Blanckenburg 1994:21; McCandless and Abitbol 1997:27; Palmer 1990:175). A few were among the largest landowners the country had ever seen.[93] In addition, several hundred more leased commercial farms purchased ostensibly for resettlement from the government.[94] Von Blanckenburg (1994:21)

---

were evicted without any plans being made for their resettlement (Deve 1993:22).

89 The Minister of Agriculture pointed out that acquiring land was not in itself a solution to poverty. In addition, people needed the wherewithal to make land productive—namely, capital investment. Lack of capital was one of the main causes of under-utilised land, which existed in all of Zimbabwe's agricultural sectors. The United Nations Development Programme (UNDP 1998:35) presented a similar argument regarding land reform as a solution to Zimbabwe's unemployment problems.

90 In 1997, 2209 farms were identified, of which 1471 were gazetted. Earlier in 1993, land councils in each district, which included CFU representatives, had identified 10 farms in each province for acquisition according to criteria laid down by the government. When the list was gazetted, however, only half of these farms were on it. Productive and single-owner farms had been substituted for the rest (von Blanckenberg 1994:36).

91 Proximity to communal areas proved controversial and was downplayed by the government as the land acquisition process progressed.

92 The black population of 700 000 in 1901 had risen to more than 7 million in 1982, 10 million in 1992 and 11.6 million in 2002 (see Appendix Table 1) (CSO 1994:164; UNDP 1998:6). Thus, between 1982 and 1992, the population growth rate was more than 3 per cent, exceeding that of the sub-Saharan region as a whole (CSO 1994:1; UNDP 1998:14). This slowed considerably, however, between 1992 and 2002 due in part to the impact of HIV/AIDS and emigration.

93 For instance, far and away the largest owners of land identified for compulsory acquisition in 1997 were Anglo American Corporation (427 200 ha, which represented 11.89 per cent of identified land) and Vice-President Nkomo's Development Trust of Zimbabwe, which owned the three properties making up Nuanetsi Ranch (319 929 ha or 8.02 per cent of identified land). Indeed, it would have been possible for the State to acquire 60 per cent of the 5 million ha it wanted from fewer than 300 large or multiple-farm owners (Moyo 1998b:36). The size of landholdings identified in 1997 then dropped to several companies and individuals who owned between 40 000 and 60 000 ha, and fell again to a much greater number of black and white large-scale farmers, who held less than 30 000 ha (Moyo 1998b:30–1). Neither Anglo American nor Nkomo, however, lost their properties. Anglo American came to a private agreement with the government, while Nkomo's land was de-listed.

94 Some 300 000–400 000 ha of land acquired during the 1980s for resettlement had been leased for commercial enterprises by successive Ministers of Agriculture—not to black graduates of Zimbabwe's agricultural colleges, but to members of the political elite. The farms were not surrendered nor were officials sacked after this became public in 1994.

noted that, while the productive capacity of a minority of them compared favourably with their white counterparts, many without training carried on farming in the manner of the communal areas. More than half were absentee farmers with little interest in agriculture, and many were politicians. Thus, given the identification criteria spelt out above, land redistribution in 1997 could have meant, for some members of the political elite, redistributing their own properties[95] (Palmer 1990:175).

Notwithstanding the recent entry of blacks into the commercial agricultural sector, land continued to be disaggregated into the categories of 'white' commercial and 'black' communal. In reality, the nature of landholding was much more complex.[96] First, although it was variously held that about 4000 to 4500 white farmers[97] 'dominated the agrarian economy' (Moyo 1998b:1), the large-scale farming sector included multinational plantations, some large state-owned estates and the already mentioned black commercial farmers. Second, landholding among whites was highly differentiated. There were some very large, white-dominated landowning companies in addition to 1000 smaller-sized white-owned family farms or companies (Moyo 1998a:38–40). It might, therefore, have been more useful to talk, as Moyo (1998a:38) suggested, of Zimbabwe's landed gentry—a term encompassing both black and white commercial landowners.

Nonetheless, the debate proceeded along the lines of white or non-indigenous farmers, where 'white' agriculture, built on freehold tenure, was perceived as capital intensive and highly productive, and linked to local and international markets (von Blanckenburg 1994:21, 29). White farmers and representatives of government set up a one-on-one relationship between these factors, which, while not totally unwarranted, went some way in legitimating large-scale commercial landholding. For instance, by the late 1990s, the large-scale agricultural sector accounted for between 35 per cent and 45 per cent of all exports, 40 per cent of the country's foreign exchange earnings and about 11–15 per cent of gross domestic product (GDP) (von Blanckenberg 1994:27; Bratton and Burgess 1987:201; Grant 1998:50; Government of Zimbabwe 1998a:5; UNDP 1998:23). Furthermore, growth in the industrial and services sectors was directly linked

---

95 Equally, political considerations played a part in the failure to designate. For instance, the Minister of Agriculture had not seen fit to sign the papers necessary to allow fellow Minister Msipa's farm, bought on the outskirts of Harare in 1981 and declared derelict in 1989, to be acquired (*Parade*, February 1991, p. 21).
96 Zimbabwe's five agricultural subsectors comprised large and small-scale commercial farmers, state farms, communal and resettlement areas (see Land Tenure Commission 1994). Individually held land (urban title and large and small farmland) made up 35 per cent of the national land, unalienated state land made up 15 per cent, communal land 42 per cent and national parks 8 per cent (*Parliamentary Debates*, 12 March 1992, col. 4347).
97 The number of white commercial farmers peaked at 6255 in 1955 (von Blanckenburg 1994:17) and then fell to about 4000 by 1982. Disaggregated 1992 census figures indicate the bald number of local white farmers to be 2224 (see Appendix Table 3). This figure reveals nothing, however, about the number or size of their farms.

to expanding agricultural production. For these reasons, some in government circles argued that it would be a 'massively destructive blow to expropriate white commercial farmers en masse' (Chung 1989:9). This was also the position held by most whites. 'The CFU has kept this country afloat for years,' explained an informant: 'Land distribution is acceptable if the land goes to those who need it and use it productively. But indications are that it will go to the politicians and *chefs*.'[98] This informant did not argue that the white agricultural sector remain untouched, but, rather, that acquisition should proceed as a transparent and ongoing, staggered process. Similarly, an urban white with close links to the CFU complained that 'on the one hand the government keeps saying foreign exchange earned from tobacco sales will bail the country out and, on the other, the government is threatening the goose that lays the golden egg. It defies logic.' She was, however, equally critical of the CFU, saying:

> The CFU should have grasped the nettle a long time back. Local CFU councils should have identified under-utilised and derelict farms and multiple ownership. They should have talked to the farmers and got together and offered excess land to the government. They should have worked to defuse the situation and made a conciliatory gesture in the interest of future stability, but then the Afrikaner[99] farmers would never give up land voluntarily. It's in their souls, just like the Africans.

Her remarks point to differences of opinion within the CFU and to unrealistic expectations on the part of many Afrikaner and African men that, as males, they have an unconditional right to land. Indeed Zimbabwe's land reform programme provoked a reappraisal of the nature of land. Was it a traditional entitlement or birthright of black males whether they made good use of it or not, or an economic asset, a commodity to be bought, sold and utilised productively for the general good? For their part, some CFU officials belatedly acknowledged their failure to address the land question for, in effect, abdicating responsibility for correcting historical wrongs.[100] Late in 1997, the organisation offered—albeit under threat of compulsory acquisition—to immediately avail the government of 1.5 million hectares (of the targeted 5 million) with more forthcoming and to fund the resettlement of this land. This proposal, known as 'Team Zimbabwe', was supported by, among others, Professor Rukuni, the Chairman of the Land

---

98 The term '*chef*' came back to Zimbabwe with ZANU leaders who were in Mozambique during the liberation struggle (Meredith 2007:78). Zimbabweans, across the racial spectrum, have adopted the word to denote a man in government with status and power. In contrast, the masses are referred to as the 'povo'.

99 Hodder-Williams (1974:637) describes the 'deeply felt need for land' by the Afrikaners of Marandellas District (now Marondera), Mashonaland East Province. Countrywide, their numbers peaked in 1921 at 20 per cent of the total white population. By 1951, Afrikaners represented 13 per cent of Europeans (Blake 1978:279). In particular districts, however, such as Marandellas, they continued to make up a socially exclusive 20 per cent and were treated with some suspicion by the English speakers (Hodder-Williams 1974:613). With independence, many Afrikaners left for South Africa.

100 See McCandless 1997:27.

Tenure Commission, as the way 'to kick-start' the reform programme.[101] Robin Palmer (1998:1) described it at the time as the 'best prospect of modest but effective land reform, especially if conceived on a largely self-financing basis'. The offer highlighted the rift that existed between black liberals who pursued economic arguments and black radicals who put more weight on historical and political factors, the latter condemning the plan out of hand (Moyo 1998b:37).[102] In the event, the government failed to act on the offer.

While historical injustices underpinned the official indigenisation discourse, no distinction was made between white farmers who inherited or acquired land during the illegal colonial era and others who purchased it under the current regime. In neither case would the government pay compensation for 'stolen land', with Mugabe saying it was up to the British Government to compensate 'their cousins' and 'its children'.[103] In this way, the President metaphorically conferred on white Zimbabweans an external mother country responsible for their wellbeing.[104] It was also extremely doubtful whether the Zimbabwean Government was in a financial position to compensate farmers for improvements, such as housing, dams, tobacco barns and irrigation, as well as the schools and clinics that served the farm workers and surrounding rural communities. Legally, the State was required to do so,[105] although the government had allocated very little finance to land acquisition or resettlement in its budget[106] (Ministry of Lands and Agriculture 1998:4; Moyo 1998b:10). Some of the complexities flowing from compulsory acquisition are illustrated in the next informants' accounts of events.

> We borrowed heavily to buy a farm two and a half years ago after government issued the necessary certificate of nil interest.[107] It's a single ownership. Then two bad seasons followed. Our farm was designated,

---

101 Rukuni 1998:16; Grant 1998:51; *Parliamentary Debates*, 17 March 1998, col. 4157.
102 'Nauseating spectacle', *The Sunday Mail*, 25 January 1998, p. 8.
103 'ZANU PF's Byo conference bars western diplomats', 'Mugabe unlikely to carry out land threats', *The Financial Gazette*, 19 December 1996, p. 1, and 16 October 1997, p. 5, respectively.
104 His comment is a far cry from Nkomo's (1984:166) recollection of Lancaster House, where the nationalist delegation argued that they did not consider whites to be settlers but Zimbabweans. At that time, Zimbabwe's new leaders hoped to negotiate a land scheme similar to Kenya's, where, under a British-subsidised programme, most of the 3500 white-owned farms passed into black hands within two decades of independence (Fitzgerald 1982; Palmer 1990:165).
105 Although the government talked in terms of land designation, the farms were in fact gazetted in 1997 under Section 5 of the *Land Act*, which governed compulsory acquisition, or expropriation, and not according to Section 12, which determined designation. As such, the State was legally obliged to compensate the farmers for the land and improvements (Nherere 1998). While compulsory acquisition may apply to any land in Zimbabwe, rural or urban, designation applies only to rural land.
106 Resettlement was an expensive and time-consuming undertaking, involving as many as 15 different government departments.
107 The government had the right of first refusal for rural land. If not interested, the government issued a certificate of no present interest and the seller could then proceed to put the land on the open market. Kriger (2007:65) noted that the government availed itself of less than one-third of the 1800 commercial farms offered between 1985 and 1992.

but who now owns the debt: the government, the new owners, the bank or ourselves? The farm has been on and off the list ever since.[108] I console myself that this designation is unreasonable and therefore won't happen. But then I know the unreasonable does happen.

This woman's argument appealed to legality and financial rationality. Compulsory acquisition without compensation for the land or improvements threatened to destabilise Zimbabwe's financial sector and undermine its agro-based industries. The next farmer's appeal was made differently, on the basis of a long association with the land, utility and political allegiance. The man, whose family had farmed a property for five generations, described his position thus:

> I am a Zimbabwean, I don't want to go anywhere else, I belong to this country, I am committed to farming and building up my country. We've always said we can work with government, we want to work with government, it is our government, let's get together and make it work, it's our future. I regard myself as…indigenous, I believe I can make a contribution to this country, the only people who can develop this country properly are all the indigenous people to this country. (CCJP 1995)

The farmer chose his words carefully, yet his seemingly positive remarks were perceived as provocative by militant blacks. Why this was the case reflected, in part, the processes by which whites could acquire, in the eyes of blacks, authenticity as indigenes. During the Rhodesian era, 'working for' Africans was considered paternalistic by politically aware blacks (Hancock 1984:22). Instead, whites were reminded that to 'work with' Africans, or the government, was preferred because these terms reflected relations of partnership and equality. Today neither is acceptable. Both smack of the 'outside-in, top-down' colonial orientation that is deeply resented (Betts 1998:80). Thus, it was no longer sufficient for the CFU, the Confederation of Zimbabwe Industries or whites generally to speak of wanting 'to work with blacks' or 'working with the government'. Instead, they were told to be part of Zimbabwean society—a point I return to below.

---

108   Many identified white farms were delisted and then later re-listed as the Minister of Lands and Agriculture (Kangai), the ZANU PF National Chairman (Msipa) and others argued the merits and demerits of acquiring various farms (see *The Herald*, 11 June 1998, p. 5, 29 June 1998, p. 7, 5 July 1998, p. 1). While some black-owned farms were gazetted in 1997, they were delisted, as were identified plantations and state farms, on the grounds that their acquisition went against the aims of indigenisation (Moyo 1998b:44, 46; Ministry of Lands and Agriculture 1998:7; *Parliamentary Debates*, 18 May 1999, col. 5582). Delisted farms did not, however, escape invasion. The bulk (70 per cent) of farms remaining on the list were single, white Zimbabwean-owned farms of less than 1500 ha (Moyo 1998a:7, 1998b:50, 53). Given that each family may hold one reasonably sized farm, 70 per cent appear to have been mistakenly identified (Moyo 1998b:42). The CFU gave a lower figure of 609 of the 1471 farms incorrectly listed (*The Herald*, 7 September 1998, p. 5).

Meanwhile, land reform late in 1997 brought the distinction between the indigenous and non-indigenous sharply into focus. In order to create a more racially balanced representation in the commercial agricultural sector, the government committed itself to promoting the entry of blacks into commercial farming.[109] This was also the section of black society that had benefited from state loans since the introduction of the ESAP, and it was their claims to land, rather than those of poorer black Zimbabweans, that were the most visible in the media (Moyo 1998a:32, 1998b:10). Indeed, the land acquisition process appeared to be driven by blacks interested in becoming commercial farmers producing for global markets[110] (Moyo 1998b:9). Not all key figures in the debate shared the government's priorities. Some, such as the Chairman of the Land Tenure Commission, talked of the largest proportion—maybe 75 per cent— being settled by the landless, disadvantaged and the poor (Rukuni 1998:16). Others believed the government should transfer the land to the 'better-off' but still small-scale black farmers, in particular those with the skills and capability to use the land productively (UNDP 1998:17). War veterans forcefully presented the position that the government had overlooked their needs in violent street demonstrations and sit-ins during 1997.[111] They believed the land was theirs on account of promises made to them during the liberation war. So a shared or unitary vision of the sort of redistribution Zimbabweans would like to see eventuate from land reform was lacking. State officials also treated ancestral claims to land as 'impractical'.[112] For this and a number of other reasons, the general public had little faith in transparent land reform.[113]

What needs to be remembered is that it was not simply white farmers who were threatened with dispossession as non-indigenes during Zimbabwe's land acquisition exercise. The place of farm workers—invariably referred to by their countries of origin and accounting for about one-quarter of Zimbabwe's formal work force—was also being challenged and denied. Estimates were that between one-half and two-thirds were descended from introduced 'foreign' African labour, mentioned earlier in this chapter. This 'invisible minority' (Muzondidya 2004:213) had been largely ignored since 1980. Colonial domestic arrangements

---

109 Friedrich Ebert Stiftung/Zimbabwe Economics Society 1998a:6; *Parliamentary Debates,* 25 July 1990, col. 1223.
110 About half of all the farms gazetted grew tobacco, Zimbabwe's major export crop.
111 Riot police had to be called when countrywide meetings between the war veterans and MPs turned hostile. Ministers were shown fleeing out back doors to their waiting Mercedes. Recognising the gravity of the situation, Mugabe, in a seven-hour meeting, agreed to an unbudgeted compensation package that included promises of land. According to Kriger (2007:70), the gratuities alone cost double the government's spending on land reform since 1980. See 'Meeting with war veterans turns nasty', *The Herald,* 21 July 1997, p. 1, and 'War veterans package is agreed', *The Herald,* 22 August 1997, p. 1.
112 'State will not renew leases', *The Sunday Mail,* 15 December 1996, p. 6.
113 Leased farms were not identified for acquisition in 1997 as the government considered the land already available for redistribution to 300 black 'tenant' commercial farmers (Moyo 1998b:10, 20). Some, such as Buttercombe Farm, earmarked for resettlement in 1992 but leased to Harare Councillor Mrs Hativagone, were invaded in 1998.

continued on the commercial farms and the government, perceiving labour as 'belonging' to the white farmer, left the responsibility for providing health care, schooling, transport and so forth to them (Rutherford 2001:231). While this provided farm labourers with some claim to resources and patronage, it also left them outside the national project, their uncertain status being overlooked in the 1984 renunciation of foreign citizenship exercise. Before the 1985 national election, however, ZANU PF functionaries had sold spurious one-dollar citizenship cards to foreign farm workers (Rutherford 2001:44). According to Rutherford (2001:226), this led many to assume that they were in fact citizens. One explained, 'I am originally from Mozambique, but I have been working on this farm since 1964. This farm is the only home I have in the world. If I go back to Mozambique I will be just like a stranger. I now regard myself as a Zimbabwean' (Madinah 1993:7). Another farm worker, who shared this anxiety, said 'we would like to be considered sons of this country, we fought in the liberation war, we are the same as you, we are like the Zimbabweans who live in the rural areas'.[114] Farm workers such as these, however, remained 'foreigners' despite marriages to local spouses.[115] As non–indigenes, they did not enjoy customary rights to land, and as 'migrants', they were unable to participate in government resettlement initiatives (Munyanyi 1998:71). Callers to talkback radio and Chief Chiweshe of Muzarabani District, among others, were demanding their repatriation.[116]

There were other settlers too: the 'new settlers' or blacks who either owned small farms outside their areas of historical origin or joined the rural cooperatives established by the State in resettlement areas soon after independence. Some 100 or so African 'strangers' found their farms in Mashonaland gazetted (Moyo 1998a:44). Further south, Chief Makore in Gutu[117] labelled newcomers in his district 'settlers and enemies of the people' and called for their expulsion.[118] Earlier, to the chief's chagrin, a nearby farm available for resettlement had been distributed to 'people from Bulawayo and Harare' rather than to those with an ancestral claim.[119] The terms 'stranger' and 'foreign' denote someone from

---

114   *Spotlight*, ZBC Radio 1, 24 February 1998.
115   In the past, some 'foreign' husbands have found themselves unwelcome in their wives' rural homes. On the woman's death, her husband could be asked to leave (Masina 1988:12). In view of this, Catherine Muchongwe, speaking for the Zimbabwean wives of foreign farm workers, asked 'are we to go with our husbands to Mozambique or are we going to separate' (*The Herald*, 13 April 1998).
116   'Chief asks state to repatriate foreigners', *The Herald*, 5 September 1998, p. 12.
117   Chiefs and their headmen confer use rights to land in the communal areas, which should then (but often were not) be registered with the local council, institutions imposed on and deriving legitimacy from a source different to that of traditional authorities (see Rukuni quoted in UNDP 1998:17). Rights to land in all other areas are administered by the State. Traditional leaders, however, believe the State has undermined their role and some encourage settlement or squatting on farms or game parks adjacent to their communal areas (*The Herald*, 13 August 1998, p. 8). Land as a sacred medium was rarely mentioned by anyone contributing to the debate.
118   'Resettlement exercise gives headaches in Gutu', *The Herald*, 16 February 1999, p. 6.
119   'We need our land', *The Herald*, 1 August 1997, p. 10.

another community, someone born in and deriving from outside the area. Others seeking a home outside their area of origin were physically attacked.[120] Internal migration within Zimbabwe to other districts or provinces in search of land was, however, a long-established practice. Local chiefs, or their headmen, were approached and presented with gifts or 'monetary kickbacks' in exchange for usufruct.[121] These illegal and insecure 'land sales' within the communal areas, which served to financially and politically empower traditional leaders at the same time as they thwarted and obstructed the plans of state administrators, were common and increasing in number (Moyo 1998b:11).

Indigeneity as cultural affiliation

Zimbabwe's land acquisition exercise provided, in short, an opportunity for ethnic unmixing[122] (Brubaker 1996:166–9). While various state authorities condemned ethno-regional exclusivity in the land reform programme, they supported exclusion on the basis of colonial origins. How were arguments justifying this position presented?

The Minister of Agriculture was quite frank when he said social and political factors were just as important as economic ones in decisions regarding compulsory acquisition of white-owned farms in 1997.[123] Also speaking about this at the Harare Land Conference,[124] Sam Moyo explained that

> some members of minority groups who are Zimbabwean citizens by birth or naturalisation regard themselves as being indigenous in contradistinction to foreign companies owning large estates. But, though Zimbabwean citizens, the limited social integration of most LSCF [large-scale commercial farm] owners into the social and political organisations of black communities renders them relatively isolated. This isolation tends to determine their conceptual disqualification as indigenous persons. (Moyo 1998a:43, 44)

---

120 *Parliamentary Debates,* 2 September 1997, col. 909, 2 February 1999, col. 3563.
121 See Cheater 1990:192, 194; Dzingirai 1994; O'Flaherty 1998:540.
122 Land acquisition was also unevenly dispersed across the country, with the southern areas—which had few representatives among the upper echelons of the political elite—accounting for most of the land identified (Moyo 1998b:36).
123 *Parliamentary Debates,* 4 February 1998, col. 2897.
124 The Harare Conference was convened early in 1998 in order to develop a consensus on the land acquisition programme. All stakeholders and other interested parties attended. Later in the year, the main issues were presented to an international donors' conference in the hope of attracting external funds. While donors supported land reform in principle, little financial assistance was forthcoming, as donors were unconvinced of the transparency of the land programme. Donors were, however, prepared to pledge funds for resettlement purposes.

Furthermore, in the eyes of black nationalists, white separation and reserve confirmed them as colonial settlers who were not infrequently told that 'Africa is for Africans' and they should 'go back to their original homes from whence their forefathers came'.[125]

Indeed, the question posed by educated urban blacks was 'when are the whites going to be part of the new Zimbabwe'. What did they share with the black majority? When were they going to provide proof of their rootedness by, for example, both understanding and using a vernacular language, developing an interest in soccer and demonstrating in other ways 'fellow-feeling with the indigenous peoples of Africa'?[126] Disinterest was taken as evidence of the whites' refusal of Africa. To this effect, S. Tsingo of Harare wrote:

> An unacceptable number of you, born in this country and expressing the feeling that this is your home refuse to give up your British and foreign passports…The time has come for you to change your attitudes and come out of your shells and participate…Stand up and be counted as true and genuine citizens of Zimbabwe…You say you accept the need for land reform, you say you see the merits of the indigenisation programme but…none of you has thought of offering some of the land you hold to the blacks. None of you has offered to sell you[r] businesses or equity specifically to blacks at concessional rates…your actions or lack of them are more noticeable because you are a minority. We can only view you as Zimbabwean citizens genuinely concerned with the development of this country if you show us that in your heart of hearts that is what you are.[127]

In this excerpt, Tsingo challenged whites to move beyond their familiar home to a less safe or comfortable place. His words highlight the extent to which identity as an indigene is participatory, dependent on what one enacts. Along similar lines, a former political detainee remarked: 'Remaining whites do not mix, they have withdrawn and are not seen around, they are not visible in the central business district. They should be seen so that suspicion of them dissipates.'

In part, this observation was correct. Whites, particularly housewives, had withdrawn to suburban shopping centres—hence the importance accorded holding mass evangelical gatherings, described earlier in reference to national reconciliation, at venues in the high-density suburbs. Agricultural outreach programmes also made whites visible and accessible. At the same time, however, the former detainee's comments reflect a common perception that there are more

---

125 'Two ways of dealing with racism', *The Sunday Mail*, 17 October 1994, p. 6.
126 'Racism', *MOTO*, May 1993, p. 19.
127 'No one should get away with racism', *The Sunday Mail*, 3 October 1994, p. 6.

whites in the country than in fact there are. Their number almost halved in urban and rural areas, falling from 82 000 to 47 000 (or from 0.8 per cent to 0.4 per cent of the total population) between 1992 and 2002.[128] The once-white elite suburbs and schools had for some time been overwhelmingly black. Among better-off Zimbabweans, race was no longer the factor determining where a family lived or their access to schools, clubs and so on. These borders have been reset by income (Weiss 1994:115, 148). Thus, indigeneity goes beyond class distinctions; it is a border that is simultaneously social, cultural and psychic (Brah 1996:198).

Not sharing historical origins or common descent, whites 'must develop an appreciation and understanding of the riches of African culture' (Henson 1988:10) if they are to sustain a permanent identity with the land. Contrary to the hopes of Mr Pratt from Marandellas, cited earlier in this chapter, they were not perceived as fellow nationals regardless of colour, but, because the cultural divide was too great to countenance, as aliens.[129] White Zimbabweans should 'learn to be African'[130] (Hove 1990:24) for without this 'they remain settlers, and not part of Africa' (Henson 1989:9). Tom Holloway contributed a letter:

> As Europeans we have been in Africa for plus or minus 250–300 years. But we have persisted in keeping ourselves apart, aloof and separate. I have now started calling myself a white African because that is exactly what I am. Nothing less, nothing more…There is a lot to admire in both Shona and Ndebele and for that matter any African culture. I do not know of any white man in Africa who has even attempted to bridge the gap culturally.[131]

Holloway was, however, an exception in recognising this shortcoming. The majority of whites, while claiming insider knowledge, showed no great interest in the lives of the various African peoples. They wished to retain European cultural traditions (Memmi 1965:40), making them in the eyes of the majority native-born colonisers rather then indigenes. Indeed, the continued use of the term 'settler' referred to imposition and domination and served to underline

---

128 See Appendix Table 1; CSO 2004 Tables 1.8, 1.9, 1.10.
129 On the same grounds, African-Americans on a roots journey back to Zimbabwe found to their consternation that they were referred to as white. Similarly, Maya Angelou (1987:19–23, 40–1) describes the disillusionment of African-Americans making their way back to Ghana only to find they are no longer recognised as being of the continent.
130 For instance, patrons of the Harare Repertory Theatre were told not to view themselves as 'aspiring Europeans…this yearning for London is surely based on false cultural assumptions at an immense cost' (Hove 1990:24). Following London theatrical productions was taken to reflect that whites still looked to Europe as the cultural centre. Instead, they should support local productions that developed an African theme—for instance, plays such as *Mbuya Nehanda, Citizen Chi* and *Dog Eat Dog*, at which expatriates made up the bulk of the audience.
131 'We have never bothered to be assimilated into African culture', *Zimbabwe Independent*, 23 October 1998, p. 8.

the white inability or refusal to 'integrate' or 'assimilate'. To belong and be recognised as indigenes, whites must rid themselves of 'separateness' and 'apartness'[132] or, to put it in other words, Euro-centrism and superiority. They must 'pierce the veil' (Chakrabarty 2000:150) and develop cultural affiliation not just with the African landscape but with its peoples, for indigeneity is relational, conferred by what one enacts and how roots are demonstrated.

Conclusion

In conclusion, the appearance of the terms indigene and indigeneity reflected black frustration and disappointment with the government's failure to effect social and economic transformation during Zimbabwe's first decade of independence. The subject position was mobilised out of concern that opportunities expected to derive from structural adjustment and trade liberalisation policies announced in 1990 be realised by the black majority. The application of the term indigeneity derived 'authority from an African experience of resistance to colonialism' (Chennells 1995:107), its semiotic function being to realign and set limits to the communities of beneficiaries. Paradoxically, while the language of indigeneity was often inward and backward looking, the discourse served to propel black entrepreneurs towards modernity, sanctioning their breaking time-honoured but confining social and economic customs. Thus, as an economic process, indigenisation provided a trajectory enabling blacks to embrace social and business practices that derived from outside the African continent. The revised term also referenced a politics of location that problematised the European presence by recovering and foregrounding socioeconomic and historical referents of the colonial encounter, at the same time as it juxtaposed the whites' place of origin with their place of current residence. Thus, the narrative established the borders of legitimate connection and placement by privileging historical origins and shared cultural resources (Brah 1996:204; Stasiulis and Yuval-Davis 1995:20).

Whites, cognisant that this reading of indigeneity replaced the community suggested in the discourse of national reconciliation with themes of division and persistent conflict, produced an alternative representation of the indigene. They arrogated indigeneity to themselves on the basis of birth and love of the land in order that they too might inhabit the comfortable and privileged space associated with legitimate belonging (Brah 1996:191). Their narrow and neutral image did not, however, enjoy widespread acceptance among the black majority. Whites as colonisers, or the beneficiaries of colonialism, were not disadvantaged by settler rule and were therefore not creditable as indigenes. To overturn the

---

132   *Newsline*, ZBC Radio 1, 24 February 1997.

colonial experience, they must become linguistically, culturally, socially and politically competent in the ways of the black majority and thereby develop cultural concepts that will sustain a permanent identity with Africa (Thornton 1994:12). To quote Chakrabarty[133] against the grain, whites 'to survive, should learn to speak in the [new] master's voice, and educate themselves in the conqueror's ways' and, in effect, develop the double consciousness of the once colonised (Young 2001a:274). Having failed, however, to demonstrate cultural affiliation in these ways, white Zimbabweans were described as non-indigenous and therefore not legitimately connected to the land. They were considered to be improperly placed and to have a home elsewhere to which they could always return.

---

133 Anthropology Seminar Programme 2000, The Australian National University, Canberra.

7. The loss of certainty

The affective relations of national identity and changes to the white sense of belonging since independence brought with it the renegotiation of subjectivity are discussed in this chapter. Ethnographic evidence indicates that a prior sense of being properly located and at home can give way or dissipate in the light of civil war, the reworking of national narratives and widespread emigration (Borneman 1992; Loizos 1981:130–2; Mamdani 1973). Accordingly, Gupta (1992:76) nominates that the structures of feeling that bind space, time and memory in the production of location should be studied in order to establish how certain spaces become, or cease to be, conceived as homelands. White Zimbabweans generally spoke of the slippage in associating their identity with the place Zimbabwe in tropes related to the loss of kin and community, changing cultural landscapes and a sense of 'the end of our history' generated by the process of land dispossession described in the previous chapter. Each of these will be examined below. The experience of compatriots, who, having imagined their homeland from afar, returned after independence to live in the place as home again, is then addressed. Towards the end of the chapter, steps taken by a minority of whites to counter their experiences of decentring and deracination and regain a sense of belonging in the country are outlined.

Homelessness: the loss of family and community

In Rhodesia, as in other colonial societies, the master narrative of progress reworked the physical space of the territory into which the Europeans moved, enabling and justifying their domination (Betts 1998:82). Earlier chapters referred to the pride taken in the country's development, which reflected the intense bonding between the settlers and the place Rhodesia. They had, in effect, made Rhodesia their home by naming and building. Doubling between self and place was part of the ideological work that situated the settlers at the centre, allowing them to claim, and hold onto, a homeland. The seeming naturalness of their geographical markers, coupled with the ability of later generations of Rhodesians to unselfconsciously 'step into' them, reflected settler hegemonic power (George 1996:6). Centring moments such as these offered a sense of themselves as 'at home' and belonging, and gave rise to the feeling of their being securely and properly located (Radcliffe and Westwood 1996:163).

However Rhodesia as a place had ceased to exist politically by 1980. The impending birth of Zimbabwe called into question the 'easy alliance' (Carter et al. 1993:viii) between the place and Rhodesian identity and brought in its wake significant white emigration. How did informants make sense of this turn of events and where responsibility for it lay?

One who fought for Rhodesia offered this explanation:

> The war made us all the same, made one family of us. You'd mourn for a family in another part of the country that you'd never met. Call it the enemy complex. The rest of the world was against us, not a friend in sight. It made us a very tight community in a small country. We did not think we would lose the war so we did not anticipate mass emigration; it did not occur to us that this was possible. It was only in the last year or so of the war that the question in the armed forces became 'where are you going?'. And now indigenous whites are being denied their birthright.

A civilian concurred with this assessment, saying:

> Whites did not anticipate that the end of the war and independence would lead to their families being dispersed. First, many did not think we would lose and, more importantly, did not think, in fact never dreamt, the country would fall into the hands of Mugabe. Ordinary whites were getting the wrong signals from the police and the Rhodesian forces. I went to one of their briefing sessions out at Norton [a commercial farming area near Harare]. We were told 'Don't worry, everything is under control', so whites weren't considering the implications of independence.

The white community appears to have been mentally unprepared—caught on the wrong foot as it were—at the end of the war. The departure of almost half their number in a matter of a few years[1] prompted some rethinking of the link between self, home and community, and, with the loss of family and friends, meaningful relationships with the locale began to give way. An elderly couple described the process whereby the place became 'unhomely' (Bhabha 1994:9) in the following terms:

> Prior to 1979 we were a family of 52 people, mostly living around the Harare area. All but four have gone, leaving me [the wife] alone. The place has become foreign; it no longer feels like home...friends say to us, 'Why do you want to leave, your friends are more important than your family?' We don't agree.

A year after this conversation, the couple packed up and left Zimbabwe. A friend reiterated the details of their failed application to emigrate, yet determination

---

[1] Every year for the decade 1975–84 saw between 10 000 and 20 000 whites exiting the country, with 1980–84 being peak years (Dumbutshena 1993).

to join a daughter in Australia and remain there, illegally if need be, once their tourist visas expired. He said, explaining their actions, 'We should not underestimate her [the wife's] sense of disorientation in the new Zimbabwe; it had become a foreign land to her.' She had 'lost her home when the country changed its name' and symbolically joined its identity with the black African states of the region. The couple's sense of dasein, of oneness with the place (Dallmayr 1993:151), dissolved with the nation's changing externalities and the disintegration of their extended family. In much the same way, the informant who pleaded without success for her siblings to take up local citizenship in 1985, and was now the only member of her natal family remaining in Zimbabwe, found that

> loss of my family is almost visceral. I need to be in close physical proximity to them. Before email, my family took on an almost dream-like quality, but email has helped. I have their photos on the computer. Email has changed my relationship with them; they have become more real. We visit every few years. I ask myself how does my husband put up with that? The cost of getting the two of us there and back [to Australia] equates to half my net annual salary.[2]

In this instance, advances in worldwide communication technology proved recuperative, allowing the informant to 'come home' by recreating links between people across a variety of sites. She lived, almost simultaneously, in several places (Hobsbawm 1991:66), offsetting somewhat the psychological pain of finding herself 'left behind'. In other cases, migration, as a process of social exclusion, made for bitterness and rivalry within families when some applications to emigrate were rejected while other family members were accepted and left for countries elsewhere.

Not everyone felt this degree of loss. Describing herself as a realist, a woman of Irish descent referred to the illusion of family stability when she said 'it's best if the kids go, we'll miss them but the Irish are travellers'. She, a relative newcomer, having arrived in Rhodesia in the mid 1960s on an assisted passage, continued: 'We did the same to our mothers. The young are just repeating what we did before them.' More philosophically, an older woman saw 'migration as a sacrifice parents make for the next generation. I have not a single blood relative left in Zimbabwe. Home is where the family is, but friends substitute for family.' A third person, present at the same gathering where the offspring of almost all the 30-odd guests were 'out of the country', chimed in: 'I've known everyone

---

2 A year later, because of 'the significant and persistent' slide in the local currency after the war veterans' payout in November 1997, international airlines and some cross-border bus companies had begun to quote fares in US dollars—soon to be called the parallel rate—almost doubling them overnight.

in this room for at least 35 years. That's community, that's why I don't leave.' The investment in relationships and routines developed over half a lifetime produced a sense of security and substance for her.

Each critical moment of white nationalism had, however, coincided with a wave of mass emigration. 'We debated it at every crisis,' proffered one speaking for many, 'we seem to have lived our whole lives with a wait-and-see attitude.' And, once out of the country, they dated each other by the historical events that marked their exit. These episodes threw into question the survival of the white homeland, its uncertain future reflected in its inability to keep its European population. In view of this, family relationships provided an important frame of reference for most informants and a metaphor expressing commitment and association. For 'the lucky ones', it was a source of pride to have 'all the children in the country', something by which one knew oneself 'to be blessed', although this perception was to change during the late 1990s. In the absence of family, however, a feeling of community provided others with the comforts and security of home. In view of this, the departures of people of one's own kind impacted not simply on close relatives, it resonated more generally throughout white society. An informant said of the situation in 1983: 'We felt the pressure to leave. I remember counting 40 sets of friends who had left. We felt we should also. I'd look out the window and think how can I leave this beautiful place, but I must.'

The woman also recalled being shocked at a dinner

> when a couple, also leaving like us, ran the country down. I did not do that, neither did my husband, not even to each other. We left very publicly with farewell parties given by old friends I could not imagine never seeing again, flashlight photos taken just in case. Returning was not difficult for we had not criticised the country. Fortunately we had not run the country down.

The narrative suggests the decision of others to emigrate tempers the sense of belonging and placement of those staying put because the act of emigration not unusually begins 'as the renunciation of the country' (Foerster quoted in King 1995:36). In a second instance, a young, semi-skilled man who, recognising that life was not necessarily any easier elsewhere, described himself as 'having thrown in my lot with the country', still found himself unsettled by a friend

> who could have made it here, but left in 1998. His departure gave rise to an outpouring of criticism towards life in Zimbabwe and the government…it's a way for those leaving to deal with the pain and justify their decision to go. But it sends ripples through the community. The problem for us remaining is that much of the criticism is true or real.

Calling attention to the country's blighted nature is particularly unsettling for the elderly and unskilled, some of whom find themselves being left behind or abandoned. An eighty-year-old mused, 'Never in my wildest dreams did I think I would be the last one left here.' Elderly informants worried about the imminent closure of their various clubs, which had provided some sense of stability and permanence (Malkki 1997:90):

> The bridge club because people, especially the elderly, do not feel safe driving at night, and the sailing and gliding clubs are too expensive. They will likely collapse because of our falling community numbers and little black interest in these particular hobbies [in contrast with tennis or golf]. There are just too few people with the energy to put into running these clubs.

Acerbic comments, such as 'we're an endangered species' and 'would the last one to leave please turn the lights off', reveal the perception of a failing community among a younger section of white society. One of their number remarked:

> Émigrés have sapped the strength of the white community and robbed it of expertise and skills. If everyone had stayed and stuck together then we would not have lost the war. They damaged the cohesion and pull-together attitude that the war inevitably fostered. But the camaraderie was disappearing, even before 1979.

In effect, the exodus, occurring in anticipation of the transfer of sovereignty, drained the white community of its lifeblood, leaving it changed. The sense of community as an extension of home, or home on a somewhat larger scale (George 1996:9), appeared to be giving way.

As an aside, it is worth noting that only a few people found themselves in the enviable position of feeling properly and securely located in Rhodesia. Others not part of the dominant European collective had never enjoyed an uncomplicated sense of belonging, of being at home, either in the past or currently. For instance, the young Indian businessman grateful to his great-grandfather for 'opening opportunities' by moving from one national space to another said, 'I've lived here all my life but I don't have a home.' Neither the place called Rhodesia nor the one called Zimbabwe provided a focus of significant feelings for him. How had this come about? In Rhodesia, as in other settler states, immigration and citizenship policies were built around the presumption that 'only those who embodied or could be assimilated to the culture and values' (Stasiulis and Yuval-Davis 1995:15, 21) of the dominant group were perceived as legitimate settlers and citizens. Asians did not qualify in this sense (Clements 1969:60), nor, in pre-independence black-nationalist writing, were Asians regarded as having a home in Rhodesia (Stigger 1970:3). Thus, they, like Memmi (1965:xxi), who belonged to colonial Tunisia's more or less privileged Jewish minority, found themselves 'excluded from the active structuring processes, confined to a view of the world which always decentres them' (Shurmer-Smith and Hannan 1994:3), set apart by the colonists at the same time as they were not accepted by the dispossessed majority.

Since 1980, the Zimbabwean Government has demanded evidence of commitment and loyalty from this 'fence-sitting' minority before willingly conceding them a home. The businessman continued:

> I'm Indian and I'm proud of it. But as an Indian I'm not welcome here nor in the UK. I returned [after studying in the United Kingdom] ready to invest heavily in the country. In fact, I began to do so. My wife said, 'Think carefully.' She was not as optimistic about Zimbabwe's future. While I don't think minorities will be kicked out, as in Uganda, indigenisation has certainly made life harder for us. It's the wrong concept. As a businessman, I put in 100 per cent effort, but the emergent businesspeople and the government treat me with contempt.

Like the overseas Chinese described by Ong (1993:771), this informant described his subjectivity as de-territorialised in relation to any particular country. Instead, extended family and community links, grounded in worldwide business and social networks, provided him with a sense of identity and belonging. And, following in his great-grandfather's footsteps, the informant was ready to move to other advantageous locations. In place of home thoughts, he offered a ditty recited by his sisters: 'Close your eyes, imagine you're in heaven; open your eyes, you're in Perth.' Perth, a place of future possibility, perceived as a sunny, clean city with little traffic congestion, invariably reminded informants from all races of Salisbury in the old days. While the businessman's sisters made Perth sound like paradise, he was nonetheless fearful of meeting racism in Australia, where he hoped to 'pass as Mediterranean', but his wife, 'imported six years ago from India' and still resident in Zimbabwe on a temporary visa, could not. Having lived abroad, he was aware that Australia, like the United Kingdom and other host societies, could have its own disadvantages.

After the compulsory acquisition of white farms late in 1997 and the subsequent sharp fall in the value of Zimbabwe's currency,[3] white parents had with renewed

---

3   The currency began to 'exhibit volatility' on the heels of the war veterans' payout and the announcement of compulsory land acquisition in November 1997. On 14 November 1997, the date that became known as Black Friday, the Zimbabwean dollar began a sharp decline, losing half its value in the next eight weeks (*The Economist*, 24 January 1998, p. 48). Its value tumbled again nine months later, reflecting a general lack of confidence in the government's management of the economy. Public anxiety regarding the dwindling foreign exchange reserve—rumoured to amount to about one month's import cover—was exacerbated by factors such as Zimbabwe's entry into the war in the Congo in August 1998, the collapse of Boka's United Merchant Bank as well as pressure on the South African rand (*The Herald*, 1 October 1998, p. 13).

vigour urged the younger generation to emigrate. In hindsight, a grandmother described those who faced censure and left in the 1970s as 'the brave ones' and credited them with making 'the right decision'. Contemptuous terms such as 'the chicken run', 'gapping it' and 'the Beitbridge 500'[4] had long lost their sting. Yet she said, 'the whites who remained after independence were Zimbabweans. You never heard people of my generation or even 10 years my senior talking about going "home" to the UK.'[5] The grandmother spoke here for an older generation of European women who by their very presence and willingness to break ties with 'the mother country' had made Rhodesia a white homeland (Kirkwood 1984:143).

At the same time, parents accused state leaders of employing threatening rhetoric, using terms such as 'children of Britain' that erased national belonging by 'reducing the adversary to biological' heritage (Anderson 1990:135), thereby 'driving out our children' and 'creating a Zimbabwean diaspora'.[6] Putting aside the social status attached to 'pioneer ancestors' and the negative perception of Britain described in Chapter 1, the ability to claim a British grandparent was proving to be of some practical use. The young who departed for the United Kingdom, however, found it 'an unknown country' and 'a very foreign place' and many, parents reported, hoped to move onwards to New Zealand and then to Australia. Parents therefore conjured up images of trauma and forced separation (Brah 1996:193) also suggested in the Central African Building Society (CABS) 'Saying of the day', broadcast each morning on national radio. An ironic verse, supplied by an emigrant now living in Queensland, Australia, went 'Home is not where you live, but where they understand you live'.[7] The contributor alludes to the perception that the loss of white locatedness, or sense of being 'not home', arises directly out of Zimbabwe's political process, when court judgements refute that a white appellant's 'necessary domicile', or domicile of origin, is coextensive with the domicile of choice (Hollander 1991:34).

Locally, the window of business opportunity, which had opened with economic liberalisation and trade deregulation, began to close as the government turned away from these policies, moving in the late months of 1998 to re-impose price controls and peg the value of the local currency.[8] Consumer goods and communication facilities that had become available with economic reform, and

---

4 Beitbridge is situated at a border crossing with South Africa.
5 I heard this phrase only once during fieldwork, uttered by an elderly woman going to visit her daughter. She was ridiculed and roundly castigated by her friends and news of her *faux pas* spread around the room.
6 'Home sweet home?', *The Financial Gazette,* 11 March 1993, p. 4.
7 ZBC Radio 1, 2 November 1998.
8 Zimbabwe adopted a floating exchange rate in 1994 as part of its economic liberalisation. On 15 January 1999, however, the Governor of the Reserve Bank, in an effort to stabilise the dollar, announced that the exchange rate would be pegged at Z$40 to the US dollar and Z$70 to the pound sterling. Companies would again have to apply for approval to obtain foreign exchange. The black market for foreign currency, which had operated during the 1980s and all but disappeared with economic liberalisation, reappeared.

that allowed the middle class some geographical, psychic and cultural multi-locality, started to disappear.[9] An informant who had returned to Zimbabwe when business confidence was good, 'arriving at the brink on April Fools' Day 1996', reflected a few years later, 'we've come full circle, we're back to the austerity years' of UDI and beyond—'not an attractive prospect'. For others, insularity, 'the thought of going back to the pre-1990s', is 'dreadful; as the dollar weakens we'll become isolated again'. More senior whites, who had referred to themselves as 'economic prisoners' during the 1980s, indicating they would not entertain leaving because they were not permitted to take assets out of the country,[10] found themselves to be 'prisoners' in a new sense with inflation[11] and the devaluation of the currency. However, an earlier emigrant now successfully relocated having 'put down roots and made a home' in Australia, on a return trip to her place of birth as a visitor but not yet a tourist (Taylor 1992:86), astutely noted:

---

9 Rising input costs (particularly imported components, fuel and electricity), wages and inflation, and the government's policy about-turn, all contributed to an economic recession and the reappearance of shortages, affecting in one way or another all Zimbabweans. Urban–rural remittances decreased as a result of rising living costs and higher unemployment in towns (MacGarry 1994a:24). The greater costs of transport and groceries made the 'month's end' trip home increasingly difficult for urban workers, who were unable to provide the gifts of money and goods that are an essential part of these visits. This inevitably created tension between rural and urban-based relatives.

10 The export of assets and capital had long been a bone of contention. The *Exchange Control Act* determined the export of goods by emigrants and holiday allowances payable to external travellers. Currency restrictions and limits on exporting household goods, put in place during the Rhodesian era, were tightened in 1981 and again in 1985 because emigrants were buying new household effects in order to evade exchange control restrictions on the export of currency. Thus, goods with a high foreign currency content, such as cars, electrical goods and lounge and dining suites, had to be more than four years old and used before they could be exported. This promoted illegal activities by resentful citizens and accusations of economic sabotage by authorities (see *Parliamentary Debates*, 26 August 1981, cols 1397–408, 1 September 1981, cols 1489–501; *The Herald*, 28 August 1981, p. 3, 7 January 1985, p. 3, 13 April 1985, p. 1). More recently, many émigrés had not declared their intentions to depart permanently in order to avoid the restrictions imposed by the *Exchange Control* and *Citizenship Acts*. To officially emigrate, applicants were required to lodge details of their belongings with a local bank. Where appropriate, the bank would approach the Reserve Bank Exchange Control Department for permission to export assets on behalf of its client. The Reserve Bank ruled on the ceilings allowed and the sum was discretionary. Should an applicant sell a major asset such as a house, the proceeds had to be placed in government bonds. If a house was not sold, the title deeds should be lodged with the bank—a process known as 'leaving the house in the custody of the bank'. Informants believed 'applicants can only lose; it's a power game'. Hence, many left unofficially—a logical decision given the increase in the holiday allowances to US$5000 in 1998, making this a larger sum than the allowances permitted emigrants. By 2001, however, the value of the holiday allowance had become a moot point as the extreme shortage of foreign currency—with import cover down to one week's reserve (*The Financial Gazette*, 20 May 2001, p. 1)—made lodging an application a fruitless exercise.

11 At the time, inflation figures were a matter of dispute in Zimbabwe. While the Central Statistics Office compiled an average consumer price index (CPI) for urban areas that indicated year-on-year inflation of about 30 per cent (*The Herald*, 13 June 1998, p. 6), this rate was generally met with scepticism. During my fieldwork, critics noted that the basket of goods used for this purpose was outdated, and further, urban prices did not necessarily reflect prices paid outside the main cities (MacGarry 1994a:6). Banks produced quarterly reports that suggested inflation was higher. These sources indicated rates of about 35 per cent in mid 1998, rising towards the end of the year and throughout 1999 to more than 40 per cent (*Business Herald*, 30 July 1998, p. 4; *Zimbabwe Independent*, 11 December 1998, p. 4). While all Zimbabweans were painfully aware of the erosion of their purchasing power, the rural and urban poor were least able to protect themselves from price increases. Inflation thus served to increase the gap between income groups.

Leaving is no longer a decision many need to make. The choice has been taken from them by immigration cutbacks and unemployment in Australia.[12] At the moment when they probably want to make this decision more than at any time in the last 18 years the decision is no longer available, or theirs to make.

Changing landscapes and cultural dissonance

The new national geography, appearing during the first decade of independence and reflecting the 'shifting topography of power', ineluctably changed the nature of the white community's relationship with the place (Gupta and Ferguson 1992:10; Massey 1992:11). As the government took back the country, whites found they no longer fitted its landscape. While I was in the field, the urban landscape was also altering in other significant ways. Many whites reflected upon the ever-more unfamiliar face of Harare's suburbs in which they lived, where hawkers of every description abounded. The changing scenery was a direct result of the repeal of Rhodesian local authority by-laws, which had authorised small-trader activity only in particular areas and thereby restricted participation in the informal economy to certain non-white areas of the city. Few informants, however, made a connection between their being confronted by another side of the city and the policy of indigenisation, outlined in the previous chapter. Instead, whites read the changing urban landscape as symptomatic of the country's more general deterioration and a daily reminder that they lived in the unregulated and untidy developing world. They had a sense of historical decline, a departure from a golden age (Turner 1987:150), against which Zimbabwe's contemporary situation was measured and found wanting.

In addition, whites referred to their perception of being 'stranded' and 'cut off' from the West. For instance, an employee of an international freight company worried that 'the distance between the technologically efficient Western world and Zimbabwe is increasing. Zimbabwe is becoming broken down and tatty.' For others, there was a growing sense of shame and disintegration. One remarked, 'It's the going down that is so painful. It would perhaps be easier if the country had always been down.' A younger woman, descended from French Huguenots,[13] voiced both frustration and estrangement when she said, 'I know we're in Africa, I know this is a Third-World country, but economically we were streets ahead of all other countries in the region at independence. The country had so much potential.' Reference to the country's 'potential', its

---
12   See Castles and Iredale 1994.
13   The Huguenots were French Protestants who left Europe during the 1600s to escape religious persecution, the first of whom established themselves in South Africa in the late 1680s.

capacity to become an economic hub in sub-Saharan Africa, reflects the white reading of the colonial past described towards the end of Chapter 3. She, like many others, expected the country's development to follow the European and colonial pattern. Finding this not to be the case, 'Third World' is the name, the representation, the informant gives to a location (Gupta and Ferguson 1997a:89) where she cannot imagine her identity being realised, where she is, in effect, 'not home'.

The nation's 'failure' to mimic the Western modernising narrative evinced in the headmaster of a private school a sense of being misplaced. This perception surfaced when a black parishioner, resisting the colonial civilising mission in which the European participant 'invariably knows best' (Chakrabarty 2000:28; Gandhi 1998:28), passed comment at a church meeting that 'we prefer black disorder to white order'. The headmaster and his wife had assumed that blacks shared their cultural values and that 'order', as part of the colonial code, was valued by both ruler and ruled (Nandy 1983:2). Whites commonly overlooked the fact that independence, as an act of sovereignty, meant remaining Europeans would reside on African terms. Henceforth, as an expatriate lecturer pointed out in the last days of Rhodesia (Hills 1981:167), Zimbabwe would be run as representatives of the black majority saw fit. The headmaster's confusion suggested that previously he had enjoyed some certainty regarding where he belonged. 'Now,' he remarked, 'I've come to feel that they don't want us here.' He had been 'at home' when others shared his habits and the sense of order that regulated life in Rhodesia and he had felt confident of the location's agreed values. As Shurmer-Smith and Hannan (1994:3) tellingly point out:

> [T]he world is a more comfortable place when the legitimized view of it coincides with one's own interests, when one perceives oneself to be at the centre and others at the margins, when one's own notions of hierarchy, morality, order and intelligence do not have to be strenuously defended at every turn.

Twenty years on found the headmaster disoriented and unsettled, aware that his values no longer equipped him to be a competent member of his religious congregation.

The sense of disconnectedness had come about rather differently for more liberally minded whites, as a result, they said, of 'our too high expectations'. One who identified with the causes of the black majority said, 'At first Mugabe seemed to have his finger on the pulse, he had the people's needs at heart. We had high hopes for his administration but these evaporated as the leadership lost sight of its goals.' A second[14] described at greater length her hopes of a better life for all, something she had worked for in a voluntary capacity over the preceding two decades.

> I'm old fashioned; home for me is being connected to my blood relations [although none remains in Zimbabwe]. I'm 'home' when I have aunts, uncles, grandparents and grandchildren around me to offer support and share the joys. For me, it's not a place thing at all. I had a home in Rhodesia and then Zimbabwe when the kids were here. We realised around independence that they would probably go—a gloomy prospect but we have accepted that they should. Now Zimbabwe is somewhere we reside, not more.

There was, however, more to her sense of homelessness than simply the departure of her children, as she went on to explain:

> We were longing for independence, we thought it would be wonderful, but it's just been a disappointment. Our dream was that independence would bring a better chance for the downtrodden; we were not comfortable with being a privileged minority, I am uncomfortable even now. For the first decade, I kept hope of a better future alive. But from the 1990s, the dream kept getting further away. I felt the situation in mid 1998 could lead to upturn and change. But we got to the end of the year and I became ill as nil had happened. All we had was increased repression. I can't bury my head and keep out of social issues, which is the advice friends give us. I'm angry that the [Anglican] Church has not stood up and issued statements about the situation here. The CCJP has done the most, but other religious bodies have not backed them up. My connectedness has died; we have become disappointed and disillusioned due to unfulfilled hopes. A small group of white Rhodies and black extremists make the trouble. I have no time for either, but they get the media coverage. Then you have the disillusioned blacks, the mass of poverty-stricken people. I can see no way they can get out of poverty. This is a country of no hope. I want to be part of a country of hope.

Hope had offered a hypothetical route for this woman's homecoming, the cessation of her sense of alienation with an end to black poverty and lack of privilege, the vision transcending the past and closing the door on colonial history.

---

14   This informant had just completed 20 years of voluntary work, most of it in homes for needy children and with a programme for the destitute run by the Anglican Church. Unlike many whites, she took on these projects after independence, at a time when other whites had resigned from charitable organisations.

Hopes of change had come for many liberals with the formation of the National Constitutional Association (NCA) in May 1997. With a broad civic membership that embraced church and women's groups, businesspeople, professionals, farmers and students as well as NGOs and human rights representatives, the association encouraged public participation in constitutional reform and in addressing the economic and political challenges facing the country. By June 1998, with Morgan Tsvangirai in the chair, the NCA was poised to enter reform politics. In July, the organisation submitted a paper to the government setting out its proposals. In October, however, negotiations with the government received a major setback when riot police broke up a peaceful NCA demonstration protesting Zimbabwe's involvement in the war in the Congo while also pressing the need for constitutional change (Kagoro 2004:241–8). With hopes for a better life for the majority still unrealised, liberal attachment to the country weakened. Recognising this, conservatives pointed out that they, with fewer expectations, adjusted more readily to majority rule. Blacks, no less than conservative whites, were also critical of liberal positioning. They noted that white liberals had failed to demonstrate the acts of identification, described earlier, that were required of 'active' citizens. Black radicals perceived liberals to be, at best, irrelevant to the new nation and at worst 'enemies of black liberation'[15] (Mandaza 1995:31). They attributed ulterior motives to voluntary work as liberal 'good intentions' were seen as racist and paternalistic and an integral part of the imperial system of power (Mafeje 1996:35). All in all, therefore, white liberals have not found their home in Zimbabwe to be a more comfortable place than in Rhodesia—something they had generally not foreseen in the run-up to 1980.

Coming home but 'not home'

During the first two decades of independence, however, not all whites were thinking about leaving. Some who were out of the country during the war were making a return journey in order to be part of the new Zimbabwe. And, by the mid 1980s, a few early post-independence emigrants were also on their way back, their return the ultimate rite of passage reflecting, some argued, reconciliation with independent Zimbabwe. Initially, the official reaction was encouraging. In line with the policy of national reconciliation, returnees were depicted as simply having a change of heart and a new appreciation of the good things about life in the country. Their return was taken to reflect well on the government and their skills were needed. Immigration authorities assured Zimbabwean passport holders that they could stay out of the country as long

---

15 Note, for instance, Febion Waniwa's letter 'We don't need white liberals anymore' (*Zimbabwe Independent*, 20 September 1996, p. 5). Every now and again, however, white liberals were thanked in particular for bringing world attention to bear on the Matabeleland massacres. See also 'We thank you white liberals', *Zimbabwe Independent*, 11 October 1996, p. 5.

as they liked, while permanent residents could be away continuously for seven years before their immigration status was jeopardised. The relationship with the land they called their home country had not been broken and all had an automatic right of re-entry.[16] Certainly, informants coming back in the 1980s had little trouble re-entering Zimbabwe. Permanent residents were told they 'could move around, and in and out, of the country like citizens'.[17] Thus, access to the national territory was conferred on all returnees, the only substantive difference between them being that permanent residents, unlike citizens, could face deportation.

How had informants on the way back—having imagined home in Africa from a distance—found living in the place as home again? In the following passage, a conscientious objector relates the experience of departure from his homeland and return more than a decade and a half later:

> I left in 1969 to go to Cape Town University. It was very hard to come home during the '70s because the army would pick me up. After two and a half years, I dropped out. When I realised I could not come home permanently, it broke my heart. I went to the UK from the Cape. My father wanted me to come back and do my duty. But later he relented when it became obvious that the war was not the five-minute affair whites initially expected. As people began getting killed, both parents changed their attitudes and supported my decision. But my heart was always in Africa, my family, and my roots. I always knew my sojourn overseas was temporary and that I would come back once the war was over and the country settled. I never had any doubt about this but my wife was less sure; she could have lived in the UK or Australia, though she came round once our first child was born. I did not like the British class-consciousness nor their racism—they never let me feel at home there. Getting back here was a long process. There were a number of changes making up a phase of my life. I had to sell property in the UK. I'd bought a house and then renovated it over two years. It was outrageously modern. I lived in it for six years but never attached to it, never put down roots. The house was featured in an English magazine called *House and Garden*, but I sold it and walked away without looking back. The sale represented my ticket home, the wherewithal to get back and set up a business. Arriving back was in many ways a non-event. My father had died, my brothers had emigrated and friends scattered to all corners of the world. There are very few around now. It's like 'Oh, I'm home', but there's no response. The white community will perhaps turn into a small but unique community. It will not be absorbed, but remain

---

16   'Dozens who "took the gap" applying to come back', *The Herald*, 5 April 1985, p. 3.
17   Zimbabwe Department of Information, 22 October 1984, p. 3.

separate partly because the powers that be keep impressing on the black majority how different we are. We could belong if this stopped. But, should the white community get as small as that in Kenya or Zambia, then we will try to go to Australia.

The man had sustained memories of home from afar and the sense of belonging in Africa throughout his time overseas. Yet, while yearning to return to something that once was, he discovered his home had altered in his absence. His recollections reflect the tension of being simultaneously 'home' and yet finding himself 'not home' in light of his father's death and the absence of friends. The place of his desire had become a place of no return (Brah 1996:192). His wife, returning to her place of origin as neither citizen nor stranger, proffered:

> We wanted independence and peace to return to our home, and were glad that chaos did not follow the end of the war. But we did not anticipate migration dividing our families. Many parents now have a child on every continent. Home for me is a longing, a sense of belonging. It's very important. It's a gut thing, lots of little things rolled into one, that make you feel secure. My concept is very local—a house with a garden. I returned when my home country had sorted itself out. But I find I have no right to live here. My home has been taken from me.

The informant conflates the terms home and home country, suggesting the intersection of public and private, individual and communal that George (1996:11) argues is implicit in imaging a space as home. Conceiving of home as a place of refuge, however, she found the old, settled coherence had given way. The home to which she had returned no longer felt comfortable, for the location had been appropriated in her absence. Now classified as a 'foreign spouse', she admitted to mixed feelings about putting the effort into trying to make Zimbabwe her home again.

This informant's experience of homecoming contrasts sharply, however, with that of another woman, pregnant with her second child, for whom the essential elements of her conception of home have not proved transportable (Read 1999:36). She had never 'arrived' in Australia and, when her husband was 'invited'—or, in the words of another wife, 'enticed'—back while on holiday by his former mates with promises of a job and help with finding a place to live, they returned in 1996. The informant spoke of this in specifically domestic terms, choosing not to dwell on home as a metaphor for social relations on the broader, national scale:

> I felt very isolated [in Perth] when I heard a friend, the first of my group, was pregnant. My husband also likes to share our friends' children, to know them as they grow up, to be part of their lives. I was depressed

> that I would not share those kids. That was the main reason we came back. In Australia, it's not cool once you're a teenager to spend time with the family. Here we holiday together, and eat together regularly—we hang out with our families. There was no problem returning as we hadn't officially emigrated and we only have Zimbabwean passports. I refuse to worry about the longer term. If there's a coup we can leave again. We can start all over; we've done it before, we can do it again. But our friends were shocked by our decision [to return]. They asked why were we 'so stupid'. We've been back 18 months now and we're still asked, 'Are you happy you're back?' There are a lot of post-mortems.

Relationships with family and friends provided the fundamental meaning to the young mother's life (Jackson 1995:56) and underpinned her sense of being 'at home' again in Zimbabwe. Economic liberalisation, outlined in Chapter 6, gave this couple and other younger whites the chance to return, some re-entering the country under the government's new investor provisions. But, while the couple was welcomed back by those they knew, and parents spoke of 'getting our family back together' or 'getting the children back', white strangers were more critical, saying

> those who return say they're back for the children, that this is a wonderful place to grow up. But that's a rationalisation. They want an easy life; they're lazy, incapable of change or working hard. Imagine being given a gift like that [entry to Australia] and throwing it away! Grab the chance with both hands!

Here the speaker intimates failure on the young mother's behalf and alludes to compelling pressures working against return. Yet critics such as this overlook that the place of one's origins represents the bedrock of identity in childhood (Taylor 1992:92)—something captured by a young man when he justified Zimbabwe as his home on the grounds that 'I grew up here, I went to school here, I broke my arm here, I have friends here, it's all I know'. During their absence, returnees, like their Newfoundland counterparts (Gmelch 1983:50; Richling 1985:243, 246), continued to think of Zimbabwe as their homeland and many wished to live near their families. They commonly re-experienced an acute sense of bonding with the place, of coming home at border crossings, with one describing how 'we always felt we'd got home once we'd crossed the bridge over the Limpopo [River, at Beitbridge]. We'd relax. South Africa is a much tenser place.' Even at the height of the civil war, many found a 'striking change of atmosphere' as the frontier with South Africa was crossed (Hudson 1981:195). A second, returning from Australia, said, 'I *know* I'm home when I touch down and meet the immigration officials. Harare is no battery-run airport. But before that, I *feel* I'm home, looking down to see if the grass is green, has there been rain, are the dams full.' She contrasts the personal and impersonal, the disorderly versus the efficient (Australian) airport, before sharing every Zimbabwean's obsession with the seasonal quality of the rains. This was the landscape in which she grew up and she was grounded by its setting. It is her emotional experience and what has shaped her.

Another, finding his 'travelling' home unsatisfactory, also took the opportunity provided by economic liberalisation to return. The young man had been taken from Zimbabwe as an adolescent in the early 1980s after his parents' divorce, but returned on holiday each year as part of the custody arrangements. He elected to return on a permanent basis as a young adult in search of a location that was more stable, or fixed, in which he could again be 'at home'. His narrative, however, suggested that he too was disturbed by the sense of finding himself 'not home', his hopes dashed in part by political realities. Speaking metaphorically, he said:

> My home for the last five years has been a canvas bag, a tent. It would probably have been better if I had left at age thirteen and never come back. I'm torn between two countries; it is a daily crisis I live with. I feel at home here as soon as I arrive at the airport, and see the Africans on the streets and climbing into ETs [emergency taxis]. I spent my childhood here, it is familiar, I know many people, black and white; it's a face-to-face community. In Australia, you have to get your information from the Yellow Pages; it's anonymous and impersonal. I never felt at home in Perth, another reason being that it lacked history, it felt like nothing important had ever happened there. History is an anchoring point for being at home. Harare has history. A battle took place on the site of my old primary school and in the surrounding region there are many remains of early Shona settlements. History is also important to my sense of identity; it helps me with who I am, locates me in the scheme of things. Trees are important too. Then there was two-faced Australian racism. In outback Western Australia, I've seen bars for Aboriginals and bars for whites. But Australians have the nerve to be critical of things in Zimbabwe. They come here as tourists to scrutinise and judge, all by Australian and CNN standards. In Africa, we live in the real world, with real poverty and real suffering. The international community holds double standards also. They didn't criticise Mugabe for sending tanks into Chitungwiza during the riots.[18] Returning has put me in an aggressive mode. I'm very upset by the government's white conspiracy theories. Even the people in the communal areas don't blame the whites for all the problems. It's orchestrated from the top. I know my [economic]

---

18   While tanks and troops were deployed extensively throughout Harare's shopping areas after rioting in early 1998, local television had shown a convoy moving along the highway towards the satellite town of Chitungwiza, angering the public, who perceived the State to be 'moving against its own people'.

goals, but the path is blocked. It's a Rubik's cube. But it's better to try at this age [young and unmarried], otherwise I would never [have] known if I could have made a life here. Friends and relatives thought I was mad or 'cooked' to return as all they want to do is get out.

The informant's testimony suggests that home, perhaps contrary to his expectations, is an inherently unstable space. His narrative reflects the ambivalence that comes with the recognition that the coherence, the comfort and safety—the imagined consonance between self and place—are an illusion. He shares the double vision, the crisis of identity, of many returnees. Caught between homes and national affiliations (George 1996:70), he constructed the place of return in part as alien by making strange what was once familiar (Taylor 1992:86). As 'an African', he knows 'real' hardship in a way Westerners do not and is insulted by the ignorance and prejudice of those originating from other settler societies whose colonial histories are no more commendable than his own. At the same time, he was aware that his kind, as perpetrators of the suffering of others (Shurmer-Smith and Hannan 1994:43), could expect little international sympathy on account of their folly or the predicament in which they now found themselves. Nonetheless, he was distressed to find white businessmen unreasonably blamed for 'hatching a plot to make the lives of the masses unbearable' by the Minister of Information, Comrade Chen Chimutengwende, for in effect inciting the countrywide price and food riots in December 1997 and January 1998.[19] The protests in fact marked the breakdown of the contract set at the beginning of economic reform in 1990 between labour, government and employers. While labour had kept its word to belt tighten and accept declining wages, the government had failed to demonstrate its commitment by cutting expenditure or meeting free-market targets (Friedrich Ebert Stiftung/Zimbabwe Economics Society 1998c). Continuing its profligate ways, the government had raised taxes on basic commodities to fund the war veterans' payout and later that year entered the war in the Congo.

The informant's sense of homecoming was also diminished by the inability to recover his former assurance of being 'at home' in Zimbabwe, for, by the year of his return, black attitudes towards returnees had hardened. The indigenisation

---

19 Whites found themselves blamed in remarks made by Comrade Chen Chimutengwende, the Minister of Information, Posts and Telecommunications, and in statements made by the Harare ZANU PF Provincial Office for the price/food riots in December 1997 and January 1998. A joint investigation by the Zimbabwe Economics Society and Friedrich Ebert Stiftung (1998c:2) concluded, however, that these accusations were unfounded. The price rises in maize and other basic food commodities were triggered by several factors. Chief among them were an increase in government sales tax from 2.5 per cent to 17 per cent to finance the war veteran gratuities, an increase in the Grain Marketing Board's (a para-statal) selling price of maize due to seasonal grain shortages and the depreciation of the Zimbabwean dollar against all major currencies ('Minister warns over price hikes', *Sunday Mail*, 11 January 1998, p. 1; 'Looting as food riots hit Harare', *The Herald*, 20 January 1998, p. 1; 'Give whites a break, Chen', *The Financial Gazette*, 29 January 1998, p. 7; 'Government insecurity catalyst for riots', *The Financial Gazette*, 29 January 1998, p. 9).

lobby saw them as competitors, referred to them as 'new immigrants' and opposed the return of supposedly 'large numbers' wanting to come back from Europe, America, Australia and South Africa.[20] The ruling party voiced its concern that 'Rhodesians' were 'in constant touch with each other world-wide, keeping the tribe together, cultivating a sense of community' on the Internet, while 'implanting the idea of [a] return "home" in the younger generation'.[21] Not only were these white messages anti-government, they were also part and parcel of keeping 'Rhodesian' identity alive. Officials were therefore reluctant to let whites come back for they had 'run away from a black government'.[22] By 'rejecting' Zimbabwe's national space for another, seemingly more desirable location, émigrés had effectively 'unwritten' the State's national project (George 1996:186). Inevitably, some applicants found their return path blocked, while whites more generally came to realise that access to one's home country, conceived as a place of origin and imminent return (Hobsbawm 1991:65), was no longer assured. The community began to refer to having 'our birthright cancelled', their sense of displacement 'made emotionally more resonant' through the State's process of othering (Jess and Massey 1995:134).

Homelessness as political process: subject formation and 'the end of our history'

Whites' claims to an automatic right of domicile and the inalienable right to a home on the basis of having been born in the country (see Chapter 5) are rich with connotations of origin and entitlement. Theirs is a conception of home as a place of rightful settlement—a 'natural' right and something one should not have to deserve or defend (Hollander 1991:33). Places, however, as systems of meaning constructed through the production of geographical locatedness, lack fixity and are therefore open to reworking and transformation (Massey 1995a:3; Hall 1995:178). Material presented up to this point suggests that white Zimbabweans, in common with the Ugandan Asians expelled in 1972 by Idi Amin (Mamdani 1973) and the Greek Cypriots who 'lost' their homeland after the 1974 coup and subsequent Turkish invasion of Cyprus (Loizos 1981:120–1), have heard a lot about themselves in policy statements and political speeches. These served to reshape white perceptions of their position in Zimbabwe.

---

20 'Returnees face tough task', *The Daily Gazette*, 1 November 1994, p. 1; 'Many Rhodies undergo a change of heart', *The Sunday Mail*, 11 December 1995, p. 1; 'Proceed with care with new immigrants', *The Herald*, 10 January 1997, p. 8.
21 'Ex-Rhodesians intensify anti-Zimbabwe campaign', *The People's Voice*, 26 July 1998, p. 1.
22 'Many Rhodies undergo a change of heart', *The Sunday Mail*, 11 December 1995, p. 1; *Parliamentary Debates*, 8 May 1996, cols 5135–42.

Contradictory statements made by political leaders led to confusion and rumour and drew whites into a process that shifted their sense of belonging, their unease growing steadily throughout the 1990s.

The government's handling of the land question proved critical in producing 'the break…the maiming' (Breytenbach 1991:74) that psychologically uncoupled whites from what they had thought of as their homeland. A farmer reflected that 'reconciliation was a promise made to minorities that we would be treated like any other citizen. We stayed after independence and did what was asked of us, we kept farming productively.' Indeed, farmers put money into dams and infrastructure as well as worker facilities during the 1990s in order to secure ownership and earn their place in the post-colonial state. They had tried in effect to 'enracinate' themselves by investing their profits in a 'hydrological revolution' described by Hughes (2006a:271) and through developing the land. Their being mobilised in the State's discourse as agents of productivity and economic development had provided farmers with moments of centring and belonging, and situated them within the national project. The informant said, however, that 'land designation represents a broken promise by government; the land question is not just about the past, it is also about our citizenship in the future'. He had put his faith in a civic concept of citizenship that extended legal and administrative protection to the private property of citizens. In common with other whites, he overlooked the fact that, to politically aware blacks, the Western and liberal language of individual rights rang of the defence of settler privilege. Another elderly farmer, alluding to the displacement of his community, which he had hitherto perceived as rooted in particular localities across the country, said, 'It's their continent. I used to think farming was a viable occupation. Not now.' He had also thought of himself as integrated, even indispensable, by virtue of the farmers' contribution to the national economy, only to find this was not so. A third, putting pen to paper with regard to the compulsory acquisition of productive white-owned farms, wrote 'when you take a man's house and his means of production, then you have certainly expelled him psychologically at the very least'.[23]

The farmers' distress was reminiscent of Doris Lessing's sense of loss on learning she had been declared a prohibited immigrant in absentia many years earlier by the Garfield Todd government. She found her exclusion from the land in which she grew up almost impossible to comprehend:

> It never crossed my mind I could be: the impossibility was a psychological fact, nothing to do with daylight realities. You cannot be forbidden the land you grew up in, so says the web of sensations, memories, experience, that binds you to that landscape. (Lessing 1992:11)

---

23 'Mugabe's many colours', *Zimbabwe Independent*, 19 December 1997, p. 6.

In essence, she belonged to Rhodesia and Rhodesia therefore belonged to her (Breytenbach 1991:74). Being designated a prohibited person in 1956 shattered this nexus, reproducing Lessing as 'an exile' and 'forcing a rift between a human being and a native place, between the self and its true home' (Said 1990:357). Returning briefly in 1982, Lessing was asked by a journalist whether she felt she was coming back home. 'Yes,' she said, 'very much so. It's very painful to be locked out of the country you were brought up in' (Katiyo 1982:43). Banished as punishment for her political opinions, Lessing's remarks echo Malkki's (1997:89) perception that exiles can be conceived as people who have 'been driven from their homes', 'disconnected' from what they consider to be 'their natural setting, their cultural home, their indigenous region' and 'their place of origin'.

By the time my research was well under way, many members of the white community had 'neither an unequivocal sense of membership in their community of origin, nor an uncomplicated conviction of having left it behind' (Ferguson 1992:90). A farm manager drew attention to his community's sense of alienation, of being dislodged from national belonging, when he described the situation in Mazowe, an agricultural region close to Harare:

> Only 5 per cent of farmers are reinvesting.[24] Most of us are holding back, unsure of the future. What is happening now has no logic. We attended the local CFU meeting in the district at the end of last year.[25] The reaction of farm owners was [of being] sick and tired. Their sons and farm managers said, 'That's it, I'm off.' Since independence, farmers have been repeatedly knocked down [through, for example, the lack of foreign exchange with which to purchase agricultural equipment, droughts, the tobacco levy, the forthcoming water bill, and so on] and managed to get up again. But I wonder if we will ever come out of this one [land designation]. So many single-owner, productive farms were listed. Why? I can't believe that it was a mistake and they would later be de-listed. I have no problem with the government buying multiple farms but don't just take them. Our citizenship means nothing. The farm workers are devastated. I read the newspapers. I know I am not wanted in my own country. I'm not a first generation; my family [father's side] has been in Africa for generations. We've done a lot for the country. I'm a fatherly figure for my workers and help them with medical facilities, a store and financially on a daily basis. I'm not saying I'm a hero but, while the farm workers appreciate what I am doing, my efforts are

---

24 Banks were also wary of lending to farmers whose property had been designated.
25 After the gazetting of farms for compulsory acquisition in late 1997, the CFU toured the country and addressed closed farmer meetings. Officials explained the implications of compulsory land acquisition and outlined the legal and administrative options open to those affected.

not recognised by government. We're written up in the papers as bad people. Politicians make wild promises that can't be met. This is my home, although the government tries to convince us otherwise.

The farm manager's words suggest that he had 'interiorised' (Brah 1996:115) much that the country's leaders and the media had told him about himself and his difference as a white. The manager's wife averred:

We made our decision to emigrate about nine months ago. At first we kept quiet about it, only telling our parents. Now that it is certain, we're telling more and more people. While some have tried to convince us to stay, to our surprise, many have not. Instead, they say that if they were in our shoes they'd be off; some even tell us they've got their papers in too! Now they tell me! Ours is a joint decision that was prompted by land designation and the price riots. The long term looks too uncertain. Before that we thought we'd always be here. Farming was to be our future and the kids' future. It now seems too risky. Once we started to consider the option, the reasons for leaving snowballed; we found so many reasons to go.

Others candidly admitted to finding 'living with this uncertainty frankly, very difficult', their conception of home as a durable place, a site of some permanence and safety, was rapidly giving way (Rapport 1995:268) with each political crisis—for rural and urban whites alike.

A white urban dweller said:

The sense of gloom and despondency is greater now than in the war. At least in the war we had the chance to win, which kept hope alive. Not now. This is the end of our home and our life here. I have no roots anywhere else. What are the farmers supposed to do?

Compulsory land acquisition, followed by farm invasions by war veterans and their supporters, thus gave rise to despair for these events were read by the white community as the nadir signalling 'the end of our history, the end of hope' and 'the end of our way of life', the spectre of their irrelevance to the country already before them.

Moving on: the search for simultaneity

While arguing for the discursive right to a place in the land, whites were now confronted with a critical question, namely whether it was possible, and if so how, for them to turn the page, leave their once-familiar home and move on. Generally speaking, defensive attitudes held by elderly whites made it difficult for them to think of or imagine a way out of their sense of 'unhomeliness'. Yet around this time there were a number of anti-government protests and mass stay-aways. Standing in 1998 with three elderly women waiting for the local library to open, they had said to each other that 'the current situation can't go on much longer' and 'it will all be over by Christmas'. While their conversational tone was full of anticipation, even eager, they exchanged few concrete ideas regarding how political change would come about or who would replace the current leadership. Instead, most whites held that it was up to disenchanted blacks, rather than themselves, to take the lead in the NCA and support anti-government protests, thereby abdicating responsibility for finding a route out of their deracination. A civil rights activist elaborated upon his compatriots' reluctance to participate:

> Whites here are part of the problem. They live in a laager, moving between Borrowdale, Kariba and such like. They will not recognise their contribution to the government's anger over reconciliation. It is so easy not to do anything on the grounds that the government is angry with them, or the government's own contribution to reconciliation is flawed… they act like victims…it is so easy to complain about the government but they [whites] won't join the opposition parties or the civil rights groups.

He suggests that active engagement could go some way in dispelling the whites' sense of themselves as victims while at the same time supporting their own enracination. But, according to Karen Alexander (2004:194), whites live 'off' rather than 'in' Zimbabwe, picking and choosing what they will allow into their lives. Certainly, the activist acknowledged that he 'knew only about a handful of others who think like I do'. A few high-profile whites, such as Mike Auret of the CCJP, lawyer and human rights activist David Coltart and critic Trudy Stevenson, had refused intimidation and joined in constitutional reform. The NCA's civil rights agenda was, however, dismissed by the ruling party as simply a manifestation of neo-colonialism and they were taunted with belonging to the 'unwanted section of society'.[26] As founding members of a new political party—and in the case of Coltart and Stevenson, soon to be opposition politicians—they also put up with ridicule and heckling at public meetings.

Nonetheless, after land designation, while nothing would be quite the same again, a new drift began to enter the conversation of a few younger whites with no intention of leaving. The optimistic note, commonly heard in the early

---

26 Government representatives took the position that modern transnational civil rights rhetoric espoused by the educated elite found within the CCJP, the Amani Trust and other civil rights groups was nothing more than a neo-colonial imposition, inconsistent with African cultural traditions and an example of white paternalism. See also ZANU PF Harare Province advertisements in *The Herald*, 11 August 1997, p. 8. Instead, the State argued that the rights of individuals should be understood as embedded in the communities to which they belonged.

1990s, that Zimbabwe's problems 'will all pan out' or 'come right in the end', even if the ways and means were obscure, was replaced with assertions of a new realism. For instance: 'I've now come to believe that the country has to hit rock bottom before it will start to turn around', or alternatively, 'I've now got used to the idea that the country will always be like this: politically unstable and with a declining currency'. These informants intimated that while larger political and economic factors appeared beyond their control, they might not be beyond their accommodation (Bhabha 1994:12). Although being 'at home' could no longer be as they had previously known it, the 'end of our history' could perhaps herald a period of homecoming if they were able to let go of the past and embrace the antithesis of all that they had held familiar (George 1996:27).

This idea was taken on board by the 'new breed' of urban white Zimbabweans—notably, those who were younger and openly critical of the 'continual carping' by their parents' generation. Tired of the 'unfair criticism of blacks' and the 'bitter pleasure' evident in stories of how the black government 'has messed it all up', some were ready to get involved in opposition politics. One of this group remarked:

> The current debate on the state of the nation is circumscribed. Whites argue in terms of their needs, not the needs and future of the country as a whole. For example, they don't back the ZCTU [Zimbabwe Confederation of Trade Unions]. It's a good thing if we hit rock bottom, for that's the only way people will learn.

'Hitting rock bottom' would perhaps stimulate critical reflection regarding the state of the country and national goals by all Zimbabweans, and make 'people think Zimbabwean'. This informant implies an interstitial passage (Bhabha 1994:4) for whites, in which the move from one home to another begins with new priorities and ways of thinking that create sets of relationships with the capacity to generate non-hierarchical links between people and places. He and a small number of others put store in experiences of control and connectedness, of homecoming through simultaneity with the black majority, during the turbulent events taking place at the time.

The young man mentioned earlier as having 'thrown his lot in with the country' provides a case in point. He spoke of belonging and not belonging in different urban locales during the first trade unions' day of mass action on 9 December 1997, called to protest the government's proposal to raise taxes in order to finance gratuities and pensions paid to ex-combatants. This protest shut down all commercial and industrial sites across Zimbabwe as well as much of the public sector. Without much forward planning, he had hurriedly closed his business and headed towards Africa Unity Square in central Harare, where demonstrators were converging. Access roads, however, were blocked and he found nowhere to leave his beaten-up, old car.

> There were so many riot police and gas, I felt at risk. I couldn't find a place to park and I can't afford to lose the car. The violence was too much. I wanted to show solidarity with the people. I went home utterly frustrated and impotent. But in the suburbs it was a different story. There was harmony and togetherness. Black and white strangers were smiling and talking to each other, much more than usual; we were together on this issue, we all know that it is the government who is oppressing the people, not another racial group.

The young man's longing for wholeness and unity was a pervasive theme in his conversation. Conscious of living in an 'unhomely world', he was 'looking for the join' (Bhabha 1994:18); his words expressed his desire for social solidarity. Within the space of a few hours, the informant's sense of city alienation gave way to suburban equivalence, generated by the small acts of recognition and kindness that had some capacity to restrain schismogenesis (Bateson 1973:43–4).

The success and support shown on this and other days of ZCTU protest that continued into 1998 had a huge psychological impact. Sachikonye (1998:8) remembers 9 December as 'much more than just a massive national shut-down' and describes it as 'a coalescence of the public mood'. White businesspeople allowed workers time off with pay and supported the various days of mass action for an assortment of reasons. Some agreed with the political issues behind the protest and believed workers' grievances to be genuine. Others had been approached and asked by union officials to close, felt a hint of intimidation should they refuse and, as business owners, decided shutting up shop was preferable to paying for damages should looting occur. As it turned out, most demonstrations were generally peaceful, despite provocations by the security forces that prompted a change of ZCTU tactics. To avert confrontations with the State, striking workers were told to stay at home or stay away rather than congregate in the city centre.

The government for its part talked of a 'white conspiracy' and 'an unholy alliance' between white employers and the unions, accused workers of teaming up with 'the oppressors' and, likening it to a 'happy marriage', asked angrily 'why is there so much harmony' between employers and union leaders. A year later, the government was still talking of this 'strange and queer relationship' between capital and labour, not previously seen in Zimbabwe.[27] Yet black employers gave their workers the day off under similar conditions as white bosses. They too shared

---

27 *The Herald,* 13 December 1997, p. 1, 12 December 1998, p. 1.

the belief that the 'government must learn to manage money responsibly' and 'stop overspending'. When asked why they did not challenge the government's notion of a white conspiracy, however, they responded that they would rather 'let whites take the heat'. Not so Mr Kunjeku of the Employers' Confederation, who disputed ZANU PF's racialisation of the conflict. He publicly questioned the government's interpretation of events, angrily asking aren't 'black bosses able to make their own decisions, aren't they autonomous', and 'aren't workers able to think for themselves, don't they have legitimate grievances'? Kunjeku also pointed out that the overwhelming majority of all employers and employees were black and not 'the slaves' of whites.[28]

Other whites, aware of being highly visible targets on the streets, phoned in messages supporting the stay-aways to a local radio station, 'honked' their horns as they passed protesters on their way to town and submitted letters of encouragement to the local papers. These marginal activities reflect shared concerns and 'difference within' an imagined collectivity (Bhabha 1994:13)—a perception also apparent in a second episode in which the young man above 'felt grounded, a Zimbabwean'. He had become 'fed up with planes flying low' over his house late one night and rang the air traffic controllers. The woman taking the call 'listened to my concerns, and talked openly and frankly about it. I was impressed for even though she could do nothing about the problem she did not give me "the blank face". I wasn't dismissed as just another unreconciled white.' Here the invitation to contribute existed and the traffic controller accepted the informant's attempts at authorship. Her recognition generated in him the feeling of being at home and of belonging. He was not interpellated simply as a white racist—where, as Shotter (1993:126) notes, the first question to be asked would be 'is he one of us'—but listened to seriously as was warranted of a fellow national or countryman. Consequently, the incident proved a pleasing experience, contributing to a perception of agency and formative of a sense of belonging within the national collective.

Occasionally, members of the black majority also publicly recognised and gave voice to black and white interconnectedness. For instance, the following excerpt refers to the common ground, rather than the difference, that is critical to a mutually recognised sense of belonging to the same country. More conscious of this with the benefit of distance, Munyaradzi wrote encouragingly from the United Kingdom: 'I know it's hard for them as it is for me to admit that, in spite of everything, we are inexorably related by the country we both call our own.' Then, after supporting in principle the redistribution of land, his letter went on:

---

28 *Issues and Views*, ZBC TV, 8 March 1998.

> [S]o, for my white brothers, all I can say is hang on in there and try to make the best of a horrible situation. You have been through this before when you had your backs to the wall through sanctions…Because I am away from home I can look at the stupidity of white arrogance and the annoyance of black scapegoating with a clearer perspective…White and urban black Zimbabweans are closer in perceptions to each other than they are to Europeans or rural blacks. So, behave yourselves out there and stop poking sticks into each other's eyes.[29]

Distance—being away from home—contributed to the writer's definition of a shared place as a source of belonging. Here again an act of recognition opened up social relations. In effect, Munyaradzi gave up 'the absolutes' and moved away from a binary conception of society (Bhabha 1994:14). His passage offered a space, a home, to whites once urban interconnectedness was acknowledged. This was an important and frequently overlooked idea in Zimbabwe. At some level, the author implicitly accepted the interrelatedness of black and white history and the fluidity, or unboundedness, of culture that gives birth to hybridity (Gupta and Ferguson 1997a:3).

The recognition of mutuality, of 'one's self in the other, the other in one's self' (Jackson 1995:118), articulated by a small number of blacks and whites was, however, the *sotto voce* to the Manichean starkness of the official narrative, in which notions of home were drafted into the service of nationalism (Bammer 1992:xi). Some months before the publication of Munyaradzi's letter Mugabe had described 'those who belong to one another' as those 'who fought the liberation struggle together'[30] when outlining the historical importance of the armed struggle. These comrades in arms, represented at Heroes' Acre by sculptures of the freedom fighters described in Chapter 4, possess dynamism and vitality. With noble heads held high, they appear 'to breathe' and 'blend naturally with their surroundings showing that they are at home' (Ministry of Information, Posts and Telecommunications 1998:4). The figures' confidence in being 'at home' differentiates them from those who 'participated on the opposite side', 'the people's one common enemy',[31] who remain under an obligation to prove political commitment, loyalty and patriotism.

Most whites, however, were unwilling to take up this political burden and its articulation of the past, which contributed only closure and fixity to their future. In view of the exclusivity of this state narrative and recriminations in the aftermath of the 1985 election, some had long argued that the white community should steer clear of politics. Others, however, made common

---

29 'Be more analytic and substantive', *Zimbabwe Independent*, 12 December 1997, p. 5.
30 'How Zimbabwe was won', *The Sunday Mail*, 16 February 1997, p. 1.
31 Ibid.

cause and supported the alliance of the NCA and labour leaders out of which a new political party, the Movement for Democratic Change (MDC), emerged in September 1999. The new party, with Morgan Tsvangirai, the ZCTU's Secretary-General, at the helm, evolved out of the trade unions' leading role in the civics movement. This newly formed cross-class and multiracial alliance committed itself to the rule of law and democratic process (Alden and Makumbe 2001:215, 233). The President had by this time let it be known that the policy of reconciliation would be revisited. 'Whites,' he said, 'are here at the sufferance of the blacks' and, evincing the State's power of eviction, could 'have all been expelled in 1980'.[32] While some whites advocated that they should 'unanimously follow a passive course' and decline to vote in the forthcoming 2000 election, in order that they not be blamed for the result, others were galvanised by their community's alienation from the nation They therefore supported the MDC and subverted Mugabe's message, saying 'Vote for a home—if you want a home, vote wisely', suggesting the wisdom of votes cast for the opposition. Thus 'home', operating in the same mythic field as family and nation, is a concept with profound emotional legitimacy (Anderson 1990:15, 31; Bammer 1992:x). As a metaphor for belonging, the term has an indeterminate referential quality (Bammer 1992:vii), allowing it to represent social relations at the domestic or at the enlarged national field (George 1996:13) while, in Zimbabwe, conferring or rejecting claims to a location as home provides a means of establishing minority difference (George 1996:2).

Conclusion

In sum, informants' ideas of home and home country coalesced around issues of entitlement and familiarity. The use of these terms conveyed the importance of family and community ties, tradition, history, agreed values, contentment, security, refuge, a rightful place of settlement and return, and so on. In each instance, the notion of home represented a territorial core and mythic space (Bammer 1992:ix) that had been shaped by people's experiences as well as the narratives that interpreted those experiences for them. During my fieldwork, however, the whites' sense of place and certainty was giving way within the wider political context of independence (Rose 1995:88). State-sponsored 'patriotic history' (Ranger 2004) constituted its villains and heroes out of the colonial memory, interpellating whites in such a way that triggered the dialectics of colonialism, disallowed doubling and thereby preventing whites from placing themselves within the national frame (Bammer 1992:xii). By freezing national belonging in the moment of the anti-colonial struggle, a hostile and combative dualism had been set up that worked against the recognition of

---

32 'Reconciliation policy may be revisited', *The Sunday Mail,* 28 February 1999, p. 1; Deve 1993:21.

racial interconnectedness and the permeability of boundaries (Massey 1992:14). The concept of home was thus implicated in the xenophobic resonance of Zimbabwean nationalism and, as whites saw it, their homelessness was part of the party's national agenda.

At the same time, understanding themselves as not belonging or feeling 'not home' in the country of their birth and residence was also of their own doing—produced by their reluctance to give up Euro-centrism and historicism (Chakrabarty 2000:7). For, generally speaking, white Zimbabweans have not stepped beyond the colonial hierarchy; they have failed to 'fit in' and accommodate themselves to the ways of the black majority. Instead, they have expected the formerly colonised to continue to accommodate them. Not recognising this, most had few ideas about how to retrieve agency and come home again by untying their identity from the isolation inherent in racial and cultural difference. While being at home had never been equally accesible to all those who were born in and inhabited the country, white narratives also suggested their displacement was 'a condition rarely experienced as absolute, unambivalent or final' (Ferguson 1992:90). There was not so much a definite break in their sense of belonging as a partial and conditional awareness of growing uncertainty, their experience of displacement being, as Ferguson (1992) avers, full of ambiguity and indeterminacy, even where the process was marked by significant events.

8. Zimbabwe's governance and land reform crises—a postscript

In a bid to disrupt and confuse the work of the people's National Constitutional Assembly (NCA), Mugabe's government set up its own Constitutional Commission of Inquiry to draw up a new constitution in April 1999. The Commission's work was presented to the public as bringing the final break with colonialism. Just months before the 2000 general election, ZANU PF's draft document was put to a referendum and rejected. This represented the first electoral defeat for ZANU PF in 20 years. The proposed constitution would have, among other things, increased executive powers, and so strengthened Mugabe's grip on power and protected his regime from prosecution for any illegalities committed while in office. Kagoro (2004:249) and others read the 'no' vote as a protest against the government itself as well as against its handling of the constitution-making process and the economy.

A second major challenge came when the Movement for Democratic Change (MDC), having contested the June 2000 election, broke ZANU PF's exclusive control of the House and brought an effective opposition party into Parliament. Zimbabwe's political landscape had changed forever. Intimidation of rural health workers and teachers in the run-up to the vote led to the closure of schools, clinics and hospitals, and saw political re-education sessions organised by war veterans for white farmers and farm workers—all features reminiscent of the liberation war era. By this time, however, the 1997 war veterans' payout had made for new alignments. Alexander and McGregor (2004:96) point to the merging of some former ZIPRA combatants with their ZANLA counterparts. Putting aside bitter rivalries, they found common cause in the use of unspeakable violence against the political opposition, doing untold damage to the social fabric by destroying property, invading and harassing local councils, state offices, company and public service personnel (McGregor 2002). Former combatants could thus be said to have intimidated and terrorised the communities that supported them during the liberation war and which, in the case of Matabeleland, had also voted overwhelmingly for the MDC. A blanket amnesty announced in October 2000 then pardoned all politically motivated crimes committed for the most part by war veterans, ZANU PF thugs and its youth militia (Eppel 2004:50).

The regime, using its power 'to name, to inscribe, to describe and *essentialise*', proceeded to invoke 'a world of moral relationships' (Werbner 1997:239) in its analysis of these electoral results. Mugabe blamed whites for the 'no' vote in the referendum and harked back to the 'unholy alliance' and 'white conspiracy' evidenced during the 1997 general strike. The MDC, he said, represented continuing imperial and settler influence in Zimbabwean politics.

Opposition supporters, derided in liberation struggle terminology as 'sell-outs' who preferred a colonial-style constitution, were tied conceptually to 'whites' and other 'stooges of Western imperialists' intent on recolonising the county. 'White', reflected Paul Nyathi, former ZIPRA commander and MDC MP, had by this time become in Zimbabwe's 'distorted political lexicon' a 'generic term for evil'.[1] The perpetrators of violence were heralded as patriotic 'super-citizens' (Hammar and Raftopoulos 2003:27), and in the case of war veteran leader and MP Chenjerai Hunzvi, made a national hero after his death in 2001. The victims being in the main opposition sympathisers found themselves branded 'Western puppets' and 'unpatriotic enemies' and were blamed for their own victimisation. Falling outside the boundaries of citizenship, these newly named internal enemies should not expect protection from the State or to benefit from land redistribution or indigenisation initiatives. A brutal crackdown on the independent press, civic organisations and intimidation of the judiciary had already begun after a local paper published a report of a likely coup in early 1999. Attacks directed towards anyone supporting the opposition intensified towards the 2000 election but did not abate thereafter. Meredith (2007:211–14) catalogues the hundreds of businesses and factories associated with whites, as well as NGOs, embassies and hospitals targeted for invasion, intimidation, humiliation and extortion during the first six months of 2001.

Ranger (2004:218, 234) highlights the centrality and importance to ZANU PF's electoral campaign of its particular telling of the past. As soon as the election was over, Zimbabwe's media was restructured and the newly named Department of Information and Publicity was subsumed within the Office of the President. The promulgation of repressive media laws, the deportation of almost all foreign journalists and closure of independent papers in order to stifle criticism and debate then followed (Chuma 2004:133–5). The new department launched a multimedia operation in support of the ruling party, land reform and its anti-colonial version of history. With the State now dominating the electronic media, the general public was 'saturated' with television and radio programmes in which 'Zimbabwe's history is Mugabe and Mugabe is Zimbabwe's history' (Chiumbu 2004:33). 'New history' books were introduced in schools, which were themselves to be renamed after national heroes and other figures important to the struggle. A youth militia was created under the guise of the National Youth Service in order to instil patriotism and impart moral education to the young (Chiumbu 2004:219). Its graduates together with the 'new' war veterans are given priority in teachers' training colleges and journalism courses (Chiumbu 2004:34). All of this illustrates that the President and the ZANU PF political elite are prepared to invest heavily in their version of history and suggests they

---

1 Paul Nyathi, Director of the Zimbabwe Project Trust and soon to be MDC Member of Parliament, quoted in Alden and Mukumbe (2001:235); 'Zimbabweans must stop name calling', *Zimbabwe Independent,* 22 June 1999.

are intent on staying in office regardless of what might be involved (Alden and Makumbe 2001:233). Indeed, some would argue that, given their plundering of the country, it would be very dangerous for them to give up power.[2]

This pattern has been repeated at every election in the past nine years; none could be called free and fair. Excesses condemned earlier as part and parcel of colonial rule have been repeated endlessly, often utilising Rhodesia's notorious *Law and Order Maintenance Act*. A rigged ballot returned Mugabe to the Presidency in 2002. In view of white support for the opposition candidate, Mugabe publicly rescinded his previous policy of reconciliation towards them in a speech later that year (Raftopoulos 2004a:164)—something he had threatened to do on and off since the 1985 general election. Soon afterwards, the European Union, the United States and other Western governments applied 'smart' sanctions to Mugabe and about 90 of his close associates, and an increasingly isolated Zimbabwe left the Commonwealth. Politically inspired intimidation, murder, violence, vote rigging and gerrymandering marred the 2005 and 2008 general elections and saw people pouring out of the country. Nevertheless, the MDC consistently produced a strong showing among workers, professionals, big business and the intelligentsia in urban areas across the country. In the countryside, the party found favour among commercial and better-off small-scale farmers, farm labourers and public servants (Hammar and Raftopoulos 2003:30). Matabeleland also voted overwhelmingly for this new party despite the populace being threatened with the return of *Gukurahundi* atrocities in every election since the MDC's inception (McGregor 2002:29; Eppel 2004:47). In contrast, ZANU PF took the rural ballot across Mashonaland, relying on partisan chiefs and headmen to deliver the vote (Hammar 2005:14). The MDC found it almost impossible to campaign in that part of the country because of disruption and intimidation by ZANU PF's henchmen.

Would-be MDC voters were discouraged and excluded in various other ways. During 2000, the Registrar-General, Tobaiwa Mudede, in office since 1980, refused to renew many Zimbabwean passports until the holder showed proof of having renounced entitlement to foreign citizenship. Various commentators suggested that this was a move to disenfranchise white and other MDC supporters prior to the 2002 Presidential election.[3] A test case concluded in 2001 found, however, that Zimbabwean law made no such requirement.[4] In disregard of the Supreme Court's judgement, amendments to citizenship legislation came into effect giving six months for citizens-by-registration and all those with a parent or parents born elsewhere to provide documentary evidence of their

---

2 'Blunt weapons', *The Economist*, 3 February 2001, p. 49.
3 See Zimbabwe Lawyers for Human Rights, 13 March 2009; Muzondidya and Alexander, 'The ghost voters, the exiles, the non-citizens: an election of exclusion', *Cape Times*, 31 March 2005. Muzondidya and Alexander estimate a higher figure of more than two million black descendants of foreign labour who have been affected.
4 *Carr vs Registrar General*, (2) ZLR 433, 2000, *Zimbabwe Law Reports*.

having renounced citizenship under the legal provisions of the foreign country or automatically lose their Zimbabwean citizenship. The measure potentially involved somewhere between 20 000 and 30 000 whites, the bulk of the Asian and coloured communities, as well as hundreds of thousands of blacks born in Zimbabwe and carrying local identity cards and passports, but whose parent(s) or grandparents came from neighbouring Malawi, Zambia, Mozambique and South Africa. These governments indicated to Zimbabwean authorities that they did not have the administrative capacity to comply with the deadline and, furthermore, applicants frequently had no documentation, such as birth certificates or national registration cards, to substantiate claims to a right to citizenship in their countries. Malawian and Zambian officials also pointed out that during the federal era no travel papers were required, as the three participating territories were at the time legally one country. The issue therefore created tension between Harare and other regional governments. Britain also expressed its irritation, saying it took up to six months for the Home Office to process and issue certificates of renunciation. To a lesser extent, the exercise also implicated the Government of India.

Back in Zimbabwe, Justice Adam in the High Court ruled a right to citizenship by descent that had never been activated could not be given up.[5] Renunciation applied only when citizenship had in fact been held. Furthermore, the Law Society noted Zimbabwean statute law did not incorporate in its provisions the requirements of foreign law and therefore renunciation under Zimbabwean law alone entailed complete fulfilment. Taking no heed, the Registrar-General, who is also the overseer of the electoral role, repeatedly and wilfully misinterpreted the citizenship provisions, bringing to court whites and Asians, as well as blacks with unusual sounding names.[6] In view of this, Justice Adam found it necessary to take him—'a mere public functionary'—to task for having 'arrogantly and unashamedly arrogated to himself the functions of the legislature and the power of the judiciary'.[7] With the renunciation exercise bogged down in legal challenges and administrative confusion, Zimbabwean passports were being invalidated at points of entry and exit and applications for their renewal refused if certificates of renunciation could not be produced. Some clarity came in November 2002 when the rules governing foreign renunciation were gazetted (Government of Zimbabwe, 22 November 2002). As legal minds had expected, these rules established that renunciation requirements applied only to a

---

5 See 'Judgment in *Morgan Tsvangerai vs Registrar General*', Zimbabwe Lawyers for Human Rights, 21 March 2003, p. 2.
6 Zimbabwe Lawyers for Human Rights, 28 November 2002; 'Zimbabwe: whether Zimbabwe recognises dual citizenship, in particular in the case of a person who detains the Zambian citizenship', *Refworld*, 8 February 2002.
7 Justice Adam quoted by Justice Mungwira in *Todd vs Registrar General of Citizenship and Another* (HC55/2002). See also 'Mudede ordered not to tamper with voters' roll', Zimbabwe Independent, 4 January 2002.

Zimbabwean citizen who was in fact presently a citizen of a foreign county. Not deterred, and still refusing direction by Cabinet and the courts, the Registrar-General continued to waste taxpayers' money by bringing many such cases to the courts in Harare and Bulawayo (Zimbabwe Human Rights and Law 2007). Having its rulings repeatedly flouted in this way obviously undermines the role of the judiciary.

Once citizenship is lost, its restoration is a costly and lengthy process. Numerically the largest group affected was the descendants of foreign labour, many of whom were at the time employed as farm workers. The colonial heritage produced arrangements that limited their horizons by anchoring their identity to a location—namely, the country's commercial farms (Rutherford 2003:192). Being 'paired to the farmer', however, marginalised them in the nation at large (Rutherford 2001:234). Falling outside the normal governance structures, their citizenship rights were never clearly defined during the colonial or post-independence eras (Muzondidya 2004:221). As farm and mine workers or urban industrial labourers, this group was also among the least able to access information or contribute resources to the renunciation exercise. Some protection for those whose parents were born within the Southern African Development Community (SADC) region was offered in 2003. Where a parent(s) had arrived before 1980 as migrant labour, either as general or farm labour, mine employee or domestic worker, a descendant, having failed through inertia or ignorance to comply with renunciation provisions, could renounce his or her foreign citizenship and thereby confirm Zimbabwean citizenship by signing a prescribed form. As the Zimbabwe Human Rights NGO Forum (4 August 2005) pointed out, however, without retrospective effect, there was nothing for these people to confirm as they had already lost their Zimbabwean citizenship. As non-citizens, they can neither participate fully in society nor benefit from state initiatives. Many are now stateless, as most countries of the region have no provision for dual citizenship, nor do they grant automatic citizenship to children born abroad to foreign-born parents. Although black and locally born, the descendants of Zimbabwe's migrant labour force are taunted as 'people without rural homes' (Muzondidya 2004:226). Without a claim to a rural home, they remain 'foreigners' or 'aliens', but never indigenes. Furthermore, the 2003 safety net was not all encompassing. The provisions excluded others deriving from SADC countries on the grounds that their forebears moved to Rhodesia for reasons of employment unrelated to labour migration.

Land reform: 'fast track' and war veterans

At independence, Zimbabwe's newly elected government inherited the 'historical burden of race-based inequalities' (Alden and Makumbe 2001:215).

Land ownership in particular had long provided a historical trope for colonial subjugation. While constrained by Lancaster House provisions until 1990, the land issue invariably received attention around elections, only to fall away soon after. Local district studies by Alexander (2006), Moore (2005) and Rutherford (2001), as well as contributions to the 1998 Land Conference referred to in Chapter 6, all illustrate the point that the land question is in reality many questions (Hammar and Raftopoulos 2003:18–19). This is something reflected in the sheer diversity of Zimbabwe's land and resources conflicts, not all of which can be explained in terms of the colonial legacy (Hammar and Raftopoulos 2003:21). Nonetheless, in media coverage and political discourse, the focus fell squarely on the country's commercial farming sector where land distribution provided 'visible testimony' of the continuing racial structure of landholding in the country (Alden and Makumbe 2001:224), as well as the government's failure to address this challenge adequately.

By 2000, ZANU PF, faced with growing discontent and the MDC's electoral challenge, needed to win back voters. A sweetener tacked on late in the referendum campaign would have, if ratified, absolved Zimbabwe from paying compensation for white farms, but it failed to turn the vote. Regardless, two months later in April, constitutional amendments were passed permitting the government to expropriate land without paying compensation—that responsibility being handed to the British Government. 'Fast-track' procedures for land alienation and resettlement began soon after. Sachikonye (2003:3) describes this programme 'as being executed between 2000 and 2002 with vigour, considerable violence and chaos'. In November 2001, the President ordered a halt to agricultural work on designated white commercial farms and Section 8 (Preliminary Notices of Compulsory Acquisition) orders came into force in May the next year. By June 2002, the majority of white farms had been listed for redistribution. Farm workers were put on forced leave and owners had three months to vacate their homesteads or be in violation of the law. War veterans set up bases on the commercial farms, from which they, together with the recently formed youth militia and peasants, launched waves of intimidation, violence and in some cases murder, disrupting agricultural work and clearing the farms of their white owners, managers and farm labour. The police refused to intervene, provide protection or lay charges, saying 'it was a political matter'. Judges were threatened and sacked for not toeing the party line and courts had their rulings ignored.

In the light of these events, a former ZIPRA commander Paul Nyathi (2004:74–5) argues that the war veterans have been co-opted to do ZANU PF's dirty work and keep Mugabe in power. The Central Intelligence Organisation and the ruling party directed them and the youth militias, known as the 'new vets' of this third *Chimurenga*, to specific farms (Alexander 2006:186). Veteran leaders also worked hand in hand with the army. Representatives of these groups clashed, however, over the control of farms. In some instances, the war veterans have been unable to hang on to the property in the face of claims by members of the political and military elite who, together with diplomats, judges and senior civil servants, have moved into the former white homesteads. Disturbed by these events, veterans' groups in Mashonaland and Matabeleland split from the main lobby group, Zimbabwe National Liberators War Veterans' Association. Having gone to war to put an end to an unjust racially ordered system of government and to contribute to the creation of a larger democratic space (Nyathi 2004:63), they distanced themselves from both the land invasions and political violence and spoke up for the rule of law[8] (Hammar 2005:12).

Fast track, along partisan lines and on the basis of immediate occupancy, thus went ahead before compensation for improvements was sorted out and without 'lease, permit or legal documentation or formal process' for the new settlers (Rukuni and Jensen 2003:246–7). Little compensation has been forthcoming to cover land improvements or commercial farm equipment, with the government machinery for administering these matters 'taxed to the limit' (Utete 2003:5). By late 2002, 11.5 million hectares of land had changed hands in the space of two and a half years (Sachikonye 2003:3)—twice the amount under stakeholders' discussion at the 1998 Land Conference. The *Utete Report*, coming out of the Office of the President, asserted that 4.2 million hectares had been offered to 127 192 households who were settled as small subsistence farmers by July 2003. The take-up rates among these 'new settlers' was very good, averaging 97 per cent. A further 7260 beneficiaries were said to have been offered commercial farms of varying sizes. This figure had to be revised downwards to 1672 a few months later.[9] The take-up rate among these 'new farmers' averaged about 66 per cent, suggesting that land not taken up was lying idle[10] (Utete 2003:5). Moreover, the government's one man, one farm policy had not been respected. Multiple farms of prime land appear to have been registered in the names of wives, children and relatives of 178 senior officials. An annex to the *Utete Report* outlining this problem has been withheld from publication. While Mugabe has ordered excess farms be surrendered, compliance is unclear.

Constitutional Amendment (No. 17) of 2005 vests all land acquired under Zimbabwe's 2000 reform programme as state land. In effect, landowners and occupiers lose security of tenure and become tenants at will and therefore beholden to the State. Technically, leases can be cancelled at the government's discretion. All that is required is for a property to be gazetted, followed by a 30-

---

8   'War veterans attack Hunzvi', *Zimbabwe Independent,* 20 March 1998, p. 1.
9   'Zimbabwe: focus on Utete committee report on agricultural reform', *IRIN,* 6 November 2003.
10 Take-up rates ranged from 42 per cent in Manicaland to 100 per cent in Matabeleland South (Utete 2003:5). Reasons for the low take-up included failure by officials to notify successful applicants, their disappointment at the lack of farm infrastructure, resource constraints and continuing court hearings (Utete 2003:25).

day grace period during which the farmer must leave the farm. The insecurity associated with this form of tenure does little to enhance investment and productivity (Rukuni and Jensen 2003:258). As a form of clientism, however, it allows ZANU PF control and patronage over its new farmers (Kriger 2007:73). After the passage of this amendment, the remaining white farmers were served with eviction notices and enforcement was stepped up. Access to the courts by owners intent on challenging the order was specifically denied[11] and appeals pending in the Administrative Court were struck off the rolls (Kriger 2007:72). Refused a hearing in Zimbabwe, 70-plus farmers whose land was to be expropriated appealed in early 2007 to a SADC Tribunal,[12] of which Zimbabwe is a signatory. The tribunal upheld the farmers' case finding in December 2008 that the Zimbabwean Government had contravened SADC's founding treaty's human rights and property rights provisions.[13] The government, however, ignored the tribunal, increasing the pace of eviction orders during its hearing. The farmers spearheading the appeal were abducted and badly beaten. One was then ordered to surrender his farm, which was earmarked for Nathan Shamurariya, a senior ZANU PF stalwart.[14] Refusing to vacate his property or bow to intimidation, the appellant's homestead and workers' housing were burned to the ground in September 2009.

Farm workers along with white farmers have been the notable losers. Workers and their dependants made up about two million people for whom no contingency plans were made (Sachikonye 2003:13). Sachikonye (2003:3) suggested that less than 5 per cent were offered land. Zimbabweans-by-descent among them could in most cases recover a place in the communal areas. More than one-quarter of this total are, however, descended from migrant labour. As 'puppets of the white man', their interests are set against those of the black majority. Anti-colonial nationalists condemn them for this relationship—for being under the influence of the farmer and sharing his interests—calling it false consciousness (Rutherford 2001:234, 2003:194). Having lost jobs, income, accommodation and access to health and educational services once provided by large-scale commercial farmers, this section of Zimbabwe's population has sunk into chronic poverty. Some remain in the farm compounds where, according to the *Utete Report* (2003:6), their presence creates 'numerous problems' as they try to survive from gold panning, hunting, fishing and other 'criminal activities'. Others depend on casual agricultural or piecework. Not all of Zimbabwe's new

---

11 Zimbabwe Human Rights NGO Forum, 4 August 2005, p. 2.
12 The tribunal was created as a peer-review mechanism to ensure the objectives of SADC's founding treaty were upheld by member states.
13 'Zimbabwe: white farmers appeal to SADC', *bilaterals.org*, 12 October 2007; 'SADC tribunal has no legal mandate to nullify member states' laws', *Race and History.com*, 19 July 2008; 'SADC tribunal rules 78 white farmers can keep Zimbabwe land', *newzimbabwe.com*, 28 November 2008.
14 'A brutal toll', *Newsweek*, 30 June 2008.

commercial farmers, however, see fit to pay the minimum wage,[15] claiming that casual farm labour is too expensive (FAO/WFP 2009:10). Other former farm workers attempt to eke out a precarious living as peri-urban squatters in areas targeted in Mugabe's infamous clean-up campaigns (Hammar 2005:2). A number have sought to disentangle themselves and escape their conceptual incarceration by establishing new dependencies and lines of patronage with the ruling party and invading war veterans (Rutherford 2003:210). Hoping for land of their own, they have endeavoured to get back on the politically correct side of patriotic history. While this path offers in all probability a less secure and lucrative relationship than previously existed with the commercial farmer, Rutherford (2008a:73) suggests it could provide farm workers with 'a new form of conditional belonging'.

In short, land reform enabled the ruling party to 'raise its ideological status' and posture as the revolutionary nationalist party (Kriger 2007:74). While taking back land in the name of the aggrieved, however, ownership remains highly skewed (FAO/WFP 2009:7). Sachikonye (2004:14) suggests that much less than half of those who applied for land have become beneficiaries. Female-headed households were sidelined, being allocated only 18 per cent of the small-scale farms and 12 per cent of the commercial farms (Utete 2003:25). On the other hand, the programme saw a massive but inequitable redistribution of wealth to privileged individuals on the basis of political patronage—the rise of a 'new regime of accumulation from above' (Hammar and Raftopoulos 2003:23). This result, justified using the discourse of anti-colonialism, was also accompanied by the destruction of capital invested in the agricultural and horticultural industries. Although farm infrastructure and implements were to remain on the property, politicians, senior government officials and war veterans had on occasion engaged in asset stripping (Davies 2004:34), confiscating and removing agricultural machinery.

Farms have also proved to be a reward for contributors to the liberation struggle, in addition to ZANU PF loyalists. Mugabe's lectures on the debt owed to the former freedom fighters by all Zimbabweans are legendary. Yet the pitch of ZANU PF's 'patriotic' history is far too high for some. Chiumbu (2004:34) argues that millions of young people born in the 1970s and since independence do not identify with the anti-colonial struggle. In addition, the wish of many raised in the urban areas is for a good job in town—not for them the tedium of life in the rural areas. Other ordinary Zimbabweans are alienated from ex-combatants by recent events—the polarisation between the comrades and the general public, according to Nyathi (2004:75), having never been greater. With Zimbabwe in the process of painful economic reform throughout the 1990s, those suffering from the effects of structural adjustment saw the focus on war

---

15 'Zimbabwe: land reform omits farm workers', *IRIN*, 26 July 2009.

veterans as misplaced. The majority of former combatants, who remained poor and ill educated after independence, are perceived to be suffering the hardships and precarious existence typical of many rural dwellers; 'their problems are our problems'. Furthermore, war veterans are today found in all walks of life. While most were recruited from the rural poor, there is now a small but highly educated elite holding senior posts in government and the civil service. They could be said to have found their post-independence rewards (Nyathi 2004:64).

Food security

At the stakeholders' Land Conference, concerns were raised that land acquisition and resettlement could reduce Zimbabwe's food security, at least in the short term (Government of Zimbabwe 1998a:59). Other ex-settler economies have faced the dilemma of how to proceed with redistribution and poverty reduction without compromising food production (Cousins 2003:266). In Zimbabwe, an ongoing, staggered process was suggested as offering some protection and a good way to move forward; however, the Deputy Minister of Lands and Agriculture and 'patriotic agrarianists' (Rutherford 2008a:3) such as Sam Moyo[16] rejected the idea as 'lacking foresight' or 'vision', intimating that this preoccupation somehow demeaned the historical legacy (Friedrich Ebert Stiftung/Zimbabwe Economics Society 1998a:7). While a regional drought in the early years did not help the resettlement programme get off to a good start, recent Food and Agriculture/World Food Programme (FAO/WFP) reports (2008, 2009) indicate that serious food shortages continue to haunt rural and urban areas. The communal farmers' maize yield—once producing the bulk of this staple crop—is one-quarter of what it was 10 years ago, while commercial farms are producing one-tenth of their 1990s' yields (FAO/WFP 2009:7). Wheat, another important crop historically grown under irrigation by large-scale commercial farmers, has fallen by about two-thirds (FAO/WFP 2008:13).

FAO/WFP nominate many reasons for this poor showing. These include the shortage of credit, fuel and draft power as well as the untimely delivery of seeds, fertilisers and chemicals by the government, absenteeism of newly settled farmers, failure to weed, which compromises crop yields, and the deteriorating agricultural infrastructure. In addition, many new commercial farmers cultivate only part of the prime land allocated to them. Some have found diverting tractors to other uses and selling their diesel allocation more lucrative options (FAO/WFP 2009:10).[17] Communal farmers have also suffered from the loss 'of their symbiotic relationship with the former large-scale commercial agricultural sector' and the

---

16 See Moyo (1998a:33) and the contribution of the Deputy Minister, Dr Muchena, to Friedrich Ebert Stiftung/Zimbabwe Economics Society, Vol. 2 (1998a:11).
17 See also 'Ripping the heart out of the heartland', *The Economist*, 25 August 2007.

demise of a healthy agro-input industry (FAO/WFP 2008:1). So, while allowing war veterans and the land hungry to move onto farmland for some years now and confiscating land in their name, the government has failed to provide these would-be farmers with sufficient agricultural assistance. Unable to meet their own food needs or produce a surplus, some have moved back to the communal areas (Alexander 2003:112). As a result of these shortcomings, the contribution of agriculture to total exports decreased from 39 per cent in 2000 to 13 per cent in 2007, although some small relative improvement was expected in 2008–09 (FAO/WFP 2009:6). With widespread famine, the country has become a food importer as well as a receiver of humanitarian food aid. Until very recently, there has been a severe scarcity in the marketplace, with shop shelves standing bereft of all food products. Inevitably, Zimbabwe has an unsustainable trade deficit and is dependent on South Africa for electricity, for which it cannot pay. Serious 'knock-on' effects from the country's agricultural revolution are also being felt in the industrial, manufacturing, finance and tourism sectors—the last now all but moribund.

While Zimbabwe's commercial land issue was mired in confusion and controversy, and attacks escalated in some areas, white farmers in other parts of the country, however, received 'offer letters'. Issued by the Ministry of Lands, these specify a farm allocated to beneficiaries on the basis of either a 99-year lease for agricultural land or 25 years for wildlife conservancies. The letters allow the bearer to evict others who might have already occupied the land but they are otherwise 'devoid of any transparent procedure' (Kriger 2007:73). In April 2009, 13 white commercial farmers were offered land in Guruve District, a fertile agricultural region close to Harare. Touring the country to assess agricultural production, Advocate Dinha, Governor of Central Mashonaland, stressed the letters 'were imperative' as most 'new farmers' were 'failing to occupy the farms they were allocated, thereby affecting production'.[18] He urged the white farmers to share their knowledge with other newly resettled farmers, noting that whites had more than a century of commercial farming expertise to draw on. Here Dinha parodies the Rhodesian trade unions' protectionist claim that the white artisan had 'a century of training in his bones' (Phimister 1988:192). Once again white farmers were instructed to integrate and be seen participating in all national events. Two months later, another 40 farmers received lease offers for wildlife conservancies in the southern Masvingo area and were directed to share their expertise by forming consortiums with 'indigenous players' before the 2010 World Cup in South Africa.[19] There have, however, been repeated calls for an independent land audit, to find out whose name is on which parcel of

---

18 'White farmers get offer letters', *The Herald*, 27 April 2009.
19 'Forty white farmers get offer letters', *The Herald*, 17 June 2009.

land before long leases are locked in. With the government still working out the fine detail,[20] the general public remains wary. The land register, like the voters' roll,[21] is known to have been in disarray for some considerable time.

Only 200 or so large-scale white commercial farms now remain in Zimbabwe (FAO/WFP 2009:8). Some lie idle awaiting court decisions, farmers on others cultivate only a fraction of their former holding and a few have come to 'fragile' agreements with the land occupiers such that profits are shared (Kriger 2007:72). Most farmers have left with their families for the safety of the towns. Where Mugabe had over the years made much political capital out of white rootlessness and lack of commitment, Presidents elsewhere saw something different and set out to actively recruit Zimbabwe's white farmers. Not insignificant numbers have relocated to develop new properties or rehabilitate degraded agricultural land in other parts of Africa—most notably in neighbouring Zambia, Mozambique and Malawi. A Zambian Government official said 'white farmers have shown their commitment to land in Zimbabwe and we feel that Zambia could gain from their professionalism'.[22] Predictably, Mugabe chastised the Zambian President for taking in 'racist colonialists'. With a highly urban population, however, and with only an estimated 10 per cent of its arable land under cultivation, Zambia faces recurrent food shortages. Zimbabwe's former commercial farmers today grow maize, tobacco, coffee, fruit, vegetables and flowers reportedly with good results on land leased from the Zambian Government. Further afield in Nigeria in West Africa, President Obasanjo was also encouraging, saying 'we don't want to take away what is good for Zimbabwe, but we don't want what is good for Africa taken away'.[23] The Governor of Nigeria's Kwara State, Mr Saraki, has pursued Zimbabwe's dispossessed farmers and actively supports them in dealings with the country's bureaucracy. With his help, their farm ventures are also proving a success.[24] Others have emigrated to New World settler societies where, as often as not, they have entered non-farming occupations.

Economic empowerment

A decade of black economic empowerment (see Chapter 6) produced limited results. Zimbabwe's economy in fact shrank in real terms by 50 per cent between

---

20 'Zimbabwe: government working on new land lease format', *The Herald,* 21 July 2009.
21 See Independent MP Margaret Dongo speaking in the run-up to the 2000 election about the operation of the Registrar-General's Office and how particular individuals and parties benefit from the 'shambles' and 'chaos' of the voters' roll (*Parliamentary Debates,* 19 May 1999, cols 5839–48).
22 'Zambia wants farmers to fight famine', *BBC News,* 3 February 2003.
23 'Bad luck continues to stalk Zambia's white farmers, hounded from Zimbabwe', *guardian.co.uk,* 27 February 2006, p. 4.
24 'White farmers bring progress in Nigeria', *Christian Science Monitor,* 2 May 2008, vol. 100, no. 111, pp. 1–4.

1998 and 2008 as businesses closed and the country experienced significant de-industrialisation (FAO/WFP 2009:2, 5). The government never properly implemented policy recommendations, bureaucratic meddling impeded the flow of funds and a lack of transparency clouded the whole indigenisation process (Raftopoulos and Compagnon 2003:23). Some multinationals such as Olivine, a subsidiary of Heinz and producer of the basic staple cooking oil, sold out to the government and left Zimbabwe altogether.[25] Unemployment has been running at about 80 per cent for a number of years. Indeed, Raftopoulos and Compagnon (2003:25) write that Mugabe has been more concerned with promoting cronyism than introducing broad-based economic empowerment. Business opportunities opened up by the indigenisation programme provided the ruling elite with another form of patronage and political reward. The interest of Zimbabwe's new entrepreneurs, also cloaked in the language of indigenisation, lay in harassing white-owned companies and seizing corporate properties for personal gain, rather than in wealth creation through economic growth (Raftopoulos and Compagnon 2003:22–3). The ruling party diverted attention away from these disappointing results with the political slogan 'Land is the economy, the economy is land' in the run-up to the 2000 elections and afterwards with land reform.

The government also proved slow to enact measures needed to stabilise the economy. The local currency, which began to exhibit volatility after Black Friday on 14 November 1997, collapsed. The Zimbabwean dollar officially traded at US$1 to Z$30 000 in May 2008, while on the parallel market, US$1 fetched in the region of Z$4 million (FAO/WFP 2008:4) Understandably, nobody wanted to touch the local currency, preferring hard currencies or petrol coupons. Barter also became commonplace as hyperinflation reached 56 million per cent in 2008 (FAO/WFP 2009:1). Farm workers hoped to return to the colonial practice of payment in kind (FAO/WFP 2008:9), landlords wanted rents paid in groceries such as sugar and cooking oil if they could be found. New bank notes with values of up to Z$100 trillion had to be printed, although this denomination was barely enough to buy a loaf of bread. Zimbabwe slashed 12 zeros from the currency in early 2009.[26] Economic indices such as these indicate that the majority of ordinary Zimbabweans are worse rather than better off after indigenisation and land reform, which, at their inception, were discussed in terms of equity and poverty reduction. It appears that by looking back and focusing on the wrongs of the past, Zimbabwe's leaders might have squandered the country's economic wellbeing for the foreseeable future (Davies 2004:40).

---

25 'Blackening the economy', *The Economist*, 15 September 2007.
26 'A worthless currency', *The Economist*, 19 July 2008; 'Zimbabwe removes 12 zeros from the currency', *CNN.com/world,* 10 July 2009.

Only with the passage of the *Indigenisation and Economic Empowerment Act* in March 2008 did attention return to other sectors of the economy. The description of an indigene—somewhat hazy in the late 1990s—firmed up as

> any person who before 18 April 1980 was disadvantaged by unfair discrimination on the grounds of his or her race, and any descendant of such a person, and any company, association, syndicate or partnership in which such persons hold the controlling interest or are the majority of members. (Government of Zimbabwe, 22 June 2007)

This is indigenisation not so much as the 'first people', disenfranchisement or non-dominance (Hodgson 2002), but rather as an act of recognition and bitter memory. Rights derive from opportunities denied before 1980, of life chances forgone due to colonial racial oppression. Concomitantly, post-independence economic hurdles are also attributed to white recalcitrance (Raftopoulos and Compagnon 2003:24).

As part of bio-politics (Worby 2003:59, 72), the State plans to reorder the population in terms of wealth and access to resources. The act directs a minister to transfer the majority share of any public company owned by non-indigenous Zimbabweans to those who qualify as indigenes.[27] The company could be anything from a backyard garage, video shop or factory to a bank or mine. It is, however, widely held that mining—the main export earner in 2009—is the sector of primary interest to the country's 'new accumulators' (Hammar and Raftopoulos 2003:40). The Chamber of Mines President, Victor Gapare, views these recently introduced government measures as ill timed and unlikely to work in Zimbabwe's current economic and political climate. The provisions come when the mining sector is operating well below capacity (FAO/WFP 2009:5). Gold production, for instance, peaked in 1999 at 27 tonnes and then fell to 3 tonnes in 2008. Base-metal mines are operating on a 'care and maintenance basis' in part due to the global downturn.[28] According to Gapare, fewer than 10 of Zimbabwe's 88 mines are 'foreign'-owned, leaving little room for economic empowerment through wealth redistribution or dispossession. Nor have financial institutions the money to advance to those wanting to engage in empowerment deals.[29] Gapare would prefer to see wealth creation through growing the sector. The head of the Chamber of Commerce, Cain Mpofu, and Reserve Bank chief, Gideon Gono, concurred. Importantly, Gono warned that this new law could be derailed and abused by individuals with government contacts. Although the act confers

---

27 See interview with the Minister for Indigenisation and Economic Empowerment, Paul Mangwana ('Foreign firms to fund own take-overs', *Zimbabwe Independent*, 14 March 2008). The Department of Indigenisation and Empowerment plans to assign a rating for each company in every sector of the economy. Companies will be required to contribute a levy to an economic empowerment fund, the proceeds of which will be used to provide finance for the acquisition of shares, working capital and other forms of finance to indigenes.
28 'Experts urge caution on black empowerment in mining', *Zimbabwe Independent*, 25 June 2009.
29 Ibid.

entitlement on an aggrieved group or collective, in practice, restitution benefits will inevitably accrue to individuals (Davies 2004:39). Gono thus called on the government to ensure well-connected individuals did not 'amass wealth for themselves in a starkly greedy and irresponsible manner'.[30] War veterans have, however, forewarned that they are going to solve the industrial issue in the way they have solved the land issue (Meredith 2007:211). Captains of industry and local economists would rather lessons be learnt from land reform with regard to planning, transparency and good economic management—priorities they share with their counterparts among the white middle class.

Inevitably, Zimbabwe's challenges spilt over to its neighbours as people flocked to leave the country. Few reliable figures are available, but the Central Statistics Office (CSO) suggests 350 000 left in the six years after 2002 (FAO/WFP 2009:4). This figure represents only those who declared their intention to emigrate, rather than going on holiday, and who left legally through recognised exit points. The Reserve Bank points to three million people sending back remittances. Neither figure captures impoverished border jumpers. Huge numbers of them are now living illegally as refugees in South Africa and Botswana. Rutherford (2008b) describes the lot of more than 10 000 employed on corporate permits in the Musina area of South Africa, close to the Zimbabwean border (see also Rutherford and Addison 2007). Many more have headed deeper into the country to Gauteng and Cape Town, where they are not welcome and have been targeted in recent attacks on immigrants. Zimbabwe has also lost its educated and professional classes, who have gone in search of greener and safer pastures in the region or have sought asylum in the United Kingdom. Their right to leave was restricted in 2005 when departure not in the national, public or economic interest of the State was outlawed. Whites, however, are people Mugabe 'would prefer to do without'; he indeed 'would actually be happier if some country were [to] accept them',[31] but none, including Britain, readily acknowledged any obligation towards them. The United Kingdom agreed in 2009, however, to a humanitarian programme to repatriate elderly in need of medical and aged care in the next 18 months.[32]

In addition, there is widespread regional concern regarding the effect of Zimbabwe's disorder on other struggling economies. Yet, with a few notable exceptions, African leaders and organisations have proved unwilling to publicly criticise Mugabe's anti-colonial and anti-imperial stance, which 'strikes a

---

30   'Zimbabwe's equity law is a recipe for economic disaster', *ZWNEWS*, 10 March 2008.
31   Mugabe speaking on Independence Day 2001 and quoted by Meredith (2007:210). See also Gandhi and Jambaya quoted in Raftopoulos (2004a:164).
32   'Great Britain to remove nationals from Zimbabwe', *Afrik.com*, 18 February 2009; 'Britons repatriated from Zimbabwe', *The Zimbabwe Guardian*, 18 February 2009. The number of those eligible is believed to be between 500 and 1500 people, the latter figure representing half of the white population falling within this age bracket currently living in Zimbabwe.

deep emotional chord' (Eppel 2004:49). Various scholars have extolled the recuperative benefits of anti-colonial nationalism in Africa (Gandhi 1998:112). For others, the term 'post-colonial' does not sit easily with regard to Southern Africa's global positioning (Radhakrishnan 1996:155), in which colonialism's material after-effects are perceived to be ever present. The continuing and unequal distribution of wealth and opportunities associated with international capitalism suggest to many that colonialism is far from over (Parry 1995:93–4; Loomba 1994:308). Phimister (2004:282, 286) correctly observes that the majority of regional leaders are in agreement with Mugabe that Britain and the colonial past are the problems they still share. Most continue to recognise the legitimacy of Zimbabwe's government and Libya has helped out with fuel supplies. Young blacks are attracted by Mugabe's inflammatory rhetoric and are happy to see him lambast the British Government and other Western imperialists. His outbursts provide rich pickings for caricature in the West; but, when fed back to Africa, these add fuel to ever-more racial xenophobia and polarising schismogenesis.

The Global Political Agreement and transitional government

In March 2008, the MDC won the majority of seats in the National Assembly election and Morgan Tsvangirai took the first round of the presidential vote. The MDC could therefore legitimately claim the mandate to form a new government, but Mugabe would not concede. A sham run-off against no opposition put Mugabe back in State House. The MDC then entered into negotiations with ZANU PF in order to set up a power-sharing arrangement and a transitional government. Donor funds begun to flow again when they signed a Global Political Agreement in September 2008. The agreement, while reflecting the disparate ideologies held by ZANU PF and the two wings of the MDC, established grounds for discussions towards resolving the challenges confronting the country. The centrality of the land question as well as issues to do with the rule of law, human rights, democracy and governance were all acknowledged as key areas of contest (Kubatana.net, 15 September 2008). Among much else, the parties committed themselves to arrest the fall in living standards, reverse the decline of the economy and restore order in the agricultural sector. While President Mugabe and the MDC came to a power-sharing agreement in February 2009 under which Tsvangirai became Prime Minister as part of a transitional government, early indications suggest that this is not an easy relationship.[33] Six months into its first term, MDC ministerial appointees are still to be sworn in and provincial governor posts allocated, and the key positions of Attorney-General

---

33   See 'MDC position paper', *SW Radio Africa*, 19 January 2009.

and Governor of the Reserve Bank are yet to be agreed on. ZANU PF also appears to be deliberately frustrating the implementation of other key issues covered in the Global Political Agreement.

Some relief from Zimbabwe's economic woes came in March 2009 when the government abandoned the Zimbabwean dollar. With the introduction of convertible currencies as legal tender, hyperinflation was brought under control. Packaged food, mostly from South Africa, reappeared in supermarkets for those with sufficient purchasing power. Civil servants began to receive an 'allowance' of US$100 a month. While not a salary, this enabled a number of them to get back to work. Schools began to reopen. The BBC has been allowed back into the country after an eight-year absence. The country is, however, unlikely to attract significant foreign investment until the government addresses the issues of property rights and law and order. Confidence in social relations has also been a significant casualty of Zimbabwe's governance and food crises. During a trip to the United Kingdom in June 2009, Tsvangirai was asked by BBC reporters how he could work with Mugabe given ZANU PF's intimidation of the MDC and its supporters. In reply, Tsvangirai harked back to the now exhausted sentiments that informed the policy of reconciliation in the 1980s. Tsvangirai's audience, made up of Zimbabwean asylum seekers whom he wanted to return home and rebuild the country, clearly did not believe him and jeered him from the stage. Inevitably, a crisis of this magnitude has brought with it the breakdown of trust between fellow citizens, as well as a loss of faith in the country's social institutions and in the very idea of the nation itself.

Patriotic history and minority identity construction

Importantly, the Global Political Agreement reaffirmed the pre-eminent place in the nation 'of Zimbabwe's gallant sons and daughters' who were sacrificed in the fight against colonialism. Loyalty, patriotism and commitment were once again cited as core values, as well as the liberation struggle being foundational to sovereignty. This 'patriotic' version of history locks in colonialism and sets up a dualism that concedes only two races, two critiques of colonialism, two world views and two mutually exclusive sets of interests—namely, black and white. The party's vision, writes Raftopoulos (2004b:xx), has become trapped in the confines of this categorisation and as a result Zimbabwe's minority groups are offered only a backward-looking approach to identity construction.

ZANU PF's story of national rebirth explains present frustrations and hardships to the populace through a highly selective remembering of the past. In this way, ZANU PF shifts responsibility from itself and garners support for its increasingly autocratic government (Alden and Makumbe 2001:231). As the undifferentiated scapegoat[34] for ruling-party ineptitude and blamed for blocking black economic empowerment, whites, in league with the British, are demonised as the 'obstacle to real decolonisation' (Alexander 2006:185) and are cast on the wrong side in patriotic history. Trying to break out and find a legitimate place for themselves within the nation has been well nigh impossible given the ruling party's singular version of history, its 'iron grip' on the origin story (Hammar and Raftopoulos 2003:28), in which whites appear only as racists, thieves and oppressors. They must also contend with the co-joining of 'whites' with 'foreigners' about to be played out in the economic sector. These conceptual linkages both dis-empower and Occidentalise (Muzondidya 2004:225)—processes whites battled against throughout the 1990s. Unable to shed 'whiteness', however, this community finds itself a spent force.[35] With Zimbabwe's rulers obsessed with the past or race and origin (Muzondidya 2004:231), they, as Europeans, have no place in Zimbabwe.

Patriotic history's racial binaries also concede no middle ground for Zimbabwe's Asian and coloured communities, who are perceived to be part of the country's 'colonial residue' (Muzondidya 2005:2). The political legacy of the contradictory colonial experience is their ambiguous status as 'fence-sitters' and continued identification with white interests. As allies of the whites, they are perceived as outsiders and aliens and on these grounds denied rights, for multi-ethnicity is not a recognised part of Zimbabwe's nationhood. The Affirmative Action Group harasses Asian businesses and coloureds, who are labelled whites, must endure the 'extreme resentment of black extremists' and are told to leave for the United Kingdom (Muzondidya 2004:226–8). In sum, the difficulties faced by Zimbabwe's subject races can be traced to the inability to move beyond identity construction during the colonial period. This continues to inform post-independence nation building (Raftopoulos 2004b:xvi) and makes any association with 'whiteness' polluting.

While I was, anthropologically speaking, 'in the field', it was not always clear where decolonisation would lead or what change was 'producing' with regard to Zimbabwe's white community beyond a growing sense of estrangement, of their being disconnected and dislodged from the country they thought of as home. Race and history, however, have returned to Zimbabwe's identity politics as central and permanent, or, to employ Bonnett's (1997:177) powerful imagery, as impossible to escape and 'set outside social change'. Such is the historical burden of colonial-based identities for Europeans, Asians and coloureds who,

---

34 'Why lump together all whites?', *Zimbabwe Independent*, 12 February 1999, p. 7.
35 The *International Herald Tribune* (21 July 2008) estimated that 20 000 whites remained in the country; other sources said 30 000. Both figures should be treated with caution. Zimbabwe's CSO has declared the 2007 and 2008 inter-census figures 'unreliable', 'unusable' and 'not available' (FAO/WFP 2008:3, 2009:4).

as Rhodesia's flotsam, together made up in 2002 just 0.7 per cent of Zimbabwe's population. The ruling party underlines the continuing centrality of race and memory in their subject positioning (Raftopoulus 2004b:xx). The plurality of experience and the diversity of memories that make up 'white' in either the colonial or the post-colonial periods are not countenanced. Rather, ZANU PF blocks productive political debate and stifles dialogue by disallowing 'demeaning' questions or critical examination. Without a shared ownership of history—itself a potentially 'influential agent' of reconciliation (Clark and Reynolds 1994:1)—alternative renderings that could open up other configurations of the national collective are silenced. Thus, ZANU PF's 'iron grip' has done untold damage to civic society more generally through the loss of democratic space in which to talk about the past and the future (Raftopoulos 2004b:xiii). Reproducing crude binaries of race, as well as regional and party affiliations, has served to essentialise difference and entrench antagonisms (Hammar and Raftopoulos 2003:16), thereby obstructing the capacity to perceive oneself in the other and closing down the fragile third space of communication, negotiation and representation (Bhabha 1990b:211) identified in the preceding chapter.

9. Conclusion

Rhodesian nationalism was an assertion of belonging in and of a place and constituted the grounds for the whites' claim to a homeland. The settlers were able to depict themselves as being 'at home' because the black majority—distanced and produced as others—was 'not home' in Rhodesia. Instead, they were located elsewhere, in the peripheral spaces of the Tribal Trust Lands, urban townships and a few elite, but separate suburbs. Racism, as the highest expression of the colonial system, thus established fundamental and immutable distinctions between the colonist and the colonised. With the transfer of power, the order of the settlers' world began to be actively contested. Zimbabwe's newly installed political elite, while keeping and accepting pre-existing territorial borders, commenced a programme of decolonisation in order to claim ownership and control over the country and its institutions in the name of the black majority. Previous chapters addressed some of the challenges whites faced as political space was reconfigured and their subjectivity reconstituted within the memory of the discursive and material specificities of Rhodesian colonialism. To this end, representations inscribed in the national landscape, citizenship practices and the structure of the economy were examined. Each embodied a unique narrative, which, having been reworked, brought to the fore white 'unhomeliness', or what Bhabha (1994:9) called 'the estranging sense of the relocation of the home and the world'. Yet, while Zimbabwe's leaders set out to distance the country from the vestiges of colonialism, the point was made that 'whiteness' remained very much part of Zimbabwe's national conversation. How had this seeming paradox come about?

Zimbabwe, delimited in colonial terms, was inevitably racially and ethnically heterogeneous. To bring distinct populations together, a policy of reconciliation was introduced to promote the idea of Zimbabwe as a nation and to weld the people into a common identity and single loyalty. Its purpose was also to forestall further white emigration, with the concomitant loss of capital and skills—a factor that invariably accompanied reform after imperialism and the emergence of new states. The unmaking of Rhodesia and remaking as Zimbabwe proved no exception in this regard. Despite the departure of a sizeable proportion of the settler population around independence, reconciliation aimed to make everyone believe the country belonged to them and that all had a stake in its future wellbeing. Consequently the 1980s saw an attempt at 'civic nationalism' (Hammar and Raftopoulos 2003:25). The policy also established guidelines for managing the recent excesses committed by protagonists on all sides during the civil war. Unpalatable memories were not to be revisited and thereby made more familiar and approachable. A blanket amnesty allowed this part of the past to be put aside. The therapeutic agency of recall was not therefore an integral part of

Zimbabwe's reconciliation programme. Nonetheless, by extending an invitation to whites to stay and contribute to national reconstruction, reconciliation provided a new dialogic space within the politics of belonging. As an entreaty to resolve difference and end separation, the official discourse signalled the possibility of non-adversarial relationships binding African and European, as well as black with black, together in common awareness. A passage between fixed colonial identifications was suggested—a productive space of hope and an opportunity to move beyond Rhodesia's polarised colonial identities. As a double representation at once seductive and coercive (Gandhi 1998:14), however, the policy, while bringing minorities into the nation by flagging previously untried arrangements between them and the black government, enjoined whites to provide skills, create jobs and opportunities, co-opting them in effect to continue the symbiotic ties of the erstwhile colonial civilising mission.

The colonial legacy was also approached in other ways. The struggle for black self-determination and sovereignty began with the spatial re-inscription of the country. ZANU PF asked whites to accept African referents and national symbols as one step towards repairing social memory, of their thinking history together with the formerly colonised. In effect, decolonising the landscape provided a metaphor of cultural transformation and historical re-visioning, facilitating the reconstitution of Zimbabwe as a black African state, and beginning a process whereby the colonial past slipped away and with it the settlers' relationship with the place began to shift and weaken. Concomitantly, the State inscribed what was to be remembered, enter national consciousness and be carried forward into the future in Zimbabwe's commemorative monuments. Chapter 4 described the official critique of Rhodesia's past embedded at Heroes' Acre, today the nation's most significant architectural icon. The site records the colonial era's institutional violence, returning this to the present during ceremonies that seek to draw whites into a discourse that establishes the absolute necessity of their political re-education and loyalty. White 'liberation' entails the obligation to engage in a self-reflective recourse to history and to bring attitudes and practices into conformity. Thus, in Zimbabwe, constituting 'pastness' has proved a moral phenomenon, 'a tool' to compel whites to play an active part in their own subordination and domestication (Wallerstein 1988:78; Falzon 1998:66–8).

ZANU PF's return to the past, many Zimbabweans would perhaps argue, has been less than an honest and inclusive attempt to develop a collective history that offers some recognition of diversity and interconnectedness. Representations of the civil war—the prototypical event of Zimbabwe's inception—portray the singularity of national origins and draw an exclusionary myth of national membership. Revolutionary language from the armed struggle, linking the current political elite with war veterans, peasants and workers, suggests wrongs that can neither be undone nor forgotten. So while Heroes' Acre reflects the importance accorded by the political elite to whites liberating themselves, the monument simultaneously objectifies their difference. Otherness resonates within this anti-colonial national narrative in which state representations reassert past identities and inscribe repetition and the impossibility of going beyond old colonial habits and boundaries. The ruling elite has, in effect, revisited the colonial past in order to reclaim it in the party's interest. As an imposed, rather than a genuine recourse to, history, this self-serving rendering on behalf of its own authority and legitimacy has proved deaf to other memories of the war or, indeed, the colonial era. It is a telling that insists minorities 'forget' or discard memories incompatible with the State's narrative, thereby suppressing dialogue necessary to, and productive of, reconciliation.

The State's failure to develop a shared history has allowed, even encouraged, whites to fall back on and reassert a prior version of autochthony in defence of their community's place in the homeland. While the State appears set on having positive aspects of the Rhodesian past go unrecorded or 'remembered otherwise' (Esbenshade 1995:87), the white community had hoped to be written into the nation's history in more inclusive terms. Conceiving of national origins as deriving from before the country's recent revolutionary war, they seek to draw attention to continuity rather than rupture with the colonial past. Thus, they work to countermand the State's deconstruction of Rhodesian national identity, repudiate the degraded representations of themselves and have their era's positive contributions included in the genesis of national formation, for their future depends on the kind of past they can mobilise on this score.

Another reconstruction of the past, however, built on the illegality of the Rudd Concession and memories of colonial exploitation and dispossession, has provided the conceptual and ideological foundations to the government's economic policies and programmes. Soon after independence, practices of dis-assimilation in the public sector, based on insurmountable biological difference, were pursued in the interests of black affirmative action. A decade later, breaking the cognitive and economic confines of colonialism began to be formulated in popular, native terms. Political figures and lobbyists portrayed the nation as incomplete and referred to their responsibility to reverse previous colonial discrimination, to take remedial action and dispossess and displace in order that economic decolonisation be realised. Their creation of an insider's economic space for the formerly colonised in the name of indigenisation reflects black aspirations for materiality and modernity. The discourse references the theme of self-determination, with blacks insisting on control and exclusivity. Furthermore, black leaders intend to conduct the country's economic emancipation in a manner of their own choosing, even should the outcome appear flawed to Western eyes. This is a Pan-Africanist critique that insists on sovereignty. Yet, perversely, the discourse is not a wholly transparent rendering on the colonised's behalf. Instead, indigenisation has increasingly been seen as a movement of and for the Shona ethno-cultural and political elite, in effect an 'exclusive' or 'ethnic' nationalism driven by accumulators from above (Hammar and Raftopoulos 2003:25). In view of this, critics question who among the black majority truly qualifies as an indigene, thereby revealing regional, class and gender lines, in addition to race, along which the nation threatens to split apart.

Importantly, assertions of indigeneity as nativism—an oppositional rather than a complicit discourse—create and maintain borders between native and settler by defining social membership, not in terms of birth in a particular territory, but more authentically, into a place of cultural affinity. Hence, to speak of indigeneity in the Zimbabwean context is to belong according to genealogical, cultural and historical experiences. Chapter 6 noted the tendency in some quarters to take these criteria back to race, to biological essentialism, in tandem with claims about the fixity or boundedness of cultural criteria. The argument turns on the notion that culture represents the community of original identity to which one belongs by descent. Accordingly, whites do not belong in Zimbabwe because their cultural origins, and therefore their place, are elsewhere. This constitution of indigeneity nullifies complex identities in favour of an obligatory status ascribed according to descent. Settlers—their identities over-determined in this way—are fixed in perpetual otherness and, despite their protests, are immobilised and beholden to the culture of their ancestors.

When, as in Zimbabwe, distinctions such as these are inscribed in juridical texts and administrative practices, settlers are denied the possibility of changing their status and shifting their sense of identity. To the extent that the 1984 state-run renunciation of foreign citizenship described in Chapter 5 was conducted along Western lines, where citizenship was conceived first and foremost as a political and legal relationship, the exercise was misconceived. Western-liberal conceptions of belonging to civil society are not subjectively and emotionally convincing when a citizen, constituted as a cultural affiliate, is a 'home boy' and a person of place. Conscious of this, whites, while they claim their home country is manifest in travel documents, do not trust their identity as citizens of Zimbabwe and hold an ambivalent vision of their future under the present regime. They, in anxiety and uncertainty, remembering events in neighbouring countries when colonial populations fled or were expelled, hedge their bets and attempt to control their destinies with passports and residence stamps—behaviour contributing, in fact, to the future they most fear. Indeed, disputes about how citizenship is to be reinstated cannot be resolved on legal grounds alone when the codes of belonging are also cultural and historical. Today, cultural descent, constructed as the natural link between people and place, distinguishes black Zimbabweans from others whose ties to the country are based on other, contractual links of association.

In sum, Zimbabwe's decolonisation programme has served to highlight the role colonial memory continues to play in public life, informing certain subject positions and social boundaries and setting limits to the white community's sense of belonging and notions of home. Clearly, the process of returning to the colonial past and projecting it into the future has revealed continuing, reciprocal antagonism tending towards rupture. With the nation defined through opposition, it has proved difficult to depart from alterity—'an idea', Loomba (1998:182) astutely notes, 'that has enormous force and power in the construction of anti-colonial narratives, by subjects who are themselves complex, mixed-up products of diverse colonial histories'. The past repeats itself when decolonisation, as a search for creative autonomy, gives way to backward-looking arguments about authenticity and culture; when, just as in the colonial era, otherness is mobilised as a disposal of power to compare, contrast and invariably amplify difference. Zimbabwe's multiplicity of national discourses has become simplified into a 'paralysing dichotomy' (Loomba 1994:306) of two opposing racial voices, making the realisation of reconciliation impossible. The State's essentialism refuses ambivalence and, repeating colonial lessons, demands instead the fixity of identity. Rather than crediting the extent to which the protagonists are 'embroiled with each other', their various subject positions and class interests (Parry 1995:94), official discourses assert the 'insurmountability' of cultural difference and the incompatibility of lifestyles (Brah 1996:186). By building on difference in this way, the State has re-formed the categories of settler and native and, turning colonialism's hierarchy on its head, replaced it with its mirror image. The insider is now the outsider, the subject is resituated as the object and, in the process, bonds linking whites to locations have given way.

While the State must bear some responsibility for having failed to make room for all Zimbabweans, the white community has, of course, contributed in its own way to Zimbabwe's atmosphere of hostile schismogenesis. The point was made that deconstructing and remaking settler identity were reflexive projects, re-visioning towards induction into a new kind of social membership. As a process of social and cultural transformation, identity re-formation implicated whites in acts of distancing and association in order to establish a new relational beginning and to recover a sense of their own rightful placement in the country. Would they, for instance, engage in critical self-reflection and 'unsettle old habits and ways of thinking' (Falzon 1998:70)? Were they prepared to de-authorise and decentre themselves, accept non-leadership roles and learn the art of being minor? Would whites forgo positional authority, give up cultural arrogance and economic dominance and accept secondary positions or insist on self-centring? Would they overturn the colonial ethos, divest themselves of colonial superiority and instead embrace a role of service? Beyond disavowal, would the white community engage in acts of cultural affiliation and recognise that the politics of identification is performative, a matter of behaviours enacted or refused in everyday life? Their willingness, or otherwise, to renounce foreign citizenship was taken as a measure of their preparedness to conform not simply to externalities but, more importantly, to become habituated to deep-seated local values and customs. Would they allow themselves to be co-opted and assimilated? Would they cultivate and demonstrate organic solidarity, speaking in terms of 'we' rather than 'I', 'ours' and not 'yours'? Through these choices, the former colonists were expected to reposition themselves within the dominant normative culture by embracing practices that would re-form them as Zimbabweans.

Generally speaking, the white response was not encouraging and the pace of 'their becoming' Zimbabwean slow. They remained distrustful of reconciliation as a discourse of social, cultural and economic negotiation, readjustment and accommodation, and bulked at practising self-transformation, proving unwilling to be formed into moral subjects. Perceiving themselves as victims, rather than as the oppressors they were portrayed to be in the nationalist discourse, they also failed to understand the essentialism apparent in, for instance, Zimbabwe's current discourse surrounding indigeneity. Elsewhere, Curthoys (1999:4) has argued that the 'white blindfold' version of history works against Australian settlers understanding the colonial past. Equally, Zimbabwe's settlers' defensive articulation of the colonial period's positive worth has proved an ontological resource, myopically inhibiting their recognition that political independence has not in itself brought an end to the unequal colonial relationship. While various scholars caution that the 'new man' does not emerge immediately—rather, the colonist and colonised live on for some time—material presented in the body of the text suggests that many hold on to a prior identity, managing only partially to distance or disengage themselves from Rhodesia. To remember, though, is not solely to report on the past as to establish one's relationship towards it. The inability to repudiate the colonial era ties them, in the eyes of the once colonised, to the side of the oppressor, and makes theirs an immobilising rather than an empowering rendering of the past.

While Curthoys (1999:17) intimates that for Australians to face up to and acknowledge another, competing historical consciousness is to risk, metaphorically at least, becoming displaced, dislocated and homeless, this research suggests that, for the white settlers of Zimbabwe, lack of recognition is a path to expulsion in a more concrete sense, for far-reaching consequences arise from their lack of affinity with the time, place and history of the new Zimbabwe. White historical amnesia, or non-innocence, means they share neither the majority's colonial memories nor prevailing ideas regarding the nature of a future just society that these underpin. Many remaining in the country now sense themselves as estranged from their surroundings, 'caught in a historical limbo between home and the world' (Gandhi 1998:132). While not wishing to put too fine a point on it, males invariably spoke of loss of place in terms of their recently devalued national housekeeping tasks. Their eschewing Africa had existed alongside notions of progress and service. Women spoke more commonly of family, homemaking and their loss thereof. These unhomely moments reflect the psychic uncertainty that arises out of the disjunction between their personal history and wider political existence (Bhabha 1994:10, 12). The former coherence between themselves and the locale dissolved as families splintered and geo-cultural re-territorialisation disengaged these settlers from what was once their country. They now find themselves strangers and outsiders in the land where they were born, raised and continue to be domiciled.

Rhetorically, the question was posed whether whites could find a passage, or think, a way out of their current deracination. In common with other peoples of the diaspora (Hall 1995:206), they must come to some kind of settlement with the culture, albeit oppressive, that now immerses them. Could they countenance the unfamiliar and adjust to a life very different from the one that had given them form? Heideggar suggests the transformative quality of estrangement, of change producing encounters and confrontations with the alien as a precondition for self-discovery and relocation (Dallmayr 1993:153–5). To be at home in Zimbabwe, whites must discard the self constructed out of racial privilege and reconcile with all that they once kept separate. The majority have, however, failed to 'come home' by Heidegger's route—that is, by proximity or drawing near to that which is most alien to them, by way of a journey through otherness. While a few among them have long appreciated that to perceive oneself as securely and properly located and at home in the world depends on links created with human beings, as well as with the landscape, most refuse the disruptive, unsettling and ultimately transformative effects of association. Memmi (1965:40), writing of the need to empty one's identity in order to be reborn, comments that for settlers such as these it is 'too much to visualise one's own end, even if it is to be reborn another'. Both he and Fanon (1963:27), however, insist that this is the 'minimal demand of the colonised'. To refuse, as white Zimbabweans have found, is to reside anomalously as colonists, aliens and foreigners.

Unable to dissolve their separation or imagine the annihilation of their identity—the dissolution of the self—they have opted to remain as exiles in a state of *unheimlichkeit*, or 'not-at-homeness' (de Beistegui 1998:129–30). Not finding themselves to be at home is a matter of their reluctance to recognise that being at home in Rhodesia was an illusion grounded in colonial privilege. As those who once enjoyed dominance, most have failed to move on, to in effect leave home in order to come home. Like other refugee and exiled groups, Zimbabwe's settler population is 'marked by a loss' that 'they do not want to let go of' (Breytenbach 1991:75)—something reflected in a somewhat defiant refusal to accept the permanence of their changed status. A sizeable number share the sensibility of an era and the distress of identifying themselves with a country that no longer appears on any map and a place to which there is no return.

The crisis of legitimacy, arising between the former colonised and former colonisers, is approached differently in today's New World settler societies. With the idea of assimilation out of favour, access to the other through acts of self-negation or self-denial appears untenable (Falzon 1998:37). Instead, in Australia and New Zealand, where settler descendants remain politically dominant, sensitivity towards a recently reinstalled subaltern history and culture is located within a discourse of cultural diversity and multiculturalism. They are well positioned to represent their sense of locatedness in iconography that provides recognition of the rightful place of all the various peoples who today make up the nation. These accommodate difference within society by speaking to past and future interconnectedness. Native land title and reparations allow whites to meet colonialism's moral and economic challenges. Through acts of remembrance and compensation, state officials and scholars hope to create a hybrid consciousness and way of life for all nationals, for hybridity 'entertains difference without an assumed or imposed hierarchy' (Bhabha 1994:4). Here one-time colonists and settlers are not contained by state discourses that construct their identities and infer their anomalous presence. Instead, mutuality facilitates the permeability of boundaries and allows the construction of a number of versions of indigeneity not tied rigidly to specific colonial dates. In this way, colonial separation is erased and their legitimate placement established.

Notwithstanding this, various Third World scholars, as well as Zimbabwe's political leaders, remain unconvinced that memories of colonial violence can be transcended or replaced with readings of the era's negotiation and intimacy, arguing instead that hybridity is not the 'only enlightened resolution' to the colonial encounter (Gandhi 1998:136). They sceptically question whether hybridity overturns the colonial hierarchy, lessens the desire for retribution or establishes the equality of cultures. The concept has, as Moore-Gilbert (1997:194) cautions, been too often deployed on behalf of the dominant party and perhaps dispenses too quickly with where, and with whom, expectations of change lie. Aware that perturbing and unequal relations are not confined to the colonial past but exist currently within the North–South divide and relations of globalisation, scholars have expanded the scope of analysis, detaching ideas of hierarchy, exclusion and knowledge from the colonial context and examining them within this broader, contemporary framework. Others, writing more generally, have expressed reservations about the degree to which the indigene in settler societies is constructed within the larger narrative of the former oppressor (Griffiths 1994:84). Goldie (1989), in particular, is concerned by the extent to which the indigene is valorised, and by this means devalued and

9. Conclusion

silenced, in the acquisitive settler's desire to belong. The argument has been put that New Zealand and Australian settlers have, in effect, appropriated the icons and discourse of the colonised, thereby perpetuating the imperial process.

Clearly, the decolonisation of the colonisers' identity, as a route to legitimacy and their homecoming, is attained differently when the balance of semiotic power has been reversed. In Zimbabwe, where the State dominates the processes of subjectification, the colonial heritage has not been easily put aside. National historical, geographic and economic recovery has produced the once colonised as 'authentic' and 'at home' and whites, the former colonisers, as those who are 'different', 'out there' and 'not home'. Authenticity here relates an attitude to identity, a matter of choice and ways of being in the world, where historical re-visioning, political re-education and economic and cultural assimilation are the minimal preconditions for white social membership. The ruling party's insistence upon oneness as unity works against the legitimacy and acceptance of difference, making it instead a condition that must be done away with. Consequently, Zimbabwe's white community—with much historically and culturally in common with European settlers elsewhere—lives its unhomeliness more profoundly, for they carry the burden of colonial memory in a way their Antipodean counterparts do not. Assertions of indigeneity—central to the resolution of the settler identity crisis—cannot creditably be made simply on the basis of birth or claimed through affinity with the landscape. Rather, indigeneity in Zimbabwe is determined at the moment of colonial imposition. Being at home is, in this context, less a matter of expropriation or arrogation, something that can be taken for granted most of the time, but possible only through estrangement or exposure to otherness. Many white Zimbabweans have found this understanding or apprehending the other a tall order, particularly as this has been set against the rapid erosion of their prosperity. The State, however, argues that assimilation as a programme of profound change leads in one way or another to the minority's disappearance, thereby bringing the colonial relationship to a close. Taken as fundamental to state purposes, assimilation eliminates distinctions between the former colonisers and formerly colonised, putting an end to historical difference and leaving a way open for community.

Appendix

Table 1 Population size by ethnic group, 1901–2002, as at 30 June each year

Year	African	European	Asian	Coloured/mixed	Total
1901	700 000	11 100	1 500		712 600
1911	880 000	23 700	900	2 000	906 600
1921	1 110 000	33 800	1 300	2 000	1 147 100
1931	1 410 000	50 100	1 700	2 400	1 464 200
1941	1 930 000	69 300	2 600	4 000	2 005 900
1951	2 680 000	138 000	4 400	6 000	2 828 400
1961	3 730 000	221 000	7 100	10 400	3 968 000
1962	3 860 000	220 000	7 400	10 900	4 098 300
1969	4 880 000	130 000	9 000	15 300	5 134 300
1982	7 297 242	147 741	10 812	21 648	7 477 443
1992	10 284 345	82 797	13 386	30 063	10 412 548*
2002	115 479 986	46 743	11 492	22 146	11 631 657**

* total includes 1957 people classified as 'not stated'
** total includes 3260 people classified as 'other' or 'not stated'

Sources: Central Statistics Office 1987, *Statistical Year Book, 1987*; Central Statistics Office 1994, *Census 1992 Zimbabwe National Report*; Central Statistics Office 2004, *Census 2002 Zimbabwe National Report*.

Table 2 Zimbabwean whites by age group and level of education, 1992

Age	None	Primary	Secondary	Diploma/cert. After primary	Diploma/cert. after secondary	Grad/postgrad.	Not applicable	Not known	Total
0–4	0	0	0	0	0	0	3 390	0	3 390
5–9	1 473	2 374	0	0	0	0	5	7	3 859
10–14	26	2 927	782	0	0	0	1	6	3 742
15–19	20	167	3 524	36	132	0	0	16	3 895
20–24	38	145	2 386	31	1 050	272	0	12	3 934
25–29	37	147	2 236	53	1 513	632	0	9	4 627
30–34	86	174	2 216	54	1 516	789	1	20	4 856
35–39	57	132	1 846	36	1 273	678	0	24	4 046
40–44	50	125	1 867	52	1 177	563	1	21	3 856
45–49	51	115	1 971	52	1 176	505	0	15	3 885
50–54	48	122	2 023	59	1 178	524	0	21	3 975
55–59	31	164	2 002	55	1 045	507	0	17	3 821
60–64	41	199	2 144	82	1 014	495	0	18	3 993
65–69	29	201	1 868	76	780	406	0	40	3 400
70–74	35	277	1 482	66	579	265	0	41	2 745
75+	75	593	1 957	99	652	319	0	227	3 922
Not known	12	6	18	0	10	1	5	53	105
Total	2 109	7 868	28 322	751	13 095	5 956	4 003	547	62 651

Source: Central Statistics Office; Government of Zimbabwe.

Table 3 Occupational classification, whites, 1992

Occupation category	Number	Per cent
Government and senior officials		
Legislator	4	..
Senior government official	25	0.04
Directors, managers, company secretaries		
Director	2 686	4.3
Manager	5 377	8.6
Natural sciences		
Physicist	20	0.03
Mathematician	7	..
Astrologer	1	..
Business and finance		
Business professional	936	1.5
Finance and sales	1 331	2.1
Businessperson	1 280	2.0
Engineers and technicians		
Engineer	378	0.6
Science technician	371	0.6
Ship, aircraft technician	173	0.2
Technician (other)	419	0.7
Life sciences		
Life science professional	84	0.1
Medical doctor	174	0.3
Nurse	227	0.4
Dentist	28	0.04
Veterinarian	42	0.06
Chemist	77	0.1
Other health professional	4	..
Life science technician	83	0.1
Modern health assistant	87	0.1
Medical assistant	17	0.03
Traditional healer	15	0.02
Professionals		
Architect and associates	138	0.2
Legal professional	167	0.3
Archivist, librarian	56	0.09
Customs tax professional	61	0.1

Education		
Higher education teacher	126	0.2
Secondary education teacher	547	0.9
Primary education teacher	251	0.4
Special education teacher	17	0.03
Other teaching professional	82	0.13
Pre-primary teacher	100	0.16
Adult education teacher	11	0.02
Temporary secondary teacher	37	0.06
Temporary primary teacher	75	0.12
Other instructors	86	0.14
Law and security		
Armed forces	40	0.06
Police inspectors	43	0.07
Protective services	141	0.2
Senior special intelligence officers	37	0.06
Information		
Computer professional	320	0.5
Printing and related trade operators	100	0.16
Social science		
Social science professional	38	0.06
Artists		
Writers/artists	203	0.32
Artistic, entertainment, sports professional	6	..
Potters	9	..
Handicraft	19	0.03
Religion	128	0.2
Machine operators		
Optical and electrical machinists	95	0.15
Plant and machine operators	84	0.13
Plant and machine assemblers	2	..
Other plant and machine operators	1	..
Administration		
Administrative assistant professionals	1 884	3.01
Artistic associates	183	0.29

Clerks and secretaries		
Secretaries	2 611	4.17
Numerical clerks	945	1.51
Stock clerks	190	0.31
Library clerks	36	0.06
Other office clerks	114	0.18
Client information clerks	327	0.52
Other clerks	367	0.59
Messengers	23	0.04
Transport		
Locomotive drivers	43	0.07
Motor vehicle drivers	34	0.05
Ships' crew	2	..
Transport labourer	15	0.02
Travel attendant	76	0.12
Services		
Business services (agric.)	136	0.22
Cashier/teller	192	0.31
Street vendor	106	0.17
Restaurant/housekeeper	156	0.42
Personal care	149	0.25
Other personal service	170	0.27
Private domestic	118	0.19
Model	14	0.02
Garbage collector	24	0.04
Building caretaker	47	0.08
Domestic, not home	13	0.02
Shoe cleaner	1	..
Shop salesperson	488	0.78
Stall salesperson	7	..
Agriculture		
Commercial farmer	2 224	3.55
Subsistence farmer	386	0.62
Agriculture and other mobile plant operator	6	..
Agriculture and fish labourer	413	0.66
Fisher/hunter	95	0.15
Forest worker	11	0.02

Mining and construction		
Miner	78	0.12
Building framer	163	0.26
Building finisher	198	0.32
Painter	25	0.04
Gold panner	12	0.02
Mining and construction labourer	146	0.23
Mechanics		
Machinery mechanic	1 201	1.92
Electrical mechanic	338	0.54
Workshop attendant	68	0.11
Precision worker	24	0.04
Manufacturing		
Textile worker	109	0.17
Pelt, leather, shoes	13	0.02
Manufacturing labourer	169	0.27
Metal worker	191	0.30
Blacksmith	109	0.17
Wood treatment technician	53	0.08
Food processing	71	0.11
Other		
Other, not stated elsewhere	100	0.16
Unclassified	30 949	49.40
Not known	102	0.16
TOTAL	62 651	100.00

Source: Central Statistics Office; Government of Zimbabwe.

Appendix

Figure 1 White Zimbabweans, demographic structure, 1992

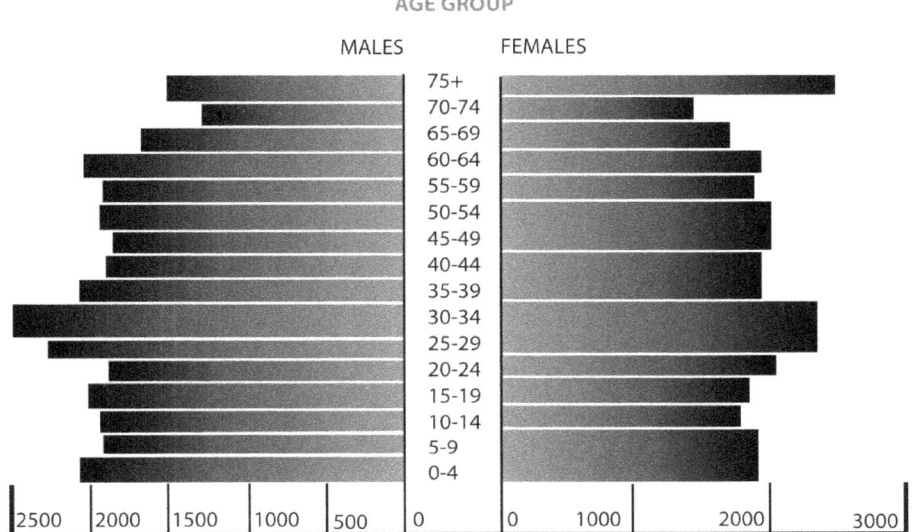

Source: Central Statistics Office; Government of Zimbabwe.

Bibliography

Agnew, J. 1987, *Place and Politics*, Allen & Unwin, Boston.

Ahmed A. 1973, 'Some remarks from the Third World on anthropology and colonialism: the Sudan', in T. Asad (ed.), *Anthropology and the Colonial Encounter*, Ithaca Press, London, pp. 259–70.

Alden, P. and Makumbe, J. 2001, 'The Zimbabwe constitution: race, land reform and social justice', in G. Cornwell and E. Stoddard (eds), *Global Multiculturalism*, Rowman and Littlefield, United States of America, pp. 215–37.

Alexander, J. 1998, 'Dissident perspectives on Zimbabwe's post-independence war', *Africa*, vol. 68, no. 2, pp. 151–79.

Alexander, J. 2003, 'Squatters, veterans and the State in Zimbabwe', in A. Hammar, B. Raftopoulos and S. Jensen (eds), *Zimbabwe's Unfinished Business*, Weaver Press, Harare, pp. 83–117.

Alexander, J. 2006, *The Unsettled Land*, James Currey, Oxford.

Alexander, J. and McGregor, J. 2004, 'War stories: guerrilla narratives of Zimbabwe's liberation war', *History Workshop Journal*, issue 57, pp. 81–100.

Alexander, J. and McGregor, J. 2005, 'Hunger, violence and the moral economy of war in Zimbabwe', in V. Broch-Due (ed.), *Violence and Belonging: The quest for identity in postcolonial Africa*, Routledge, London, pp. 75–90.

Alexander, J., McGregor, J. and Ranger, T. 2000, *Violence and Memory—One hundred years in the 'dark forests' of Matabeleland*, James Currey, Oxford.

Alexander, K. 2004, 'Orphans of the empire. An analysis of elements of white identity and ideology construction in Zimbabwe', in B. Raftopoulos and T. Savage (eds), *Zimbabwe Injustice and Political Reconciliation* Weaver Press, Harare, pp. 193–212.

Amani Trust 1997, *Narrative Report*, April–June, Amani Trust, Harare.

Amani Trust 1998, *Survivors of Organised Violence in Matabeleland: Facilitating an agenda fordevelopment*, Amani Trust, Harare.

Anderson, B. 1990, *Imagined Communities*, Verso, London.

Anderson, B. 1992, 'The new world disorder', *New Left Review*, no. 193, pp. 3–14.

Anderson, D. 1989, *The Toe-Rags: A memoir*, Andre Deutsch Ltd, London.

Angelou, M. 1987, *All God's Children Need Travelling Shoes*, Virago Press, London.

Anthias, F. and Yuval-Davis, N. 1992, *Racialized Boundaries*, Routledge, New York and Oxford.

Appadurai, A. 1988, 'Putting hierarchy in its place', *Cultural Anthropology*, vol. 3, no. 1, pp. 36–49.

Appiah, K. 1991, 'Out of Africa: topologies of nativism', in D. La Capra (ed.), *The Bounds of Race*, Cornell University Press, Ithaca, pp. 134–64.

Applegate, C. 1992, 'The question of *Heimat* in the Weimar Republic', *New Formations*, no. 17 (Summer), pp. 64–74.

Asad, T. 1973, 'Introduction', *Anthropology and the Colonial Encounter*, Ithaca Press, London, pp. 9–19.

Asad, T. 1991, 'Afterword: from the history of colonial anthropology to the anthropology of Western hegemony', in G. Stocking (ed.), *History of Anthropology: Essays on the contextualization of ethnographic knowledge. Volume 7*, pp. 314–24.

Ashcroft, B. 1997, 'Globalism, post-colonialism and African studies', in P. Ahluwalia and P. Nursey-Bray (eds), *Post Colonialism: Culture and identity in Africa*, Nova Science Publishers, Commack, NY, pp. 11–26.

Ashcroft, B., Williams, G. and Tiffin, H. (eds) 1995, *The Post Colonial Studies Reader*, Routledge, New York and Oxford.

Asmal, K. 1997, *Reconciliation Through Truth: A reckoning of apartheid's criminal governance*, James Currey Ltd, Oxford.

Astrow, A. 1983, *Zimbabwe: A revolution that lost its way?*, Zed Press, London.

Auret, D. 1992, *Reaching for Justice. The Catholic Commission for Justice and Peace 1972–1992*, Mambo Press, Gweru.

Australian Bureau of Immigration, Multicultural and Population Research 1995, *Australian Citizenship—1991 Census*, Statistical Report no. 15, Australian Government Printer, Canberra.

Bailey, F. 1983, *The Tactical Uses of Passion*, Cornell University Press, Ithaca, NY.

Balibar, E. 1987, 'Propositions on citizenship', *Ethics*, vol. 98, pp. 723–8.

Balibar, E. 1991, 'The national form: history and ideology', in E. Balibar and I. Wallerstein, *Race, Nation and Class*, Routledge, New York and Oxford, pp. 86–106.

Bammer, A. 1992, 'Editorial', *New Formations*, no. 17 (Summer), pp. vii–xi.

Barnes, T. 2004, 'Reconciliation, ethnicity and school history in Zimbabwe 1980–2002', in B. Raftopoulos and T. Savage (eds), *Zimbabwe Injustice and Political Reconciliation*, Weaver Press, Harare, pp. 140–59.

Bateson, G. 1958, *Naven*, Stanford University Press, California.

Bateson, G. 1973, *Steps to an Ecology of Mind*, Paladin Books, New York.

Batwell, J. 1996, 'A great occasion for Bulawayo: the railway comes to town', *Heritage of Zimbabwe*, no. 15, pp. 1–16.

Bauman, Z. 1997, 'The making and unmaking of strangers', in P. Werbner and T. Modood (eds), *Debating Cultural Hybridity*, Zed Books, London, pp. 46–58.

Beach, D. 1980, *The Shona and Zimbabwe*, Heinemann, London.

Berlyn, P. 1967, *Beleaguered Country*, Mitre Press, London.

Berry, B. n.d., *Flying in the Winds of Change: Flags from Rhodesia to Zimbabwe*, National Archives, Harare.

Betts, R. 1998, *Decolonization*, Routledge, New York and Oxford.

Bhabha, H. 1990a, 'Introduction: narrating the nation', *Nation and Narration*, Routledge, Oxford, pp. 1–7.

Bhabha, H. 1990b, 'The third space', in J. Rutherford (ed.), *Identity: Community, culture and difference*, Lawrence and Wishart, London, pp. 207–21.

Bhabha, H. 1990c, 'The other question: difference, discrimination and the discourse of colonialism', in R. Ferguson et al. (eds), *Out There*, MIT Press, Cambridge, Mass., pp. 71–86.

Bhabha, H. 1994, *The Location of Culture*, Routledge, Oxford.

Bhabha, H. 1997, 'Of mimicry and man', in F. Cooper and L. Stoller (eds), *Tensions of Empire*, University of California Press, Berkeley, pp. 152–60.

Bhebe, N. and Ranger, T. (eds) 1995, 'General' and 'Volume introduction', *Soldiers in Zimbabwe's Liberation War. Volume 1*, University of Zimbabwe Publications, Harare, pp. 1–23.

Blake, R. 1978, *A History of Rhodesia*, Albert Knopf Inc., New York.

Bloch, E. and Robertson, J. 1996, *Zimbabwe: Facing the facts*, Thomson Publications, Harare.

Bloch, M. 1975, 'Introduction', *Political Language and Oratory in Traditional Society*, Academic Press, London, pp. 1–28.

Bloch, M. 1996, 'Internal and external memory: different ways of being in history', in P. Antze and M. Lambek (eds), *Tense Past*, Routledge, New York and Oxford, pp. 215–34.

Bodnar, J. 1994, 'Public memory in an American city: commemoration in Cleveland', in J. Gillis (ed.), *Commemorations*, Princeton University Press, Princeton, NJ, pp. 74–90.

Bonnett, A. 1997, 'Constructions of whiteness in European and American anti-racism', in P. Werbner and T. Modood (eds), *Debating Cultural Hybridity*, Zed Books, London, pp. 173–92.

Borneman, J. 1992, 'State, territory, and identity formation in the postwar Berlins, 1945–1989', *Cultural Anthropology*, vol. 7, no. 1, pp. 45–60.

Bourdillon, M. 1987, *The Shona Peoples*, Mambo Press, Gwelo.

Bowman, G. 1994, 'A country of words: conceiving the Palestinian nation from the position of exile', in E. Laclau (ed.), *The Making of Political Identities*, Verso, London and New York, pp. 138–65.

Bowman, L. 1973, *Politics in Rhodesia: White power in an African state*, Harvard University Press, Cambridge, Mass.

Brah, A. 1993, 'Re-framing Europe: engendered racisms, ethnicities and nationalisms in contemporary Western Europe', *Feminist Review*, vol. 45, pp. 9–29.

Brah, A. 1996, *A Cartographics of Diaspora*, Routledge, New York and Oxford.

Bratton, M. and Burgess, S. 1987, 'Afro-Marxism in a market economy: public policy in Zimbabwe', in E. Keller and D. Rothchild (eds), *Afro-Marxist Regimes*, Lynne Reiner Publishers, Boulder, Colo., pp. 199–222.

Brennan, T. 1990, 'The national longing for form', in H. Bhabha (ed.), *Nation and Narration*, Routledge, Oxford, pp. 44–68.

Breytenbach, B. 1991, 'The long march from hearth to heart', *Social Research*, vol. 58, no. 1, pp. 69–83.

Broby, M. 1978, Can Rhodesia survive an exodus of skilled manpower?, Public lecture presented at the University of Rhodesia, Salisbury, pp. 1–15.

Brubaker, R. 1996, *Nationalism Reframed: Nationhood and the national question in Europe*, Cambridge University Press, Cambridge.

Burchell, G., Gordon, C. and Miller, P. (eds) 1991, *The Foucault Effect*, Harvester Wheatsheaf, London.

Burrett, R. 1996, 'Gweru and its environs: a glimpse of the Matabele uprising—First *Umvukela*, 1896', *Heritage of Zimbabwe*, no. 15, pp. 37–55.

Cabinet Task Force on the Indigenisation of the Economy 1994, *Policy on Indigenisation of the Economy*, Government Printer, Harare.

Cambridge, A. and Feuchtwang, S. 1990, *Antiracist Strategies*, Avebury, United States of America.

Carter, E., Donald, J. and Squires, J. (eds) 1993, 'Introduction', *Space and Place: Theories of identity and location*, Lawrence and Wishart, London, pp. vii–xv.

Carter, P. 1987, *The Road to Botany Bay*, Faber and Faber Ltd, London and Boston.

Cary, R. 1975, *The Story of Reps*, Galaxie Press, Salisbury.

Castles, S. 1996, 'A German dilemma: ethnic identity and the debate on citizenship', in G. Fischer, *Debating Enzensberger—Great migration and the civil war*, Stauffenberg Verlag, Tubingen, pp. 169–85.

Castles, S. and Iredale, R. 1994, 'Australian immigration between globalization and recession: conference report', *International Migration Review*, vol. xxviii, no. 2, pp. 370–83.

Catholic Commission for Justice and Peace (CCJP) 1995, *Keeping a Live Voice*, Audiovisual recording, produced by E. Spicer.

Catholic Commission for Justice and Peace (CCJP) and Legal Resources Foundation 1997, *Breaking the Silence, Building True Peace. A report on the disturbances in Matabeleland and Midlands 1980–1988*, Catholic Commission for Justice and Peace and Legal Resources Foundation, Harare.

Caute, D. 1983, *Under the Skin: The death of white Rhodesia*, Allen Lane, London.

Central Statistics Office (CSO) 1987, *Statistical Year Book*, Government Printer, Harare.

Central Statistics Office (CSO) 1994, *Census 1992, Zimbabwe National Report*, Government Printer, Harare.

Central Statistics Office (CSO) 2004, *Census 2002, Zimbabwe National Report*, Government Printer, Harare.

Chakrabarty, D. 2000, *Provincializing Europe*, Princeton University Press, Princeton, NJ.

Chambati, A. 1994, 'Zimbabwe: indigenisation of the economy—can it work?', *SAPEM*, August, pp. 12–14.

Chater, P. 1985, *Caught in the Crossfire*, Zimbabwe Publishing House, Harare.

Chaza, G. 1998, *Bhurakuwacha Black Policeman in Rhodesia*, The College Press, Harare.

Cheater, A. 1984, *Idioms of Accumulation*, Mambo Press, Gweru.

Cheater, A. 1990, 'The ideology of "communal" land tenure in Zimbabwe: mythogenesis enacted?', *Africa*, vol. 60, no. 2, pp. 188–206.

Cheater, A. 1998, 'Transcending the state? Gender and borderline constructions of citizenship in Zimbabwe', in T. Wilson and H. Donnan (eds), *Border Identities*, CUP, New York, pp. 189–214.

Cheater, A. and Gaidzanwa, R. 1996, 'Citizenship in neo-patrilineal states: gender and mobility in Southern Africa', *Journal of Southern African Studies*, vol. 22, no. 2 (June), pp. 189–99.

Chennells, A. 1989, 'White Rhodesian nationalism—the mistaken years', in C. Banana (ed.), *Turmoil and Tenacity*, College Press, Harare, pp. 123–39.

Chennells, A. 1995, 'Rhodesian discourse, Rhodesian novels and the Zimbabwe liberation war', in N. Bhebe and T. Ranger (eds), *Society in Zimbabwe's Liberation War. Volume 2*, University of Zimbabwe Publications, Harare, pp. 102–29.

Chidyausiku, G. 1998, *Report of the Commission of Inquiry into the Administration of the War Victims Compensation Act*, Government Printer, Harare, Chapter 11.16.

Childs, P. and Williams, P. 1997, *An Introduction to Post-Colonial Theory*, Prentice Hall, London.

Chipeta, C. 1998, 'Indigenous African economic system', *SAPEM*, March, pp. 23–5.

Chiumbu, S. 2004, 'Redefining the national agenda—media and identity: challenges of building a new Zimbabwe', in H. Melber (ed.), *Media, Public Discourse and Political Contestation in Zimbabwe*, Elanders Infologistics Vast, Goteborg, pp. 29–35.

Chuma, W. 2004, 'Liberating or limiting the public sphere? Media policy and the Zimbabwean transition, 1980–2004', in B. Raftopoulos and T. Savage (eds), *Zimbabwe Injustice and Political Reconciliation*, Weaver Press, Harare, pp. 119–39.

Chung, F. 1989, 'The land issue: what is to be done?', *SAPEM*, October, pp. 8–11.

Clarke, D. 1974, 'Settler ideology and African underdevelopment in postwar Rhodesia', *The Rhodesian Journal of Economics*, vol. 8, no. 1, pp. 17–38.

Clarke, D. 1977, *Distribution of Wealth and Income in Rhodesia*, Mambo Press, Gwelo.

Clarke, D. 1978, 'The pattern of white emigration/immigration and their effects on the Zimbabwean economy', *Zimbabwe Manpower Survey*, vol. 2, Patriotic Front Seminar Report, Geneva, pp. 207–16.

Clark, I. and Reynolds, H. 1994, *Sharing History: A sense for all Australians of a shared ownership of their history*, Council for Aboriginal Reconciliation, Australian Government Publishing Service, Canberra, pp. 1–43.

Clements, F. 1969, *Rhodesia*, Praeger Publishers, New York.

Clifford, J. 1988, 'On orientalism', *The Predicament of Culture*, Harvard University Press, Cambridge, Mass., pp. 255–76.

Clifford, J. 1992, 'Travelling cultures', in L. Grossberg, C. Nelson and P. Treichler (eds), *Cultural Studies*, Routledge, New York and Oxford, pp. 96–116.

Clifford, J. 1994, 'Diasporas', *Cultural Anthropology*, vol. 9, no. 3, pp. 302–38.

Clutton Brock, G. 1969, *Rekayi Tangwena 'Let Tangwena Be'*, Mambo, Gwelo.

Clutton Brock, G. 1970, *The Cold Comfort Farm Society*, Mambo, Gwelo.

Clutton Brock, G. 1987, *Guy and Molly Clutton Brock: Reminiscences by their family and friends*, Longman, Harare.

Cohen, A. 1994, *Self Consciousness. An alternative anthropology of identity*, Routledge, Oxford.

Cooke, P. 1994, 'The Southern Rhodesian air force', *Heritage of Zimbabwe*, no. 13, pp. 123–36.

Conner, W. 1986, 'The impact of homelands upon diasporas', in G. Sheffer (ed.), *Modern Diasporas in International Politics*, St Martins Press, New York, pp. 16–45.

Connerton, P. 1989, *How Societies Remember*, Cambridge University Press, Cambridge.

Cousins, B. 2003, 'The Zimbabwe crisis in its wider context: the politics of land, democracy and development in Southern Africa', in A. Hammar, B. Raftopoulos and S. Jensen (eds), *Zimbabwe's Unfinished Business*, Weaver Press, Harare, pp. 263–315.

Crapanzano, V. 1985, *Waiting: The whites of South Africa*, Random House, New York.

Curthoys, A. 1993, 'Feminism, citizenship and national identity', *Feminist Review*, no. 44, pp. 19–38.

Curthoys, A. 1999, 'Expulsion, exodus and exile in white Australian historical mythology', *Journal of Australian Studies*, Special issue: 'Imaginary Homelands', vol. 23, no. 61, pp. 1–18.

Dahrendorf, R. 1994, 'The changing quality of citizenship', in B. Van Steenbergen (ed.), *The Condition of Citizenship*, Sage, London, pp. 10–19.

Dallmayr, F. 1993, *The Other Heidegger*, Cornell University Press, Ithaca.

Dashwood, H. 1996, 'The relevance of class to the evolution of Zimbabwe's development strategy, 1980–1991', *Journal of Southern African Studies*, vol. 22, no. 1, pp. 27–47.

Davidow, J. 1979, *A Peace in Southern Africa: The Lancaster House Conference on Rhodesia*, Westview Press, Boulder, Colo.

Davies, R. 2004, 'Memories of underdevelopment: a personal interpretation of Zimbabwe's economic decline', in B. Raftopoulos and T. Savage (eds), *Zimbabwe Injustice and Political Reconciliation*, Weaver Press, Harare, pp. 19–42.

Davis, F. 1979, *Yearning for Yesterday*, The Free Press, New York.

Day, J. 1983, 'Continuity and change in the African parties of Zimbabwe during the struggle for majority rule', in P. Lyon and J. Manor (eds), *Transfer and Transformation*, Leicester University Press, Leicester, pp. 167–82.

de Beistegui, M. 1998, *Heidegger and the Political*, Routledge, Oxford.

Dembour, M. 2000, *Recalling the Belgium Congo*, Berghahn Books, New York.

Department of Immigration Promotion 1965–72, *Annual Reports*, Government of Rhodesia, Government Printers, Salisbury.

Department of Prime Minister and Cabinet 1975, *The National Anthem of Rhodesia*, 24 September 1975.

Department of State Enterprises and Indigenisation, Office of the President and Cabinet 1997, *Draft Policy Framework for Indigenisation of the Economy*, Government Printer, Harare.

Des Chene, M. 1997, 'Locating the past', in A. Gupta and J. Ferguson (eds), *Anthropological Locations*, University of California Press, Berkeley, pp. 66–85.

Deve, T. 1993, 'Zimbabwe: politicising the land issue', *SAPEM*, July, pp. 21–2.

Deve, T. 1997, 'War veterans: the forgotten people', *SAPEM*, August, pp. 8–9.

De Waal, V. 1990, *The Politics of Reconciliation*, Longman, Harare.

Dhalla, P. 1993, 'Contesting the future: Indian ethnic politics and the competing moral of nonracialism and multiracialism in South Africa', in S. Falk Moore (ed.), *Moralizing States and the Ethnography of the Present*, American Ethnological Society Monograph (no. 5), Arlington, Va, pp. 17–54.

Di Perna, A. 1978, *A Right to be Proud*, Books of Rhodesia Publishing Company, Rhodesia.

Dominey, M. 1990, 'Cultural politics in New Zealand', *Anthropology Today*, vol. 6, no. 3, pp. 3–21.

Dominey, M. 1993, 'Lives were always here: the inhabited landscape of the New Zealand high country', *Anthropological Forum*, vol. VI, no. 4, pp. 567–85.

Dominey, M. 1995, 'White settler assertions of native status', *American Ethnologist*, vol. 22, no. 2, pp. 358–75.

Driver, F. 1992, 'Geography and power: the work of Michel Foucault', in P. Burke (ed.), *Critical Essays on Foucault*, Scolar Press, Aldershot, Hants, pp. 147–56.

Drury, A. 1967, *A Very Strange Society*, Hollen Street Press, United Kingdom.

Dumbutshena, T. 1993, 'White exodus, white return', *SAPEM*, April, pp. 4–6.

During, S. 1987, 'Postmodernism or post-colonialism', *Textual Practice*, no. 1, pp. 32–47.

Dzimba, J. 1998, *South Africa's Destabilisation of Zimbabwe, 1980–1990*, St Martin's Press, New York.

Dzingirai, V. 1994, *Politics and ideology in human settlement*, Occasional Papers—NRM Series, CASS, University of Zimbabwe, Harare, pp. 1–9.

Eddy, J. and Schreuder, D. (eds) 1988, 'Introduction', *The Rise of Colonial Nationalism*, Allen & Unwin, Sydney, pp. 1–14.

Eley, G. and Suny, G. (eds) 1996, 'Introduction', *Becoming National*, Oxford University Press, New York, pp. 3–37.

Elsener, J. 1965, *My Life Tomorrow—A teachers' guide*, Mambo Press, Gwelo.

Emmanuel, A. 1972, 'White settler colonialism and the myth of investment imperialism', *New Left Review*, no. 73, pp. 35–57.

Eppel, S. 2004, '*Gukurahundi* the need for truth and reparation', in B. Raftopoulos and T. Savage (eds), *Zimbabwe Injustice and Political Reconciliation*, Weaver Press, Harare, pp. 43–62.

Esbenshade, R. 1995, 'Remembering to forget: memory, history, national identity in postwar East–Central Europe', *Representations*, vol. 49, pp. 72–96.

Faber, M. 1961, 'The distribution of income between racial groups in Southern Rhodesia', *Race*, vol. 2, no. 2, pp. 41–52.

Falk Moore, S. 1987, 'Explaining the present: theoretical dilemmas in processual ethnography', *American Ethnologist*, vol. 14, pp. 727–37.

Falk Moore, S. (ed.) 1993, 'Introduction', *Moralizing States and the Ethnographic Present*, American Ethnological Society Monograph Series (no. 5), Arlingon, Va, pp. 1–17.

Falk Moore, S. 1994, *Anthropology and Africa: Changing perspectives on a changing scene*, University Press of Virginia, Charlottesville.

Falzon, C. 1998, *Foucault and Social Dialogue*, Routledge, New York and Oxford.

Fanon, F. 1963, *The Wretched of the Earth*, Penguin, Harmondsworth.

Fanon, F. 1965, 'Algeria's European minority', *A Dying Colonialism*, Penguin, Harmondsworth, pp. 143–58.

Ferguson, J. 1992, 'The country and the city on the Copperbelt', *Cultural Anthropology*, vol. 7, no. 1, pp. 80–92.

Ferguson, J. 1993, 'De-moralizing economies: African socialism, scientific socialism and the moral politics of structural adjustment', in S. Falk Moore (ed.), *Moralizing States and the Ethnography of the Present*, American Ethnological Society Monograph Series (no. 5), Arlington, Va, pp. 78–92.

Ferguson, R. (ed.) 1990, 'Introduction: invisible centre', *Out There: Marginalization and contemporary cultures*, MIT Press, Cambridge, Mass., pp. 2–7.

Fitzgerald, M. 1982, 'European and Asian minorities in Kenya', *Africa Insight*, no. 2, pp. 115–17.

Flower, K. 1987, *Serving Secretly*, John Murray, London.

Food and Agriculture Organisation/World Food Programme (FAO/WFP) 2008, *Special Report Zimbabwe: Crop and food supply assessment mission*, Food and Agriculture Organisation/World Food Programme, Rome.

Food and Agriculture Organisation/World Food Programme (FAO/WFP) 2009, *Special Report Zimbabwe: Crop and food security assessment mission*, Food and Agriculture Organisation/World Food Programme, Rome.

Ford, J. 1991, 'Frederick Courteney Selous (1851–1917)', *Heritage of Zimbabwe*, no. 10, pp. 131–48.

Foucault, M. 1982, 'Afterword: the subject and power', in H. Drefus and P. Rabinow, *Michel Foucault: Beyond structuralism and hermeneutics*, Harvester Press, Brighton, pp. 208–26.

Foucault, M. 1991, 'Governmentality', in G. Burchell, C. Gordon and P. Miller (eds), *The Foucault Effect*, Harvester Wheatsheaf, London, pp. 87–104.

Frankenberg, R. and Mani, L. 1993, 'Crosscurrents, crosstalk: race, postcoloniality and the politics of location', *Cultural Studies*, vol. 7, no. 2, pp. 292–310.

Friedman, J. 1992, 'Myth, history, and political identity', *Cultural Anthropology*, vol. 7, no. 2, pp. 194–210.

Friedrich Ebert Stiftung/Zimbabwe Economics Society 1997, *The Impact of ESAP on the Communal Areas of Zimbabwe*, Friedrich Ebert Stiftung/Zimbabwe Economics Society, Harare.

Friedrich Ebert Stiftung/Zimbabwe Economics Society 1998a, *The Land Reform Challenge: An economic and social perspective. Volumes 1 and 2. Seminar Proceedings*, no. 16, Friedrich Ebert Stiftung/Zimbabwe Economics Society, Harare.

Friedrich Ebert Stiftung/Zimbabwe Economics Society 1998b, *Land reform in Zimbabwe: farmers' and academics' view point*, Working Paper no. 23, Friedrich Ebert Stiftung/Zimbabwe Economics Society, Harare.

Friedrich Ebert Stiftung/Zimbabwe Economics Society 1998c, *Staple Foods and Producer Prices: Where do they go?*, Friedrich Ebert Stiftung/Zimbabwe Economics Society, Harare.

Fulford, R. 1993, 'A post-modern dominion: the changing nature of Canadian citizenship', in W. Kaplan (ed.), *Belonging. The meaning and future of Canadian citizenship*, McGill-Queens University Press, Montreal, Quebec, pp. 104–19.

Furusa, M. 1998, 'The role of institutions in development', in E. Chiwome and Z. Gambahaya (eds), *Culture and Development: Perspectives from the South*, Mond Books, Harare, pp. 49–54.

Gaidzanwa, R. 1993, 'Citizenship, nationality, gender and class in Southern Africa', *Alternatives*, vol. 18, pp. 39–59.

Gaidzanwa, R. 1997, Indigenisation as empowerment? Gender, race, ethnicity and class in the empowerment discourse in Zimbabwe, Paper presented at the ASA Conference Power, Empowerment and Disempowerment in Changing Structures, Harare, January.

Galvin, T. 1991, Socio-cultural sources of stress in marital decision making among Zimbabweans married to foreigners, Unpublished D.Phil thesis, University of Zimbabwe, Harare.

Gandhi, L. 1998, *Postcolonial Theory*, Allen & Unwin, St Leonards, NSW.

Gann, L. 1961, 'The white settler: a changing image', *Race*, vol. 2, no. 2, pp. 28–40.

Gann, L. 1965, *A History of Southern Rhodesia*, Chatto and Windus, London.

Gates, H. 1991, 'Critical Fanonism', *Critical Inquiry*, vol. 17, no. 3, pp. 457–70.

Geertz, C. 1995, *After the Fact*, Harvard University Press, Cambridge, Mass.

George, R. 1996, *The Politics of Home*, Cambridge University Press, New York.

Gillis, J. (ed.) 1994, 'Introduction—memory and identity: the history of a relationship', *Commemorations*, Princeton University Press, Princeton, NJ, pp. 3–24.

Gilroy, P. 1996, 'One nation under a groove: the cultural politics of "race" and racism in Britain', in G. Eley and G. Suny (eds), *Becoming National*, Oxford University Press, New York, pp. 352–69.

Gmelch, G. 1983, 'Who returns and why: return migration behaviour in two North Atlantic societies', *Human Organisation*, vol. 42, no. 1, pp. 46–54.

Godwin, P. 1996, *Mukiwa: A white boy in Africa*, Picador, London.

Godwin, P. and Hancock, I. 1993, *Rhodesians Never Die*, Oxford University Press, Oxford.

Goldie, T. 1989, *Fear and Temptation*, McGill-Queens University Press, Kingston, Ontario.

Goldin, I. and van der Mensbrugghe, D. 1993, *Trade liberalisation: what's at stake?*, Policy Brief no. 5, OECD Development Centre, Organisation for Economic Cooperation and Development, Paris.

Good, K. 1974, 'Settler colonialism in Rhodesia', *African Affairs*, vol. 73, pp. 10–36.

Gordon, D. 1966, *The Passing of French Algeria*, Oxford University Press, London.

Government of Zimbabwe 1981, *Growth With Equity—An economic policy statement*, February, Government Printer, Harare.

Government of Zimbabwe 1982, *National Development Plan 1982–1985*, Government Printer, Harare.

Government of Zimbabwe 1991, *Zimbabwe: A framework for economic reform 1991–1995*, Government Printer, Harare.

Government of Zimbabwe 1998a, *Land Reform and Redistribution Programme: Progress report*, Government Printer, Harare.

Government of Zimbabwe 1998b, *ZIMPREST Zimbabwe's Programme for Economic and Social Transformation*, Government Printer, Harare.

Grant, D. 1994, 'Focus on aspects of the last stand of the Wilson Patrol and its aftermath', *Heritage of Zimbabwe*, no. 13, pp. 97–100.

Grant, J. 1998, 'The land reform issue: social and economic challenges', *The Land Reform Challenge. Seminar Proceedings. Volume 2*, Friedrich Ebert Stiftung, Harare, pp. 50–6.

Grant, S. 1998, '"The charter of its birthright": the Civil War and American nationalism', *Nations and Nationalism*, vol. 4, no. 2, pp. 163–85.

Gray, J. 1990, 'Address on the occasion of the unveiling of the Livingstone Memorial', *Heritage of Zimbabwe*, no. 9, pp. 103–7.

Griffiths, G. 1994, 'The myth of authenticity', in C. Tiffin and A. Lawson (eds), *De-scribing Empire*, Routledge, New York and Oxford, pp. 70–85.

Grillo, R. 1993, 'The construct of "Africa" in "African socialism"', in C. Hann (ed.), *Socialism: Ideals, ideologies and local practice*, ASA Monographs 31, Routledge, New York and Oxford, pp. 59–76.

Gupta, A. 1992, 'The song of the nonaligned world: transnational identities and the reinscription of space in late capitalism', *Cultural Anthropology*, vol. 7, no. 1, pp. 63–79.

Gupta, A. 1995, 'Blurred boundaries: the discourse of corruption, the culture of politics, and the imagined state', *American Ethnologist*, vol. 22, no. 2, pp. 375–402.

Gupta, A. and Ferguson, J. (eds) 1992, 'Beyond "culture": space, identity and the politics of difference', *Cultural Anthropology*, vol. 7, no. 1, pp. 6–23.

Gupta, A. and Ferguson, J. (eds) 1997a, 'Culture, power, place: ethnography at the end of an era', *Culture, Power, Place: Explorations in critical anthropology*, Duke University Press, Durham, NC, pp. 1–30.

Gupta, A. and Ferguson, J. (eds) 1997b, 'Discipline and practice: "the field" as site, method, and location in anthropology', *Anthropological Locations*, University of California Press, Berkeley, pp. 1–43.

Gurr, A. 1981, *Writers in Exile*, Harvester Press, Brighton.

Hall, S. 1990, 'Cultural identity and diaspora', in J. Rutherford (ed.), *Identity: Community, culture and difference*, Lawrence and Wishart, London, pp. 222–37.

Hall, S. 1991a, 'Old and new identities', in D. King (ed.), *Culture, Globalization and the World System*, Macmillan, Basingstoke, pp. 41–68.

Hall, S. 1991b, 'The local and the global: globalization and ethnicity', in D. King (ed.), *Culture, Globalization and the World System*, Macmillan, Basingstoke, pp. 19–39.

Hall, S. 1995, 'New cultures for old', in D. Massey and P. Jess (eds), *A Place in the World?*, The Open University, Milton Keynes, pp. 175–213.

Hall, S., Critcher, C., Jefferson, T., Clarke, J. and Roberts, B. 1978, *Policing the Crisis*, Macmillan, London.

Hamber, B. 1997, 'Truth: the road to reconciliation', *Cantilevers*, vol. 3, pp. 5–6.

Hammar, A. 2003, 'The making and unma(s)king of local government in Zimbabwe', in A. Hammar, B. Raftopoulos and S. Jensen (eds), *Zimbabwe's Unfinished Business*, Weaver Press, Harare, pp. 119–54.

Hammar, A. 2005, *Disrupting democracy? Altering landscapes of local government in post-2000 Zimbabwe*, Discussion Paper no. 9, Crisis States Development Research Centre, London School of Economics and Political Science, London, pp. 1–35.

Hammar, A. and Raftopoulos, B. 2003, 'Zimbabwe's unfinished business: rethinking land, state and nation', in A. Hammar, B. Raftopoulos and S. Jensen (eds), *Zimbabwe's Unfinished Business*, Weaver Press, Harare pp. 1–48.

Hancock, I. 1984, *White Liberals, Moderates and Radicals in Rhodesia 1953–1980*, Croom Helm, London.

Handleman, D. and Shamgar-Handelman, L. 1993, 'Aesthetics versus ideology in national symbolism: the creation of the emblem of Israel', *Public Culture*, vol. 5, no. 3, pp. 431–49.

Handler, R. 1988, *Nationalism and the Politics of Culture in Quebec*, University of Wisconsin Press, Madison.

Hansen, K. (ed.) 1992, 'Introduction', *African Encounters with Domesticity*, Rutgers University Press, New Brunswick, pp. 1-33.

Harris, P. 1972, 'Economic incentives and European immigration in Rhodesia', *Rhodesian Journal of Economics*, vol. 25, no. 2, pp. 61–74.

Harris, P. 1974, 'Ten popular myths concerning the employment of labour in Rhodesia', *Rhodesian Journal of Economics*, vol. 8, no. 1, pp. 39–48.

Harvey, C. 1998, The impact on Southern Africa of the financial crisis in Asia and Russia, Paper presented at ZCC, CZI and FES Seminar Globalisation: Challenges and Opportunities for Zimbabwe, Harare, November.

Henson, P. 1988, 'The white minority then and now', *MOTO*, December, pp. 9–10.

Hills, D. 1981, *The Last Days of White Rhodesia*, Chatto and Windus, London.

Hills, J. 1999, 'Language, race and white public space', *American Anthropologist*, vol. 100, no. 3, pp. 680–9.

Hintjens, H. 1995, *Alternatives to Independence: Explorations in post-colonial relations*, Dartmouth, Aldershot, Brookfield.

Hirschkop, E. 1996, 'Editorial', *New Formations*, no. 30, pp. v–vii.

Hobsbawm, E. 1983, 'The mass-producing traditions: Europe, 1870–1914', in E. Hobsbawm and T. Ranger (eds), *The Invention of Tradition*, Columbia University Press, New York, pp. 1–14.

Hobsbawm, E. 1991, 'Introduction to exile: a keynote address', *Social Research*, vol. 58, no. 1, pp. 65–8.

Hodder-Williams, R. 1974, 'Afrikaners in Rhodesia: a partial portrait', *African Social Research*, vol. 18, pp. 611–42.

Hodder-Williams, R. 1980, 'Independent Zimbabwe', *Africa Insight*, vol. 10, nos 3–4, pp. 104–8.

Hodge, B. and Mishra, V. 1990, *Dark Side of the Dream*, Allen & Unwin, Sydney.

Hodgson, D. 2002, 'Introduction: comparative perspectives on the indigenous rights movement in Africa and the Americas', *American Anthropologist*, vol. 104, no. 4, pp. 1037–49.

Hollander, J. 1991, 'It all depends', *Social Research*, vol. 58, no. 1, pp. 3–63.

Hooks, B. 1992, 'Representing whiteness in the black imagination', in L. Grossberg, C. Nelson and P. Treichler (eds), *Cultural Studies*, Routledge, New York, pp. 338–46.

Horowitz, D. 1991, *A Democratic South Africa?*, University of California Press, Berkeley.

Hove, C. 1990, 'Cultural development', *SAPES*, April, pp. 23–4.

Howman, R. 1990, 'Patriotism and pioneering problems', *Heritage of Zimbabwe*, no. 9, pp. 75–102.

Hudson, M. 1981, *Triumph or Tragedy? Rhodesia to Zimbabwe*, Hamish Hamilton Ltd, London.

Huggan, G. 1989, 'Decolonizing the map: post-colonialism, post-structuralism and the cartographic connection', *Ariel*, vol. 20, pp. 115–31.

Hughes, D. 2005, 'Third nature: making space and time in the Great Limpopo Conservation Area', *Cultural Anthropology*, vol. 20, no. 2, pp. 157–84.

Hughes, D. 2006a, 'Hydrology of hope: farm dams, conservation, and whiteness in Zimbabwe', *American Ethnologist*, vol. 33, no. 2, pp. 269–87.

Hughes, D. 2006b, 'Whites and water: how Euro-Africans made nature at Kariba', *Journal of Southern African Studies*, vol. 32, no. 4, pp. 823–38.

Hunter, G. and Hunter, L. 1959, *Report on Adult Education in the Federation of Rhodesia and Nyasaland, and Kenya: Proposal for colleges of citizenship*, Beit Trustee, Salisbury.

Hutson, H. 1978, *Rhodesia: Ending an era*, Springwood Books, London.

Inglis, K. 1998, *Anzac Remembered*, University of Melbourne History Monographs no. 23, Parkville, Vic.

Intercessors for Zimbabwe 1997–98, *The Prayer Informer*, Intercessors for Zimbabwe, Harare.

Jackson, M. 1995, *At Home in the World*, Duke University Press, Durham, NC.

Jenkins, C. 1997, 'The politics of economic policy making in Zimbabwe', *Journal of Modern African Studies*, vol. 35, no. 4, pp. 575–602.

Jess, P. and Massey, D. 1995, 'The contestation of place', in D. Massey and P. Jess (eds), *A Place in the World?*, The Open University, Milton Keynes, pp. 133–74.

Kabweza, M. 1987, 'People with two homes', *MOTO*, August, pp. 12–13.

Kagoro, B. 2004, 'Constitutional reform as social movement: a critical narrative of the constitution making debate in Zimbabwe', in B. Raftopoulos and T. Savage (eds), *Zimbabwe Injustice and Political Reconciliation*, Weaver Press, Harare, pp. 236–56.

Kaplan, C. 1990, 'Reconfigurations of geography and historical narrative', *Public Culture*, vol. 3, no. 1, pp. 25–32.

Kaplan, M. and Kelly, J. 1994, 'Rethinking resistance: dialogics of "disaffection" in colonial Fiji', *American Ethnologist*, vol. 21, pp. 123–51.

Kaplan, W. (ed.) 1993, 'Who belongs? Changing concepts of citizenship and nationality', *Belonging—The meaning and future of Canadian citizenship*, McGill-Queens University Press, Montreal, Quebec, pp. 245–63.

Katiyo, W. 1982, 'Doris Lessing visits home', *MOTO*, October, p. 43.

Kemper, S. 1993, 'The nation consumed: buying and believing in Sri Lanka', *Public Culture*, vol. 5, no. 3, pp. 377–93.

Kennedy, D. 1987, *Islands of White. Settler society and culture in Kenya and Southern Rhodesia 1890 to 1939*, Duke University Press, Durham, NC.

Kileff, C. 1975, 'Black suburbanites: an African elite in Salisbury, Rhodesia', in C. Kileff and W. Pendelton (eds), *Urban Man in Southern Africa*, Mambo Press, Gwelo, pp. 81–98.

King, R. 1995, 'Migration, globalisation and place', in D. Massey and P. Jess (eds), *A Place in the World?*, The Open University, Milton Keynes, pp. 5–44.

Kinloch, G. 1975, 'Changing group attitudes of whites as defined by the press: the process of colonial adaptation', *Zambezia*, vol. 4, no. 1, pp. 105–17.

Kirkwood, D. 1984, 'Settler wives in Southern Rhodesia', in H. Callen and S. Ardener (eds), *The Incorporated Wife*, Croon Helm, London, pp. 143–64.

Kratochwil, F. 1994, 'Citizenship: on the border of order', *Alternatives*, vol. 19, pp. 485–506.

Kraybill, R. 1994, 'Transition from Rhodesia to Zimbabwe: the role of religious actors', in D. Johnston and C. Sampson (eds), *Religion, the Missing Dimension of Statecraft*, Oxford University Press, New York, pp. 208–57.

Kriger, N. 1988, 'The Zimbabwean war of liberation: struggles within struggles', *Journal of Southern African Studies*, vol. 14, no, 2, pp. 304–22.

Kriger, N. 1995, 'The politics of creating national heroes', in N. Bhebe and T. Ranger (eds), *Soldiers in Zimbabwe's Liberation War. Volume 1*, University of Zimbabwe Publications, Harare, pp. 139–62.

Kriger, N. 2007, 'Liberation from constitutional constraints: land reform in Zimbabwe', *SAIS Review*, vol. XXVII, no. 2, pp. 63–76.

Kuper, A. 1994, 'Culture, identity and the project of a cosmopolitan anthropology', *Man*, vol. 29, no. 3, pp. 537–54.

Lambek, M. 1996, 'The past imperfect: remembering as moral practice', in P. Antze and M. Lambek (eds), *Tense Past*, Routledge, New York, pp. 235–54.

Land Tenure Commission 1994, *Report of the Commission of Inquiry into Appropriate Land Tenure Systems*, Government Printer, Harare.

Landry, D. and MacLean, G. (eds) 1996, *The Spivak Reader*, Routledge, New York and Oxford.

Lapsley, M. 1986, *Neutrality or Co-Option?*, Mambo Press, Gweru.

Laqueur, T. 1994, 'Memory and naming in the Great War', in J. Gillis (ed.), *Commemorations*, Princeton University Press, Princeton, NJ, pp. 150–67.

Lardner Burke, D. 1966, *Rhodesia. The story of the crisis*, Oldbourne Book Company, London.

Lessing, D. 1992, *African Laughter*, Harper Collins, London.

Lessing, D. 1994, *Under My Skin*, Harper Collins, London.

Lewis, Father A. 1973, *Rhodesia—Live or Die*, Rhodesian Christian Group, Salisbury, pp. 3–20.

Lewis, Father A. 1976, *Rhodesia Undefeated*, Rhodesian Christian Group, Salisbury, pp. 1–16.

Loizos, P. 1981, *The Heart Grown Bitter*, Cambridge University Press, New York.

Loney, M. 1975, *Rhodesia: White racism and imperial response*, Penguin, London.

Loomba, A. 1994, 'Overworlding the "Third World"', in P. Williams and L. Chrisman (eds), *Colonial Discourse and Post-Colonial Theory*, Harvester Wheatsheaf, New York, pp. 305–23.

Loomba, A. 1998, *Colonialism/Postcolonialism*, Routledge, New York and Oxford.

McCandless, E. 1997, 'Land tenure reform in Zimbabwe', *Cantilevers*, vol. 4, pp. 24–7 and 36–7.

McCandless, E. and Abitbol, E. 1997, 'Editorial', *Cantilevers*, vol. 3, pp. 1–2.

McCarthy, J. 1994, 'The physical energy statue', *Heritage of Zimbabwe*, no. 13, pp. 39–50.

McClintock, A. 1993, 'Family feuds: gender nationalism and the family', *Feminist Review*, vol. 44, pp. 61–80.

McFadden, P. 1994, 'Black men, white women: the politics of race and privilege', *SAPEM*, December, pp. 42–7.

McFadden, P. 1996, 'Democratising citizenship', *SAPEM*, August, pp. 40–2.

Macgaffey, J. 1987, *Entrepreneurs and Parasites: The struggle for indigenous capitalism in Zaire*, Cambridge University Press, New York.

MacGarry, B. 1994a, *Double Damage*, Silveira House Social Series no. 7, Mambo Press, Gweru.

MacGarry, B. 1994b, *Land for Which People?*, Silveira House Social Series no, 8, Mambo Press, Gweru.

McGregor, J. 2002, 'The politics of disruption: war veterans and the local state in Zimbabwe', *African Affairs*, vol. 101, pp. 9–37.

MacKenzie, J. 1974, 'Colonial labour policy and Rhodesia', *The Rhodesian Journal of Economics*, vol. 8, no. 1, pp. 1–15.

Madinah, T. 1993, 'The *Land Act*'s losers', *Horizon*, September, p. 7.

Mafeje, A. 1996, 'The national question in Southern African settler societies', *SAPEM*, vol. 9, no. 9, pp. 33–7.

Mahoso, T. 1992, 'Zimbabwe reconciled to Rhodesia?', *MOTO*, April, pp. 6–8.

Malkki, L. 1992, 'National geographic: the rooting of peoples and the territorialization of national identity among scholars and refugees', *Cultural Anthropology*, vol. 7, no. 1, pp. 24–44.

Malkki, L. 1997, 'News and culture: transitory phenomena and the fieldwork tradition', in A. Gupta and J. Ferguson (eds), *Anthropological Locations*, University of California Press, Berkeley, pp. 86–101.

Mamdani, M. 1973, *From Citizen to Refugee*, Frances Printers, London.

Mamdani, M. 1997a, *Citizen and Subject. Decentralized despotism and the legacy of late colonialism*, Oxford University Press, Delhi.

Mamdani, M. 1997b, 'Reconciliation without justice', *SAPEM*, March, pp. 22–5.

Mamdani, M. 1998, *When Does a Settler Become a Native? Reflections of the colonial roots of citizenship in Equatorial and Southern Africa*, University of Cape Town, pp. 4–15.

Mamdani, M. 2001, 'Beyond settler and native as political identities: overcoming the political legacy of colonialism', *Comparative Studies in Society and History*, vol. 43, no. 4 (October), pp. 651–64.

Mandaza, I. 1988, 'The relationship of Third World intellectuals and progressive Western scholars: an African critique', *SAPEM*, February, pp. 7–12.

Mandaza, I. 1995, 'Persistent images of white conquest and domination', *SAPEM*, January, pp. 30–1.

Mandaza, I. 1997, 'A country in crisis', *SAPEM*, August, pp. 4–7.

Mandebvu, M. 1997, 'The next stage: The World Bank Group and ZIMPREST', *SAPEM*, August, pp. 11–14.

Martin, C. 1972, 'Rhodesia: immigrants not needed', *Race Today*, pp. 151–3.

Martin, P. and Johnson, D. 1986, 'Zimbabwe: apartheid's dilemma', in D. Johnson and P. Martin (eds), *Destructive Engagement—Southern Africa at war*, Zimbabwe Publishing House, Harare, pp. 43–72.

Masina, Z. 1988, 'Now we are all Zimbabweans', *MOTO*, May, pp. 11–12.

Massey, D. 1992, 'A place called home?', *New Formations*, no. 17 (Summer), pp. 3–15.

Massey, D. 1995a, 'Imagining the world', in J. Allen and D. Massey (eds), *Geographical Worlds*, The Open University, Milton Keynes, pp. 3–51.

Massey, D. 1995b, 'Places and their pasts', *History Workshop Journal*, vol. 39, pp. 182–91.

Massey, D. and Jess, P. (eds) 1995, 'Introduction', *A Place in the World?*, The Open University, Milton Keynes, pp. 1–4.

Matchaba-Hove, R. 1993, 'The ZimRights agenda', *Social Change and Development*, nos 33–4, pp. 11–12.

Matenga, E. 1998, *The Soapstone Birds of Zimbabwe*, African Publishing Group, Harare.

Maveneka, L. 1981, 'Discrimination thriving', *MOTO*, January, p. 2.

May, J. 1987, *Changing People, Changing Laws*, Mambo Press, Gweru.

Mayer, P. and Mayer, I. 1970, 'Socialisation by peers: the youth organisation of the Red Xhosa', in P. Mayer (ed.), *Socialisation: The approach from social anthropology*, Tavistock Publishers, London and New York, pp. 159–89.

Mbembe, A. 1992, 'Provisional notes on the post colony', *Africa*, vol. 62, pp. 3–37.

Mehrez, S. 1991, 'The subversive poetics of radical bilingualism. Postcolonial francophone North Africa literature', in D. La Capra (ed.), *The Bounds of Race*, Cornell University Press, Ithaca, pp. 255–77.

Melber, H. 1993, 'Namibia: the case of a post-colonial white settler society', *SAPEM*, April, pp. 25–8.

Memmi, A. 1965, *The Colonizer and the Colonized*, Orion Press, New York.

Memmi, A. 1973, 'The impossible life of Franz Fanon', *The Massachusetts Review*, vol. XIV, no. 1, pp. 9–39.

Meredith, M. 2007, *Mugabe: Power, plunder and the struggle for Zimbabwe*, Perseus Books, United States of America.

Ministry of Immigration and Tourism 1965a, *Report of the Under Secretary for Immigration and Tourism 1964*, Government Printers, Salisbury.

Ministry of Immigration and Tourism 1965b, *Rhodesia: Assisted passages to land of sunshine and golden opportunity*, Government Printers, Salisbury.

Ministry of Information, Posts and Telecommunications 1986 [1998], *A Guide to Heroes Acre*, Government of Zimbabwe, Harare.

Ministry of Labour, Manpower and Planning and Social Welfare 1984, *Annual Review of Manpower*, Government Printer, Harare.

Ministry of Labour, Manpower and Planning and Social Welfare 1986, *Annual Review of Manpower*, Government Printer, Harare.

Ministry of Lands and Agriculture 1998, *Zimbabwe's Land Reform and Redistribution Programme: Progress report*, Government Printer, Harare.

Ministry of Public Service, Labour and Social Welfare 1995, *Poverty Assessment Study Survey*, Government Printer, Harare.

Mishra, V. and Hodge, B. 1994, 'What is post(-)colonialism?', in P. Williams and L. Chrisman (eds), *Colonial Discourse and Post-Colonial Theory*, Harvester Wheatsheaf, New York, pp. 276–90.

Mlambo, A. 1997, *The Economic Structural Adjustment Programme*, University of Zimbabwe Press, Harare.

Moore, David 1995, 'The Zimbabwe People's Army: strategic innovation or more of the same?', in N. Bhebe and T. Ranger (eds), *Soldiers in Zimbabwe's Liberation War. Volume 1*, University of Zimbabwe Publications, Harare, pp. 73–86.

Moore, Donald 2005, *Suffering for Territory: Race, place and power in Zimbabwe*, Duke University Press, Durham, NC, and London.

Moore-Gilbert, B. 1997, *Post Colonial Theory: Contexts, practices and politics*, Verso, London.

Moore-King, B. 1989, *White Man, Black War*, Baobab Books, Harare.

Mosley, P. 1983, *The Settler Economies. Studies in the economic history of Kenya and Southern Rhodesia 1900–1963*, Cambridge University Press, New York.

Moyo, S. 1998a, 'The economic and social implications of recent land designations', *The Land Reform Challenge. Volume 2. Seminar Proceedings*, Friedrich Ebert Stiftung, Harare, pp. 32–49.

Moyo, S. 1998b, *The Land Acquisition Process in Zimbabwe 1997/8*, UNDP Resource Centre, Harare.

Mulgan, R. 1989, *Maori, Pakeha and Democracy*, Oxford University Press, Auckland.

Mulgan, R. 1998, 'Citizenship and legislation in post-colonial Australia', in N. Peterson and W. Sanders (eds), *Citizenship and Indigenous Australians*, Cambridge University Press, Cambridge and New York, pp. 179–95.

Munyanyi, P. 1998, 'The social implications of the designation of commercial farms for resettlement on the farm workers', *The Land Reform Challenge. Volume 2. Seminar Proceedings*, Friedrich Ebert Stiftung, Harare, pp. 70–2.

Mupinda, M. 1995, Loss and grief among the Shona: the meaning of disappearances, Paper presented to the VII International Symposium on Torture as a Challenge to the Medical Profession, Cape Town, November.

Murapa, R. 1984, 'Race and the public service in Zimbabwe: 1890–1983', in M. Schatzberg (ed.), *The Political Economy of Zimbabwe*, Praeger Press, New York, pp. 55–80.

Murphree, M. 1979, Africanization in the '80s, Address to IPMSA National Convention, Salisbury, 19 October.

Murphree, M. 1980, Race in the new Zimbabwe, Speech to the Institute of Personnel Management, Salisbury.

Murphree, M. and Baker, D. 1976, 'Racial discrimination in Rhodesia', in W. Veenhoven (ed.), *Case Studies on Human Rights and Fundamental Freedoms: A world survey. Volume 5*, Nijhoff, The Hague, pp. 377–413.

Murray, S. (ed.) 1997, 'Introduction', *Not On Any Map*, University of Exeter Press, Exeter, pp. 1–18.

Muzondidya, J. 2002, 'Towards a historical understanding of the making of the coloured community in Zimbabwe, 1890–1920', *Identity, Culture and Politics*, vol. 3, no. 2, pp. 1–26.

Muzondidya, J. 2004, 'Zimbabwe for Zimbabweans: invisible subject minorities and the quest for justice and reconciliation in post-colonial Zimbabwe', in B. Raftopoulos and T. Savage (eds), *Zimbabwe Injustice and Political Reconciliation*, Weaver Press, Harare, pp. 213–35.

Muzondidya, J. 2005, *Walking a Tightrope: Towards a social history of the coloured community of Zimbabwe*, Africa World Press, Lawrenceville, NJ.

Naipaul, S. 1986, 'Passports to dependence', *Beyond the Dragon's Mouth*, Penguin Books, New York, pp. 221–9.

Nandy, A. 1983, *The Intimate Enemy—Loss and recovery of self under colonialism*, Oxford University Press, Delhi.

Ncube, W. 1989, *Family Law in Zimbabwe*, Legal Resources Foundation, Harare.

Ndebele, N. 1998, 'Memory, metaphor, and the triumph of narrative', in S. Nuttall and C. Coetzee (eds), *Negotiating the Past. The making of memory in South Africa*, Oxford University Press, Cape Town, pp. 19–28.

Nederveen Pieterse, J. and Parekh, B. (eds) 1995, 'Shifting imageries: decolonisation, internal decolonisation, postcolonialism', *The Decolonisation of Imagination*, Zed Books, London, pp. 1–19.

Nicol, A. 1993, 'Nationality and immigration', in R. Blackburn (ed.), *Rights of Citizenship*, Mansell Publishers, London and New York, pp. 254–68.

Ngugi wa Thiong'o 1988, *Decolonising the Mind*, Heinemann, Portsmouth, NH.

Nherere, P. 1998, 'Legal and procedural aspects of the *Land Acquisition Act*', *The Land Reform Challenge. Volume 2. Seminar Proceedings*, Friedrich Ebert Stiftung, Harare, pp. 22–31.

Nkomo, J. 1984, *The Story of My Life*, Methuen, London.

Nursey-Bray, P. and Ahluwalia, P. 1997, 'Frantz Fanon and Edward Said: decolonisation and the search for identity', in P. Ahluwalia and P. Nursey-Bray (eds), *Post Colonialism: Culture and identity in Africa*, Nova Science Publishers, Commack, NY, pp. 27–47.

Nuttall, S. and Coetzee, C. (eds) 1998, 'Introduction', *Negotiating the Past. The making of memory in South Africa*, Oxford University Press, Cape Town, pp. 1–15.

Nyathi, P. 2004, 'Reintegration of ex-combatants into Zimbabwean society: a lost opportunity', in B. Raftopoulos and T. Savage (eds), *Zimbabwe Injustice and Political Reconciliation*, Weaver Press, Harare, pp. 63–78.

O'Callaghan, M. 1995, 'Continuities in imagination', in J. Nederveen Pieterse and B. Parekh (eds), *The Decolonisation of Imagination*, Zed Books, London, pp. 22–42.

O'Flaherty, M. 1998, 'Communal tenure in Zimbabwe: divergent models of collective land holding in communal areas', *Africa*, vol. 68, no. 4, pp. 537–57.

Ogot, B. and Ochieng, W. 1995, *Decolonisation and Independent Kenya*, James Currey Ltd, London.

Okeyo, A. 1980, 'Daughters of the lakes and rivers: colonisation and the land rights of Luo women', in M. Etienne and E. Leacock (eds), *Women and Colonisation*, Praeger, New York, pp. 186–213.

Ong, A. 1993, 'On the edge of empires: flexible citizenship among Chinese in diaspora', *Positions*, vol. 1, no. 3, pp. 745–78.

Oommen, T. 1997a, *Citizenship, Nationality and Ethnicity: Reconciling competing images*, Blackwell, Cambridge, Mass.

Oommen, T. 1997b (ed.), 'Conceptualising the linkage between citizenship and national identity', *Citizenship and National Identity: From colonialism to globalization*, Sage, California, pp. 13–51.

Orizio, R. 2000, *Lost White Tribes*, The Free Press, New York.

Ortner, S. 1995, 'Resistance and the problem of ethnographic refusal', *Society for Comparative Study of Society and Culture*, vol. 37, pp. 173–93.

Oyelaran, O. and Adediran, M. 1997, 'Colonialism, citizenship and fractured national identity: the African case', in T. Oommen (ed.), *Citizenship and National Identity: From colonialism to globalization*, Sage, California, pp. 173–97.

Palley, C. 1960, *Nationality and Citizenship Laws*, Stevens and Sons, London.

Palley, C. 1970, 'Law and the unequal society: discriminatory legislation in Rhodesia under the Rhodesian Front from 1963 to 1969. Parts 1 and 2', *Race*, vol. XII (July), pp. 15–47, and (October), pp. 139–67.

Palmer, R. 1977, *Land and Racial Domination*, Heinemann, London.

Palmer, R. 1990, 'Land reform in Zimbabwe', *African Affairs*, vol. 89, pp. 163–81.

Palmer, R. 1998, Mugabe's 'land grab' in regional perspective, Presented to Conference on Land Reform in Zimbabwe The Way Forward, SOAS, pp. 1–7.

Panter-Brick, K. 1983, 'Africanization in Zimbabwe', in P. Lyon and J. Manor (eds), *Transfer and Transformation*, Leicester University Press, Leicester, pp. 215–36.

Parker, J. 1972, *Rhodesia: Little white island*, Pitman Press, London.

Parry, B. 1994, 'Resistance theory/theorising resistance or three cheers for nativism', in F. Baker, P. Hulme and M. Iversen (eds), *Colonial Discourse/Post Colonial Theory*, Manchester University Press, Manchester, pp. 172–94.

Parry, B. 1995, 'Reconciliation and remembrance', *Pretexts*, vol. 5, nos 1–2, pp. 84–96.

Pascoe, F. 1969, *The Business of Living: A guide to good citizenship*, Mardon, Bulawayo.

Patel, H. 1988, 'Zimbabwe', *Survival*, vol. xxx, no. 1, pp. 38–57.

Pearson, K., Parry, B. and Squires, J. (eds) 1997, 'Introduction', *Cultural Readings of Imperialism*, St Martin's Press, New York, pp. 8–28.

Peck, J. 1992, 'Is there a German "home"?', *New Formations*, no. 17 (Summer), pp. 75–85.

Perruchoud, R. 1989, 'Family reunification', *International Migration*, vol. 27, pp. 509–22.

Peterson, N. and Sanders, W. (eds) 1998, 'Introduction', *Citizenship and Indigenous Australians*, Cambridge University Press, Cambridge and New York, pp. 1–32.

Phimister, I. 1988, *An Economic and Social History of Zimbabwe 1890–1948*, Longman Group, London and New York.

Phimister, I. 2004, 'South African diplomacy and the crisis in Zimbabwe: liberation solidarity in the 21st century', in B. Raftopoulos and T. Savage (eds), *Zimbabwe Injustice and Political Reconciliation*, Weaver Press, Harare, pp. 271–91.

Piearce, G. 1992, 'A singular piece of vanity—Livingstone's tree at the Victoria Falls', *Heritage of Zimbabwe*, no. 11, pp. 95–100.

Pile, S. and Thrift, N. (eds) 1995, 'Introduction', *Mapping the Subject: Geographies of cultural transformation*, Routledge, Oxford and New York, pp. 1–12.

Pitman, D. 1979, *You Must Be New Around Here*, Books of Rhodesia, Bulawayo.

Quandt, W. 1998, *Between Ballots and Bullets: Algeria's transition from authoritarianism*, Brookings Institution Press, Washington, DC.

Quenet, V. 1976, *Report of the Commission of Inquiry into Racial Discrimination*, Government Printers, Salisbury.

Radcliffe, S. and Westwood, S. 1996, *Remaking the Nation. Place, identity and politics in Latin America*, Routledge, London and New York.

Radhakrishnan, R. 1996, *Diasporic Mediations: Between home and location*, University of Minnesota Press, Minneapolis.

Raftopoulos, B. 1992, 'Beyond the house of hunger: democratic struggle in Zimbabwe', *Review of African Political Economy*, no. 54, pp. 59–74.

Raftopoulos, B. 2003, 'The state in crisis: authoritarian nationalism, selective citizenship and distortions of democracy in Zimbabwe', in A. Hammar, B. Raftopoulos and S. Jensen (eds), *Zimbabwe's Unfinished Business*, Weaver Press, Harare, pp. 217–42.

Raftopoulos, B. 2004a, 'Nation, race and history in Zimbabwean politics', in B. Raftopoulos and T. Savage (eds), *Zimbabwe Injustice and Political Reconciliation*, Weaver Press, Harare, pp. 160–75.

Raftopoulos, B. 2004b, 'Unreconciled differences: the limits of reconciliation politics in Zimbabwe', in B. Raftopoulos and T. Savage (eds), *Zimbabwe Injustice and Political Reconciliation*, Weaver Press, Harare, pp. viii–xx.

Raftopoulos, B. and Compagnon, D. 2003, 'Indigenization, the state bourgeoisie and neo-authoritarian politics', in S. Darnolf and L. Laakso (eds), *Twenty Years of Independence in Zimbabwe*, Palgrave Macmillan, Basingstoke, Hampshire, pp. 15–33.

Ranger, T. 1983, 'The invention of tradition in colonial Africa', in E. Hobsbawm and T. Ranger (eds), *The Invention of Tradition*, Cambridge University Press, New York, pp. 211–62.

Ranger, T. 1985, *Peasant Consciousness and Guerrilla War in Zimbabwe*, James Currey, London.

Ranger, T. 1989, 'Missionaries, migrants and the Manyika: the invention of ethnicity in Zimbabwe', in L. Vail (ed.), *The Creation of Tribalism in Southern Africa*, James Currey, London, pp. 118–49.

Ranger, T. 1992, 'Afterword: war, violence and healing in Zimbabwe', *Journal of Southern African Studies*, vol. 18, no. 3, pp. 698–707.

Ranger, T. 1999, *Voices From the Rocks*, Indiana University Press, Bloomington, Ind.

Ranger, T. 2004, 'Nationalist historiography, patriotic history and the history of the nation: the struggle over the past in Zimbabwe', *Journal of Southern African Studies*, vol. 30, no. 2, pp. 215–34.

Rapport, N. 1995, 'Migrant selves and stereotypes', in S. Pile and N. Thrift (eds), *Mapping the Subject: Geographies of cultural transformation*, Routledge, New York and Oxford, pp. 267–82.

Read, P. 1996, *Returning to Nothing*, Cambridge University Press, Melbourne.

Read, P. 1998, 'Whose citizens? Whose country?', in N. Peterson and W. Sanders (eds), *Citizenship and Indigenous Australia*, Cambridge University Press, Cambridge and New York, pp. 169–78.

Read, P. 1999, 'Leaving home', *Journal of Australian Studies*, Special issue: 'Imaginary Homelands', vol. 23, no. 61, pp. 35–46.

Renan, E. 1990, 'What is a nation?', in H. Bhabha (ed.), *Nation and Narration*, Routledge, London, pp. 8–22.

Rhodesia National Tourist Board 1972, 'Decided to stay', *Rhodesia Calls*, March–April.

Richling, B. 1985, '"You'd never starve here": return migration to rural Newfoundland', *Canadian Review of Sociology and Anthropology*, vol. 22, no. 2, pp. 236–49.

Roberts, R. 1978, 'The settlers', *Rhodesiana*, no. 39, pp. 55–61.

Rodman, M. 1992, 'Empowering place: multilocality and multivocality', *American Anthropologist*, vol. 94, pp. 640–56.

Rose, G. 1995, 'Place and identity', in D. Massey and P. Jess (eds), *A Place in the World?*, The Open University, Milton Keynes, pp. 87–132.

Rosenberg, T. 1999, 'Afterword: confronting the pain of the past', in M. Meredith, *Coming to Terms. South Africa's search for truth*, Public Affairs, New York, pp. 327–70.

Rothchild, D. 1973, *Racial Bargaining in Independent Kenya*, Oxford University Press, London.

Rouse, J. 1994, 'Power/knowledge', in G. Gutting (ed.), *The Cambridge Companion to Foucault*, Cambridge University Press, New York, pp. 92–113.

Rouse, R. 1995, 'Questions of identity', *Critique of Anthropology*, vol. 15, no. 4, pp. 351–80.

Rowlands, M. 1996, 'Memory, sacrifice and the nation', *New Formations*, no. 30, pp. 8–17.

Rukuni, M. 1998, 'Alternatives models of land reform', *The Land Reform Challenge. Volume 2. Seminar Proceedings*, Friedrich Ebert Stiftung, Harare, pp. 13–21.

Rukuni, M. and Jensen, S. 2003, 'Land, growth and governance: tenure reform and visions of progress in Zimbabwe', in A. Hammar, B. Raftopoulos and S. Jensen (eds), *Zimbabwe's Unfinished Business*, Weaver Press, Harare, pp. 243–62.

Rutherford, B. 2001, *Working on the Margins*, Zed Books, London.

Rutherford, B. 2003, 'Belonging to the farm(er): farm workers, farmers, and the shifting politics of citizenship', in A. Hammar, B. Raftopoulos and S. Jensen (eds), *Zimbabwe's Unfinished Business*, Weaver Press, Harare, pp. 191–216.

Rutherford, B. 2008a, 'Conditional belonging: farm workers and the cultural politics of recognition in Zimbabwe', *Development and Change*, vol. 39, no. 1, pp. 73–99.

Rutherford, B. 2008b, 'Zimbabweans living in the South African border-zone: negotiating, suffering, and surviving', *concerned.africascholars.org*, 13 December.

Rutherford, B. and Addison, L. 2007, 'Zimbabwean farm workers in northern South Africa', *Review of African Political Economy*, vol. 34, no. 114, pp. 619–35.

Rutherford, J. (ed.) 1990, 'A place called home: identity and the cultural politics of difference', *Identity: Community, culture, difference*, Lawrence Wishart, London, pp. 9–27.

Ryan, S. 1994, 'Inscribing the emptiness', in C. Tiffin and A. Lawson (eds), *De-Scribing Empire*, Routledge, New York and Oxford, pp. 115–30.

Sachikonye, L. 1998, 'The crisis of governance in Zimbabwe', *SAPEM*, March, pp. 31–2.

Sachikonye, L. 2003, 'Land reform for poverty reduction? Social exclusion and farm workers in Zimbabwe', *IDMP*, April, Manchester University.

Sachikonye, L. 2004, 'The promised land: from expropriation to reconciliation and *Jambanja*', in B. Raftopoulos and T. Savage (eds), *Zimbabwe Injustice and Political Reconciliation*, Weaver Press, Harare, pp. 1–18.

Sadie, J. 1967, *Planning for the Economic Development of Rhodesia*, Government Printers, Salisbury.

Safran, W. 1991, 'Diasporas in modern societies: myths of homeland and return', *Diaspora*, vol. 1, no. 1, pp. 83–99.

Said, E. 1978, *Orientalism*, Routledge and Kegan Paul Ltd, London.

Said, E. 1986, *After the Last Sky*, Pantheon Books, New York.

Said, E. 1989, 'Representing the colonised: anthropology's interlocutors', *Critical Inquiry*, vol. 15, pp. 205–25.

Said, E. 1990, 'Reflections on exile', in R. Ferguson (ed.), *Out There*, MIT Press, Cambridge, Mass., pp. 357–66.

Said, E. 1993, *Culture and Imperialism*, Vintage, New York and London.

Said, E. 2000, *Out of Place*, Granta Books, London.

Sanjek, R. 1993, 'Anthropology's hidden colonialism', *Anthropology Today*, vol. 9, no. 2, pp. 13–17.

Sartre. J.-P. 2001, *Colonialism and Neocolonialism*, Routledge, New York and Oxford.

Saunders, R. 2007, 'Trade union struggles for autonomy and democracy in Zimbabwe', in J. Kraus (ed.), *Trade Unions and the Coming of Democracy in Africa*, Palgrave Macmillan, Basingstoke, Hampshire, pp. 157–98.

Savage, K. 1994, 'The politics of memory: black emancipation and the Civil War monument', in J. Gillis (ed.), *Commemorations*, Princeton University Press, Princeton, NY, pp. 127–49.

Scarritt, J. 1970, The adjustment of Europeans to Zambian independence and its implications for Southern Africa, Paper presented at the 13th Annual Meeting of the American Studies Association.

Schultz, B. 1975, 'Homeward bound?', *Ufahamu*, vol. 5, no. 3, pp. 81–117.

Schwartz, B. 1982, 'The social context of commemoration: a study in collective memory', *Social Force*, pp. 374–400.

Scott, J. 1986, *Weapons of the Weak*, Yale University Press, New Haven.

Scott, J. 1990, *Domination and the Arts of Resistance*, Yale University Press, New Haven.

Settles, B. 1993, 'The illusion of stability in family life: the reality of change and mobility', in B. Settles, D. Hanks and M. Sussman (eds), *Families on the Move: Migration, immigration, emigration, and mobility*, The Haworth Press, New York, pp. 5–29.

Shamuyarira, N. 1966, *Crisis in Rhodesia*, Transatlantic Arts, New York.

Shamuyarira, N., Kumar, N. and Kangai, K. (eds) 1995, *Mugabe's Reflections*, Har-Anand Publications, New Delhi.

Shaw, A. 1993, *Kandaya. Another time, another place*, Baobab Books, Harare.

Shotter, J. 1993, 'Psychology and citizenship: identity and belonging', in B. Turner (ed.), *Citizenship and Social Theory*, Sage, California, pp. 115–38.

Shurmer-Smith, P. and Hannan, K. 1994, *Worlds of Desire, Realms of Power*, Edward Arnold, London.

Sichone, O. 1997, 'Afterword to "Reconciliation without justice": what about reciprocity?', *SAPEM*, February, p. 26.

Simpson, J. (ed.) 1995, *The Oxford Book of Exile*, Oxford University Press, Oxford.

Sinamayi, A. 1998, 'Heritage in politics: Great Zimbabwe in the struggle for self determination', in E. Chiwome and Z. Gambahaya (eds), *Culture and Development: Perspectives from the South*, Mond Books, Harare, pp. 93–8.

Sinclair, M. 1979, 'The brain drain from Rhodesia to Canada: the issue of compensation payments', *Issue*, vol. 19, no. 4, pp. 41–3.

Sithole, M. 1987, 'State power consolidation in Zimbabwe: party and ideological development', in E. Keller and D. Rothchild (eds), *Afro-Marxist Regimes*, Lynne Rienner Publishers, Boulder, Colo, pp. 85–106.

Sithole, M. 1991, 'Book reviews', *Africa*, vol. 61, pp. 552–4.

Smart, B. 1986, 'The politics of truth and the problem of hegemony', in D. Hoy (ed.), *Foucault: A critical reader*, Basil Blackwell, Oxford and New York, pp. 157–73.

Smith, A. 1994, 'Colonialism and the poisoning of Europe: towards an anthropology of colonists', *Journal of Anthropological Research*, vol. 50, pp. 383–93.

Smith, I. 1997, *The Great Betrayal: The memoirs of Ian Douglas Smith*, Blake Publishers, London.

Spencer, P. 1965, *The Samburu*, Routledge and Kegan Paul, London.

Spillman, L. 1997, *Nation and Commemoration: Creating national identities in the United States and Australia*, Cambridge University Press, Cambridge.

Spitulnik, D. 1993, 'Anthropology and mass media', *Annual Review of Anthropology*, vol. 22, pp. 293–315.

Spivak, G. 1990, 'The intervention interview', *The Post-Colonial Critic*, Routledge, New York, pp. 113–32.

Stasiulis, D. and Yuval-Davis, N. (eds) 1995, 'Introduction', *Unsettling Settler Societies*, Sage, London, pp. 1–38.

Stedman, S. 1991, *Peacemaking in Civil War*, Lynne Rienne Publishers, Boulder, Colo.

Stigger, P. 1970, 'Asians in Rhodesia and Kenya: a comparative political history', *Rhodesian History*, vol. 1, pp. 1–8.

Stocking, G. (ed.) 1991, 'Colonial situations: essays on the contextualization of ethnographic knowledge', *History of Anthropology. Volume 7*, University of Wisconsin Press, Madison, pp. 3–8.

Stoneman, C. and Cliffe, L. 1989, *Zimbabwe*, Pinter Publishers, London and New York.

Strong, G. 1985, *Keys to Effective Prayer*, Marshall, Morgan and Scott Ltd, Basingstoke.

Stubbs, C. 1994, 'The history of Zimbabwe's indigenous cattle', *Heritage of Zimbabwe*, no. 13, pp. 137–40.

Sylvester, C. 1990, 'Simultaneous revolutions: the Zimbabwean case', *Journal of Southern African Studies*, vol. 16, no. 3, pp. 452–75.

Sylvester, C. 1991, *Zimbabwe: The terrain of contradictory development*, Westview Press, Boulder, Colo.

Sylvester, C. 1995, 'Whither opposition in Zimbabwe?', *The Journal of Modern African Studies*, vol. 33, no. 3, pp. 403–23.

Sylvester, C. 2000, *Producing Women and Progress in Zimbabwe*, Heinemann, Portsmouth, NH.

Talmu, S. 1994, 'Campus tribalism: the Tutsification and Hutufication of UZ', *MOTO*, October, pp. 8–9.

Tavuchis, N. 1991, *Mea Culpa. A sociology of apology and reconciliation*, Stanford University Press, Stanford, California.

Taylor, J. 1992, 'Re-locations from Bradford to Brighton', *New Formations*, no. 17 (Summer), pp. 86–94.

Timbe, A. 1991, The Zimbabwe public service: theory and practice of the Presidential Directive on African advancement, Unpublished M.Phil thesis, University of Zimbabwe, Harare.

Thomas, D. 1997, 'Constructing national and cultural identities in sub-Saharan francophone Africa', in S. Murray (ed.), *Not On Any Map*, University of Exeter Press, Exeter, pp. 115–34.

Thomas, N. 1994, *Colonialism's Culture*, Polity Press, Cambridge.

Thornton, R. 1994, 'South Africa: countries, boundaries, enemies and friends', *Anthropology Today*, vol. 10, no. 6, pp. 7–15.

Tobaiwa, E. 1998, 'A study of shareholding structure and contribution to GDP of selected large companies in Zimbabwe', Friedrich Ebert Stiftung, Harare, pp. 1–28.

Tredgold, R. 1968, *The Rhodesia That Was My Life*, George Allen & Unwin, London.

Tuhiwai Smith, L. 1999, *Decolonizing Methodologies*, Zed Books, London and New York.

Turner, B. 1987, 'A note on nostalgia', *Theory, Culture and Society*, vol. 4, pp. 147–56.

United Nations Development Programme (UNDP) 1998, *Human Development Report—Zimbabwe*, Printopak, Harare.

Ushewokunze, H. 1984, *An Agenda for Zimbabwe*, Redwood Burn Ltd, United Kingdom.

Utete, C. 2003, *Report of the Presidential Land Review Committee on the Implementation of the Fast Track Land Reform Programme*, Government of Zimbabwe, Harare.

Uusihakala, K. 2008, *Memory Meanders: Place, home and commemoration in an ex-Rhodesian diaspora community*, University of Helsinki.

Vambe, L. 1972, *An Ill-Fated People*, Heinemann Ltd, London.

Van Der Merwe, H. 1997, 'Reconciliation: what role for victims and perpetrators', *Cantilevers*, vol. 3, pp. 7–8.

Vekris, J. 1991, 'Calling a spade a spade', *Social Change*, vol. 26, pp. 13–14.

von Blanckenburg, P. 1994, *Large Commercial Farms and Land Reform in Africa: The case of Zimbabwe*, Avebury, United States of America.

Waldron, J. 1992, 'Historic injustice: its remembrance and suppression', in G. Oddie and R. Perrett (eds), *Justice, Ethics and New Zealand Society*, Oxford University Press, Auckland, pp. 139–70.

Wallerstein, I. 1988, 'The construction of peoplehood: racism, nationalism, ethnicity', in E. Balibar and I. Wallerstein, *Race, Nation and Class*, Routledge, New York and Oxford, pp. 71–85.

Weiss, R. 1994, *Zimbabwe and the New Elite*, British Academic Press, London.

Weitzer, R. 1990, *Transforming Settler States*, University of California Press, Berkeley.

Welsh, S. 1997, '(Un)belonging citizens, unmapped territory: black immigration and British identity in the post-1945 period', in S. Murray (ed.), *Not On Any Map*, University of Exeter Press, Exeter, pp. 43–66.

Werbner, P. 1997, 'Essentialising essentialism, essentialising silence: ambivalence and multiplicity in the constructions of racism and ethnicity', in P. Werbner and T. Modood (eds), *Debating Cultural Hybridity*, Zed Books, London, pp. 226–54.

Werbner, P. 1998, 'Exorcising citizenship', *Canberra Anthropology*, vol. 21, no. 2, pp. 1–27.

Werbner, R. 1992, *Tears of the Dead*, Baobab Books, Harare.

Werbner, R. 1995, 'Human rights and moral knowledge: arguments of accountability in Zimbabwe', in M. Strathern (ed.), *Shifting Contexts: Transformations in anthropological knowledge*, Routledge, London and New York, pp. 99–116.

Werbner, R. 1998 (ed.), 'Introduction. Beyond oblivion: confronting memory crisis' and 'Smoke from the barrel of a gun: postwars of the dead, memory and reinscription in Zimbabwe', *Memory and the Postcolony. African anthropology and the critique of power*, Zed Books, London and New York, pp. 1–17 and 71–101.

Wermter, O. 1987, 'Families torn between town and country', August, p. 12.

Whaley, W. 1973, 'Race politics in Rhodesia', *Zambezia*, vol. 3, no. 1, pp. 31–7.

Wilkinson, A. 1980, 'The impact of war', in W. Morris-Jones (ed.), *From Rhodesia to Zimbabwe*, Frank Cass, London, pp. 110–23.

Wilson, R. 2000, 'Reconciliation and revenge in post-apartheid South Africa', *Current Anthropology*, vol. 41, no. 1, pp. 74–98.

Wilson, T. and Donnan, H. (eds) 1998, 'Nation, state and identity at international borders', in *Border Identities*, Cambridge University Press, New York, pp. 1–30.

Wiseman, H. and Taylor, A. 1981, *From Rhodesia to Zimbabwe*, Pergamon Press, Oxford.

Wood, R. 1997, 'Contemplations on the Harare Club's centennial', *Heritage of Zimbabwe*, no. 16, pp. 137–40.

Worby, E. 2003, 'The end of modernity in Zimbabwe? Passages from development to sovereignty', in A. Hammer, B. Raftopoulos and S. Jensen (eds), *Zimbabwe's Unfinished Business*, Weaver Press, Harare, pp. 49–81.

Young, R. 1990, *White Mythologies: Writing history and the West*, Routledge, London and New York.

Young, R. 2001a, *Postcolonialism: An historical introduction*, Blackwell, Oxford, UK.

Young, R. 2001b, 'Preface', in J.-P. Sartre, *Colonialism and Neocolonialism*, Routledge, London and New York, pp. vii–xxiv.

Zaffiro, J. 1984, 'Broadcasting and political change in Zimbabwe 1931–1984', Universal Microfilms International, Ann Arbor, Mich.

Zerubavel, Y. 1994, 'The death of memory and the memory of death: Masada and the holocaust as historical metaphors', *Representations*, vol. 45, pp. 72–97.

Zimbabwe Human Rights and Law 2007, *Zimbabwe and citizenship; what the law says*, Submission on the Interpretation of Citizenship Laws to the Parliamentary Committee on Defence and Home Affairs, 7 March 2007, Harare.

Zimbabwe Human Rights NGO Forum 2005, *Constitutional Amendment (no. 17) Bill*, Presentation to the Portfolio Committee on Justice, Legal and Parliamentary Affairs, 4 August 2005, Harare.

Zimbabwe Women Lawyers' Association 1996, *Response to Clause 8 of Constitution of Zimbabwe Amendment (No 14) Bill, 1995*, Zimbabwe Women Lawyers Association.

Zinyama, L. 1990, 'International migrations to and from Zimbabwe and the influence of political change on population movements, 1965–1987', *IMR*, vol. xxiv, no. 4, pp. 748–67.

Zvarevashe, Reverend I. 1994, 'Religion: the missing element in national celebrations', *MOTO*, August, pp. 5–7.

Other reports and publications

Zimbabwe Government Gazette

'Indigenisation and Economic Empowerment Bill (General notice 147/2007)', *Government Gazette*, 22 June 2007.

'Citizenship of Zimbabwe (General notice 584/2002)', *Government Gazette*, 22 November 2002.

Kubatana.net – The NGO Network Alliance Project

'Agreement between the Zimbabwe African National Union Patriotic Front and the two Movement for Democratic Change Formations, on resolving the challenges facing Zimbabwe', 15 September 2008.

'Indigenisation and Economic Empowerment Bill', 22 June 2007.

'Citizenship of Zimbabwe Amendment Bill', 14 February 2003.

Rhodesian Information Service

Rhodesian Commentary

'Immigration policy is successful', vol. 4, no. 22 (November 1970).

'Indigenous Nkone cattle create beef interest', vol. 4, no. 3 (February 1970).

'The accidental immigrants', vol. 5, no. 9 (May 1971).

'Message to associations from the Prime Minister of Rhodesia', vol. 5, no. 13 (June 1971).

'Indigenous cattle becoming more prominent', vol. 5, no. 19 (September 1971).

'Indigenous pigs equal to exotic', vol. 6, no. 16 (August 1972).

'Immigrants wanted', vol. 8, no. 2 (January 1974).

'New immigrants volunteer for immediate military service', vol. 9, no. 21 (October 1975).

'National anthem lyrics chosen', vol. 9, no. 21 (October 1975).

'Black and white are here to stay for all time', vol. 9, no. 23 (November 1975).

Zimbabwe Department of Information

Press statements

Prime Minister Elect Mugabe, 'Greetings in the name of freedom', 4 March 1980.

'Prime Minister speaks on pensions', 11 June 1981.

'Reconciliation a reciprocal process', 7 April 1982.

'Alien employment regulations tightened', 1 March 1984.

'PM praises Asian community', 25 April 1984.

Mubako, 'Immigration staff must promote tourism', 22 October 1984.

'Co-operation between government and private sector is vital', 2 December 1985.

Shave, 'Black advancement not impressive', 18 February 1986.

'Sanyangare attends ZNCC meeting', 24 March 1986.

'Constitutional changes—for better government', 3 August 1987.

'Housing situation in commercial farms', 10 December 1987.

Nkomo, 'Train workforce for skilled manpower', 21 January 1990.

Hon. E. D. Mnangagwa, Minister of Justice, Legal and Parliamentary Affairs, 'Constitution of Zimbabwe Amendment (no. 14) Bill, 1996', 9 March 1996.

Zimbabwe Lawyers for Human Rights

'The path to disenfranchisement—2002 Presidential elections', *Pambazuka News*, issue 58, 13 March 2009.

'Citizenship, renunciation and passport issues', 28 November 2002.

Zimbabwe Law Reports

Principal Immigration Officer vs O'Hara, (1) ZLR 69 (s), 1993.

Hambly vs The Chief Immigration Officer, Judgment no. SC 147/98, 1998.

Carr vs Registrar-General, (2) ZLR 433, 2000.

Todd vs Registrar-General of Citizenship and Another, HC 55/2002, 2002.

www.ingramcontent.com/pod-product-compliance
Lightning Source LLC
Chambersburg PA
CBHW060928170426
43192CB00031B/2867